THE BIG BOOK OF JEWISH HUMOR

edited and annotated by

WILLIAM NOVAK

MOSHE WALDOKS

HarperPerennial

A Division of HarperCollins*Publishers*

THE
BIG
BOOK *of*
JEWISH
HUMOR

Copyright acknowledgments will be found on page 306, which constitutes a continuation of this copyright page.

First Perennial Library edition published 1981.   First HarperPerennial edition published 1990.

Library of Congress Cataloging-in-Publication Data
Main entry under title:
The Big book of Jewish humor.
    1. Jewish wit and humor. I. Novak, William II. Waldoks, Moshe.
PN6231.J5B45 1981   808.88′2.   81–47234
                         AACR2
ISBN: 0-06-014894-2
ISBN: 0-06-090917-X (pbk)

90 91 92 93 94 MPC 10 9 8 7 6 5 4 3 2 1
        93 94 MPC 10 9 8 7 6   (pbk.)

For our parents and children

Other Books by William Novak and Moshe Waldoks

The Big Book of New American Humor

Other Books by William Novak

High Culture: Marijuana in the Lives of Americans

The Great American Shortage and Other Roadblocks to Romance

Other Books with William Novak

Iacocca: An Autobiography, by Lee Iacocca

Goodbye to the Low Profile, by Herb Schmertz

Mayflower Madam, by Sydney Biddle Barrows

Man of the House, by Tip O'Neill

My Turn, by Nancy Reagan

Acknowledgments

A great many people helped us to compile this collection by telling jokes, laughing at jokes (or not laughing at them), commenting on the manuscript, and making all kinds of helpful suggestions. We want to thank Donald Altschiller, Steven and Amy Broder, Ann Close, Leo Cohen, Robin Cohen, Steven M. Cohen, Stephen P. Cohen, Stuart Copans, Susan Devins, Amram Ducovny, Michael Fixler, Everett Fox and Cherie Koller-Fox, J. J. Goldberg, Albert Goldman, Martin S. Goldman, Janet Goldstein, Ted and Lillian Gorman, Allan Gould, Elinor Grumet, Carol Kur, Larry Kushner, Paul Levenson, Bill Levy, Rafi Lieberman, Martin and Paula Manaly, Jacob Rader Marcus, Leonard Michaels, Naomi Katz Mintz, Hana Wirth-Nesher, Sol and Marjorie Pomerantz, Joel Rosenberg, Gary Rosenblatt, David Roskies, Mark Shechner, Kurt Schlesinger, Howard Schwartz, Samuel Silver, Michael Strassfeld, Jeffrey Summit and Gail Kaufman, Phil Waldoks and Amy Persky, Jonathan Wolf, and Leon Wieseltier.

We are especially grateful to Leonard Fein, Lewis Mintz, Matthew Nesvisky, and Elsie and Bob Summit. Richard Siegel provided early encouragement for this book. And we thank Stephen Whitfield for his many rich insights and valuable suggestions.

Our involvement in this book over the past three years was made easier by the active encouragement and helpful advice of our wives, Linda Manaly Novak and Anne Pomerantz Waldoks.

Steven Axelrod, our agent, provided steady support throughout. Linda Rogers at Harper & Row untangled the intricacies of rights and permissions with ruthless efficiency and constant good cheer. Finally, we are indebted to Ted Solotaroff, whose acute literary sensibilities and superb editorial judgment were invaluable.

Contents

PROMISED LANDS PART THREE

PART FOUR   MAKING A LIVING

PART FIVE   FIRST THINGS LAST

With drawings by:
Diana Bryan, John Caldwell, Dick Codor,
Sherry Flenniken, Devis Grebu, S. Gross, Kirschen, David
Levine, Lou Myers, Mark Podwal, George Price, Richter, Maurice
Sendak, Ralph Steadman, Howard Weiss, Jack Ziegler

From *Running A Muck,* copyright © 1978 by John Caldwell. By permission of Writer's Digest Books.

Introduction

We see this book as a kind of gregarious family reunion which brings together disparate and dispersed relatives and guests of all ages and orientations. At the long and crowded dinner table, the Wise Men of Chelm and Hershele Ostropoler swap jokes with the Marx Brothers and Mel Brooks. Sholom Aleichem, at the other end of the table, pokes Philip Roth in the ribs, as the impertinent waiter, assisted by Sam Levenson, clears away the first course. Off in a corner, Isaac Babel chats about Cossacks with Woody Allen, while back at the table, Yankele the *schnorrer,* reaching for a boiled potato for tomorrow's lunch, inadvertently spills his soup on S.J. Perelman's lap.

This arrangement allows us to take full advantage of the marvelously broad spectrum of Jewish humor. Although the conventional wisdom associates it mostly with nineteenth-century Eastern Europe, the fact is that we are currently in the midst of a second golden age of Jewish humor which has been unfolding throughout twentieth-century America. While these two periods are in some ways very different, their essential concerns are the same, and at the family reunion their various representatives mingle amicably and talk together late into the night.

NINETEENTH-CENTURY JEWISH HUMOR

The justly celebrated humor of the European *shtetl* is typically referred to as "traditional" Jewish humor. Except for Sholom Aleichem and occasional pieces by other Yiddish writers, most of this material belongs to the realm of folk humor—jokes and anonymous funny stories, together with an assortment of proverbs and curses—all of which was passed along and developed over several generations. Some of its roots can be traced as far back as the medieval Purim *shpils*—comic plays based on the story of Esther and other Biblical tales. Indeed, it is even argued that the Bible and the Talmud, as the original repositories of Jewish humor, are replete with humorous tales and witty exchanges. This claim may hold true for a few of the commentaries that the Biblical text continues to generate, but the Bible itself is fundamentally a sober work, while the Talmud contains all too few truly funny passages.

A predominant misconception about traditional Jewish humor is that it is essentially composed of "laughter through tears." Along with its heartwarming appeal, the phrase enjoys a ring of cogency; after all, the humor of the Russian and Polish

Jews arose out of one of the grimmest stretches in all of Jewish history. Persecution, poverty, and uprootedness, three of the major conditions of that era, gave rise to much of the humor that is associated with Eastern Europe and that came to America in successive waves of immigration.

But despite the enduring popularity of the idea, "laughter through tears" is an incomplete description of traditional Jewish humor. It is true that these jokes deal with actual events, and it is also true that these events are frequently unpleasant —or worse. But the phrase wrongly emphasizes the humor that developed through suffering and implies that the Jew's endless struggle with adversity provides its dominant theme.

The evidence suggests otherwise. For every joke about anti-Semitism, poverty, or dislocation, there are several others dealing with less melancholy topics: the intricacies of the Jewish mind, its scholars, students, and *schlemiels;* the eternal comedy of food, health, and manners; the world of businessmen, rabbis, and *schnorrers* (beggars); the concerns of matchmaking, marriage, and family. What all these jokes have in common, aside from a remarkable combination of earthiness and subtlety that appeals to common folk and intellectuals alike, is not that they are primarily sad or wistful, but that they are wise and—no small matter for nineteenth-century humor—genuinely funny even today.

This is not to say that traditional Jewish humor is typically joyful or celebratory; far from it. Like the Jewish people, Jewish humor is optimistic in the long run, but pessimistic about the present and the immediate future. Running through many of these jokes are twin currents of anxiety and skepticism that can become so strong that even the ancient sources of Jewish optimism are swept up in them. "Don't worry," goes one punch line. "God has protected us from Pharaoh and Haman. He will protect us from the Messiah too."

TWENTIETH-CENTURY JEWISH HUMOR

Jewish humor of twentieth-century America is more difficult to identify and define. Like the Jews themselves, its very success in permeating the general society has diluted its ethnic identity, and its degree of "Jewishness" varies widely and sharply. Although it began as an extension of the folk humor of Eastern Europe, twentieth-century Jewish humor underwent certain immediate changes and transformations in America. To take the most obvious example, anti-Semitism became far less central a theme to the immigrants in America, as jokes about assimilation, name-changing, and even conversion soon took its place. Jokes about fundraisers replaced stories of *schnorrers.*

Jokes about mothers became popular, replacing jibes at mothers-in-law. The twitting of pretentious rabbis and the well-to-do was broadened as economic and social opportunities enabled the common people to become targets of satire.

Still, to a remarkable degree, the fundamental themes of Jewish humor did not change, though so much else did for the Jews who came to America. What did change, however, were the forms it took. While the folk process of Jewish humor continued to operate in the American setting, the more creative energies came from another source: comedians and writers. Some of them continued to work, more or less, within the oral tradition, but increasingly they would provide their own material, based not only on the collective Jewish experience but also on the conditions and tensions—Jewish and otherwise—of their own lives. Their primary loyalties were not always to the Jewish community, and there began a complicated and often adversary relationship between the community and its humorists, a relationship that has grown more problematic with every passing decade.

This brings us to a central misunderstanding about contemporary American Jewish humor: that it is largely self-hating. According to this view, traditional Jewish humor is warm, sweet, nostalgic, and unthreatening; contemporary Jewish humor, by contrast, is seen as harsh, vulgar, neurotic, and increasingly masochistic.

Like the myth of laughter through tears, the charge of masochism has some truth to it, especially with regard to jokes about anti-Semitism. Jewish humor is frequently self-critical and sometimes even self-deprecating. Still, the negative element of recent Jewish humor is characteristically overstated, just as traditional Jewish humor was subject to similar criticisms in its own time. As the folklorist Dan Ben-Amos has observed: "Perhaps the only validation of the Jewish-masochism thesis is its mass acceptance by Jewish intellectuals, for the actual evidence derived from the jokes themselves does not support it." And a scholar of our acquaintance who is often asked to lecture on this subject now responds to the inevitable question "Isn't Jewish humor masochistic?" by saying: "No, and if I hear that line once more I'm going to kill myself!"

Freud, perhaps the first serious student of Jewish humor, correctly identified a self-critical component in many of the jokes, noting: "I do not know whether there are many other instances of a people making fun to such a degree of its own character." Some of Freud's followers—most notably Theodor Reik in his book *Jewish Wit*—and various other commentators have taken Freud's observation and expanded it into a general insight into Jewish character. According to this view, Jewish humor arose as a way for Jews to cope with the hostility they found all around them, sometimes by using that hostility against themselves. In the words of the psychoanalyst Martin Grotjahn: "Aggression turned against the self seems to be an essential feature of the truly Jewish joke. It is as if the Jew tells his enemies: 'You do not need to attack us. We can do that ourselves—and even better.'"

The allegation of Jewish masochism (otherwise known as self-hatred) has been made with increasing frequency in recent years (especially against Philip Roth), and while there are certainly elements of it among other contemporary Jewish humorists, it is important to ask whether this reductive concept is the best way to describe an uninhibited and frequently critical treatment of Jewish life. Jewish humor, after all, is an extension of the Jewish mind, which has traditionally been a highly self-critical instrument, reluctant to accept anything at face value, and not unwilling to search for evidences of the storm beneath the surface tranquillity of everyday life. It is no accident that the pioneer of psychoanalysis was especially interested in Jewish jokes.

In addition, the established Jewish community, in the absence of severe anti-Semitism in America, has at times been overly sensitive to those Jewish artists and writers who are occasionally unflattering in their depictions of Jewish middle-class life. It is sometimes suggested that such descriptions provide "ammunition" for anti-Semites, but one suspects that the real sin lies elsewhere. Jewish comedians and writers may be critical of the Jewish community, but as we have said, there is nothing new about that. What may also disturb the official Jewish community is that some of the contemporary humorists, such as Lenny Bruce and Wallace Markfield, taunt not only the Jews but also the *goyim.* *

The point, then, is that the real offense of the contemporary humorists is not in their dwelling on Jewish inferiority, but rather their revealing the more or less secret feelings of Jewish superiority. And so, for example, Sam Levenson and Harry Golden, who have stressed the similarity of Jews to other Americans, have been far more readily embraced by a nervous

---

Goy (plural: *goyim*) means "nation" in Biblical Hebrew. In Yiddish, however, *goy* has come to mean a non-Jew—sometimes with a denigrating connotation. But culturally, *goy* has also been the standard way that Jews refer to non-Jews without any connotation, and it is in that sense that the word is used in these pages.

Along the same lines, *yid* (which means "Jew" in Yiddish) has denigrating connotations *outside* of Yiddish. In fact, many Jewish jokes, when told in their original Yiddish, begin: "*A yid iz geven . . .*" (literally, "A Jew was . . .," but actually, "A man was . . ."), for in Eastern Europe, a person was assumed to be Jewish (and male) unless it was otherwise specified. In our renditions of these jokes, all characters are Jewish unless otherwise noted.

community than, say, Lenny Bruce and Philip Roth, who have made much of the differences.

Finally, and perhaps more obviously, contemporary Jewish comedians have unprecedented access to the general public and no longer depend upon the approval of the Jewish community. Traditional Jewish humor, by contrast, was primarily in Yiddish, which functioned as a kind of secret Jewish parlance which permitted one to saying *anything* without worrying about what the *goyim* would think. For better or worse, those days are over.

JEWISH HUMOR IN AMERICA

One of the complicating factors in identifying American Jewish humor is that American Jews themselves have been strangely reluctant to recognize it and appreciate it for what it is. Even people who own records by Lenny Bruce and Allan Sherman, who go to see movies by Woody Allen and Mel Brooks, who read novels by Philip Roth, Bruce Jay Friedman, and Wallace Markfield, and who watch television performers like Myron Cohen, Buddy Hackett, and David Steinberg, still seem to think of Jewish humor as belonging to the world of Eastern Europe and to the early stages of acculturation in America—more or less like Yiddish itself. It is true that not all the material of these contemporary humorists can properly be called Jewish, but even by the strictest measures, there is much that can.

Gentiles have little difficulty in recognizing the Jewish slant of Lenny Bruce's hipsters, or Woody Allen's *schlemiels,* or Philip Roth's compulsive intellectuals. Why is the Jewish audience more equivocal? Part of the reason may be the reluctance of these humorists to see themselves as part of Jewish America. But if this is true of the performers and writers, it is perhaps no less true of their audiences; American Jews in general have been reluctant to take seriously their own Jewishness. According to this prejudice (and here is a compelling case of self-deprecation), Eastern Europe represents an idealized and "authentic" Judaism, and not incidentally, a Yiddish-speaking culture, next to which Judaism in America seems artificial, watered-down, and decidedly second best. For some aspects of Jewish culture, this bias is valid, although less so with each passing year. But in no area has it been less true than for Jewish humor.

Adding to the confusion is that while the themes of Jewish humor have not changed dramatically since Eastern Europe, America has made available (and Jews have helped to create) a host of new forms which make twentieth-century Jewish humor appear to have little in common with its nineteenth-century origins. Whereas traditional Jewish humor emerged anonymously from a collective consciousness, America has provided a multitude of new conduits for its transmission: public meetings and lectures, vaudeville, the Borscht Belt, Broadway, nightclubs, radio, record albums, movies, and most especially television, as well as widely circulating books, newspapers, and magazines. America has made available a popular culture that has been not only open to Jews but positively *inviting* to Jewish performers and Jewish themes to a degree that was unimaginable in Eastern Europe. There has been, of course, a price to pay for accepting this invitation, which has resulted in the *parevezation,* or neutering, of much of the material.

Then there is the language difference. Yiddish has frequently been celebrated for being so rich in comic possibilities that even those who don't understand it are apt to chuckle at many of its terms; F. Scott Fitzgerald, so the story goes, used to wander into a Jewish delicatessen just to hear the word "knish." While the immigrant generation of American Jews retained Yiddish—and there was even a weekly humor magazine called *Groyser Kundes* ("Big Stick"), published between 1909 and 1927—it soon became clear that Jewish life in America would be conducted in English.

It happened that English, too, was rich in comic possibilities—at least the English spoken by Jews of immigrant background, who took the new language and enriched it not only with Yiddish phrases but also with Jewish rhythms, much as blacks had done with American music. The result was a kind of verbal equivalent to jazz that is best exemplified in the *sphritzes* (spontaneous monologues) of Jewish comedians and novelists.

As the vehicles of humor have changed, so have the modes of its circulation. "A new joke," Freud wrote in 1905, "is passed from one person to another like the news of the latest victory." Freud's analogy is not altogether obsolete; a wave of jokes about changing light bulbs swept across North America as this book was being completed. But one of the casualties of a mass society is that jokes are more likely to gain instant exposure on the *Tonight* show than to be passed along from one individual to another. "Today," observes a veteran of Jewish organization life, "the only time I hear Jewish jokes is during conventions, usually while standing at urinals in the men's room."

But while the telling of jokes may be on the decline, Jewish humor is now more popular than ever. It is even possible to argue that Jewish humor, which once represented a secular corner of many otherwise religious Jewish lives, has now come full circle to fulfill a kind of religious need in the lives of many nonpracticing Jews. "Of all the Jewish holidays," goes one contemporary witticism, "I observe only the Jascha Heifetz concerts." A similar phenomenon may be true for Jewish jokes. In an age when the great classical and religious texts of Judaism speak only to a minority, it is Jewish jokes that are known, enjoyed, and treasured by Jews of all shades of identification and religious observance, and it is surely significant that traditional Jewish jokes are told and read more often in America than they were in their country of origin. Jewish humor, in other words, has in some ways come to replace the standard sacred texts as a touchstone for the entire Jewish community. Not all Jews can read and understand a page of Talmud, but even the most assimilated tend to have a special affection for Jewish jokes.

At the same time, Jewish humor continues to occupy a special place in American popular culture, and the contributions of twentieth-century Jews to American humor can hardly be overstated.* Indeed, it is difficult to imagine what would remain of American humor in the twentieth century without its Jewish component. This has been especially true since World War II, and today even Gentile comedians like Robin Williams and Danny Thomas have found it advantageous to include some Jewish material in their repertoires. Johnny Carson often mentions his tax accountants, H. & R. Goniff, and his stockbroker, E. F. Schnorrer. Steve Allen's material is so Jewish that audiences are often surprised to learn that he isn't. For the purposes of this volume, however, we have adopted a fairly narrow definition of Jewish humor, and have included only those selections that are explicitly Jewish in content or in form.

*A preliminary list might include, in addition to hundreds of unheralded gag writers and creators of situation comedies for radio and television, the following names: Joey Adams, Woody Allen, Morey Amsterdam, Joe Ancis, Phil Baker, Sandy Baron, Belle Barth, Jack Benny, Gertrude Berg, Milton Berle, Shelley Berman, Joey Bishop, Ben Blue, Victor Borge, David Brenner, Fanny Brice, Marshall Brickman, Albert Brooks, Mel Brooks, Lenny Bruce, Art Buchwald, George Burns, Abe Burrows, Red Buttons, Sid Caesar, Eddie Cantor, Al Capp, Jack Carter, Bennett Cerf, Myron Cohen, Irwin Corey, Rodney Dangerfield, Marshall Efron, Stanley Elkin, Jules Feiffer, Totie Fields, Phil Foster, Bruce Jay Friedman, Rube Goldberg, Harry Golden, Shecky Green, Dan Greenburg, Milt Gross, Sam Gross, Buddy Hackett, Goldie Hawn, Joseph Heller, Harry Hershfield, Abbie Hoffman, Lou Holtz, Willie Howard, Lou Jacobi, George Jessel, Mickey Katz, Danny Kaye, Georgie Kaye, Alan King, Robert Klein, Arthur Kober, Paul Krassner, Harvey Kurtzman, Bert Lahr, Louise Lasser, Norman Lear, London Lee, Fran Lebowitz, Jack E. Leonard, Jerry Lester, Sam Levenson, David Levine, Jerry Lewis, Robert Q. Lewis, Wallace Markfield, the Marx Brothers, Jackie Mason, Lou Mason, Bette Midler, Henry Morgan, Zero Mostel, Jan Murray, Lou Myers, Nichols and May, Parkyakarkas (Harry Einstein), S. J. Perelman, Gilda Radner, Carl Reiner, Don Rickles, the Ritz Brothers, Joan Rivers, Leo Rosten, Philip Roth, Mort Sahl, Soupy Sales, Dr. Seuss, Dick Shawn, Al Shean, Allan Sherman, Max Shulman, Phil Silvers, Shel Silverstein, Neil Simon, Smith and Dale, Arnold Stang, David Steinberg, Saul Steinberg, the Three Stooges, Barbra Streisand, Larry Storch, Gerald Sussman, Calvin Trillin, Sophie Tucker, Betty Walker, Nancy Walker, Ira Wallach, Billy Wilder, Gene Wilder, Paul Winchell, Ed Wynn, and Henny Youngman.

What, then, do we mean by Jewish humor? To begin, it is humor that is overtly Jewish in its concerns, characters, definitions, language, values, or symbols. (A Jewish joke, goes one definition, is one that no *goy* can understand and every Jew says he has already heard.) But not all Jewish humor derives from Jewish sources, just as not all humor created by Jews is necessarily Jewish. In these matters it is best to examine not the singer but the song.

Jewish humor is too rich and too diverse to be adequately described by a single generalization. Jewish theologians used to say that it is easier to describe God in terms of what He is *not;* the same process may be useful in understanding Jewish humor. It is not, for example, escapist. It is not slapstick. It is not physical. It is generally not cruel, and does not attack the weak or the infirm. At the same time, it is also not polite or gentle. But individual humorists come to mind immediately to negate each of these tendencies: the Marx Brothers are slapstick performers; Jerry Lewis and Sid Caesar are physical; Don Rickles is cruel; Sam Levenson is polite, and Danny Kaye is playful. So much for generalizations.

What Jewish humor *is* may be even more difficult to determine, and we offer the following broad statements in full awareness of the possible futility of the exercise:

● Jewish humor is usually substantive; it is *about* something. It is especially fond of certain specific topics, such as food (noshing is sacred), family, business, anti-Semitism, wealth and its absence, health, and survival. Jewish humor is also fascinated by the intricacies of the mind and by logic, and the short if elliptical path separating the rational from the absurd.

● As social or religious commentary, Jewish humor can be sarcastic, complaining, resigned, or descriptive. Sometimes the "point" of the humor is more powerful than the laugh it delivers, and for some of the jokes, the appropriate response is not laughter, but rather a bitter nod or a commiserating sigh of recognition. This didactic quality precludes laughing "for free," as in slapstick humor, which derives its laughter from other people's misfortunes.

● Jewish humor tends to be anti-authoritarian. It ridicules grandiosity and self-indulgence, exposes hypocrisy, and kicks pomposity in the pants. It is strongly democratic, stressing the dignity and worth of common folk.

From *Running A Muck,* copyright © 1978 by John Caldwell. By permission of Writer's Digest Books.

● Jewish humor frequently has a critical edge which creates discomfort in making its point. Often its thrust is political—aimed at leaders and other authorities who cannot be criticized more directly. This applies to prominent figures in the general society, as well as to those in the Jewish world, such as rabbis, cantors, sages, intellectuals, teachers, doctors, businessmen, philanthropists, and community functionaries. A special feature of Jewish humor is the interaction of prominent figures with simple folk and the disadvantaged, with the latter often emerging triumphant. In general, Jewish humor characteristically deals with the conflict between the people and the power structure, whether that be the individual Jew within his community, the Jew facing the Gentile world, or the Jewish community in relation to the rest of humanity.

● Jewish humor mocks everyone—including God. It frequently satirizes religious personalities and institutions, as well as rituals and dogma. At the same time, it affirms religious traditions and practices, seeking a new understanding of the differences between the holy and the mundane.

We began working on this project because we love Jewish humor and did not believe that its full range had been successfully captured in book form. No collection prior to this one, for example, has drawn significantly upon American Jewish humor of the post–World War II period, and very few have included *any* Jewish humor from America beyond the standard jokes from the Lower East Side and the garment industry. No other collection of Jewish humor has been illustrated except in the most perfunctory way. And very few books have included anything beyond the standard jokes, proverbs, and curses.

When we began talking about the need for a new volume of Jewish humor, each of us immediately recalled the same book—a book we had read again and again, first as children, then as adolescents, and finally as adults. The book, published in 1948, was *A Treasury of Jewish Folklore* by Nathan Ausubel. Today, after three dozen or so reprintings and a recently issued paperback edition, it still stands alone as the most influential book of Jewish humor ever published in English.

Ausubel later edited a second collection, entitled *A Treasury of Jewish Humor,* but the folklore volume contains the best humor. The book played a special role in our lives as children and, we have come to learn, in the lives of many of our friends and peers as well. The jokes, which have aged exceedingly well, provided us with laughter and enjoyment, of course, but they did something else: they offered us a link to a rich heritage of humor which, it turned out, was itself linked to other traditions of history, literature, and religion. In the *shtetl* of Eastern Europe, young children were introduced to the Hebrew letters with a taste of honey; for us, Ausubel's book served a similar purpose, as an appealing and inviting point of entry into Judaism and the Jewish people. We hope, among other things, that our book will offer a similar benefit.

But while Ausubel's anthology remains indispensable, it has also become dated in that it does not adequately reflect contemporary Jewish life. *A Treasury of Jewish Folklore* has the look and feel of the 1940s, and while thirty or forty years is normally a mere blink in the longer span of Jewish history, these past four decades have represented a stunning exception. Reading through Ausubel's jokes, for example, one would have little awareness of the Holocaust (for yes, even the Holocaust is represented in Jewish humor), and one would know nothing of the State of Israel, or the contemporary Jewish community in

America, or the liberation movement of Soviet Jews—four of the most significant developments in all of Jewish history.

While our book is able to include material on each of these recent topics, our primary purpose is to provide an entertainment. This book is not intended as a definitive or complete collection of Jewish humor, nor does it pretend to be a history or a textbook. While we have tried to include a good variety of authors and topics, there are numerous omissions, due both to a lack of space and to our own personal preferences.

SOURCES

All humor collections borrow from their predecessors, and in compiling this book we have drawn upon a variety of sources. We began by reading through every book of Jewish humor published in English, as well as several in Hebrew and Yiddish. We have already noted Ausubel's two collections. Leo Rosten successfully tells a good many jokes in *The Joys of Yiddish.* Henry Spaulding provides an enormous quantity of jokes in his two collections, *Encyclopedia of Jewish Humor* and *A Treasure-Trove of American Jewish Humor,* although both books are disappointing in their quality and presentation. The various collections by Mendelsohn and Learsi were also useful, as were *Isaac Asimov's Treasury of Humor* and several other anthologies. *The Day God Laughed* by Hyam Maccoby was helpful in its presentation of humorous passages from the Talmud. An especially valuable and little-known source were two articles by the folklorist Richard Dorson.* From these and many other collections we drew a wide compilation of jokes, all of which we have rewritten for this volume.

Next, we contacted dozens of friends, acquaintances, Jewish professionals, rabbis, joke collectors, and other interested parties. Our hope was to collect good jokes that had never before appeared in print. To appeal for still more jokes, we placed notices in Jewish newspapers and in *The New York Times Book Review.* The results of this search were disappointing. In all, we received close to a hundred letters, but we found very few jokes that were both new and good. "Good," of course, is a subjective judgment, while "new" is no less problematic; it is said that Cain killed Abel because his brother told him a joke he had known since childhood.

The interesting thing about the jokes we received in the mail, nearly all of which we already knew, was that many of our correspondents sincerely believed that they were composed

---

*"Jewish American Dialect Stories on Tape," *Studies in Biblical and Jewish Folklore,* ed. Raphael Patai, Francis L. Utley, and Dov Noy (Bloomington, Ind., 1960), pp. 111–174; "More Jewish Dialect Stories," *Midwest Folklore* X (1960), pp. 133–146.

by a family member—usually a parent or a grandparent. Similarly, several times we were told "new" jokes by friends and well-placed sources, only to discover the identical story a few days later in one of the many anthologies we had collected.

Our favorite reply to the notice in the *Times Book Review* came from an anonymous reader:

Gentlemen:
My favorite story is about the two Boston *schnorrers* who got the innocent *Times* to published their "Query." These guys hoped to get enough material from unsuspecting *schlemiels* to put together an anthology. Now, that's *chutzpah!*

Fortunately, we were not dependent upon the jokes we received in the mail; otherwise, this book would have been issued as a tiny pamphlet.

Our third source proved to be impractical. We had hoped to publish selections from radio and television shows, movies, record albums, plays, and the routines of famous comedians. But all too often, what is effective on the stage or on television feels flat on the page and loses much of its appeal. As for comedians, it proved virtually impossible to find selections that at the same time were original, overtly Jewish, of high quality —*and* worked well in print. As we were constantly reminded, much of a joke's appeal lies in how it is told, and nobody has yet discovered an effective way to transfer that quality to the printed page.

Happily, our fourth source proved much more successful. Jews have been especially active in American literary culture during the last thirty years or so, and we were able to find a number of selections from the works of such writers as Saul Bellow, Bernard Malamud, Max Shulman, Joseph Heller, Judith Viorst, and many others that worked very well on the page—which, of course, is how they were intended.

HOW TO READ THIS BOOK

We have divided the book into five parts, according to topics and themes rather than styles or periods. Part One ("Deeper Meanings") is about the life of the mind, including jokes about trains (which for some curious reason form the setting for many jokes about logic), scholarship, the Talmud, intellectuals, the Wise Men of Chelm, Hershele Ostropoler, Einstein and other savants, and psychiatrists, our latter-day rabbis. Part Two ("Jewish & Goyish") includes a large body of humor about anti-Semitism, as well as material on the differences between Jews and Gentiles as seen from a Jewish perspective.

Part Three ("Promised Lands") is about America and Israel. "America" in this context includes jokes about organized Jewish life, synagogues, assimilation, dialect, Yiddish, and verbal communication. The section on Israel is shorter than we would have liked, for several reasons. Much of Israeli humor does not translate well into English because a great deal of it is "insider" humor that would be meaningless to American readers. It also tends to be topical and is thus quickly outdated. Another large body of Israeli humor is not at all Jewish, while those parts that are recognizably Jewish tend to derive from the traditional humor of Eastern Europe, which is already represented in these pages.

Part Four ("Making a Living") includes jokes about business and money, from *schnorrers* (poor Jews with middle-class values) to rabbis and doctors. Part Five ("First Things Last") includes such basics as God and the Bible, animals, bar mitzvahs, marriage, men and women, family, food, death, and the world to come.

To accompany the various texts we have written a commentary which provides background information and occasional interpretations (but never explanations) of the jokes and stories. In the commentaries are a great many jokes that are related to those in the main text, but whose inclusion there might have made the book seem repetitive. Often, though not always, we have put the best-known jokes, the classics, into the commentary. And for the reader who wishes to read straight through without any intrusions of seriousness, we have set all the jokes in the commentary in bold type.

Two caveats to the reader: First, the issue of "bad taste" in humor is a matter of opinion; some readers may be offended by some of the material or language in this book. We have excluded selections that, in our view, were more offensive than funny, or that were self-deprecating with little redeeming comic value. We hope that readers will keep in mind that much of Jewish humor is *intended* to give offense, and to express that which cannot always be discussed in more delicate ways.

And finally, we repeat that the jokes we have brought together here are merely our own versions of jokes and stories that often exist in many variations. We encourage the reader to experiment with these jokes and to make them his or her own by adding whatever personal touches or details seem natural and appropriate. Many of the selections in these pages work best when read (or told) aloud, especially, of course, those containing a great deal of dialogue. We have not attempted to reproduce dialects or accents on the page, but we encourage readers to do so if they are so inclined.

Dick Codor © 1981

TRAINS • LOGIC • THE WISE MEN
OF CHELM • HERSHELE OSTROPOLER •
INTELLECTUALS • PSYCHIATRISTS •
PILPUL

MAURICE SENDAK • DEVIS GREBU •
SHOLOM ALEICHEM • DICK CODOR •
STANLEY ELKIN • EPHRAIM KISHON •
ISAAC BABEL • DAVID LEVINE • PHILIP
ROTH • WOODY ALLEN • SHERRY
FLENNIKEN • JOHN CALDWELL • RALPH
STEADMAN • ELIEZER BEN TAM • MARK
PODWAL

Illustration by Maurice Sendak. *From Zlateh The Goat and Other Stories* by Isaac Bashevis Singer. Pictures copyright © 1966 by Maurice Sendak. Reprinted by permission of Harper & Row, Publishers, Inc.

PART ONE

DEEPER MEANINGS

A classic. Minsk and Pinsk, which appear in many jokes because of the sound of their names, were important commercial centers and Jewish communities in White Russia.

This joke appears in Freud's book *Jokes and Their Relation to the Unconscious*. After explaining the joke's literal meaning, Freud goes on to comment on the issue it raises: "Is it the truth if we describe things as they are without troubling to consider how our hearer will understand what we say? Or is this only jesuitical truth, and does not genuine truth consist of taking the hearer into account and giving him a faithful picture of our own knowledge?"

This classic story comments not only on the intricacies of the Jewish mind, but also on the ravenous social curiosity that is part of modern Jewish life, making "Jewish geography" a ritual in almost every encounter between two Jewish strangers.

In a related joke:

•

A weary traveler relaxing in a train compartment is greeted by a stranger with the customary "sholom aleichem."

But instead of responding with the common reply "aleichem sholom," the traveler launches into a monologue: "Listen closely, my friend. I come from Kiev and I'm on my way to Warsaw. I'm in the grain business, but I'm strictly a small-time operator. My name is Cohen, Moshe Cohen. I have a son who has just had a bar mitzvah, and two daughters. One of my daughters is married, with two children; the other is engaged. I don't play cards, drink, or smoke. I have no political opinions. Now, I hope I haven't left anything out, but if I have, let's take care of it now, because I'm dead tired and I'm going to take a nap!"

•

TWO rival businessmen meet in the Warsaw train station. "Where are you going?" says the first man.

"To Minsk," says the second.

"To Minsk, eh? What a nerve you have! I know you're telling me you're going to Minsk because you want me to think that you're really going to Pinsk. But it so happens that I know you really *are* going to Minsk. *So why are you lying to me?*"

AFTER months of negotiation, a Jewish scholar from Odessa was granted permission to visit Moscow. He boarded the train and found an empty seat. At the next stop a young man got on and sat next to him. The scholar looked at the young man and thought:

This fellow doesn't look like a peasant, and if he isn't a peasant, he probably comes from this district. If he comes from this district, he must be Jewish because this is, after all, a Jewish district. On the other hand, if he is a Jew, where could he be going? I'm the only one in our district who has permission to travel to Moscow.

Wait—just outside Moscow there is a little village called Samvet, and you don't need special permission to go there. But why would he be going to Samvet? He's probably going to visit somebody there, but how many Jewish families are there in Samvet? Only two—the Bernsteins and the Steinbergs. The Bernsteins are a terrible family, so he must be visiting the Steinbergs. But why is he going?

The Steinbergs have only girls, so maybe he's their son-in-law. But if he is, then which daughter did he marry? Sarah married that nice lawyer from Budapest and Esther married a businessman from Zhadomir, so it must be Sarah's husband. Which means that his name is Alexander Cohen, if I'm not mistaken. But if he comes from Budapest, with all the anti-Semitism they have there, he must have changed his name. What's the Hungarian equivalent of Cohen? Kovacs. But if he changed his name, he must have some special status. What could it be? A doctorate from the university.

At this point the scholar turned to the young man and said, "How do you do, Dr. Kovacs?"

"Very well, thank you, sir," answered the startled passenger. "But how is it that you know my name?"

"Oh," replied the scholar, "it was obvious."

A PASSENGER on a train in Israel watched in astonishment as the old man across the aisle kept repeating the same pattern. First he would mumble a few words to himself, then he would smile, and finally he would raise his hand and stop talking for a few moments.

After observing this unusual behavior for close to an hour, the passenger finally brought himself to address the stranger. "Excuse me, sir, but I couldn't help noticing what you were doing. Is anything wrong?"

"Not at all," replied the old man. "You see, whenever I take a trip, I get bored. And so I always tell myself jokes, which is why you saw me smiling."

"But why did you keep raising your hand?"

"Oh, *that.* It's to interrupt myself because I've heard that joke before."

Devis Grebu © 1981

LEVINGER, a businessman from Utica, goes to the train station to catch the eleven-thirty express to Philadelphia. A cautious man, he arrives a full hour early, and begins to wander around the station in search of some amusement.

But Utica, a small city, has a rather modest train station, and after visiting the small newsstand, Levinger is reduced to putting a penny into a scale that promises: "Your weight and fortune. One cent."

"What have I got to lose?" Levinger asks himself as he fishes for a penny. He steps on the scale, drops the penny in the slot, and retrieves a little card. "Your name is Seymour Levinger," says the card, "you're Jewish, and you weigh 170 pounds."

Levinger is incredulous. He goes off to buy a magazine, but he is drawn back to the scale, and he climbs on again, and inserts another penny. Again the same card: "Your name is Seymour Levinger, you're Jewish, and you weigh 170 pounds."

Levinger is astonished. He calls a porter, and asks him to step up on the scale. Levinger pays. The card reads: "Your

They say that when you tell a joke to a peasant,
he laughs three times—
> *once when you tell the joke,*
> *again when you explain it,*
> *and yet again when he understands it,*
>> *for peasants love to laugh.*

> *When you tell a joke to a landowner,*
> *he laughs twice—*
>> *once when you tell him the joke,*
>> *and again when you explain it,*
>>> *for he never really understands it.*

>> *When you tell a joke to an army officer,*
>> *he laughs only once—*
>>> *when you tell it.*
>> *He never lets you explain it,*
>>> *and it goes without saying that*
>>>> *he is unable to understand it.*

name is Leroy Jackson, you're black, and you weigh 155 pounds."

"That's right," says the porter, as Levinger stands there shaking his head in disbelief. There is only one other passenger in the station, and Levinger runs over to him, and begs the man to weigh himself on the scale. The man complies. "Your name is Tony Callaghan," says the card, "you're Irish, and you weigh 200 pounds."

"Correct," says Callaghan. Now Levinger is growing irritated. He is determined to fool the machine. Next to the station is a post office, and Levinger knows one of the clerks, an Armenian dwarf with one leg. Finally he will defeat the machine. Levinger goes to find the dwarf, and convinces him to come to the station to be weighed. The dwarf agrees, and as he hobbles onto the scale, Levinger drops in another penny. The card reads: "Your name is Stefan Mongoosian, you're Armenian and a dwarf, and you weigh 85 pounds."

Levinger is furious. Grabbing his suitcase, he jumps into a cab. Ten minutes from the station he knows a certain Chinese restaurant, and in the restaurant is a waitress whose father comes from Egypt, and whose mother is from Hawaii. Levinger implores the woman to come to the station with him, and she agrees. When they arrive, Levinger inserts another penny in the machine. The card reads: "Your name is Liana Mahfooz, you're half Egyptian and half Hawaiian, and you weigh 125 pounds."

Levinger sends her back in the cab. Around the corner from the station is a theatrical shop, and Levinger goes in, coming out ten minutes later in blackface, wearing a false mustache, a blond wig, sunglasses, and carrying a cane. In his coat pocket are bricks he has found in the street.

Weighed down by the bricks, Levinger pads up to the machine and drops in another penny. Out comes the card: "Your name is Seymour Levinger, you're Jewish, and you just missed your train."

•

Sam and Max are traveling in fine style from New York to Chicago, by train. Along the way, they keep the porter busy with dozens of small requests: a glass of water, a shoeshine, a telegram, the morning paper. As they're getting off the train, Sam turns to Max and says, "I forgot to give George a tip. Did you take care of him?"

"No," says Max. "I thought *you* did." Max quickly runs back onto the train and hands George a twenty-dollar bill.

"Now I know that you people didn't crucify the Lord," says George. "You just *worried* him to death."

•

But when you tell a joke to a Jew—
even before you've had a chance to finish it
he's already interrupting you.
    First, he's heard it before.
    Second, why are you telling it wrong?
So he decides to tell you the joke—but in a much better version than yours.

One of the basic principles of Jewish logic is that things could always be worse:

A poor man goes to the rabbi and complains: "My house is much too small for my family of ten."

"Bring in your goat," says the rabbi, and the man complies. A week later he returns: "Rabbi, it's even worse!"

"Bring in your chickens," says the rabbi.

The man returns in another week, and the rabbi tells him to bring in his cow as well. The next time the man comes, he is at his wits' end. "I can't stand it any longer," he says.

"In that case," says the rabbi, "go home and take all your animals back into the barn."

"Thank you, Rabbi," the man says a few days later. "Lately we've had so much room. . . ."

These jokes have hundreds of cousins. A sampling:

Sholom Aleichem's most famous character, Tevye the dairyman, addressing the Lord: "You have made us a little lower than the angels. That depends on what you call a little, doesn't it? Lord, what is life, and what are we, and to what may a man be compared? A man may be compared to a carpenter; a carpenter lives and lives and lives, and finally he dies. And so does a man."

Levine brings a package to the post office.

"It's too heavy," says the clerk. "You'll have to put more stamps on it."

"And if I put more stamps on it," says Levine, "that'll make it lighter?"

Two partners from the garment industry are vacationing in Florida. On the balcony of their hotel is a bouquet of tropical flowers. "Just look at these beautiful flowers," says the first man. "I wonder what kind they are."

"How should I know?" replies his friend. "What am I, a milliner?"

WHEN Yankel met Mendel on the train, he was surprised to find his friend in pain, yelling "Oy" every minute or two.

"What's the matter with you?" asked Yankel.

"It's my feet," replied Mendel. "My feet are killing me. It's because my shoes are too small."

"But that's crazy," replied Yankel. "Then why do you wear them?"

"I'll tell you why. My partner made off with all our profits. My daughter is about to marry a goy. My other daughter is so ugly and unpleasant that she'll never get married. My son is nothing more than a bum. My wife doesn't stop nagging. And bills—every day I come home and there are more bills to be paid. Right now I'm out of work. And so every night I go home, and then I take off these shoes—and Yankel, believe me, I feel like a million dollars!"

A POOR Talmud scholar approached his rabbi with his masterpiece: a commentary on the Mishnah.

"Better you should stop writing," said the rabbi. "It won't get you anywhere."

"And if I stopped writing," replied the scholar, "would it get me anywhere?"

AN elderly Jew walked up to the window at the main post office in Pinsk. "Excuse me," he began timidly, "but how often does the mail go from here to Warsaw?"

"To Warsaw? Every day."

The old man was silent for a moment, and then asked, "Thursdays too?"

KATZ is sitting naked in his room, wearing only a top hat, when Cohen walks in.

"Why are you sitting here naked?"

"It's all right," says Katz. "Nobody comes to visit."

"But why the hat?"

"Well, maybe somebody will come."

TWO Jews are sitting silently over a glass of tea.

"You know," says the first man, "life is like a glass of tea with sugar."

"A glass of tea with sugar?" asks his friend. "Why do you say that?"

"How should I know?" replies the first man. "What am I, a philosopher?"

SOMEBODY once asked Motke Chabad, the legendary wit: "Tell me, Motke, you're a smart fellow. Why is *kugel* called *kugel?*"

Motke lost no time in responding. "What kind of silly question is that? It's sweet like *kugel*, isn't it? It's thick like *kugel*, isn't it? And it tastes like *kugel*, doesn't it? So why *shouldn't* it be called *kugel?*

"SAM, please close the window. It's cold outside."

"Nu, and if I close the window, will it be warm outside?"

A WOMAN on a train walked up to a distinguished-looking gentleman across the aisle. "Excuse me," she said, "but are you Jewish?"

"No," replied the man.

A few minutes later the woman returned. "Excuse me," she said again, "but are you sure you're not Jewish?"

"I'm sure," replied the man.

But the woman was not convinced, and a few minutes later she approached him a third time. "Are you absolutely sure you're not Jewish?" she asked.

"All right, all right," the man said. "You win. I'm Jewish."

"That's funny," said the woman. "You don't *look* Jewish."

A merchant bought a sack of prunes from his competitor. Opening the sack, he saw that the prunes had begun to go rotten. He went back to the seller and demanded his money back. The seller refused, and the two men went to see the rabbi to settle their dispute.

The rabbi sat down at a table between the two men and emptied the sack in front of them. Then he put on his eyeglasses, and without saying a word, he went to work, slowly and carefully tasting one prune after another and each time shaking his head.

After some time had passed, the plaintiff finally spoke up: "Nu, Rabbi, what do you think?"

The rabbi, who was about to consume the last of the prunes, looked up and replied sharply: "Why are you fellows wasting my time? What do you think I am—a prune expert?"

•

"That pot you borrowed from me? It's damaged. You'll have to buy me a new one!"

"What?! First of all, it was in perfect condition when I gave it back to you. Second, it was broken when you gave it to me. And third, I never borrowed your lousy pot!"

•

The same joke is told about an Orthodox Jew who goes to China and attends a synagogue service there. "Ah, so," says the rabbi. "Are you Jewish?" "Of course I'm Jewish," the man replies, and the rabbi responds with: "Funny, you don't look Jewish."

The old man wouldn't stop complaining: "Oy, am I thirsty! Oy, am I thirsty!" But while the train was in motion, there was nothing that could be done. At the first stop, three passengers rushed out to bring the old man a glass of water. When the train pulled out of the station, the car was blessedly quiet, until suddenly the old man's voice broke through, hoarsely: "Oy, was I thirsty!"

•

On Account of a Hat

Sholom Aleichem (his real name was Sholom Rabinowitz) was born in the Ukraine in 1859, and died in New York in 1916. The most famous of all Yiddish writers, he began his career writing in Hebrew, and translated *Robinson Crusoe* into Hebrew at the age of fifteen. When he switched to Yiddish, he invented his pseudonym (a traditional greeting meaning "peace unto you") so that neither relatives nor friends would know that he was writing in a language that was considered unworthy of serious writing. (The pseudonym would become even more useful when Sholom Aleichem became a businessman associated with influential citizens in Kiev who had no use for any writers—let alone a writer who wrote in Yiddish.)

"On Account of a Hat" is an elaborate version of a well-known and simple joke. "Out of this insubstantial matter," writes Ruth Wisse in the Introduction to *The Best of Sholom Aleichem,* "Sholom Aleichem has woven a masterpiece with a dozen interpretations: it is the plight of the Diaspora Jew, an exposure of rootlessness, a mockery of tyranny, the comic quest for identity, a Marxist critique of capitalism, and of course, an ironic self-referential study of literary sleight of hand."

"Did I hear you say absentminded? Now, in our town, that is, in Kasrilevke, we've really got someone for you—do you hear what I say? His name is Sholem Shachnah, but we call him Sholem Shachnah Rattlebrain, and is he absentminded, is this a distracted creature, Lord have mercy on us! The stories they tell about him, about this Sholem Shachnah—bushels and baskets of stories—I tell you, whole crates full of stories and anecdotes! It's too bad you're in such a hurry on account of the Passover, because what I could tell you, Mr. Sholom Aleichem —do you hear what I say?—you could go on writing it down forever. But if you can spare a moment I'll tell you a story about what happened to Sholem Shachnah on a Passover eve—a story about a hat, a true story, I should live so, even if it does sound like someone made it up."

These were the words of a Kasrilevke merchant, a dealer in stationery, that is to say, snips of paper. He smoothed out his beard, folded it down over his neck, and went on smoking his thin little cigarettes, one after the other.

I must confess that this true story, which he related to me, does indeed sound like a concocted one, and for a long time I couldn't make up my mind whether or not I should pass it on to you. But I thought it over and decided that if a respectable merchant and dignitary of Kasrilevke, who deals in stationery and is surely no *litterateur*—if he vouches for a story, it must be true. What would he be doing with fiction? Here it is in his own words. I had nothing to do with it.

This Sholem Shachnah I'm telling you about, whom we call Sholem Shachnah Rattlebrain, is a real estate broker—you hear what I say? He's always with landowners, negotiating transactions. Transactions? Well, at least he hangs around the landowners. So what's the point? I'll tell you. Since he hangs around the landed gentry, naturally some of their manner has rubbed off on him, and he always has a mouth full of farms, homesteads, plots, acreage, soil, threshing machines, renovations, woods, timber, and other such terms having to do with estates.

One day God took pity on Sholem Shachnah, and for the first time in his career as a real estate broker—are you listening?—he actually worked out a deal. That is to say, the work itself, as you can imagine, was done by others, and when the time came to collect the fee, the big rattler turned out to be not Sholem Shachnah Rattlebrain, but Drobkin, a Jew from

Minsk province, a great big fearsome rattler, a real estate broker from way back—he and his two brothers, also brokers and also big rattlers. So you can take my word for it, there was quite a to-do. A Jew has contrived and connived and has finally, with God's help, managed to cut himself in—so what do they do but come along and cut him out! Where's justice? Sholem Shachnah wouldn't stand for it—are you listening to me? He set up such a holler and an outcry—"Look what they've done to me!"—that at last they gave in to shut him up, and good riddance it was, too.

When he got his few cents, Sholem Shachnah sent the greater part of it home to his wife, so she could pay off some debts, shoo the wolf from the door, fix up new outfits for the children, and make ready for the Passover holidays. And as for himself, he also needed a few things, and besides, he had to buy presents for his family, as was the custom.

Meanwhile the time flew by, and before he knew it, it was almost Passover. So Sholem Shachnah—now listen to this—ran to the telegraph office and sent home a wire: *Arriving home Passover without fail.* It's easy to say "arriving," and "without fail," at that. But you just try it! Just try riding out our way on the new train and see how fast you'll arrive. Ah, what a pleasure! Did they do us a favor! I tell you, Mr. Sholom Aleichem, for a taste of Paradise such as this you'd gladly forsake your own grandchildren! You see how it is: until you get to Zolodievka there isn't much you can do about it, so you just lean back and ride. But at Zolodievka the fun begins, because that's where you have to change, to get onto the new train, which they did us such a favor by running out to Kasrilevke. But not so fast. First there's the little matter of several hours' wait, exactly as announced in the schedule—provided, of course, you don't pull in after the Kasrilevke train has left. And at what time of night may you look forward to this treat? The very middle, thank you, when you're dead tired and disgusted, without a friend in the world except sleep—and there's not one single place in the whole station where you can lay your head, not one. When the wise men of Kasrilevke quote the passage from the Holy Book, *"Tov shem meshemen tov,"* they know what they're doing. I'll translate it for you: We were better off without the train.

To make a long story short, when our Sholem Shachnah arrived in Zolodievka with his carpetbag, he was half dead; he had already spent two nights without sleep. But that was nothing at all to what was facing him—he still had to spend a whole night waiting in the station. What shall he do? Naturally he looked around for a place to sit down. Whoever heard of such a thing? Nowhere. Nothing. No place to sit. The walls of the station were covered with soot, the floor was covered with spit.

It was dark, it was terrible. He finally discovered one miserable spot on a bench where he had just room enough to squeeze in, and no more than that, because the bench was occupied by an official of some sort in a uniform full of buttons, who was lying there all stretched out and snoring away to beat the band. Who this Buttons was, whether he was coming or going, he hadn't the vaguest idea—Sholem Shachnah, that is. But he could tell that Buttons was no dime-a-dozen official. This was plain by his cap, a military cap with a red band and a visor. He could have been an officer or a police official. Who knows? But surely he had drawn up to the station with a ringing of bells, had staggered in, full to the ears with meat and drink, laid himself out on the bench as in his father's vineyard, and worked up a glorious snoring.

It's not such a bad life to be a Gentile, and an official one at that, with buttons, thinks he—Sholem Shachnah, that is—and he wonders, dare he sit next to this Buttons, or hadn't he better keep his distance? Nowadays you never can tell whom you're sitting next to. If he's no more than a plain inspector, that's still all right. But what if he turns out to be a district inspector? Or a provincial commander? Or even higher than that? And supposing this is even Purishkevitch himself, the famous anti-Semite (may his name perish)? Let someone else deal with him, and Sholem Shachnah turns cold at the mere thought of falling into such a fellow's hands. But then he says to himself—now listen to this—Buttons, he says, who the hell is Buttons? And who gives a hang for Purishkevitch? Don't I pay my fare the same as Purishkevitch? So why should he have all the comforts of life and I none? If Buttons is entitled to a delicious night's sleep, then doesn't he—Sholem Shachnah, that is —at least have a nap coming? After all, he's human too, and besides, he's already gone two nights without a wink. And so he sits down on a corner of the bench and leans his head back, not, God forbid, to sleep, but just like that, to snooze. But all of a sudden he remembers he's supposed to be home for Passover, and tomorrow is Passover eve! What if, God have mercy, he should fall asleep and miss the train? But that's why he's got a Jewish head on his shoulders—are you listening to me or not? So he figures out the answer to that one too—Sholem Shachnah, that is—and goes looking for a porter, a certain Yeremei (he knows him well), to make a deal with him. Whereas he, Sholem Shachnah, is already on his third sleepless night and is afraid, God forbid, that he may miss his train, therefore let him— Yeremei, that is—in God's name, be sure to wake him, Sholem Shachnah, because tomorrow night is a holiday, Passover. "Easter," he says to him in Russian, and lays a coin in Yeremei's mitt. "Easter, Yeremei, do you understand, *goyisher kop?*

Our Easter." The peasant pockets the coin, no doubt about that, and promises to wake him at the first sign of the train—he can sleep soundly and put his mind at rest. So Sholem Shachnah sits down in his corner of the bench, gingerly, pressed up against the wall, with his carpetbag curled around him so that no one should steal it. Little by little he sinks back, makes himself comfortable, and half shuts his eyes—no more than forty winks, you understand. But before long he's got one foot propped up on the bench and then the other; he stretches out and drifts off to sleep. Sleep? I'll say sleep, like God commanded us: with his head thrown back and his hat rolling away on the floor. Sholem Shachnah is snoring like an eight-day wonder. After all, a human being, up two nights in a row—what would you have him do?

He had a strange dream. He tells this himself—that is, Sholem Shachnah does. He dreamed that he was riding home for Passover—are you listening to me?—but not on the train, in a wagon, driven by a thievish peasant, Ivan Zlodi we call him. The horses were terribly slow, they barely dragged along. Sholem Shachnah was impatient, and he poked the peasant between the shoulders and cried, "May you only drop dead, Ivan darling! Hurry up, you lout! Passover is coming, our Jewish Easter!" Once he called out to him, twice, three times. The thief paid him no mind. But all of a sudden he whipped his horses to a gallop and they went whirling away, up hill and down, like demons. Sholem Shachnah lost his hat. Another minute of this and he would have lost God knows what. "Whoa, there, Ivan, old boy! Where's the fire? Not so fast!" cried Sholem Shachnah. He covered his head with his hands—he was worried, you see, over his lost hat. How can he drive into town bareheaded? But for all the good it did him, he could have been hollering at a post. Ivan the Thief was racing the horses as if forty devils were after him. All of a sudden—tppprrru!—they came to a dead stop. What's the matter? Nothing. "Get up," said Ivan. "Time to get up."

Time? What time? Sholem Shachnah is all confused. He wakes up, rubs his eyes, and is all set to step out of the wagon when he realizes he has lost his hat. Is he dreaming or not? And what's he doing here? Sholem Shachnah finally comes to his senses and recognizes the peasant. This isn't Ivan Zlodi at all, but Yeremei the porter. So he concludes that he isn't on a high road after all, but in the station at Zolodievka, on the way home for Passover, and that if he means to get there he'd better run to the window for a ticket, but fast. Now what? No hat. The carpetbag is right where he left it, but his hat? He pokes around under the bench, reaching all over, until he comes up with a hat—not his own, to be sure, but the official's, with the red band and the visor. But Sholem Shachnah has no time for details and he rushes off to buy a ticket. The ticket window is jammed; everybody and his cousins are crowding in. Sholem Shachnah thinks he won't get to the window in time, perish the thought, and he starts pushing forward, carpetbag and all. The people see the red band and the visor and they make way for him. "Where to, Your Excellency?" asks the ticket agent. What's this Excellency, all of a sudden? wonders Sholem Shachnah, and he rather resents it. Some joke, a Gentile poking fun at a Jew. All the same, he says—Sholem Shachnah, that is—"Kasrilevke." "Which class, Your Excellency?" The ticket agent is looking straight at the red band and the visor. Sholem Shachnah is angrier than ever. I'll give him an Excellency so he'll know how to make fun of a poor Jew! But then he thinks: Oh, well, we Jews are in Diaspora—do you hear what I say?—let it pass. And he asks for a ticket third class. "Which class?" The agent blinks at him, very surprised. This time Sholem Shachnah gets good and sore and he really tells him off. "Third!" he says. All right, thinks the agent, third is third.

In short, Sholem Shachnah buys his ticket, takes up his carpetbag, runs out onto the platform, plunges into the crowd of Jews and Gentiles, no comparison intended, and goes looking for the third-class carriage. Again the red band and visor work like a charm; everyone makes way for the official. Sholem Shachnah is wondering, What goes on here? But he runs along the platform till he meets a conductor carrying a lantern. "Is this third class?" asks Sholem Shachnah, putting one foot on the stairs and shoving his bag into the door of the compartment. "Yes, Your Excellency," says the conductor, but he holds him back. "If you please, sir, it's packed full, as tight as your fist. You couldn't squeeze a needle into that crowd." And he takes Sholem Shachnah's carpetbag—you hear what I'm saying?—and sings out, "Right this way, Your Excellency, I'll find you a seat." "What the devil!" cries Sholem Shachnah. "Your Excellency and Your Excellency!" But he hasn't much time for the fine points; he's worried about his carpetbag. He's afraid, you see, that with all these Excellencies he'll be swindled out of his belongings. So he runs after the conductor with the lantern, who leads him into a second-class carriage. This is also packed to the rafters, no room even to yawn in there. "This way, please, Your Excellency!" And again the conductor grabs the bag and Sholem Shachnah lights out after him. "Where in blazes is he taking me?" Sholem Shachnah is racking his brains over this Excellency business, but meanwhile he keeps his eye on the main thing—the carpetbag. They enter the first-class carriage, the conductor sets down the bag, salutes, and backs away, bowing. Sholem Shachnah bows right back. And there he is, alone at last.

Left alone in the carriage, Sholem Shachnah looks around to get his bearings—you hear what I say? He has no idea why all these honors have suddenly been heaped on him—first class, salutes, Your Excellency. Can it be on account of the real estate deal he just closed? That's it! But wait a minute. If his own people, Jews, that is, honored him for this, it would be understandable. But Gentiles! The conductor! The ticket agent! What's it to them? Maybe he's dreaming. Sholem Shachnah rubs his forehead and while passing down the corridor glances in the mirror on the wall. It nearly knocks him over! He sees not himself but the official with the red band. That's who it is! "All my bad dreams on Yeremei's head and on his hands and feet, that lug! Twenty times I tell him to wake me and I even give him a tip, and what does he do, that dumb ox, may he catch cholera in his face, but wake the official instead! And me he leaves asleep on the bench! Tough luck, Sholem Shachnah, old boy, but this year you'll spend Passover in Zolodievka, not at home."

Now get a load of this. Sholem Shachnah scoops up his carpetbag and rushes off once more, right back to the station, where he is sleeping on the bench. He's going to wake himself up before the locomotive, God forbid, lets out a blast and blasts his Passover to pieces. And so it was. No sooner had Sholem Shachnah leaped out of the carriage with his carpetbag than the locomotive did let go with a blast—do you hear me?—one followed by another, and then, good night!

The paper dealer smiled as he lit a fresh cigarette, thin as a straw. "And would you like to hear the rest of the story? The rest isn't so nice. On account of being such a rattlebrain, our dizzy Sholem Shachnah had a miserable Passover, spending both *Seders* among strangers in the house of a Jew in Zolodievka. But this was nothing—listen to what happened afterward. First of all, he has a wife—Sholem Shachnah, that is—and his wife—how shall I describe her to you? *I* have a wife, *you* have a wife, we all have wives, we've had a taste of Paradise, we know what it means to be married. All I can say about Sholem Shachnah's wife is that she's A number one. And did she give him a royal welcome! Did she lay into him! Mind you, she didn't complain about his spending the holiday away from home, and she said nothing about the red band and the visor. She let that stand for the time being; she'd take it up with him later. The only thing she complained about was the telegram! And not so much the telegram—you hear what I say?—as the one short phrase *without fail.* What possessed him to put that into the wire: *Arriving home Passover without fail.* Was he trying to make the telegraph company rich? And besides, how dare a human being say 'without fail' in the first place? It did him no good to answer and explain. She buried him alive. Oh, well, that's what wives are for. And not that she was altogether wrong—after all, she had been waiting so anxiously. But this was nothing compared with what he caught from the town—Kasrilevke, that is. Even before he returned, the whole town—you hear what I say?—knew all about Yeremei and the official and the red band and the visor and the conductor's Your Excellency—the whole show. He himself—Sholem Shachnah, that is—denied everything and swore up and down that the Kasrilevke smart alecks had invented the entire story for lack of anything better to do. It was all very simple: the reason he came home late, after the holidays, was that he had made a special trip to inspect a wooded estate. Woods? Estate? Not a chance—no one bought *that!* They pointed him out in the streets and held their sides, laughing. And everybody asked him, 'How does it feel, Reb Sholem Shachnah, to wear a cap with a red band and a visor?' 'And tell us,' said others, 'what's it like to travel first class?' As for the children, this was made to order for them—you hear what I say? Wherever he went they trooped after him, shouting, 'Your Excellency! Your excellent Excellency! Your most excellent Excellency!'

"You think it's so easy to put one over on Kasrilevke?"

Translated by Isaac Rosenfeld

Devis Grebu © 1981

STANLEY ELKIN

The Meaning of Life

Morty sat propped up in bed. Behind his head was the bulging
knapsack he used for a pillow. He read the Yellow Pages until
two in the morning and had just finished TAXIS when he had the
inspiration. He went to Eighth Avenue and 164th Street, to the
Manhattan garage of the largest cab company in the city. He
chose one ramp and followed it down until he came to an enormous room where there were more cabs than he had ever seen.
I could have used one of these in the jungle, he thought absently.

Despite the vastness of the room and the dim light, the
yellow machinery lent a kind of brightness to the place. Everywhere there were drivers, alone or in groups, writing up log
sheets or talking together. Men stood in line in front of the
coffee machines along the wall. Inside some of the cabs, the
doors open wide on their hinges, Morty could see drivers reading newspapers. He heard the steadily registering bells on the
gas pumps. It was three-thirty in the morning.

Morty walked toward the center of the cavernous room and
climbed up on top of a cab.

"Hey, what's the matter with you? Get down from there," a man yelled.

"New York cabdrivers are world famous," Morty shouted from the roof of the cab, "for their compassion and their oracular wisdom. I am Morty Perlmutter, fifty-seven years old, fifty-seven-time loser of the Nobel Prize for Everything, and I'm here to find out what you know." They stared up at him, astonished. "I got the idea from the Yellow Pages," he added sweetly.

"That's my cab that nut is up on," a driver said. "Come on, nut, off and out."

"I challenge you to a debate, sir," Morty shouted. "I challenge *all* of you to a debate. Let's go, every man on his taxicab." He watched them carefully. Someone moved forward threateningly but stopped, still several feet away from the taxi on which Morty stood. It was the Perlmutter Dipsy Doodle, the dependable mock madness, one of his most useful techniques. He told them that frankly. He told them to their faces. He didn't hold back a thing.

"It's a known fact," he said. "People have a lot of respect for insanity. Madmen are among the least persecuted members of any society. It's because they're not a *part* of society. They're *strangers.* The Greco-Persian ethic of hospitality lies behind that. Listen, I didn't read *Hamlet* until I was forty-two years old, but I learned the lesson. When does Hamlet die? *During the single moment in the play he's completely sane,* that's when! Figure it out." He folded his arms and hugged himself and did a little dance on the roof. He was completely safe. "Come on, up on your cabs. Everybody."

A man laughed and put a knee on his fender. "What the hell," he said, "I'm a sport. A sport's a sport." He scrambled onto the hood and made his way over the windshield to the roof of the cab and stood up uncertainly. "Hey," he said, "you guys look goofy down there."

Morty applauded, and below him the drivers were grinning and pointing up at the two of them. Soon others were climbing over their cabs, and in a few minutes only the man whose roof Morty had taken was without a cab to stand on. He seemed disappointed. Morty shrugged.

Perlmutter waited until the others stopped giggling and became accustomed to their strange positions. "All right," he said. "You men have lived in this city all your lives, most of you. What do you know? Tell me." He pointed to a fat driver on a taxicab across from him, but the man looked back blankly and smiled helplessly. Morty waited for one of the others to speak. At last a tall driver in a green cap started to say something.

"Louder, sir," Morty shouted. "It's hard to hear pronouncements in this cave."

"I was just saying that if you want I could talk about what's wrong with the traffic in this town."

The drivers groaned. Morty joined them. "Small-time," he said, "but that's an interesting demonstration of the limited world view. Thank you."

"I'll tell you how I give up smoking," another driver said.

"Why did you?"

"I went out and bought a whole carton and dipped them in the old lady's chicken soup and let them dry out on the radiator overnight. Then when I'd go for a smoke—"

"Why did you give it up?" Morty interrupted him.

". . . you can imagine for yourself. They tasted—"

"I asked *why*. Why did you give it up?"

The driver stared at him. "Well, who needs the aggravation of a lung cancer?" he said. "I got a brother-in-law in Queens he's got three dry-cleaning plants, a daughter away at school. Forty-eight years old he gets this cough he can't get rid of it."

"Self-preservation," Morty said, bored. "Nothing. *Nothing.*" The man sat down on the roof of his cab. "Look," Morty said, "I'm asking the meaning of life. This one says traffic congestion, that one lung congestion. I won't be sidetracked." Morty wiped his forehead. "New Yorkers, Cabdrivers, Big-Mouths: I'm Morton Perlmutter from the world's cities and jungles and seas and poles. I come, a genius, but humble, willing to learn, you understand, to the largest city in the world—that's crap about London: they count everybody from Scotland to Surrey; Tokyo the same—*the largest city in the world,* a capstone of the planet, melting pot for the tired, the poor, the huddled masses, the not so huddled, the works. And if anyone should know, *you* should know. What's the meaning of life?"

Morty watched a driver cup his hands against his mouth and he saw it coming.

"Life?" the driver shouted. "Life's a fountain."

"Yeah, yeah," Morty said, getting down from the cab. "I know that one too."

Stanley Elkin was born in 1930 in New York, and has been teaching at Washington University in Saint Louis for the past twenty years. He is the author of many acclaimed short stories, and several novels, including *Boswell, A Bad Man, The Dick Gibson Show,* and *Searches and Seizures.*

This selection is from "Perlmutter at the East Pole," the tale of an eccentric and independent anthropologist who wanders through the world searching for truth. Fittingly, Morty arranges his itinerary so that New York is the final stop on his voyage. This story appears in Elkin's collection *Criers and Kibitzers, Kibitzers and Criers.*

"Life is a fountain," at the end of this excerpt, refers to this famous story:

•

A rabbinical student is about to leave Europe for a position in the New World. He goes to his rabbi for advice, and the rabbi, a great Talmud scholar, offers an adage which, he assures the younger man, will guide him throughout his life: "Life is a fountain."

The young rabbi is deeply impressed by the profundity of his teacher's remarks, and departs for a successful career in America. Thirty years later, hearing that his mentor is dying, the younger man returns for a final visit.

"Rabbi," he says to his old teacher, "I have one question. For thirty years, every time I have been sad or confused I have thought of the phrase you passed on to me before I left for America. It has helped me through the most difficult of times. But to be perfectly honest with you, rabbi, I have never fully understood the meaning of it. And now that you are about to enter the World of Truth, perhaps you would be so kind as to tell me what these words really mean. Rabbi, why *is* life like a fountain?"

Wearily, the old man replies, "All right, so it's *not* like a fountain!"

•

Devis Grebu © 1981

Devis Grebu © 1981

EPHRAIM KISHON

Jewish Poker

Ephraim Kishon has long been Israel's best-known humorist. Born in Budapest in 1924, Kishon came to Israel in 1949 and quickly established a successful career as a satirist, columnist, and playwright. He also wrote, directed, and produced the Israeli hit film *Sallah.*

Kishon's European sensibilities are reflected in many of his pieces, including this one. His work is known around the world, and his books have been translated into many languages. His works in English include *Wise Guy, Solomon; Look Back, Mrs. Lot;* and *Unfair to Goliath.*

For quite a while the two of us sat at our table, wordlessly stirring our coffee. Ervinke was bored.

"All right," he said. "Let's play poker."

"No," I answered. "I hate cards. I always lose."

"Who's talking about cards?" Thus Ervinke. "I was thinking of Jewish poker."

He then briefly explained the rules of the game. Jewish poker is played without cards, in your head, as befits the People of the Book.

"You think of a number; I also think of a number," Ervinke said. "Whoever thinks of a higher number wins. This sounds easy, but it has a hundred pitfalls. *Nu!*"

"All right," I agreed. "Let's try."

We plunked down five piasters each, and leaning back in our chairs, began to think of numbers. After a while Ervinke signaled that he had one. I said I was ready.

"All right." Thus Ervinke. "Let's hear your number."

"Eleven," I said.

"Twelve," Ervinke said, and took the money. I could have kicked myself, because originally I had thought of Fourteen, and only at the last moment had I climbed down to Eleven; I really don't know why.

"Listen." I turned to Ervinke. "What would have happened had I said Fourteen?"

"What a question! I'd have lost. Now, that is just the charm of poker: you never know how things will turn out. But if your nerves cannot stand a little gambling, perhaps we had better call it off."

Without saying another word, I put down ten piasters on the table. Ervinke did likewise. I pondered my number carefully and opened with Eighteen.

"Damn!" Ervinke said. "I have only Seventeen!"

I swept the money into my pocket and quietly guffawed. Ervinke had certainly not dreamed that I would master the tricks of Jewish poker so quickly. He had probably counted on my opening with Fifteen or Sixteen, but certainly not with Eighteen. Ervinke, his brow in angry furrows, proposed we double the stakes.

"As you like," I sneered, and could hardly keep back my jubilant laughter. In the meantime a fantastic number had occurred to me: Thirty-five!

"Lead!" said Ervinke.

"Thirty-five!"

"Forty-three!"

With that he pocketed the forty piasters. I could feel the blood rushing into my brain.

"Listen," I hissed. "Then why didn't you say Forty-three the last time?"

"Because I had thought of Seventeen!" Ervinke retorted indignantly. "Don't you see, that is the fun in poker: you never know what will happen next."

"A pound," I remarked dryly, and, my lips curled in scorn, I threw a note on the table. Ervinke extracted a similar note from his pocket and with maddening slowness placed it next to mine. The tension was unbearable. I opened with Fifty-four.

"Oh, damn it!" Ervinke fumed. "I also thought of Fifty-four! Draw! Another game!"

My brain worked with lightning speed. "Now you think I'll again call Eleven, my boy," I reasoned. "But you'll get the surprise of your life." I chose the surefire Sixty-nine.

"You know what, Ervinke"—I turned to Ervinke—"you lead."

"As you like," he agreed. "It's all the same with me. Seventy!"

Everything went black before my eyes. I had not felt such panic since the siege of Jerusalem.

"Nu?" Ervinke urged. "What number did you think of?"

"What do you know?" I whispered with downcast eyes. "I have forgotten."

"You liar!" Ervinke flared up. "I know you didn't forget, but simply thought of a smaller number and now don't want to own up. An old trick. Shame on you!"

I almost slapped his loathsome face for this evil slander, but with some difficulty overcame the urge. With blazing eyes I upped the stakes by another pound and thought of a murderous number: Ninety-six!

"Lead, stinker," I threw at Ervinke, whereupon he leaned across the table and hissed into my face:

"Sixteen hundred and eighty-three!"

A queer weakness gripped me.

"Eighteen hundred," I mumbled wearily.

"Double!" Ervinke shouted, and pocketed the four pounds.

"What do you mean, 'double'?" I snorted. "What's that?"

"If you lose your temper in poker, you'll lose your shirt!" Ervinke lectured me. "Any child will understand that my number doubled is higher than yours, so it's clear that—"

"Enough," I gasped, and threw down a fiver. "Two thousand," I led.

"Two thousand four hundred and seventeen." Thus Ervinke.

"Double!" I sneered, and grabbed the stakes, but Ervinke caught my hand.

"Redouble!" he whispered, and pocketed the tenner. I felt I was going out of my mind.

"Listen"—I gritted my teeth—"if that's how things stand, I could also have said 'redouble' in the last game, couldn't I?"

"Of course," Ervinke agreed. "To tell you the truth, I was rather surprised that you didn't. But this is poker, *yahabibi*— you either know how to play it or you don't! If you are scatter-brained, better stick to croquet."

The stakes were ten pounds. "Lead!" I screamed. Ervinke leaned back in his chair, and in a disquietingly calm voice announced his number: Four.

"Ten million!" I blared triumphantly. But without the slightest sign of excitement, Ervinke said:

"Ultimo!"

And then took twenty pounds.

I then broke into sobs. Ervinke stroked my hair and told me that according to Hoyle, whoever is first out with the Ultimo wins, regardless of numbers. That is the fun in poker: you have to make split-second decisions.

"Twenty pounds," I whimpered, and placed my last notes in the hands of fate. Ervinke also placed his money. My face was bathed in cold sweat. Ervinke went on calmly blowing smoke rings, only his eyes had narrowed.

"Who leads?"

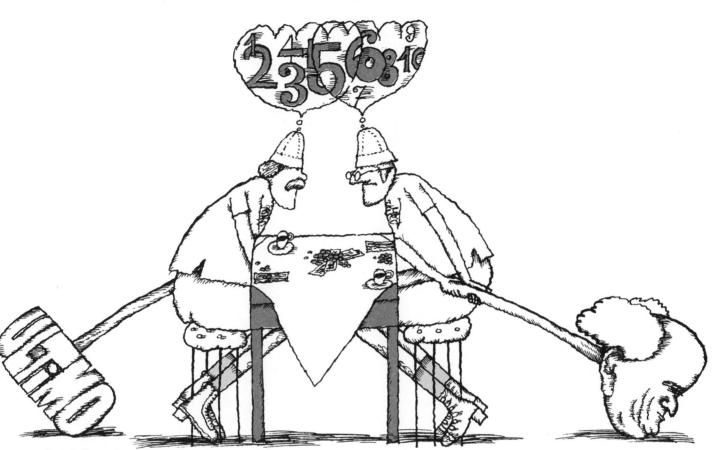

Devis Grebu © 1981

"You," I answered, and he fell into my trap like the sucker he was.

"So I lead," Ervinke said. "Ultimo," and he stretched out his hand for the treasure.

"Just a moment"—I stopped him: "Ben-Gurion!"

With that I pocketed the mint's six-month output. "Ben-Gurion is even stronger than Ultimo," I explained. "But it's getting dark outside. Perhaps we had better break it off."

We paid the waiter and left.

Ervinke asked for his money back, saying that I had invented the Ben-Gurion on the spur of the moment. I admitted this, but said that the fun in poker was just in the rule that you never returned the money you had won.

The Wise Men of Chelm

It is said that after God had created the world,

he had to fill it with people.

He sent off an angel with two sacks—
one full of wise souls, one full of foolish ones—
to be distributed equally in various communities.
But while the angel was flying over Chelm,
one of the sacks became caught on the top of a
mountain,

and all the

foolish

souls

spilled

out

and

fell

into

Chelm.

ווי אזוי כעלם איז באשאפען געווארען אויף דער וועלט

THE citizens of Chelm used to spend a good deal of time worrying—so much time, in fact, that they soon began to worry about how much they worried. The Grand Council of Wise Men convened a meeting to discuss all this worrying, and to find a solution for it.

For seven days and seven nights the wise men of Chelm discussed the problem, until finally the chairman announced a solution: Yossel, the chimney sweep, would be the official Chelm Worrier. In return for one ruble a week, he would do the worrying for everybody in Chelm.

The Grand Council members all agreed that this was the ideal solution, but just before the vote was taken, one of the sages rose to speak against the proposal. "Wait a minute," he announced. "If Yossel were to receive one ruble a week, then what would he have to worry about?"

TWO wise men of Chelm went out for a walk, when suddenly it began to rain.

"Quick," said one man. "Open your umbrella."

"It won't help," said his friend. "My umbrella is full of holes."

"Then why did you bring it in the first place?"

"I didn't think it would rain!"

IT was tax time in Chelm, and two of its leading citizens were having a discussion.

"I don't understand this business with taxes," said the first man. "Surely the Czar has enough money of his own. He even has his own royal mint, where he can make as many rubles as he likes. So why does he bother with my ruble?"

"Don't be silly," said the second. "Let me tell you a parable. It is said that every time a Jew performs a *mitzvah,* God creates an angel. So why not ask God why he needs one more angel in addition to the millions of angels he has already created? Can't God make as many angels as he likes? *Of course he can!* But why doesn't he? Because God prefers *your* angel.

"Well, the same thing is true with taxes. Of *course* the Czar can make as many rubles as he likes. But don't you understand —he prefers to take *your* ruble."

For many children, the Chelm stories represent their first exposure to Jewish humor. Although it is sometimes asserted that the Wise Men of Chelm are lacking in logic or common sense, in fact the reverse is true: they suffer from having *too much* common sense, much more so than the rest of the world. Typically, the citizens of Chelm solve their problems with a solution that is theoretically correct, but which does not succeed in practice.

Another striking characteristic of Chelm is its powerful sense of community; the citizens of Chelm are passionately interested in the common good, and in the welfare and glory of Chelm.

Whatever else it may represent, Chelm is a real city in Poland, southeast of Lublin, and the site of a Jewish community from the twelfth century until the Holocaust. But why Chelm was singled out as the home of a peculiar assortment of "wise men" has never been clear.

Equivalents to Chelm appear in several other cultures: Gotham, for example, in England, or Abdera in Greece. The stories of a town in Germany known as Schildburg were translated into Yiddish in 1597, and were very popular among the Jews of central and eastern Europe. It is possible that these tales inspired the stories of Chelm, especially if there were already stories about fools with no unifying peg on which to hang them.

Typically, observes Israel Knox, "the Chelmites talk and plan for seven days and seven nights, and then set to work carrying out their plan, and when it is done and they are about to rejoice in its consummation and to reap their reward, there is the sudden collapse of their effort and their expectation into dust and wind, into nothing. Defeat for the Chelmites is always temporary; it is not really a defeat but a misadventure. They might laugh at it, but they cannot spare the time for it, nor are they accustomed, by tradition and upbringing, to let themselves go in laughter. Without hesitation and without trepidation they are at it again, holding conclave for seven days and seven nights, in preparation for a renewed assault upon a recalcitrant world in which 'foolish things are always happening to us.'"

One of the sages of Chelm was explaining to his friend that with the miracle of the steam locomotive, a person could leave Chelm at noon and be in Warsaw at midnight.

His friend is unimpressed: "What on earth would I do in Warsaw in the middle of the night?"

TWO wise men of Chelm were deep in conversation, discussing the intricacies of modern travel.

"Let me understand you correctly," said the first man. "It takes a horse and carriage only four hours to go from here to Pinsk, is that right?"

"Exactly," said his friend. "But if you had a carriage with *two* horses, then it would take you only two hours."

"I see," replied the first. "And I suppose, then, that if you had a carriage with four horses, you'd get there in no time at all. Is that right?"

"Precisely," answered his friend. "But in that case, why bother to go to Pinsk in the first place? Better to just harness up your four horses and stay right here!"

One of the wise men of Chelm came to the rabbi with a question. "Why is it," he asked, "that a slice of bread with butter on it always falls with the buttered side down?"

"Is that so?" said the rabbi. "Let's see if it's true." The rabbi buttered a piece of bread, and let it fall. This time the buttered side was facing up. "Now, what about that?" asked the rabbi.

"But, Rabbi," came the reply. "You obviously buttered the wrong side!"

THE cantor of Chelm was about to marry off one of his daughters, but he had no money for her dowry. The congregation voted to advance him two hundred zlotys, which would be deducted from his salary over the next five years.

Because the cantor was a proud man, he insisted on appearing before the board of directors, where he made the following statement: "My friends, I want you to know that I am accepting your kind offer on two conditions. If I should live another five years, that is your good fortune. But if I should die before this debt is paid—well, that is simply my good luck!"

This story is sometimes told with other punch lines, such as: "Oh, I just put that in to fool people," or: "All right, so I exaggerated a little!"

A jokester in Chelm once thought up a riddle that nobody could answer: "What's purple, hangs on the wall, and whistles?"

When everybody in Chelm gave up, he announced the answer: a herring.

"A *herring?*" people said. "A herring isn't purple."

"Nu," replied the jokester, "*this* herring was painted purple."

"But hanging on a wall? Who ever heard of a herring that hung on the wall?"

"Aha! But this herring was hung on the wall."

"But a herring doesn't whistle," somebody shouted.

"Nu, so it doesn't whistle."

A MAN from Warsaw, in Chelm on a business trip, was walking down the street when he was stopped by Yossel the chimney sweep. "Zalman!" cried Yossel. "What has become of you? It's so long since I've seen you. Just look at yourself."

"But wait," replied the stranger, "I'm—"

"Never mind that," said Yossel. "I can't get over how much you've changed. You used to be such a big man, built like an ox. And now you're smaller than I am. Have you been sick?"

"But wait," replied the stranger, "I'm—"

"Never mind that," said Yossel. "And what has become of your hair? You used to have a fine head of black hair, and now you're completely bald. And your mustache, so black and dapper. What has become of it? You know, I don't see how I ever recognized you. Zalman, what has become of you?"

"I've been trying to tell you," the man replied. "I'm not Zalman."

"Oy," replied Yossel. "You've gone and changed your name as well."

This story has many practical applications, for those situations in life when legitimate evidence is completely ignored, or when the facts of a case are deemed irrelevant to its interpretation.

Cases of mistaken identity are frequent in Chelm:

•

Mendel the butcher is walking to his store one morning when a perfect stranger runs up and slaps him on the face. "That's for you, Yankel," the stranger calls out.

To which Mendel responds, after recovering from the shock, with a laugh.

"Why are you laughing?" asks the stranger. "Do you want me to hit you again?"

"No, please," comes the reply. "It's just that the joke's on you— I'm not Yankel!"

•

Hershele Ostropoler

One day Hershele was traveling, and he stopped for the night at an inn. The place was deserted: there were no other guests, and even the innkeeper was away, leaving his wife in charge.

"I'm dying of hunger," Hershele told her. "Please give me something to eat."

The innkeeper's wife took a good look at her guest, and she didn't like what she saw. Hershele was unkempt, his coat was torn, and he looked altogether unsavory.

This fellow will never be able to pay the bill, she thought. "I'm sorry, sir," she said to Hershele, "but we're all out of food tonight."

Hershele shook his head and said nothing. Then he looked straight ahead and said to the woman, "In that case, I'm going to have to do what my father did."

Immediately the woman grew frightened. "What did your father do?" she asked.

"My father," Hershele replied, "did what he had to do."

Hearing this, the woman grew even more frightened. Who knew what kind of father this man had? And she alone in the house! Perhaps his father was a thief, a murderer, or worse.

Hershele Ostropoler (1770?–1810?) is a folk figure, the hero of many tales. But he was also a real person, although what is known about him is based mostly on oral tradition and folklore. He is thought to have come from Balta, in the Ukraine, and his name is based on the small town of Ostropol, in Poland, where he served the community as *shochet* (ritual slaughterer).

According to legend, Hershele lost his job because of his constant joking, which was offensive to the leaders of the community. He then wandered through the Ukraine, and was a familiar personality at various inns and restaurants, which explains why such institutions figure so prominently in the stories about him.

Eventually he found his calling —at the court of Rabbi Boruch of Miedzibezh, grandson of the Baal Shem-Tov, the founder of Hasidism. Rabbi Boruch was plagued by frequent depressions, and Hershele served as a kind of court jester, frequently mocking the rabbi and his cronies, but delighting the common folk.

After his death, Hershele lived on through a series of Yiddish pamphlets which recorded his tales and witty remarks. He was the subject of lyric poems, a novel, a comedy performed in 1930 by the Vilna Troupe —and even an American television play in the 1950s.

"Just a minute, sir," she said, and soon returned with a full plate of chicken, *kishke,* fish, and black bread. Hershele devoured it all, as the woman looked on in amazement. When he had finished, he told her, "Lady, that was a wonderful meal, the best I've tasted since last Passover."

Seeing that her guest was finally relaxed and satisfied, the innkeeper's wife dared to ask the question that had been burning in her all evening. "Good sir," she said, "please tell me, what was it that your father did?"

"My father?" said Hershele. "Oh, yes, my father. You see, whenever my father couldn't get anything to eat—he went to bed hungry."

For dinner the next night Hershele went to an inn on the outskirts of town. It was a pretentious establishment, and when the main course was brought to him, Hershele was dismayed to see such a small portion of meat. He immediately broke into loud sobbing.

At once the innkeeper ran over to his table and asked, "Is anything wrong, sir?"

"Oy," cried Hershele. "To think that for this little morsel of meat a great big ox had to be slaughtered!"

The following day, when Hershele reached his destination, he went into a small café for lunch. The waitress came to take his order, and he asked her for two onion rolls. As soon as she brought them, he said, "I've changed my mind. I'd rather have two bagels, if that's all right."

"Very good, sir. They're even the same price."

The waitress took away the onion rolls, and returned with two bagels, which Hershele quickly consumed. As he rose to leave the café, the waitress stopped him: "Wait, sir, you haven't paid for the bagels."

"What do you mean?" replied Hershele. "Didn't I give you two onion rolls for the bagels?"

"That's right, sir, but you didn't pay for the onion rolls, either."

"Of course not," replied Hershele. "Why should I pay for the onion rolls if I didn't eat them?"

On the day after the fast of Tisha B'av, the rabbi sent for Hershele. "My disciples have told me that you were seen eating yesterday, the day of the fast. Is it true that you have committed so grave a sin?"

"Let me explain what happened," said Hershele. "As I was leaving the synagogue after morning prayers, I walked along the river where the poor women do their laundry. One of the women remarked that everybody in town was fasting today. 'Is that so?' said her friend. 'Well, I wish I had a hundred rubles for every Jew who will eat today!'

"And to make sure that this poor woman would have at least a hundred rubles, I decided that I should break the fast."

Hershele did not like to spend much time in the synagogue. One day the rabbi rebuked him: "It doesn't look right that I should spend an hour in prayer while it takes you only ten minutes."

"But, Rabbi," replied Hershele. "You have so much to be thankful for! Your carriage and your fine horses, your house, your gold and silver, your fancy dishes.

"But look at me. I have a nagging wife, my six children, and a skinny goat. And so my prayers are very simple: 'Wife, children, goat' —and I'm done."

Hershele was not skilled at any one trade, and he made his living as best he could, mostly by his wits. For a while he tried his luck in the antique business, and set up a stand in the marketplace. Prominent among his wares was a large canvas in a frame. The canvas was blank.

Eventually a customer wandered by and inquired about the canvas. "This," explained Hershele, "is an old and famous painting."

"But it's blank," replied the customer.

"No," replied Hershele. "It just looks that way. For one silver crown, I will reveal to you the mystery of this painting."

Overcome by curiosity, the customer came up with the money.

"This painting," Hershele confided in a whisper, "is an actual depiction of the crossing of the Red Sea. It was done by a close relative of Moses."

"Grandma Moses, did you say?"

"Probably a cousin. As you can guess, it's a very valuable work."

"How can that be?" asked the customer. "There's nothing there. Where, for example, are the Israelites?"

"When this picture was painted, the Israelites had already crossed over."

"And the Egyptians?"

"They hadn't yet arrived."

"Aha. But the water! Where's the water?"

"But don't you remember? The waters had already parted!"

Shabbas Nachamu

Isaac Babel (1894–1939) occupies a special place in the Jewish literature of Eastern Europe. At the age of twenty-five, he joined the Red Army as a war correspondent, and for the rest of his life—which ended in a Stalinist purge—he reflected the tensions between Cossacks and Jews. Between 1939 and 1957 Babel's name was taboo in Soviet Russia, and all mention of him was banished from schoolbooks and encyclopedias; he has since been rehabilitated. He is best known for his stories of the Jewish underworld in Odessa, and its leader, Benya Krik.

"Shabbas Nachamu" is based on a folktale about Hershele. Although there is nothing else in Babel's work resembling it, he apparently planned to write more about Hershele, as this story was originally subtitled "From the Hershele Cycle."

Shabbas Nachamu (the Sabbath of Comfort) refers to the Sabbath after the fast of Tisha B'Av, which marks the end of the summer mourning period commemorating the destruction of the first and second Temples, as well as various other tragedies in Jewish history.

The morning goes by, the evening comes—and it's the fifth day of the week. Another morning goes by, the evening comes—and it's the sixth day. On the sixth day, on Friday, you have to pray. When you've prayed, you take a stroll through the *shtetl* in your best hat and then come back home for supper. When he gets home, a good Jew has a glass of vodka—neither God nor the Talmud says he can't have two—and eats his gefilte fish and his currant cake. After supper he feels good. He tells stories to his wife; then he goes to sleep with one eye closed and his mouth open. He sleeps, but his wife in the kitchen hears music, as though the blind fiddler had come from the *shtetl* and was standing under the window playing.

That's how it is with every Jew. But Hershele was different from other Jews. No wonder he was famous in all of Ostropol, in all of Berdichev, and in all of Vilyuisk. Hershele celebrated only one Friday in six. On the others he sat with his family in the darkness and cold. His children cried, and his wife gave him hell. Each reproach was as heavy as a cobblestone. Hershele used to answer back in verse.

Once, so the story goes, Hershele thought he would look ahead a little. He went off to the fair on Wednesday to earn some money for Friday. Where there's a fair you'll find a *pan*, and where there's a *pan* you'll find ten Jews. But you'd be lucky to earn three pennies from ten Jews. They all listened to Hershele's funny stories, but when it was time to pay, they weren't around anymore. Hershele went back home with a belly as empty as a wind instrument.

"What did you earn?" his wife asked.

"I earned life everlasting," he said. "Both the rich and the poor promised it to me."

Hershele's wife had only ten fingers. She bent them back one by one. Her voice was like thunder in the mountains. "Every other wife has a husband like everybody else's. But I have a husband who feeds his wife on funny stories. May God take away the use of his tongue, and his hands, and his feet in the New Year."

"Amen," Hershele said.

"In everybody else's windows the candles burn as if they'd set fire to oak trees in the house, but I have candles as thin as matches, and there's so much smoke from them it shoots up to heaven. Everybody else has white bread, but all my husband brings me is firewood as wet as newly washed hair—"

Hershele said not a single word in reply. Why add fuel to

the flames when they're burning so brightly as it is? That's point number one. And then, point number two, what can you say to a cantankerous wife when she's right? When she got tired of shouting, Hershele went and lay down on his bed and thought: Maybe I should go and see Rabbi Boruchl? (Everybody knew that Rabbi Boruchl suffered from black melancholia and that only Hershele with his talk could make him feel better.) Maybe I should go to Rabbi Boruchl? It's true the *tsaddik's* servants give me only bones and keep the meat for themselves. Meat is better than bones, but bones are better than air. I'll go to Rabbi Boruchl."

Hershele got up and went out to harness his mare. She gave him a stern and sad look.

"It's all very well, Hershele," her eyes said, "you didn't give me any oats yesterday, you didn't give me any oats the day before yesterday, and I didn't get anything today, either. If you don't give me any oats tomorrow, I'll have to start thinking about whether I'm going to live."

Hershele flinched before her searching look, lowered his eyes, and stroked her soft lips. Then he sighed so loud that the mare understood everything, and he said, "I'll go to Rabbi Boruchl on foot."

When Hershele set off, the sun was high in the sky. The

Drawing by David Levine, Copyright © 1969 by Nyrev, Inc. By permission of *The New York Review of Books.*

On being scolded for drinking too much, Hershele replied:
"Whenever I take a drink, I become somebody else.
And doesn't that fellow also deserve a drink?"

When promised a ruble by a rich man if he could tell a lie
without thinking, Hershele responded:
"A ruble? But you just said two!"

After pawning his watch to pay his creditors,
Hershele appeared one night at the pawnshop and knocked on the shutters.
"What do you want?" shouted the pawnbroker,
who had been awakened by the noise.
"I want to know what time it is," Hershele replied.
"And for this you woke me up?"
"I'm sorry," said Hershele, "but I only trust my own watch."

When asked if the stories were really true
that he beat his wife with a stick while she bopped him over the head
with a rolling pin, he replied:
"Not really; sometimes we switch."

sweltering road ran on ahead. Carts drawn by white oxen and piled with sweet-smelling hay lumbered slowly along. Peasants sat on these high carts, dangling their legs and swishing their long whips. The sky was dark blue, and the whips were black. When he'd gone about five miles, Hershele reached a forest. The sun was already leaving its place in the sky, which was ablaze with gentle fires. Barefoot girls were bringing the cows in from the fields. The cows' pink udders, heavy with milk, swayed to and fro.

The forest met Hershele with cool shade and soft twilight. Green leaves bent over and stroked each other with their flat hands, whispered together faintly up there in the treetops, and then fell back, rustling and quivering, into their places. Hershele did not hear their whispering. The orchestra playing in his belly was as big as anything hired by Count Potocki for a gala evening. He still had a long way to go. Dusk was hurrying in from the edges of the earth, closing in over Hershele's head, and spreading out across the world. Unblinking lamps lit up in the sky, and the earth fell silent.

It was night when Hershele arrived at an inn. A light was burning in a small window. Zelda, the landlady, was sitting in her warm room by this window, sewing baby clothes. Her belly was so big it looked as if she were going to have triplets. Hershele looked at her small red face with its light-blue eyes and wished her good evening. "Can I stop here and rest for a while, ma'am?"

"Sure you can."

Hershele sat down. His nostrils heaved like a pair of blacksmith's bellows. There was a red-hot fire blazing in the stove. Water was boiling in a large caldron and frothing over snow-white dumplings. A fat chicken was bobbing up and down in a golden broth. There was a smell of currant cake from the oven. Hershele sat on a bench writhing like a woman in labor. More plans were hatching in his head at that moment than King Solomon ever had wives. It was quiet in the room, the water was boiling, and the chicken tossed and pitched on its golden waves.

"Where is your husband, ma'am?" Hershele asked.

"My husband has gone to the *pan* to pay his rent," she said, and paused. Her childlike eyes grew round and large. Suddenly she went on: "And I am sitting here at the window thinking. I would like to ask you a question. I suppose you travel up and down the world, and you've studied with the rabbi, and you know about our Jewish ways. But nobody ever taught me anything. Tell me: will *Shabbas Nachamu* be coming soon?"

Oho, thought Hershele, a very good question indeed. All kinds of potatoes grow in God's garden.

"I'm asking because my husband promised me that when Shabbas Nachamu comes, we'll go and visit my mother. And I'll buy you a dress, he says, and a new wig, and we'll go to Rabbi Motalemi to ask him for a son to be born to us instead of a daughter. But that will only be when Shabbas Nachamu comes. I suppose he's a man from the other world, this Shabbas Nachamu?"

"You are quite right, ma'am," Hershele replied. "God himself put those words into your mouth. You will have both a son and a daughter. I am Shabbas Nachamu, ma'am."

The baby clothes slipped from Zelda's knees. She got up and bumped her head on a rafter, because she was tall, Zelda was, and plump and red and young. Her high breasts looked like two bags tightly packed with grain. Her light-blue eyes opened wide like a child's.

"I am Shabbas Nachamu," Hershele repeated. "For two months now I've been doing my rounds, helping people. It's a long journey from heaven down to earth. My shoes are all worn out. I bring you greetings from all your people up there."

"From Aunt Pesya?" Zelda shouted. "And from Father, and from Aunt Golda? You know them?"

"Who doesn't know them?" Hershele said. "I often talk with them just like I'm talking with you now."

"How are they getting on up there?" Zelda asked, clasping her trembling hands on her belly.

"Not too well," Hershele replied sadly. "What sort of life do you think it is for a dead person? There isn't much fun up there."

Zelda's eyes filled with tears.

"They're cold," Hershele went on, "and hungry. They eat the same as angels, you see. They're not supposed to eat more than the angels. And how much do angels eat? They're quite happy with a drink of water. You wouldn't get a glass of vodka up there once in a hundred years."

"Poor Father," Zelda whispered, quite shaken.

"At Passover you get a *latke,* and one blintz has to last you twenty-four hours."

"Poor Aunt Pesya." Zelda shuddered.

"I have to go hungry myself," Hershele continued, and turned his face away as a tear rolled down his nose and fell into his beard. "There's nothing I can do about it, you see: up there I'm treated like everybody else—"

Hershele didn't manage to get any further. With a patter of her large feet, Zelda bore down on him with plates, bowls, glasses, and bottles. When Hershele began to eat, she saw that he really was a man from the other world.

To start off with, Hershele had chicken liver garnished with fat and chopped onion. He drank it down with a glass of high-class vodka flavored with orange peel. Then he had fish, mashing soft boiled potatoes into the savory sauce that went with it and putting half a jarful of red horseradish on the side of his plate—a horseradish at the mere sight of which five *pans* in all their finery would have wept tears of envy.

After the fish Hershele did his duty by the chicken and the broth with blobs of fat swimming in it. The dumplings, bathed in molten butter, jumped into Hershele's mouth like hares fleeing from a hunter. We don't have to say anything about what happened to the currant cake. What do you think happened to it, if you consider that Hershele sometimes never saw a currant cake from one end of the year to the other?

When he had finished, Zelda got together all the things that she had decided to ask Hershele to take to the other world for Father, Aunt Pesya, and Aunt Golda. For her father she put out a new prayer shawl, a bottle of cherry brandy, a jar of raspberry jam, and a pouch full of tobacco. For Aunt Pesya she got out some warm gray socks, and for Aunt Golda an old wig, a large comb, and a prayer book. Lastly, she gave Hershele a pair of boots, some goose cracklings, and a silver coin.

"Give them our regards, Mister Shabbas Nachamu, give them all our kind regards," were her parting words to Hershele as he set off with the heavy bundle. "Or would you like to wait a little until my husband comes back?"

Dick Codor © 1979

"No," said Hershele. "I must be on my way. You don't think you're the only one I have to look after, do you?"

When he had gone about a mile, Hershele stopped to draw breath, threw the bundle down, sat on it, and took stock of the situation. "As you well know, Hershele," he said to himself, "the world is full of fools. The landlady in that inn was a fool. But perhaps her husband is not a fool, perhaps he has large fists, fat cheeks, and a long whip. If he comes home and chases after you in the forest, what then?"

Hershele wasted no time seeking an answer to this question. He immediately buried the bundle in the ground and marked the spot so that he would be able to find it again.

Then he ran back the way he had come, stripped naked, put his arms around a tree, and began to wait. He did not have to wait long. At dawn Hershele heard the crack of a whip, the smacking lips of a horse and the thud of its hooves. This was the innkeeper in hot pursuit of Mister Shabbas Nachamu.

When he reached the naked Hershele with his arms around a tree, the innkeeper stopped his horse and looked as silly as a monk on meeting the devil.

"What are you doing here?" he asked.

"I am a man from the other world," Hershele replied gloomily. "I have been robbed of important papers which I was taking to Rabbi Boruchl."

"I know who robbed you," shouted the innkeeper. "I have a bone to pick with him too. Which way did he go?"

"I cannot tell you which way he went," Hershele whispered bitterly. "If you will lend me your horse I will soon catch up with him, while you wait for me here. Undress and stand by this tree. Hold it up and do not leave it until I return. It is a holy tree, and many things in our world depend on it."

Hershele only had to take one look at a man to see what he was made of. He had seen right away that the innkeeper was not much brighter than his wife. And sure enough, the innkeeper got undressed and stood by the tree. Hershele climbed onto the cart and drove back to where he had left the bundle. He dug it up and went on to the edge of the forest.

Here Hershele shouldered the bundle again, left the horse, and took the road which led to the house of the holy Rabbi Boruchl. It was morning already. The roosters were crowing with their eyes shut. The innkeeper's horse wearily plodded back with the empty cart to the place where she had left her master.

He was waiting for her, huddled against the tree, naked under the rays of the rising sun. He was cold, and he kept shifting from foot to foot.

●

Letters to Einstein

These letters are drawn from the first section of a long and little-known story by Philip Roth entitled "On the Air," which appeared in *New American Review* 10 (1970). The story, an homage to certain radio programs, such as *The Answer Man* and *Duffy's Tavern,* from the author's childhood, contains some of Roth's most outrageous and funny writing, especially on the subject of Gentiles and Jews. Although Lippman takes his wife and son on a motor trip to Princeton to visit Einstein, the story is concerned not with the encounter (which never takes place), but with a bizarre series of misadventures en route.

In Jewish folk culture, Einstein is the modern-day secular equivalent to the great sages of old, who were renowned for their learning and intelligence. But unlike these rabbis, who were occasionally mocked or criticized in traditional Jewish jokes, Einstein—so far, at least—has remained a wholly positive figure.

Dear Mr. Einstein:

I am writing you with a wonderful suggestion that I know would bring about gigantic changes in the world and improve the lot of Jews everywhere. Mr. Einstein, I am a fellow Jew, and proud of it. Your name is sacred to me as to people of our faith around the globe. That the Nazis chased you from Germany is our gain and their loss a million times over, if they even know what a loss is, and I only hope and pray that you are happy here in "the land of the free."

Here is my suggestion. Why don't you go on the radio every week with your own show? If you would agree I would like to manage you, so that your famous mind would not have to be cluttered up with business and so on. I am ashamed to say this in the same breath with your name, but probably you are aware of "The Answer Man" program which is on every night from seven to seven-fifteen. If you're not, just listen for a minute some night. Children all over America think this fake is "an Einstein" probably, when the real Einstein is something they would faint to hear in person. I would like them to know that THE GENIUS OF ALL TIME IS A JEW! This is something the world must know, and soon.

Respectfully yours,
M. Lippman,
Talent Agent

P.S. You will probably want to know what right I have even to suggest myself as a manager to the great Einstein. And all I can say is that if I had a list of the greatest names in the entertainment industry as my clientele, I would be as ashamed of my credentials as I am right now where you are concerned, the Great Albert Einstein. I feel it is even a sin to write out your whole name, that it is too holy for me to utter. But if I didn't write it out, how would you even get this letter? So forgive me. Until now, I have to tell you, I have not had a famous list of acts. Mostly I represent colored. I probably have most of the best tap dancing talent in the state under contract to me at this very moment, and am helping some of these young men—for instance, the famous Famous Brothers (Buck and Wing)—to raise themselves into a respectable life. With my new talent discoveries since Buck and Wing, I am changing their old names to

Drawing by David Levine. Copyright © 1966 by Nyrev, Inc.
By permission of *The New York Review of Books.*

There are many jokes and stories about Einstein.

Little Sammy tells his grandfather about the great scientist and his theory of relativity.

"Oh, yes?" says the grandfather. "And what does this theory have to say?"

"Our teacher says that only a few people in the whole world can really understand it," the boy explains. "But then she told us what it means. Relativity is like this: If a man sits for an hour with a pretty girl, it feels like a minute. But if he sits on a hot stove for a minute, it feels like an hour. And that's the theory of relativity."

Grandpa is silent, and slowly shakes his head. "Sammy," he says softly, "from this your Einstein makes a living?"

In an allegedly true story, Einstein and his wife were visiting the Mount Wilson Observatory in California. "And what's that one for?" asked Mrs. Einstein, pointing to a complex piece of machinery.

She was told that the machine in question was used to determine the shape of the universe. "Oh, really," she replied. "My husband does that on the back of an old envelope!"

Einstein is seated at dinner with a slightly naive and stagestruck lady. "Tell me, Professor," she says. "What is the difference between time and eternity?"

"Madam," replies the great scientist, "if I should devote all my time to explaining it, it would take an eternity for you to begin to understand."

the names of famous American Presidents, only backwards. This way I think they still sound colored, which they should as tap dancers, and yet have a little class. Also I attend an average of two to three *bar mitzvah* parties of a single Saturday, in my endless search for young Jewish talent in singing, bandleading, et cetera.

I hope I will be hearing from you soon, and favorably, about "The Albert Einstein Show."

Again respectfully,
M. Lippman

Dear Mr. Einstein:

I can understand how busy you must be thinking, and appreciate that you did not answer my letter suggesting that I try to get you on a radio program that would make "The Answer Man" look like the joke it is. Will you reconsider, if the silence means no? I realize that one of the reasons you don't wear a tie or even bother to comb your hair is because you are as busy as you are, thinking new things. Well, don't think that you would have to change your ways once you became a radio personality. Your hair is a great gimmick, and I wouldn't change it for a second. It's a great trademark. Without disrespect, it sticks in your mind the way Harpo Marx's does. Which is excellent. (Now I wonder if you even have the time to know who the Marx Brothers are? They are four zany Jewish brothers, and you happen to look a little like one of them. You might get a kick out of catching one of their movies. Probably they don't even show movies in Princeton, but maybe you could get somebody to drive you out of town. You can get the entire plot in about a minute, but the resemblance between you and Harpo, and his hair and yours, might reassure you that you are a fine personality in terms of show business just as you are.)

The kind of program I have in mind is something I would certainly have to talk with you about before embarking upon making the right contacts. For instance, should we follow "The Answer Man" format with questions sent in? Should we have a theme song? Would you object to another personality asking the questions? Something strikes me right about the idea of you being interviewed by Tony Martin, the singer. He has a beautiful speaking voice and makes a wonderful impression in a dinner jacket, and is also (contrary to the belief that he is of Italian extraction) a Jewish boy with whom you would feel completely at home. Easygoing is his whole style, *but with respect.* Whether I can get him is another story. I don't want to

When
Rabbi Joshua
ben Hanania went to Athens
to dispute with the philosophers there,
they asked him many questions and he
answered them all successfully. ¶One of
their questions was: "Where is the center
of the earth?" ¶Rabbi Joshua pointed with
his forefinger to a spot on the ground nearby,
and said, "**Here.**" ¶They said, "How do
we know that you are right?" ¶He said,
"Bring your measuring rods, and
measure it for your-
selves."

•

Talmud
(Bechorot 8B)

make promises I can't deliver so as to entice the famous Einstein. I wouldn't dare. But what I'm saying is that the sky is the limit once I get an okay from you. I am tempted to spell that with a capital letter. You. But in the middle of the sentence.

Perhaps I should have told You that my fee is ten percent. But truly and honestly I am not in this business for money. I want to help people. I have taken colored off the streets, shoeshine kit and all, and turned them into headline tap dancers at roadhouses and nightclubs overnight. And my satisfaction comes not from the money, which in all honesty is not so much, but in seeing those boys getting dressed up in dinner jackets and learning to face an audience of people out for a nice time. Dignity far more than money is my business.

With you, Mr. Einstein, I think I could really break through into something of worldwide importance in terms of doing good. Who better than you knows the persecution the Jews have taken around the globe? It will only stop when they look up to us and recognize that when it comes to smart, we are the tops. It will only stop when our own little Jewish boys and girls realize that there is an Einstein in the world who is a Jew just like them, and is a million times smarter than some *goy* radio announcer with a stuffy voice who they also give the answers to anyway. Do we want our children to grow up admiring such fakes? I have a little boy of my own, and I know what it would mean to me if I could sit with him at night once a week and listen to the Famous Albert Einstein talking around a fireside with someone of the caliber of a Tony Martin.

If you are too busy to write and discuss these matters, how about if I came to see you some Sunday? It would be a thrill if I could bring my son along.

Respectfully yours,
M. Lippman
Agent to
The Famous Brothers,
Roosevelt Franklin,
Jefferson Thomas,
Cleveland Grover, &
Monroe James

Dear *Dr.* Einstein:

No word, but I understand. I hope and pray you were not offended that I have been addressing you all along as Mister. I cannot express all my admiration for you, and it breaks my heart if you think any disrespect was intended. I am not an educated person, though I try to make up in hard work and quick thinking what I don't know from books. Every day, and this is no exaggeration, I have a hundred wonderful ideas that could improve the world. My idea to encourage you to go on the air on a regular basis is only one, Doctor.

I am sure that you are naturally nervous about me and the millions of others who probably write to you looking for "an easy buck." I have to assure you, *the money is secondary.* Uppermost is getting you on the radio and showing those *goyim* what smart really means. Why hide under a barrel something that could change the life of *every Jew alive and their children to come?* This is how strongly I believe in the power of radio. I think sometimes that the Bible stories of God talking from above to the people down below is just what they had in those days instead of radio. People, whether then or now, like to hear "the real thing." Hearing is believing! (Maybe that could be our motto for the show—if you approve. For a theme song I have been thinking along robust lines, but still meaningful—something like "The Whole World Is Singing My Song.") Today we don't *hear* God as they did in the Bible—and what is the result? It is impossible for some people to believe He is there. There. The same holds true with you, Doctor Einstein, I'm sorry to say. To the general public, who is Einstein? A name who doesn't comb his hair (not that I have any objection) and is *supposed* to be the smartest person alive. A lot of good that does the Jews, if you understand what I'm saying. At this stage of the game, I'm afraid that if an election were held tonight between you and The Answer Man, more people would vote for him than for you. I have to be honest with you.

Here is my proposal. I will drive to Princeton next Sunday, arriving around two P.M. If you are not home, fine. If you are, and you happen to be at the window, and you happen to feel only like waving and that's all, well let me tell you, that would be a wonderful experience in itself. But if you want to ask a question or two about my suggestion, even through the window if that's all you have the time for, fine with me, I'll do that too, from the lawn. I will leave my wife and child in the car so that they don't bother you, though if you should want to wave at the boy, I would be most appreciative. And he of course would remember it for life.

To make a joke, don't put on a tie for my account, Doctor.

Your fellow Jew and humble admirer,
M. Lippman

●

The astronomer was concluding his lecture at the synagogue: "And some of my colleagues believe that our own sun will probably die out within four or five billion years."

"*How* many years did you say?" asked Mrs. Siegel from the back of the room.

"Four or five billion," replied the scientist.

"Whew!" said Mrs. Siegel. "I thought you said *million!*"

●

A few years before the death of the great Hebrew poet Chaim Nachman Bialik, the newspapers of the day were full of speculation that he would be awarded the Nobel Prize for Literature.

When the prize was awarded to another writer, Bialik was asked for his reaction. "I'm very glad I didn't win the prize," he said. "Now everybody's my friend and feels sorry for me. My, my, how angry they are on my behalf! 'Now isn't that a scandal!' they say. 'Imagine such a thing—Bialik, the great poet Bialik, doesn't get the Nobel Prize! And—tsk! tsk!—just look who they gave it to! To X, that so-and-so! Why, he can't even hold a candle to Bialik!'

"On the other hand, what if I had been awarded the Nobel Prize? Then, I'm sure, some of the very same people who are now so indignant on my account would have said, 'Nu, nu, what's so wonderful about getting the Nobel Prize? Why, even that poet Bialik got one!'"

Drawing by David Levine. Copyright © 1978 by Nyrev, Inc. By permission of *The New York Review of Books*.

WOODY ALLEN

The Whore of Mensa

One thing about being a private investigator, you've got to learn to go with your hunches. That's why when a quivering pat of butter named Word Babcock walked into my office and laid his cards on the table, I should have trusted the cold chill that shot up my spine.

"Kaiser?" he said. "Kaiser Lupowitz?"

"That's what it says on my license," I owned up.

"You've got to help me. I'm being blackmailed. Please!"

He was shaking like the lead singer in a rumba band. I pushed a glass across the desktop and a bottle of rye I keep handy for nonmedicinal purposes. "Suppose you relax and tell me all about it."

"You . . . you won't tell my wife?"

"Level with me, Word. I can't make any promises."

He tried pouring a drink, but you could hear the clicking sound across the street, and most of the stuff wound up in his shoes.

"I'm a working guy," he said. "Mechanical maintenance. I build and service joy buzzers. You know—those little fun gimmicks that give people a shock when they shake hands?"

"So?"

"A lot of your executives like 'em. Particularly down on Wall Street."

"Get to the point."

"I'm on the road a lot. You know how it is—lonely. Oh, not what you're thinking. See, Kaiser, I'm basically an intellectual. Sure, a guy can meet all the bimbos he wants. But the really brainy women—they're not so easy to find on short notice."

"Keep talking."

"Well, I heard of this young girl. Eighteen years old. A Vassar student. For a price, she'll come over and discuss any subject—Proust, Yeats, anthropology. Exchange of ideas. You see what I'm driving at?"

"Not exactly."

"I mean, my wife is great, don't get me wrong. But she won't discuss Pound with me. Or Eliot. I didn't know that when I married her. See, I need a woman who's mentally stimulating, Kaiser. And I'm willing to pay for it. I don't want an involvement—I want a quick intellectual experience, then I want the girl to leave. Christ, Kaiser, I'm a happily married man."

"How long has this been going on?"

"Six months. Whenever I have that craving, I call Flossie.

Although he is best known for his films, Woody Allen is also considered a master of literary humor, and has published three collections of short pieces: *Getting Even, Without Feathers,* and *Side Effects.* Most of these stories, including this one, appeared originally in *The New Yorker.*

Woody Allen (Allen Konigsberg) was born in Brooklyn in 1935, and became a comedy writer after dropping out of college during his freshman year. After serving as a writer for Sid Caesar's *Your Show of Shows,* he began performing his own material in 1964.

The personal ads which accompany this piece are from *The New York Review of Us,* a *National Lampoon* parody.

She's a madam, with a master's in comparative lit. She sends me over an intellectual, see?"

So he was one of those guys whose weakness was really bright women. I felt sorry for the poor sap. I figured there must be a lot of jokers in his position, who were starved for a little intellectual communication with the opposite sex and would pay through the nose for it.

"Now she's threatening to tell my wife," he said.

"Who is?"

"Flossie. They bugged the motel room. They got tapes of me discussing *The Waste Land* and *Styles of Radical Will,* and, well, really getting into some issues. They want ten grand or they go to Carla. Kaiser, you've got to help me! Carla would die if she knew she didn't turn me on up here."

The old call-girl racket. I had heard rumors that the boys at headquarters were on to something involving a group of educated women, but so far they were stymied.

"Get Flossie on the phone for me."

"What?"

"I'll take your case, Word. But I get fifty dollars a day, plus expenses. You'll have to repair a lot of joy buzzers."

"It won't be ten G's' worth, I'm sure of that," he said with a grin, and picked up the phone and dialed a number. I took it from him and winked. I was beginning to like him.

Seconds later, a silky voice answered, and I told her what was on my mind. "I understand you can help me set up an hour of good chat," I said.

"Sure, honey. What do you have in mind?"

"I'd like to discuss Melville."

"*Moby Dick* or the shorter novels?"

"What's the difference?"

"The price. That's all. Symbolism's extra."

"What'll it run me?"

"Fifty, maybe a hundred for *Moby Dick.* You want a comparative discussion—Melville and Hawthorne? That could be arranged for a hundred."

"The dough's fine," I told her, and gave her the number of a room at the Plaza.

"You want a blonde or a brunette?"

"Surprise me," I said, and hung up.

I shaved and grabbed some black coffee while I checked over the Monarch College Outline series. Hardly an hour had passed before there was a knock on my door. I opened it, and standing there was a young redhead who was packed into her slacks like two big scoops of vanilla ice cream.

"Hi, I'm Sherry."

They really knew how to appeal to your fantasies. Long

straight hair, leather bag, silver earrings, no makeup.

"I'm surprised you weren't stopped, walking into the hotel dressed like that," I said. "The house dick can usually spot an intellectual."

"A five-spot cools him."

"Shall we begin?" I said, motioning her to the couch.

She lit a cigarette and got right to it. "I think we could start by approaching *Billy Budd* as Melville's justification of the ways of God to man, *n'est-ce pas?*"

"Interestingly, though not in a Miltonian sense." I was bluffing. I wanted to see if she'd go for it.

"No. *Paradise Lost* lacked the substructure of pessimism." She did.

"Right, right. God, you're right," I murmured.

"I think Melville reaffirmed the virtues of innocence in a naive yet sophisticated sense—don't you agree?"

I let her go on. She was barely nineteen years old, but already she had developed the hardened facility of the pseudo-intellectual. She rattled off her ideas glibly, but it was all mechanical. Whenever I offered an insight, she faked a response:

THE UNHAPPIEST MAN IN NEW YORK

He had an Irish psychiatrist and a Jewish bartender.

Reprinted by permission from *National Lampoon*, September, 1979 issue

CLASSIFIED ADS

PERSONAL

LOST IN SANTA CRUZ radical blather, need coherent conversation, intellectual traction. Interests: Mandelstahm, Eliot, Pound, Berryman, Jong, languages, music, opera, backgammon. If unintimidated, write NYR, Box 10773.

SHEILAH! We dined June 13. You brought spam jelly, I made carrot yogurt; we ate chinks. Lost your number. Help me, please! NYR Box 88331.

YOUNG MARRIED BUSINESS PROFESSOR and vice-president of a well-known liberal arts college seeks female companionship for quiet luncheon, light shopping, and dry humping. Must be discreet and immaculately confidential. Thomas Parker, General Delivery, North Bennington, Vt. 05201.

HOT, DIFFICULT TO HANDLE, OVERWEIGHT MAN seeks lonely, sensitive, ethical woman with enormous breasts. Write NYR, Box 33811.

TIMID AND SHY young Bronx Jewish student, glasses, from reserved, sedate, conserv. family, seeks relations with fedayeen. NYR, Box 732.

EXTRAORDINARILY HIGH I.Q. physicist/lit. historian, fun-loving, sensual, sensitive, quiet, timid almost, with gigantic genitalia, seeks discreet relations with women from Ohio or Pennsylvania. NYR, Box 391.

PUBLISHED HISTORIAN and professor of comp. lit. (slight acne scars on right temple, lower back) seeks sexual freedom in the form of controlled napalm warfare. If you follow, write NYR, Box 22199.

HUNGARIAN PROFESSOR of radiology at Technical College of Odobestio, congenial, intense, ironic, laconic, independent, occasionally redundant, with redundant tendencies seeks pen-friend outside Soviet bloc with whom to discuss stamps and oral sex. NYR, Box 551

SOMEWHAT HOSTILE MUTE with M.A. in organismic physiognomy needs attention in form of female who can endure such doses of mature, physical stress. Asbestos. NYR, Box 31.

BOOKLOVING, TV HATING Brooklyn man. Unattached again, long unemployed, diffident, with a little psoriasis but not much, takes long shits, naps, reads Jewish-Buddhist newspapers, was once interested in the Hittites, hates smoking, sex in the morning, listening to anyone else, has bad breath from smoking Camels, washes own socks whenever, roll of existential bellyfat, wen, baldspot, into his own hangups, vulnerable, cries a lot, mugged twice, broken shoelace, rumpled sheets, teacup, cracker crumbs, bathroom tap. Seeks nonsmoking, blond, voluptuous glamorgirl with intellectual tolerances and blue eyes to keep house for him and share the rent, gas, elec., be understanding and (hopefully) invest herself in a deep, durable, and sensually abandoned relationship. Write Moise Tvechka, NYR, Box 87678.

AM I LOOKING FOR YOU? Speak up. I'm weary of this frantic social whirl, garden parties, convertibles, highballs at the Ritz in my squash shorts. The effete Nob Hill world makes me languid with ennui. Graceless, arch, and pertinacious females swigging gossip and daquiris and trying to impress one with their breeding and intellect at the same time as they are rolling their eyes and inching toward the bedroom door towards which I will not move from my wingback chair to take a step—from these and their kidney, spare and deliver me. I long to meet a sweet, unspoiled young thing, about nineteen, with all her virtues and ideals intact, laughing gayly over one shoulder as she comes in from tennis. Fresh of mind, fresh of body. If you are such, I am rich beyond measure, and not yet forty. Randolph is my name, despoilation my game. But I'm sincere. So few are. NYR at once! Box 65432.

SHOCK ABSORBER insertion and Saul Bellow technique. If you honestly understand what this means, please contact immediately. NYR, Box 81102.

HUMANISTIC, IRONIC, teleological, proleptic, heuristic, typological, dichotomistic, transumptive or metaleptic, eclectic, Thomistic, neocritiological male seeks unkempt slattern with big nipples and strong bowed legs to raise a mess of brats with. Write NYR, Box 88654.

FREELANCE WRITER, POET DESIRES occasional beatings from attractive, well-educated, professionally oriented Japanese. NYR, Box 997.

OVER 40, WELL-READ, SLIGHTLY WAN yet tenacious business exec likes certain literature and seeks younger females (under 13) for light work. NYR, Box 11.

SOLID BOSTONIAN, F. SCOTT FITZGERALD TYPE, double Ph.D., published abroad, tenured professor, well-versed with unusual face, schooled in Gt. Britain, needs female who likes good gums. NYR, Box 88711.

WELL-VERSED BUT BORED Indiana U. prof. of entomology seeks responsible male for short conversations, light baby sitting, some clitoral stimulation. NYR, Box 8890.

GROISSE ZETZ; TUCHUS. If you really understand, please send detailed, confidential reply to NYR, Box 11045.

JEWISH

ORTHODOX PSYCHOLOGIST who knows how to live well seeks woman to share bleeding ulcer. NYR, Box 8775.

AGING YIDDISH STORY WRITER seeks young man for light enema work. Some typing. Other. NYR, Box 441.

REFORM LIBERAL, outspoken, Long Island Congregational rabbi and wife seek well-educated, literary black woman for racial repartee, intensive interviews, light housework. NYR, Box 3218.

SOMEWHAT UNHAPPILY MARRIED orthodox, well-mannered gentleman seeks shame. Reply NYR, Box 22910.

I'M A PETITE, CUDDLY, AFFECTIONATE, red-headed Hasid diamond merchant who seeks everlasting matrimony within sacred covenant. Will provide carfare. NYR, Box 7892.

BISEXUAL RENTALS

ENGLISH COUNTRY BISEXUAL for rent. In quiet, coastal village in Somerset. Fully modernized and equipped. 3 mos. Phone 212-819-4927 after 2 A.M.

FUNKY BISEXUAL resembling Harold Bloom for weekly or monthly rentals and small gatherings. Must be Ph.D. NYR, Box 99873.

LOVELY, SPACIOUS PROVINCIAL FARM BISEXUAL. Appliances. Library. NYR, Box 9900137.

ESTABLISHED BISEXUAL WRITER for lease during 1976-77, available for sabbatical. Will exchange ideology and matters pertaining to creative subconscious for other stimulation. NYR, Box 881.

RESTORED, HILLTOP HOMOSEXUAL in well-developed area, private locations, complete. NYR, Box 44211.

BEAUTIFULLY FURNISHED London townhouse homosexual. Also, renovated early 20th century bisexual. Town and Country Real Estates. Avail. 6 mos. Security. NYR, Box 1718.

JEWISH/GOYISH
GOYISH/JEWISH

JEWISH-GOYISH/JEWISH MAN, 33, seeks Roman-type goy to share experiences and some knocking around on Purim and other festival days, Simchat Torah, or anytime. NYR, Box 9722.

JEWISH-GOYISH/MALE Jew, 29, looks to break Sabbath and High Holy Day traditions with non-Jewish young woman who speaks very little English. NYR, Box 443.

GOYISH-JEWISH/GOYISHE, bilingual Roman Catholic girl, 29, pretty, likes Mailer, Malamud, McKuen, seeks young male who will consent to pose as ham radio operator in exchange for physical love. NYR, Box 2311.

JEWISH-GOYISH, Tired, tense Jewish woman seeks hyperactive, guilty Greek to share urinary tract infection and school holidays. Strong. NYR, Box 299.

PROTESTANT FREE-LANCE WRITER needs info for booklet on anal retention, expulsives. Jewish preferred. Possible participation. Write Prof. M. NYR, Box 5.

BROOKLYN YESHIVA, 63, PROFESSOR of Kabbalah and Tractates from Lubovitch family of fabric merchants is fed up with smelly rituals. Seeks to trade Yartzeit candles for open-minded relations with young gentlemen from upstate. NYR, Box 55113.

SERVICES

UNDER RABBINICAL SUPERVISION: Williamsburg, Brooklyn J.H.S. teacher, expert on Torah, seeks to convert homosexuals using simple prayer and other techniques. No electricity. NYR, Box 32998.

SUFFERING WRITERS! I CAN HAVE YOUR MATERIAL PUBLISHED, printed, and distributed on colorful cocktail napkins. Send 75¢ for free booklet.

BENNINGTON COLLEGE, CLASSICIST, teacher of literature and languages desires discreet encounter with modest or comely reptiles for special research project. Confidential. NYR, Box 80.

SPARE TIME

HOW TO MAKE MONEY INVENTING SMALL WORDS. I'll tell you how to do it and where to go. Barrett, P.O. Box 332, Grand Central Station, NYC.

PERFORM VASECTOMIES in your spare time! Learn how. Make your own hours. Increase your income. Wilson's, Box 223, Greenvale, Fla.

TUCHIS? YENTA? GEY KOCKEN? SHTUP?? You can actually earn a living reading Yiddish words out loud in your spare time in the southern U.S. Start with simple home course. Yiddish Division, La Salle Extension University, Grand Rapids, Mich.

RUMORS AND UNPLEASANT FILLERS for Jewish or Yiddish short stories. Inexpensive outlines for unpleasant characters, odors, etc. Write Knish & Kasha Filler Co., Box 559, Brooklyn, N.Y.

SCAPEGOATS AND OTHER RELATED IDEAS can actually solve your problems practically overnight. Send for details. Free Press, Box 66, Orlando, Fla.

SICKNESS, ACCIDENTS, MILD DISEASE needed for your story? We have everything for the ethnic author. Simple insertions fit into any story or essay effortlessly. Instructions. Rank Fillers, Box 12, Acton, Ohio.

PROTESTANT? Walking around feeling insulated by the cotton of insensivity? Have invigorating, Yiddish Tension Massage by overweight woman. Creplach massages. NYR, Box 30.

OUT OF PRINT

PALIMPSESTS, INCUNABULA, hieroglyphs, scrolls, papyri, cave paintings, teepee drawings, and other preliterate shit. Ya want it, we got it! If it ain't in our large stock, you get our free soich soivice. Let us whip our catalogue to ya! Da Book Bug, Galloshers, Ore. 20887.

HANG-A-POET—I'll hang and frame your favorite living poet, you, or other essayist. Send for important brochure. We've done Berryman, Plath, Roethke, Anne Sexton. Become well known overnight away! Barrett, P.O. Box 332, Grand Central Station, NYC.

"Oh, yes, Kaiser. Yes, baby, that's deep. A Platonic comprehension of Christianity—why didn't I see it before?"

We talked for about an hour and then she said she had to go. She stood up and I laid a C-note on her.

"Thanks, honey."

"There's plenty more where that came from."

"What are you trying to say?"

I had piqued her curiosity. She sat down again.

"Suppose I wanted to—have a party?" I said.

"Like, what kind of party?"

"Suppose I wanted Noam Chomsky explained to me by two girls?"

"Oh, wow."

"If you'd rather forget it . . ."

"You'd have to speak with Flossie," she said. "It'd cost you."

Now was the time to tighten the screws. I flashed my private investigator's badge and informed her it was a bust.

"What!"

"I'm fuzz, sugar, and discussing Melville for money is an 802. You can do time."

"You louse!"

"Better come clean, baby. Unless you want to tell your story down at Alfred Kazin's office, and I don't think he'd be too happy to hear it."

She began to cry. "Don't turn me in, Kaiser," she said. "I needed the money to complete my master's. I've been turned down for a grant. *Twice.* Oh, Christ."

It all poured out—the whole story. Central Park West upbringing, Socialist summer camps, Brandeis. She was every dame you saw waiting in line at the Elgin or the Thalia, or penciling the words "Yes, very true" into the margin of some book on Kant. Only somewhere along the line she had made a wrong turn.

"I needed cash. A girl friend said she knew a married guy whose wife wasn't very profound. He was into Blake. She couldn't hack it. I said sure, for a price I'd talk Blake with him. I was nervous at first. I faked a lot of it. He didn't care. My friend said there were others. Oh, I've been busted before. I got caught reading *Commentary* in a parked car, and I was once stopped and frisked at Tanglewood. Once more and I'm a three-time loser."

"Then take me to Flossie."

She bit her lip and said, "The Hunter College Book Store is a front."

"Yes?"

"Like those bookie joints that have barbershops outside for show. You'll see."

Drawing by David Levine. Copyright © 1969 by Nyrev, Inc. By permission of *The New York Review of Books.*

I made a quick call to headquarters and then said to her, "Okay, sugar. You're off the hook. But don't leave town."

She tilted her face up toward mine gratefully. "I can get you photographs of Dwight Macdonald reading," she said.

"Some other time."

I walked into the Hunter College Book Store. The salesman, a young man with sensitive eyes, came up to me. "Can I help you?" he said.

"I'm looking for a special edition of *Advertisements for Myself.* I understand the author had several thousand gold-leaf copies printed up for friends."

"I'll have to check," he said. "We have a WATS line to Mailer's house."

I fixed him with a look. "Sherry sent me," I said.

"Oh. In that case, go on back," he said. He pressed a button. A wall of books opened, and I walked like a lamb into that bustling pleasure palace known as Flossie's.

Red flocked wallpaper and a Victorian decor set the tone. Pale, nervous girls with black-rimmed glasses and blunt-cut hair lolled around on sofas, riffling Penguin Classics provocatively. A blonde with a big smile winked at me, nodded toward a room upstairs, and said, "Wallace Stevens, eh?" But it wasn't just intellectual experiences—they were peddling emotional ones too. For fifty bucks, I learned, you could "relate without getting close." For a hundred, a girl would lend you her Bartók records, have dinner, and then let you watch while she had an anxiety attack. For one-fifty, you could listen to FM radio with twins. For three bills, you got the works: A thin Jewish brunette would pretend to pick you up at the Museum of Modern Art, let you read her master's, get you involved in a screaming quarrel at Elaine's over Freud's conception of women, and then fake a suicide of your choosing—the perfect evening, for some guys. Nice racket. Great town, New York.

"Like what you see?" a voice said behind me. I turned and suddenly found myself standing face to face with the business end of a .38. I'm a guy with a strong stomach, but this time it did a back flip. It was Flossie, all right. The voice was the same, but Flossie was a man. His face was hidden by a mask.

"You'll never believe this," he said, "but I don't even have a college degree. I was thrown out for low grades."

"Is that why you wear that mask?"

"I devised a complicated scheme to take over *The New York Review of Books,* but it meant I had to pass for Lionel Trilling. I went to Mexico for an operation. There's a doctor in Juarez who gives people Trilling's features—for a price. Something went wrong. I came out looking like Auden, with Mary McCarthy's voice. That's when I started working the other side of the law."

Quickly, before he could tighten his finger on the trigger, I went into action. Heaving forward, I snapped my elbow across his jaw and grabbed the gun as he fell back. He hit the ground like a ton of bricks. He was still whimpering when the police showed up.

"Nice work, Kaiser," Sergeant Holmes said. "When we're through with this guy, the FBI wants to have a talk with him. A little matter involving some gamblers and an annotated copy of Dante's *Inferno.* Take him away, boys."

Later that night, I looked up an old account of mine named Gloria. She was blond. She had graduated *cum laude.* The difference was she majored in physical education. It felt good.

Drawing by David Levine. Copyright
© 1975 by Nyrev, Inc. By permission of
The New York Review of Books.

In Jewish humor of the past several decades, the psychiatrist has gradually come to take the place of the rabbi. Like rabbis, psychiatrists are often mocked or denounced in jokes, especially for their allegedly magical or mystical powers.

"There is something intensely Jewish about the very nature of Freudianism," writes Chaim Bermant in *The Jews.* "Traditional Jewish scholarship was never content with deriving the obvious from the evident. Things are not always what they seem, words do not always mean what they say. One was trained to read between the lines, and between the words, and indeed, within the words, for hints, clues and hidden meanings, so that it was almost inevitable that if someone was to force the subconscious to surface it would be someone like Freud."

•

A man comes to see a psychiatrist.

"Doctor, I've been talking to myself."

"Don't worry about that," says the doctor. "Many people do the same thing."

"Yes," responds the patient, "but you don't know what a *nudnik* I am!"

•

Two psychiatrists are leaving their building together after a long day. The younger man is completely worn out, with rumpled hair, wrinkled clothing, and a tired, sweaty face. The older man, however, looks as if he has just enjoyed a siesta.

"Meyers," says the younger man, "I don't understand you. Here you've been working a full day and you look like you're ready for another eight hours. I don't know how you do it. My patients are driving me crazy. All day they come in and bring all the problems of the city with them. It must be the same with your patients. Don't you get tired and depressed, having to sit there all day and listen to them?"

"*Aha,*" replies Meyers. "Who listens?"

•

These are the ABC's of psychiatry:
Neurotics build castles in the air,
psychotics live in them, and
psychiatrists collect the rent.

From *Running A Muck*, copyright © 1978 by John Caldwell. By permission of Writer's Digest Books.

I HAD the strangest dream last night," a man was telling his psychiatrist. "I saw my mother, but when she turned around to look at me, I noticed that she had your face. As you can imagine, I found this very disturbing, and in fact I woke up immediately, and couldn't get back to sleep. I just lay there in bed waiting for morning to come, and then I got up, drank a Coke, and came right over here for my appointment. I thought you could help me explain the meaning of this strange dream."

The psychiatrist was silent for a full minute before responding: "A Coke? That's a breakfast?"

What is the difference between a psychotic and a neurotic?
A psychotic thinks that 2 plus 2 makes 5.
A neurotic *knows* that 2 plus 2 makes 4
—he just can't *stand* it.

ONE fine morning at F. A. O. Schwarz, three-year-old Jennifer Berkowitz simply refused to get off the red tricycle she had been riding for close to an hour. Her mother pleaded, and so did the salespeople, but the little girl flew into a rage and would not be budged.

Suddenly, the store manager remembered that he had recently met and chatted with the renowned child psychologist Irving Green. He also remembered that Dr. Green's office was only three blocks from the toy store.

The Berkowitz girl was fast becoming impossible, and the manager decided that nothing could be lost by calling Dr. Green. Perhaps he could spare a few minutes to help with this annoying problem? Yes, said Dr. Green, he would be happy to come right over.

There was a collective sigh of relief as the distinguished psychologist marched into the store. Without talking to anybody, he made his way to the girl on the red tricycle, leaned over, smiled, and whispered something in her ear. At once, and without a word of protest, Jennifer jumped off the tricycle as though it were on fire, and ran over to rejoin her mother.

As soon as the girl and her mother had left the store, the sales force crowded around Dr. Green. They were eager to know what words of psychiatric wisdom he had uttered to get the girl off the tricycle.

"Oh, it was nothing, really," said the therapist. "I said to her: 'Listen, *tzatskelah,* if you don't get off that thing right now, I'm gonna give you such a *potch* on the *tuchis* that you won't sit down for a week!'"

This joke is a special favorite of older audiences, who retain a measure of skepticism about psychotherapy, and fondly recall the days when psychoanalysis was still a fancy new theory. Indeed, remarks one of Woody Allen's characters, in the old days the process was not only less formal, but considerably less expensive:

•

For five marks Freud himself would treat you. For ten marks he would treat you and press your pants. For fifteen marks, Freud would let *you* treat *him,* and that included a choice of two vegetables.

•

In 1897, the same year he joined the B'nai B'rith, Freud wrote to a colleague that he had begun a collection of Jewish jokes; two years later he announced that he was putting together an anthology, but this project was apparently never completed. A number of Jewish jokes, especially those about *schnorrers* (beggars) and *shadchans* (marriage brokers), did find their way into *Jokes and Their Relation to the Unconscious,* published in 1905.

•

Sam Levenson was especially interested in the relationship between children and their parents, especially the matter of child psychology and its popular distortions. "One mother," he recalled, "wrote a note to the teacher. If Gregory is a bad boy, she says, don't slap him. Slap the boy *next* to him. Gregory will get the idea."

•

From *Sigmund Freud* by Ralph Steadman. Reprinted by permission of the artist.
Copyright © 1979 by Ralph Steadman. All rights reserved.

From *Sigmund Freud* by Ralph Steadman. Reprinted by permission of the artist. Copyright © 1979 by Ralph Steadman. All rights reserved.

This joke appears in Theodor Reik's *Jewish Wit,* where Reik notes that he heard it from Freud while they were discussing one of Reik's patients. *Jewish Wit,* published in 1962, is the only full-length treatment of Jewish humor from a psychoanalytic perspective.

A CERTAIN patient in a mental institution had argued long and hard that he must be served only kosher food. Finally, unable to avoid the extra work and expense, the director of the institution acquiesced.

A few days later, on the Sabbath, the director was strolling around the grounds, when he came upon the same patient sitting in a chair and smoking a cigar.

"Wait a minute, Schwartz," he said. "I thought you were so religious that we had to bring in special food for you. And now, here you are smoking on the Sabbath!"

"But, Doctor," Schwartz replied. "Did you forget? I'm *meshugah!*"

From *Sigmund Freud* by Ralph Steadman. Reprinted by permission of the artist. Copyright © 1979 by Ralph Steadman. All rights reserved.

The Babylonian Talmud

with Commentaries by Rashi, Tosaphot,
etc. 20 Volumes, Vilna

Reviewed by Eliezer ben Tam

Apparently encouraged by the commercial success of the *Palestinian (Yerushalmi) Talmud,* the rabbis of Pumpedita, with Rav Ashi at the helm, have jumped onto the bandwagon with a similar enterprise, which they call, with no small hint of irony, the *Talmud Bavli.* Although this work has its merits, one hopes that we will be spared further imitations—Spanish, Polish, and Canadian Talmuds, which enterprising publishers are already reported to be commissioning.

Like its Palestinian companion, the *Bavli* is in a sense a sequel to Rabbi Yehuda HaNasi's *Mishnah* (viz. M. Maimonides' review in *Mishneh Torah,* Vol. I), following to a dubious conclusion the lives and adventures of many of our favorite characters from Rabbi Yehudah's heartwarming and grotesque book. For those of us who developed a deep affection for that mischievous ox of *Baba Qamma* (who can forget the hilarious episode in which, while attempting to gore a blind heathen, he tramples instead a pregnant woman and then escapes to the countryside, only to fall into an abandoned pit?), it is a thrill to find him still as precocious as ever, always a tail away from the stones of the Establishment. Similarly, such favorites as the Discredited Witnesses, the Nocturnal Seminal Emission, the Figs of the Sabbatical Year, and especially that inseparable trio: the Deaf-Mute, the Fool, and the Minor—these and many more will return to delight you in the present volume.

Nevertheless, there are a number of characters whose roles in the *Bavli* have been severely cut, or altogether, as it were, forgotten. In some cases, one can regard such changes with a measure of justification—for example: the Sacrifice Squad from the Temple was apparently introduced during the height of the Sin Offering fad of the forties; but who these days can really be titillated by such crude sadistic efforts? Nevertheless, even here there is cause for regret, for in doing away with the trite sacrificial scenes (apparently yielding to subtle pressures from Vespasian and his henchmen), we are also deprived of one of the most enchanting and enigmatic figures of the *Mishnah,* that of the High Priest (Cohen Gadol), whose previously superhuman posture as the Manson-like demagogue of a primitive but colorful phallic cult has been reduced almost cruelly to a *schlemiel,* now preoccupied with marital problems and domestic bickering. Such is the fate of the nonfunctional tradition in a pragmatic world.

It is also disappointing that little that is really new has

This review of the Talmud is a contemporary underground favorite known fondly in those circles—independent *havurah* groups, for example—whose members are knowledgeable about Judaism but retain a contemporary perspective on the tradition.

The review appeared originally in *Strobe,* a student magazine published irregularly by the McGill University Hillel Foundation during the late 1960s and early 1970s.

The Talmud, an encyclopedic anthology of several centuries of Jewish genius, was completed in the sixth century. In our own time, virtually every elaborate or nonconventional exercise in mind or logic has been dubbed "Talmudic reasoning"; if everyone who has used this phrase had actually read even a single page of Talmud, ours would indeed be a generation of scholars.

If classic Jewish jokes share anything with the Talmud, it is in their process rather than their content. Improbable logic, slightly convoluted arguments, skepticism, and a remarkable desire to equate intelligence with common sense—these are some of the characteristics of the rabbinic mind, as well as of Jewish humor.

Mark Podwal © 1978

been introduced to substitute for what has been discarded. Most of the action involves merely repeated elaboration and rehashing, albeit sometimes ingenious, on themes that were well discussed in the *Mishnah.* Nevertheless, new characters are introduced. By far the dominant figures are Abaye and Rava, a team whose persistent slapstick routines, corny as they might seem, mark them as suitable replacements for Rabbi Akiva and Rabbi Ishmael. Similarly, the transference of the greater part of the action to Babylonia (with the exotic names of its places and people—Nahardea, Sura, Pappa, Iddi, etc.) adds a distinct freshness which the *Yerushalmi* could not claim.

One irritating feature of the *Bavli* is particularly unforgivable in view of the *Bavli*'s own persistent efforts to remove the same fault from the *Mishnah;* I refer to the problem of unresolved themes. Such dangling prepositions filled the *Mishnah,* and the *Bavli,* with sleuthwork that would put Fearless Fosdick to shame, succeeded in identifying many of the mysterious, anonymous "Tanna Qammas" (as they whimsically call these shadowy figures, who materialize in scores of identities, taking on plurality at times), as well as to forcefully decide arguments in the most heated of conflicts. Having recognized the editors' uncanny skills along these lines, it is particularly unforgivable that the *Bavli* should stand guilty of the same literary faults. One can only assume that, at the expense of the readers' satisfaction, the publishers are trying to render inevitable the release of yet another tedious but lucrative sequel.

May I suggest that the *Talmud* would make a particularly fitting gift for anyone with three or more arms (or for someone uninhibited in the use of his feet)—such is the nature of the text that he has to keep fingers in a variety of embarrassing places simultaneously, in order to keep track of the steady counterpoint of kibbitzing that continuously emerges from the margins (cf. apparently a Hellenistic Jewish variation on the Aragonés cartoons in *Mad* magazine) in the persons of such proficient back-seat drivers as Rashi and the Tosaphot and their stooges. The former usually plays straight man. The latter, actually a well-financed dynastic corporation from France, makes one of the most consistently upheld attempts, since Socrates, to provoke a punch in the mouth.

Moreover, it is a work of, to put it succinctly, rare relevance. While avoiding overworked issues, it boldly tackles problems from which most pundits today conspicuously flee: The measure of ritual impurity that results from contact with a gonorrheal rabbit in a tent; whether an *eruv* should consist of a plank and a stake or of two stakes; whether it was Rabbi Eliezer or Rabbi Joshua who exempted the High Priest from alimony payments in the case of a kidnapped divorcee—and all the other questions that have been keeping you awake in front of your television.

In short—and the *Talmud* is certainly not—the *Bavli* contains something for everybody, and even a hell of a lot for nobody. Aside from intrigue, action, and sex (the more recent editions contain an index of "good parts" by Rabbi Hayyim of Plotsk, the eighteenth-century pilpulist and lecher), we must not forget that we are really dealing with a glorified "how to" book, in which the great Jewish minds of hundreds of years fight each other to the death to offer you recipes, legal and medical advice, and, primarily, to order you around till you're ready to cry. This perhaps is the greatness of the *Talmud*—the fact that it has embodied within itself a thousand-year-old monumental tradition of nudnikism, the minutes of countless Sunday-morning bagel-bakery symposia, the nitpicking and vacillation of generations of kvetches. Not for the squeamish.

ONCE there was a man who wanted to build a house. He went to see his rebbe and knocked on the door. The rebbe, who was studying Talmud at the time, looked up from his book. "Come in," he said.

"Rebbe," said the man, "forgive me for disturbing you. But I want to build a house, and I don't know where to begin. Can you help me out?"

"This is a most auspicious question," replied the rebbe. "For at this very moment I am sitting here studying *Masechet Batim,* the section of the Talmud that deals with houses. And here, right on this page, Rabbi Yochanan has a long digression about how to build a house. Here, take the Talmud; I have another one. Go home, follow these directions carefully, and you'll have yourself a beautiful house, and a wonderful place for your family."

The man was delighted. He took home the book, propped it up on a rock, and began reading: "Do this for four cubits, do that for six cubits." Three months later he had a truly lovely house,

Dick Codor © 1981

Dick Codor © 1981

Dick Codor © 1981

and he invited the entire community to its dedication. When it came time to put up the *mezuzah,* the man took a hammer, gave it a little tap—and the entire house fell to the ground!

Frantic, the man returned to the rebbe. "Rebbe," he said in a quivering voice, "I followed the instructions and do you know what happened? As I was putting up the *mezuzah,* the house fell down!"

The rebbe looked up from the Talmud. "What do you think the Talmud is—the daily newspaper? No! The Talmud is a holy book and it must be studied carefully. Obviously you were careless. Here's what you should do: Get yourself a friend and have him read every direction to you as you go along, and you should say each direction back to him, just to be safe and completely certain that you are following the directions exactly. Now go and build your house."

The man went right to work. This time it took five months to build his house, as his friend read every direction and he repeated it back to him. Again the man invited the entire community to the dedication of the house. Again he lifted the hammer to affix the *mezuzah*—and again the entire house fell down!

This time the man was furious with the rebbe. He went to the rebbe's house and opened the door without knocking. He threw the big volume of the Talmud down on the table in front of the rebbe.

"Again it happened!" the man shouted. "I carefully followed all of Rabbi Yochanan's directions. Why is it that every time I put up the house it fell down?"

The rebbe studied the appropriate page of the Talmud for a few moments. "Wait a *minute,*" he finally said. "Rashi asks the same question!"

●

Rashi, of course, is the famous eleventh-century Biblical commentator whose exegesis is still used today in studying Torah and Talmud. Yeshiva youngsters are often told that God has given them two hands—one to study the text, the other to follow the comments of Rashi, without whose explanation the text is often incomprehensible.

Among audiences already familiar with the Talmud, this joke is more effective with Tosaphot—a commentary on the Talmud—instead of the more elementary Rashi.

TALMUDIC LOGIC

If one man saw a *koy*
   [an animal that was believed to be intermediate
   between a kid and a gazelle,
   and which, consequently, the rabbis were uncertain
   to classify as wild or domestic, or both or neither],
and said,
   "I vow to be a Nazarite if this is a wild animal,"
and another man said,
   "I vow to be a Nazarite if this is not a wild animal,"
and a third man said,
   "I vow to be a Nazarite if this is a domestic animal,"
and a fourth man said,
   "I vow to be a Nazarite if this is not a domestic animal,"
and a fifth man said,
   "I vow to be a Nazarite if this is both a wild animal and a domestic animal,"
and a sixth man said,
   "I vow to be a Nazarite if this is neither a wild animal nor a domestic animal,"
and a seventh man said,
   "I vow to be a Nazarite if one of you six people is a Nazarite,"
and an eighth man said,
   "I vow to be a Nazarite if none of you seven people is a Nazarite,"
and a ninth man said,
   "I vow to be a Nazarite if all you eight people are Nazarites"
—then they are all Nazarites.

Mishnah (Nazir 5:7)

Dick Codor © 1980

Dick Codor © 1979

IN 1914, when war threatened to engulf all of Europe, two yeshiva students were discussing the situation. One was completely pessimistic; the other was trying to console him:

"As yet there's no reason to worry. This whole crisis may blow over, but even if war comes, there are still two possibilities: either you will be drafted or you won't. If you're not drafted, there's nothing to worry about. But if you *are* drafted, there are still two possibilities: you may be sent to the front or you may not. If you are sent to the front, there are still two possibilities: you may be wounded or you may not. If you're not wounded, you have nothing to worry about. If you *are* wounded, there are still two possibilities: you may be wounded seriously or you may not. If not, you have nothing to worry about. If you *are* wounded seriously, there are still two possibilities: you may die from your wounds or you may not. If you don't die, you have nothing to worry about. If you *do* die, there are still two possibilities: you may go to the good place or to the bad place. If you go to the good place, you have nothing to worry about. But even if you go to the bad place, there is still one other possibility: there may be no war at all, so you have nothing to worry about!"

This is one of those rare cases where the term "Talmudic logic" is accurate and appropriate. "Every stick has two ends," says the proverb, and there are several jokes based on this tendency to allow for every possibility.

The most famous of these stories has to do with the two litigants who come before the rabbi. After hearing the first testimony, the rabbi says, "It seems that you are right." But after the second man speaks, the rabbi says, "It seems that *you* are right too."

"How can this be?" says the rabbi's wife, who has been listening to the arguments. "How can both of these men be right?"

"Hm," says the rabbi. "You're right too."

Rabbi Jeremiah asked: If one foot of the fledgling is within the limit of fifty cubits, and one foot is outside it, what is the law?

The Mishnah states: If a fledgling bird is found within fifty cubits of a dovecote, it belongs to the owner of the dovecote. If it is found outside the limit of fifty cubits, it belongs to the person who finds it.

It was for this question that Rabbi Jeremiah was thrown out of the House of Study.

Talmud (Bava Batra 23b)

ANTI-SEMITISM • DISPUTATIONS • THE GOYISH PERSUASION

S. GROSS • LENNY BRUCE • DICK CODOR • BERNARD MALAMUD • MAX APPLE • ROMAIN GARY • JOHN CALDWELL • DAVID LEVINE • KIRSCHEN • MARK PODWAL • WALLACE MARKFIELD • PHILIP ROTH

"It's a goy!"

© 1981 S. Gross

PART TWO

JEWISH & GOYISH

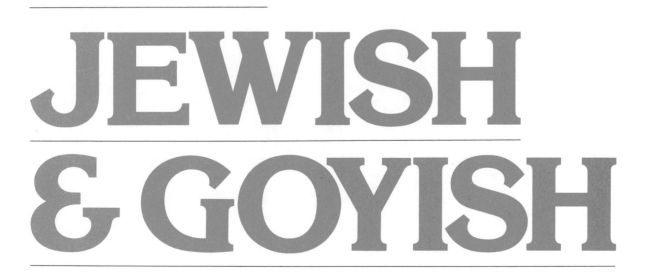

JEWISH AND GOYISH

Dig: I'm Jewish. Count Basie's Jewish. Ray Charles is Jewish. Eddie Cantor's goyish. B'nai B'rith is goyish; Hadassah, Jewish.

If you live in New York or any other big city, you are Jewish. It doesn't matter even if you're Catholic; if you live in New York, you're Jewish. If you live in Butte, Montana, you're going to be goyish even if you're Jewish.

Kool-Aid is goyish. Evaporated milk is goyish even if the Jews invented it. Chocolate is Jewish and fudge is goyish. Fruit salad is Jewish. Lime jello is goyish. Lime soda is *very* goyish.

All Drake's Cakes are goyish. Pumpernickel is Jewish and, as you know, white bread is very goyish. Instant potatoes, goyish. Black cherry soda's very Jewish, macaroons are *very* Jewish.

Negroes are all Jews. Italians are all Jews. Irishmen who have rejected their religion are Jews. Mouths are very Jewish. And bosoms. Baton-twirling is very goyish.

Underwear is definitely goyish. Balls are goyish. Titties are Jewish.

Celebrate is a goyish word. Observe is a Jewish word. Mr. and Mrs. Walsh are *celebrating* Christmas with Major Thomas Moreland, USAF (ret.), while Mr. and Mrs. Bromberg *observed* Hanukkah with Goldie and Arthur Schindler from Kiamesha, New York.

Lenny Bruce

THE ESSENTIAL ANTI-SEMITISM JOKES

A FEW months after the end of World War I, the premier of Poland had a meeting with President Woodrow Wilson. "If you don't meet our nation's demands at the peace conference," warned the premier, "I foresee great troubles ahead. The Polish people will be very angry, and they'll go out and massacre the Jews."

"And if your demands *are* met?" asked Wilson.

"In that case," responded the premier, "my people will be delighted. They'll go out in the streets and get drunk—and *then* they'll massacre the Jews."

TWO Jews sat in a coffeehouse, discussing the fate of their people.

"How miserable is our lot," said one. "Pogroms, plagues, quotas, discrimination, Hitler, the Klan . . . Sometimes I think we'd be better off if we'd never been born."

"Sure," said his friend. "But who has that much luck—maybe one in fifty thousand?"

FOUR friends are sitting in a restaurant in Moscow. For a long time, nobody says a word. Finally, one man groans, "Oy."

"Oy vey," says a second man.

"Nu," says the third.

At this, the fourth man gets up from his chair and says, "Listen, if you fellows don't stop talking politics, I'm leaving!"

DURING the Second World War, after three months of waiting in Casablanca, Lowenthal had almost given up hope of getting a visa for America. The American consulate was constantly filled with refugees, and it was virtually impossible even to get an interview with an American official. Finally, Lowenthal was able to make an appointment.

"What are my chances of entering your country?" he asked.

"Not very good, I'm afraid," said the official. "Your country's quota is completely filled. I suggest you come back in ten years."

"Fine," replied Lowenthal impassively. "Morning or afternoon?"

ALTMANN and his secretary were sitting in a coffeehouse in Berlin in 1935. "Herr Altmann," said his secretary. "I notice you're reading *Der Stürmer!* I can't understand why you're carrying a Nazi libel sheet. Are you some kind of masochist, or, God forbid, a self-hating Jew?"

"On the contrary, Frau Epstein. When I used to read the Jewish papers, all I learned about were pogroms, riots in Palestine, and assimilation in America. But now that I read *Der Stürmer,* I see so much more: that the Jews control all the banks, that we dominate in the arts, and that we're on the verge of taking over the entire world. You know—it makes me feel a whole lot better!"

Humor about anti-Semitism is frequently a peculiar cohabitation of hope, irony, and skepticism. Jewish jokes about survival are particularly poignant:

•

An Austrian Jew, sensing Hitler's imminent takeover of his country, is considering various options for emigration. He goes to a travel agent for advice, and the agent takes out a large globe and begins discussing the entry requirements of various countries. It soon becomes clear that many of the options are beset with difficulties. One country requires a labor permit; the second country does not recognize the Austrian passport; the third has a strict money requirement for new arrivals, while the fourth doesn't want any immigrants at all—especially not Jews. Finally, in desperation, the Jew asks, "Haven't you got another globe?"

•

The traditional Jewish world view is so close-knit that in spite of all his efforts toward separation, the Jew still does not feel that there is any objective reason to be considered different from other people. A similar situation prevailed among European Jews who emigrated to eastern American cities:

•

A Hasidic rabbi makes a business trip to a small town in Mississippi. As soon as he steps off the train, small children follow him through the streets, fascinated by his appearance. They begin teasing him. Finally he turns to them and says, "Whatsa matter, you kids never seen a Yenkee before?"

•

Dick Codor © 1979

ALTER SCHOENBAUM, an old Hasid, was preparing to leave his village to do business in Warsaw. Before his departure, the old man decided to make himself presentable; he bought a new long black caftan, had his fur hat cleaned and blocked, and replaced the fringes on his prayer shawl. As he boarded the train, he looked like a Rembrandt portrait of an Orthodox Jew.

Two weeks later, Alter returned home in a sullen mood. His business partner was concerned, and asked, "What happened, Alter? Did the deal fall through, God forbid?"

"No, thank God, it went fine," Alter replied. "But on the way home, on the train, I was very disturbed when I heard several young Poles making fun of our people and our ways. They were drinking, and yelling obscenities and laughing, and I was very upset."

"I hope you left them alone," said Alter's partner. "They could have torn you to pieces."

"Of course I left them alone," said Alter. "I didn't say a word. I just sat back and pretended I wasn't Jewish."

TWO Jews are walking through an anti-Semitic neighborhood one evening, when they notice that they are being followed by a pair of hoodlums.

"Sam," says his friend, "we better get out of here. There are two of them and we're alone!"

BERNARD MALAMUD

The Jewbird

Bernard Malamud was born in Brooklyn in 1914. His novels include *The Assistant, The Fixer, A New Life, The Tenants,* and *Dubin's Lives.* He is also the author of several collections of short stories, including *The Magic Barrel* and *Idiots First,* where "The Jewbird" appeared.

The window was open so the skinny bird flew in. Flappity-flap with its frazzled black wings. That's how it goes. It's open, you're in. Closed, you're out and that's your fate. The bird wearily flapped through the open kitchen window of Harry Cohen's top-floor apartment on First Avenue near the lower East River.

On a rod on the wall hung an escaped-canary cage, its door wide open, but this black-type long-beaked bird—its ruffled head and small dull eyes, crossed a little, making it look like a dissipated crow—landed if not smack on Cohen's thick lamb chop, at least on the table close by. The frozen-foods salesman was sitting at supper with his wife and young son on a hot August evening a year ago. Cohen, a heavy man with hairy chest and beefy shorts; Edie, in skinny yellow shorts and red halter; and their ten-year-old Morris (after her father)—Maurie, they called him, a nice kid though not overly bright—were all in the city after two weeks out, because Cohen's mother was dying. They had been enjoying Kingston, New York, but drove back when Mama got sick in her flat in the Bronx.

"Right on the table," said Cohen, putting down his beer glass and swatting at the bird. "Son of a bitch."

"Harry, take care with your language," Edie said, looking at Maurie, who watched every move.

The bird cawed hoarsely and with a flap of its bedraggled wings—feathers tufted this way and that—rose heavily to the top of the open kitchen door, where it perched staring down.

"Gevalt, a pogrom!"

"It's a talking bird," said Edie in astonishment.

"In Jewish," said Maurie.

"Wise guy," muttered Cohen. He gnawed on his chop, then put down the bone. "So if you can talk, say what's your business. What do you want here?"

"If you can't spare a lamb chop," said the bird, "I'll settle for a piece of herring with a crust of bread. You can't live on your nerve forever."

"This ain't a restaurant," Cohen replied. "All I'm asking is what brings you to this address?"

"The window was open," the bird sighed; adding after a moment, "I'm running. I'm flying but I'm also running."

"From whom?" asked Edie with interest.

"Anti-Semeets."

"Anti-Semites?" they all said.

"That's from who."

"What kind of anti-Semites bother a bird?" Edie asked.

"Any kind," said the bird, "also including eagles, vultures, and hawks. And once in a while some crows will take your eyes out."

"But aren't you a crow?"

"Me? I'm a Jewbird."

Cohen laughed heartily. "What do you mean by that?"

The bird began dovening. He prayed without Book or tallith, but with passion. Edie bowed her head, though not Cohen.

And Maurie rocked back and forth with the prayer, looking up with one wide-open eye.

When the prayer was done, Cohen remarked, "No hat, no phylacteries?"

"I'm an old radical."

"You're sure you're not some kind of a ghost or dybbuk?"

"Not a dybbuk," answered the bird, "though one of my relatives had such an experience once. It's all over now, thanks God. They freed her from a former lover, a crazy jealous man. She's now the mother of two wonderful children."

"Birds?" Cohen asked slyly.

"Why not?"

"What kind of birds?"

"Like me. Jewbirds."

Cohen tipped back in his chair and guffawed. "That's a big laugh. I've heard of a Jewfish but not a Jewbird."

"We're once removed." The bird rested on one skinny leg, then on the other. "Please, could you spare maybe a piece of herring with a small crust of bread?"

Edie got up from the table.

"What are you doing?" Cohen asked her.

"I'll clear the dishes."

Cohen turned to the bird. "So what's your name, if you don't mind saying?"

"Call me Schwartz."

"He might be an old Jew changed into a bird by somebody," said Edie, removing a plate.

"Are you?" asked Harry, lighting a cigar.

"Who knows?" answered Schwartz. "Does God tell us everything?"

Maurie got up on his chair. "What kind of herring?" he asked the bird in excitement.

"Get down, Maurie, or you'll fall," ordered Cohen.

"If you haven't got matjes, I'll take schmaltz," said Schwartz.

"All we have is marinated, with slices of onion—in a jar," said Edie.

"If you'll open for me the jar I'll eat marinated. Do you have also, if you don't mind, a piece of rye bread—the spitz?"

Edie thought she had.

"Feed him out on the balcony," Cohen said. He spoke to the bird: "After that, take off."

Schwartz closed both bird eyes. "I'm tired and it's a long way."

"Which direction are you headed—north or south?"

Schwartz, barely lifting his wings, shrugged.

"You don't know where you're going?"

"Where there's charity I'll go."

"Let him stay, Papa," said Maurie. "He's only a bird."

"So stay the night," Cohen said, "but no longer."

In the morning Cohen ordered the bird out of the house but Maurie cried, so Schwartz stayed for a while. Maurie was still on vacation from school and his friends were away. He was lonely and Edie enjoyed the fun he had, playing with the bird.

"He's no trouble at all," she told Cohen, "and besides, his appetite is very small."

"What'll you do when he makes dirty?"

"He flies across the street in a tree when he makes dirty, and if nobody passes below, who notices?"

"So all right," said Cohen, "but I'm dead set against it. I warn you he ain't gonna stay here long."

"What have you got against the poor bird?"

"Poor bird, my ass. He's a foxy bastard. He thinks he's a Jew."

"What difference does it make what he thinks?"

"A Jewbird—what *chutzpah!* One false move and he's out on his drumsticks."

At Cohen's insistence, Schwartz lived out on the balcony in a new wooden birdhouse Edie had bought him.

"With many thanks," said Schwartz, "though I would rather have a human roof over my head. You know how it is at my age. I like the warm, the windows, the smell of cooking. I would also be glad to see once in a while the *Jewish Morning Journal* and have now and then a schnapps because it helps my breathing, thanks God. But whatever you give me, you won't hear complaints."

However, when Cohen brought him a bird feeder full of dried corn, Schwartz said, "Impossible."

Cohen was annoyed. "What's the matter, cross-eyes, is your life getting too good for you? Are you forgetting what it means to be migratory? I'll bet a helluva lot of crows you happen to be acquainted with, Jews or otherwise, would give their eyeteeth to eat this corn."

Schwartz did not answer. What can you say to a *grubber yung?*

"Not for my digestion," he later explained to Edie. "Cramps. Herring is better, even if it makes you thirsty. At least rainwater don't cost anything." He laughed sadly in breathy caws.

And herring, thanks to Edie, who knew where to shop, was what Schwartz got, with an occasional piece of potato pancake, and even a bit of soup meat when Cohen wasn't looking.

When school began in September, before Cohen would once again suggest giving the bird the boot, Edie prevailed on him to wait a little while until Maurie adjusted.

"To deprive him right now might hurt his schoolwork, and you know what trouble we had last year."

"So okay, but sooner or later the bird goes. That I promise you."

Schwartz, though nobody had asked him, took on full responsibility for Maurie's performance in school. In return for favors granted, when he was let in for an hour or two at night, he spent most of his time overseeing the boy's lessons. He sat on top of the dresser near Maurie's desk as he laboriously wrote out his homework. Maurie was a restless type and Schwartz gently kept him to his studies. He also listened to him practice his screechy violin, taking a few minutes off now and then to rest his ears in the bathroom. And they afterwards played dominoes. The boy was an indifferent checker player and it was impossible to teach him chess. When he was sick, Schwartz read him comic books, though he personally disliked them. But Maurie's work improved in school and even his violin teacher admitted his playing was better. Edie gave Schwartz credit for these improvements, though the bird pooh-poohed them.

Yet he was proud there was nothing lower than C minuses on Maurie's report card, and on Edie's insistence celebrated with a little schnapps.

"If he keeps up like this," Cohen said, "I'll get him in an Ivy League college for sure."

"Oh, I hope so," sighed Edie.

But Schwartz shook his head. "He's a good boy—you don't have to worry. He won't be a *shicker* or a wife-beater, God forbid, but a scholar he'll never be, if you know what I mean, although maybe a good mechanic. It's no disgrace in these times."

"If I were you," Cohen said, angered, "I'd keep my big snoot out of other people's private business."

"Harry, please," said Edie.

"My goddamn patience is wearing out. That cross-eyes butts into everything."

Though he wasn't exactly a welcome guest in the house, Schwartz gained a few ounces although he did not improve in appearance. He looked bedraggled as ever, his feathers unkempt, as though he had just flown out of a snowstorm. He spent, he admitted, little time taking care of himself. Too much to think about. "Also outside plumbing," he told Edie. Still, there was more glow to his eyes, so that though Cohen went on calling him cross-eyes, he said it less emphatically.

"After this, the second seder is going to seem anti-climactic."

Liking his situation, Schwartz tried tactfully to stay out of Cohen's way, but one night when Edie was at the movies and Maurie was taking a hot shower, the frozen-foods salesman began a quarrel with the bird.

"For Christ sake, why don't you wash yourself sometimes? Why must you always stink like a dead fish?"

"Mr. Cohen, if you'll pardon me, if somebody eats garlic he will smell from garlic. I eat herring three times a day. Feed me flowers and I will smell like flowers."

"Who's obligated to feed you anything at all? You're lucky to get herring."

"Excuse me, I'm not complaining," said the bird. "You're complaining."

"What's more," said Cohen, "even from out on the balcony I can hear you snoring away like a pig. It keeps me awake at night."

"Snoring," said Schwartz, "isn't a crime, thanks God."

"All in all, you are a goddamn pest and freeloader. Next thing you'll want to sleep in bed next to my wife."

"Mr. Cohen," said Schwartz, "on this rest assured: A bird is a bird."

"So you say, but how do I know you're a bird and not some kind of a goddamn devil?"

"If I was a devil you would know already. And I don't mean because of your son's good marks."

"Shut up, you bastard bird," shouted Cohen.

"Grubber yung," cawed Schwartz, rising to the tips of his talons, his long wings outstretched.

Cohen was about to lunge for the bird's scrawny neck but Maurie came out of the bathroom, and for the rest of the evening until Schwartz's bedtime on the balcony, there was pretended peace.

But the quarrel had deeply disturbed Schwartz and he slept badly. His snoring woke him, and awake, he was fearful of what would become of him. Wanting to stay out of Cohen's way, he kept to the birdhouse as much as possible. Cramped by it, he paced back and forth on the balcony ledge, or sat on the birdhouse roof, staring into space. In the evenings, while overseeing Maurie's lessons, he often fell asleep. Awakening, he nervously hopped around, exploring the four corners of the room. He spent much time in Maurie's closet, and carefully examined his bureau drawers when they were left open. And once when he found a large paper bag on the floor, Schwartz poked his way into it to investigate what the possibilities were. The boy was amused to see the bird in the paper bag.

"He wants to build a nest," he said to his mother.

Edie, sensing Schwartz's unhappiness, spoke to him quietly.

"Maybe if you did some of the things my husband wants you, you would get along better with him."

"Give me a for instance," Schwartz said.

"Like take a bath, for instance."

"I'm too old for baths," said the bird. "My feathers fall out *without* baths."

"He says you have a bad smell."

"Everybody smells. Some people smell because of their thoughts or because of who they are. My bad smell comes from the food I eat. What does his come from?"

"I better not ask him or it might make him mad," said Edie.

In late November, Schwartz froze on the balcony in the fog and cold, and especially on rainy days he woke with stiff joints and could barely move his wings. Already he felt twinges of rheumatism. He would have liked to spend more time in the warm house, particularly when Maurie was in school and Cohen at work. But though Edie was goodhearted and might have sneaked him in, in the morning, just to thaw out, he was afraid to ask her. In the meantime Cohen, who had been reading articles about the migration of birds, came out on the balcony one night after work when Edie was in the kitchen preparing pot roast, and peeking into the birdhouse, warned Schwartz to be on his way soon if he knew what was good for him. "Time to hit the flyways."

"Mr. Cohen, why do you hate me so much?" asked the bird. "What did I do to you?"

"Because you're an A-number-one troublemaker, that's why. What's more, who ever heard of a Jewbird? Now scat or it's open war."

But Schwartz stubbornly refused to depart, so Cohen embarked on a campaign of harassing him, meanwhile hiding it from Edie and Maurie. Maurie hated violence and Cohen didn't want to leave a bad impression. He thought maybe if he played dirty tricks on the bird he would fly off without being physically kicked out. The vacation was over, let him make his easy living off the fat of somebody else's land. Cohen worried about the effect of the bird's departure on Maurie's schooling but decided to take the chance, first, because the boy now seemed to have the knack of studying—give the black bird-bastard credit—and second, because Schwartz was driving him bats by being there always, even in his dreams.

The frozen-foods salesman began his campaign against the bird by mixing watery cat food with the herring slices in Schwartz's dish. He also blew up and popped numerous paper bags outside the birdhouse as the bird slept, and when he had got Schwartz good and nervous, though not enough to leave, he brought a full-grown cat into the house, supposedly a gift for little Maurie, who had always wanted a pussy. The cat never stopped springing up at Schwartz whenever he saw him, one day managing to claw out several of his tail feathers. And even at lesson time, when the cat was usually excluded from Maurie's room, though somehow or other he quickly found his way in at the end of the lesson, Schwartz was desperately fearful of his life and flew from pinnacle to pinnacle—light fixture to clothes tree to doortop—in order to elude the beast's wet jaws.

Once when the bird complained to Edie how hazardous his existence was, she said, "Be patient, Mr. Schwartz. When the cat gets to know you better he won't try to catch you anymore."

"When he stops trying we will both be in Paradise," Schwartz answered. "Do me a favor and get rid of him. He makes my whole life worry. I'm losing feathers like a tree loses leaves."

"I'm awfully sorry, but Maurie likes the pussy and sleeps with it."

What could Schwartz do? He worried but came to no decision, being afraid to leave. So he ate the herring garnished with cat food, tried hard not to hear the paper bags bursting like firecrackers outside the birdhouse at night, and lived terror-stricken, closer to the ceiling than the floor, as the cat, his tail flicking, endlessly watched him.

Weeks went by. Then on the day after Cohen's mother had died in her flat in the Bronx, when Maurie came home with a zero on an arithmetic test, Cohen, enraged, waited until Edie had taken the boy to his violin lesson, then openly attacked the bird. He chased him with a broom on the balcony and Schwartz frantically flew back and forth, finally escaping into his birdhouse. Cohen triumphantly reached in, and grabbing both skinny legs, dragged the bird out, cawing loudly, his wings wildly beating. He whirled the bird around and around his head. But Schwartz, as he moved in circles, managed to swoop down and catch Cohen's nose in his beak, and hung on for dear life. Cohen cried out in great pain, punched the bird with his fist, and tugging at its legs with all his might, pulled his nose free. Again he swung the yawking Schwartz around until the bird grew dizzy, then with a furious heave, flung him into the night. Schwartz sank like a stone into the street. Cohen then tossed the birdhouse and feeder after him, listening at the ledge until they crashed on the sidewalk below. For a full hour, broom in hand, his heart palpitating and his nose throbbing with pain, Cohen waited for Schwartz to return, but the broken-hearted bird didn't.

That's the end of that dirty bastard, the salesman thought, and went in. Edie and Maurie had come home.

"Look," said Cohen, pointing to his bloody nose, swollen to three times its normal size, "what that sonofabitchy bird did. It's a permanent scar."

"Where is he now?" Edie asked, frightened.

"I threw him out and he flew away. Good riddance."

Nobody said no, though Edie touched a handkerchief to her eyes and Maurie rapidly tried the nine-times table and found he knew approximately half.

In the spring, when the winter's snow had melted, the boy, moved by a memory, wandered in the neighborhood, looking for Schwartz. He found a dead black bird in a small lot near the river, his two wings broken, neck twisted, and both bird-eyes plucked clean.

"Who did it to you, Mr. Schwartz?" Maurie wept.

"Anti-Semeets," Edie said later.

●

MAX APPLE

The Purple Gang

Who knows about this world of Mafia gangsters? Now, if these were Jewish gangsters, like the old Purple Gang that Frieda and Abe used to talk about, then who would be afraid? Before I was born, Frieda lived in their neighborhood. "They were perfect gentlemen. They didn't carry guns; they made less noise than regular neighbors." Whenever there was talk about crime, Frieda always mentioned them. It was the Golden Age of Crime. The way Momma carried on about them, it's surprising that I didn't become an outlaw. If any course in school had been called "Preparing for the Purple Gang," I, Ira Goldstein, would have been the first to sign up. What they did she never talked about. But drive up on a dark night and they are there to open the car door for you. Need a blood transfusion in an emergency, the Purple Gang is there to help faster than the Red Cross. A small loan, a little food—this is the Depression, don't forget—always the Gang is there to count on. And on the Sabbath and the Holy Days: "You should have seen them. It was like a parade. They took off their wide-brimmed felt hats and put on black skullcaps. They wore flowers in their lapels; their faces shined. You saw them walking down Livernois Avenue early in the morning and you knew there was a God in heaven. And if ever in a real pinch you needed a tenth man to make up that quorum for prayer, that *minyan*, then the Purple Gang would never let you down."

Max Apple, a writer living in Texas, is the author of the novel *Zip*, from which this selection is taken, and *The Oranging of America*, a collection of stories. *Zip* is the story of Ira Goldstein, a Jewish student from Detroit, who becomes the manager of Jesus, a middleweight boxer.

There was a "Purple Gang" in Detroit during the 1920s and 1930s; originally formed around Samuel "Sammie Purple" Cohen, the gang began with shoplifting and extortion before moving into the bootlegging business during Prohibition.

•

Sam "Killer" Kaplan, a hit man for Murder Inc., a notorious Jewish gang which operated in the Brownsville section of Brooklyn in the 1930s, was caught in a crossfire during a gang war. Severely wounded, he managed to escape and crawl the three blocks to his mother's house. Barely able to climb the stairs and bleeding profusely, he used all his strength to bang on the door. "Mama," he cried, "it's me, Sammy. I'm hurt bad!"

"Sit down and eat," his mother said. "Later we'll talk."

•

Dick Codor © 1979

I used to think that the reason they were such successful criminals, Momma, was because God watched over them because of their piety and politeness. And anyway, what sorts of crimes did Jewish criminals commit? They didn't murder or rob. Probably they just roughed up anti-Semites who without the Purple Gang would have roamed Detroit in those days being junior Nazis. Yes, at an early age I knew all about Father Coughlin, about the German Bundt groups and Henry Ford. Because of him our pickups were always Chevys. "Not a dollar to such an anti-Semitic *momzer,*" Momma said. "Never a Ford, not even a used one." I used to daydream that the Purple Gang would one day get their hands on Hitler, [Mr.] Solomon, and Henry Ford, and rush them off to the synagogue all dressed up to listen to a two-hour sermon. Then, if they didn't change their ways, the Gang would do what the Gang had to do. They would do it the way Rev Lieberman used to handle the chickens. First you say a blessing. Then you twist Henry Ford's neck back and slit his jugular until all the blood shoots out. Every chicken that I watched him slaughter for us had the name of one of our enemies. I understood history. I never used this for personal vengeance. Only enemies of America, Democracy, and the Jewish people got this treatment. I could take care of my own battles; the Purple Gang stood way back in the mountains of the thirties, like Robin Hood in the forest. When we needed them, they would strike for us. "When will there be another Purple Gang, Momma," I used to ask her, "and where are they now?"

"Some are in jail. Some moved away from Detroit and went into other business. Who knows? I never knew any of them personally by name." But if not for the Purple Gang, Momma, what other Jewish heroes would I have had?

The Gang moved quickly against the enemies of Zion. They came out of retirement, closed their other businesses, escaped from prisons where they were unjustly held. They met in the middle of the night, not far from our house, near the bakery on Six Mile Road, the very bakery where Zeide of blessed memory once worked and where you, Momma, were attacked on that warm afternoon by the lust-crazed Solomon. The Gang meant business. "There are too many Hitlers," the Gang said. "Everywhere you look there are little Hitlers. They are ruining Abe's business, they are causing prices to rise, and coercing people—even Jews—to drive Ford automobiles. And the Jewish Hitlers—like Solomon—these are even more troublesome. Against them it's a regular civil war."

The Gang invaded Europe. They erased the numbers from the arms of the camp victims. They resettled people by the millions in northwest Detroit and in Chicago too, on the west side in the big apartments near Cousin Sophia, where there were always vacancies because the *shvartzes* lived so close. The original Hitler they tortured for two weeks, and when he was dead, his eternal job was to shine the shoes of the scribes in heaven. And Solomon, for him the Gang decreed poverty. A life of a scrap peddler and battery picker-upper. Like Abe, only worse. A life marked by many flat tires, faulty alternators, a life of much grease and little company on long, boring rides. A life of no hitchhikers and all meals taken at roadside EAT signs from homely waitresses. Yes, this was the decree of the Gang. Throughout the land they dispersed. They appeared at B'nai B'rith meetings and gave autographs. These were not one-sided men. They could talk about more than crime and Hitler. At the B.B. meetings they were full of warm anecdotes about the Tigers and the great Jewish slugger, Hank Greenberg.

●

IN a small village in the Ukraine, a terrifying rumor was spreading: a Christian girl had been found murdered.

Realizing the dire consequences of such an event, and fearing a pogrom, the Jewish community instinctively gathered in the synagogue to plan whatever defensive actions were possible under these circumstances.

Just as the emergency meeting was being called to order, in ran the president of the synagogue, out of breath and all excited. "Brothers," he cried out, "I have wonderful news! The murdered girl is Jewish!"

ROMAIN GARY

The Dance of Genghis Cohn

There are but a very few things I haven't already taught my friend Schatz about our history and our beliefs, and he knows all there is to know about that familiar phenomenon which everyone who has studied our tradition has come across: the dybbuk. Schatz, Commissioner First Class, knows that he is possessed by a dybbuk. It is an evil spirit, a demon who grabs you, gets within you, and starts to reign and lord it over you, as

This joke is admittedly in bad taste, but then so is much of Jewish history, and it is virtually inevitable that such jokes would emerge. Routinely, the death or disappearance of a Christian child would give rise to accusations that the Jews used the blood of Christian children for sacramental purposes, such as baking matzoh and making wine. Known as blood libels, these fears go back at least to the twelfth century (and are mentioned in Chaucer's "Prioress's Tale"), and extend to the Beilis case in Russia in our own century—the subject of Bernard Malamud's *The Fixer.*

So-called sick humor in response to anti-Semitism is hardly a new phenomenon. Sholom Aleichem has one of his characters write a letter to a friend in America after the notorious Kishinev pogrom of 1903:

Dear Yankel: You ask me to write at length, and I'd like to oblige, but there's really nothing to write about. The rich are still rich and the poor are dying of hunger, as they always do. What's new about that? And as far as pogroms are concerned, thank God we have nothing more to fear, as we've already had ours—two of them, in fact, and a third wouldn't be worth while. . . . All our family got through it safely, except for Lippi, who was killed with two of his sons, Noah and Mordecai; first-class artisans, all three of them. Oh, yes, and except Hersh. Perel was found dead in the cellar together with the baby at her breast. But as Getzi used to say: "It might have been worse; don't think of the better, because there's no limit to that." You ask about Heshel. He's been out of work now for over half a year. The fact is they won't let him work in prison. . . . Mendel did a clever thing; he up and died. Some say of hunger, others of consumption. Personally, I think he died of both. I really don't know what else to write about, except the cholera, which is going great guns. . . .

Romain Gary, born in Lithuania of Russian parents, died in 1980 at the age of sixty-six. He was the author of several novels, including *The Roots of Heaven, The Ski Bum,* and *European Education.*

During the war, Gary flew for Britain's Royal Air Force and the Free French forces, and was decorated for heroism. Later, he served in the French delegation to the United Nations and as consul general in Los Angeles.

The Dance of Genghis Cohn is an astonishing novel, a savagely dark and brilliant comic story of a Jewish comedian who is killed by the Nazis, and who returns as a *dybbuk* to torment the soul of a Nazi officer after the war.

Gary's work is in the tradition of *galgenhumor* (gallows humor), which has been part of the Jewish response to anti-Semitism for centuries.

master. To drive him away, one needs prayers, ten pious Jews, venerable ones, known for their saintliness, who will throw their weight into the balance and chase the demon away.

Schatz has often spent hours prowling around a synagogue, but he's never dared to go inside. The truth is that this is the first time in the history of thought and religion that a pure Aryan, a former SS, has been possessed by a Jewish dybbuk. I suppose I'll have to go find myself a rabbi and plead to be delivered from my horrible destiny: being obliged to haunt the German conscience. That's the reason why normally Schatz waits on me, hand and foot. He wants to coax me. He wants me to free him, under pretext of freeing myself. But this time, with the help of alcohol and exasperation, he has really thrown caution to the winds. He can't control himself anymore. He's not even afraid of being seen by witnesses talking to a murdered Jew who isn't there. . . .

Do German doctors have the right to liquidate a Jewish *dybbuk?* It is certain that from a strictly nationalistic viewpoint, the final solution to a problem raised by six million psychic parasites of the German conscience is a desirable thing, a requirement of public hygiene. New drugs, particularly prazimine, for example, in large doses, have proven deeply efficient in this particular domain. But this new suppression of suppressed Jews can only be a governmental decision. The new German government must face its responsibilities. It must free the German conscience from its Jewish parasites. Anyway, everyone knows that the Jews weren't assassinated. They died *voluntarily.* I keep abreast of the news, as I have nothing else to do, and I recently discovered some reassuring evidence about that in the book of a certain Jean-François Steiner, *Treblinka:* We stood obligingly in line, in front of the gas chambers, we never resisted extermination. There were but a few rebels, here and there, particularly in the Warsaw ghetto, but as a whole, there was an eager, obedient will to disappear. There was a will to die. Collective suicide, that's what it was. Soon a new best seller will demonstrate that the Nazis were only an instrument in the hands of smart Jewry. You see, Jews who wanted to die, while making some profit on the side. How? I'll tell you how. We didn't commit suicide with our own hands, as the insurance company wouldn't pay up, and our survivors couldn't have recovered any damages. So . . . It is time someone wrote a definitive work on this question, showing how we manipulated the Germans, both to make a profit and to satisfy our perverted taste for self-destruction. Somewhere there must be an author willing to unveil our diabolical maneuver, and describe how we transformed the Nazis into a blind and obedient tool in our hands. . . .

When we were digging our grave, while the SS were leveling their machine guns, I asked my neighbor at the graveside, Sioma Kapelusznik, what he thought of culture, if he could give me a good definition of the word "culture," so that I would know I wasn't dying for nothing, but was leaving at least some kind of heritage behind me. He obliged, but all those brats yelling in their mothers' arms—the mothers who were holding their babies were excused from digging their graves—at first prevented me from hearing his answer. So, while digging, Sioma Kapelusznik moved a bit closer to me, winked, and then said:

"Culture is when mothers who are holding their babies in their arms are excused from digging their own graves before being shot."

It was a good *chochme,* and we both had a good laugh. I'm telling you, there's no funnyman like the Jewish funnyman.

"She had only one purpose in life: culture!"

I was, I remember, a bit piqued at the thought that it was a colleague and not I who had made such a good crack before dying, so I tried to think of an even better *vitz,* but they had already started shooting us, so I had to make do with a visual effect, showing the Germans my *tuchis.* Since then, thank God, I have had all my leisure to reflect peacefully on exactly what "culture" meant, and I finally found a rather good definition, when reading the newspapers a year or so ago. At that time the German press was full of accounts of atrocities committed by the savage Simbas, in the Congo. The civilized world was indignant. So let me put it this way: the Germans had Schiller, Goethe, Hölderlin, and the Simbas of the Congo had nothing. The difference between the Germans, heirs to an immense culture, and the savage Simbas is that the Simbas ate their victims, whereas the Germans turned theirs into soap. *This need for cleanliness, that is culture.*

There have undoubtedly been more worthy and noble last words in history than "Kiss my ass," but I have never made any claim to greatness and, besides, I'm quite pleased with my effort and only hope that my message will go down to posterity and that I will have thus contributed a little something to our spiritual heritage. I do not wish to sound bitter, but I do believe that six million Jews left without any help at all by the civilized world could not address the latter a more heartfelt and befitting message than "Kiss my ass," or that the civilized world deserved anything more noble and dignified. Anyone who thinks otherwise should have his conscience examined.

●

THE DESPONDENT RUSSIAN NOVELIST PLANNED TO HANG HIMSELF BY LEAPING FROM ATOP HIS SUICIDE NOTE.

CALDWELL

From *Running A Muck,*
copyright © 1978 by John Caldwell.
By permission of Writer's Digest Books.

THE HUMOR OF SOVIET JEWS

A LONG line has formed outside a Moscow meat market, where a large shipment of meat is due to arrive. It is a cold day, and the crowd is stamping its feet and clapping its hands to keep warm. After two hours of this, the manager of the meat market makes an appearance. "Comrades," he announces, "the shipment is on the way, but I have counted the number of people in line and there are too many people and not enough meat. And so I must ask that all the Jews go home." A large group then leaves the line.

After another hour, the manager comes out again. "Comrades, the meat has still not arrived, but I must tell you that there won't be enough. Therefore those of you who are not party members will please leave the line." Again a large group goes home.

After another hour, the manager appears once more. "Comrades," he says, "I have bad news. The truck has broken down 40 kilometers away, and we won't have meat today. You might as well go home."

Whereupon one party member turns to another and mutters, "Those damn Jews have all the privileges!"

A JEW in Moscow was awakened in the middle of the night by a loud knock on the door.

"Who's there?" he asked.

"The mailman," came the reply.

The man got out of bed and opened the door, and found two KGB agents. "Are you Goldstein?" asked one of the agents.

"Yes," replied Goldstein.

"And did you make an application to go to Israel?"

"That's right."

"Do you have enough food to eat here?"

"Yes, we do."

"Don't your children get a good Communist education?"

"Certainly."

"Then why do you want to leave Russia?"

"Because," replied Goldstein, "I don't like to live in a place where they deliver mail at three in the morning!"

AN elderly man is sitting on a Moscow park bench studying a Hebrew book. A KGB agent walks by, looks over the man's shoulder, and says, "What is that strange writing?"

"This is Hebrew," says the old man. "It's the language of Israel."

"Don't be silly," says the agent. "At your age you'll never get to Israel."

"Perhaps not," sighs the old man. "But Hebrew is also the language of heaven."

The agent replies, "What makes you so sure you're going to heaven?"

"Maybe I'm not," says the old man. "But I already know Russian."

THREE Soviet citizens, a Pole, a Czech, and a Jew, were accused of spying and sentenced to death. Each was granted a last wish.

"I want my ashes scattered over the grave of Pilsudski," said the Pole.

"I want my ashes scattered over the grave of Masaryk," said the Czech.

"And I," said the Jew, "want my ashes scattered over the grave of Comrade Kosygin."

"But that's impossible," he was told. "Kosygin isn't dead yet."

"Fine," said the Jew. "I can wait."

A good deal of Soviet Jewish humor centers around the mythical Abram Rabinovich, a sort of latter-day Hershele Ostropoler who delights in outwitting Soviet officials.

THE census taker comes to the Rabinovich house.

"Does Abram Rabinovich live here?" he asks.

"No," replies Rabinovich.

"Well, then, comrade, what is your name?"

"Abram Rabinovich."

"Wait a minute—didn't you just tell me that Rabinovich doesn't live here?"

"Aha," says Rabinovich. "You call this living?"

RABINOVICH applies for membership in the Communist Party, and he is required to answer a few questions.

"Who was Karl Marx?"

"I don't know," replies Rabinovich.

"Lenin?"

"Sorry, I don't know him, either.

"What about Leonid Brezhnev?"

"Never heard of him."

"Are you playing games with me?" asks the official.

"Not at all," says Rabinovich. "Do you know Hershel Salsberg?"

"No," says the official.

"What about Yankel Horowitz?"

"Never heard of him."

"Nahum Davidovich?"

"No."

"Well," says Rabinovich, "I guess that's the way it goes. You've got your friends and I've got mine."

SARA RABINOVICH emigrates but Abram stays behind in Russia. Before they part, the couple work out a code. "Anything I write in black ink is true," Abram explains. "And anything in red ink is false."

Some time later, Sara receives a letter in black ink. "Life here in Russia is getting better every day. This year's selection of clothing is stylish and affordable. Meat is so plentiful that you can't make up your mind which cut of beef to buy. My main problem must seem trifling by comparison—I just can't find red ink anywhere."

RABINOVICH sits down in a café and orders a glass of tea and a copy of *Pravda.*

"I'll bring the tea," the waiter tells him, "but I can't bring you a copy of *Pravda.* The Soviet regime has been overthrown and *Pravda* isn't published anymore."

"All right," says Rabinovich, "just bring me the tea."

The next day, Rabinovich comes to the same café and asks for tea and a copy of *Pravda.* The waiter gives him the same answer.

On the third day, Rabinovich again orders tea and *Pravda,* and this time the waiter says to him, "Look, sir, you seem to be an intelligent man. For the past three days you've ordered a copy of *Pravda,* and three times now I've had to tell you that the Soviet regime has been overthrown, and *Pravda* isn't published anymore."

"I know, I know," says Rabinovich. "But I just like to hear it."

Drawing by David Levine. Copyright © 1965 by Nyrev, Inc. By permission of *The New York Review of Books.*

© 1979 Kirschen

AS soon as Hitler came into power, and before he had the chance to act upon his infamous plans, the country was deluged by anti-Nazi jokes. Hitler was furious, and ordered that whoever was responsible for these jokes be brought to him personally. Several weeks later, the police arrested Kaufman, a Jewish comic.

"What's your name, Jew?" asked Hitler.

"Kaufman."

"And are you responsible for the joke about me and the pig?"

"Yes."

"What about the joke in which whenever I die will be a Jewish holiday?"

"Yes, that one's mine."

"What about the joke in which I'm saved from drowning, and when I offer the Jew who saved me a reward, his request is simply that I don't tell anybody what he did?"

"Oh, yes, that one is also mine."

"Jew, how dare you make these jokes? How dare a Jew be so impudent? Don't you know who I am—the leader of the Third Reich, which is destined to last a thousand years?"

"Now wait a minute," said Kaufman. "Don't blame me for that joke—I've never heard it before!"

TWO Jews had a plan to assassinate Hitler. They learned that he drove by a certain corner at noon each day, and they waited for him there with their guns well hidden.

At exactly noon they were ready to shoot, but there was no sign of Hitler. Five minutes later, nothing. Another five minutes went by, but no sign of Hitler. By twelve-fifteen they had started to give up hope.

"My goodness," said one of the men. "I hope nothing's happened to him!"

EMIL FORMSTECHER was on his way to the market in Munich with a chicken under his arm. He was accosted in the street by a Nazi bully, who demanded, "Jew, where are you going?"

"I'm going to the market to buy some feed for my chicken."

"What does he eat?" the Nazi asked.

"Corn," replied Formstecher.

"Corn? The nerve of you people. German soldiers go hungry while you Jews feed your chickens on native German corn!" He then slapped Formstecher in the face and continued on his way.

A moment later, another Nazi stopped Formstecher.

"Where are you going, Jew dog?"

"To the market, to buy some feed for my chicken."

"What does he eat?"

"Perhaps some wheat."

"Wheat? Of all things! The Jew's chicken eats wheat while German children go hungry." And he promptly knocked Formstecher to the ground.

Formstecher picked himself up and continued on his way, when he was approached by yet another Nazi.

"Where are you going, kike?"

"To the market, to buy some feed for my chicken."

"Feed for your chicken? What does he eat?"

"Look," said Formstecher, "I don't know. I figure I'll give him a couple of *pfennigs* and let him buy whatever he wants!"

Jewish jokes about Hitler seem, in retrospect, perversely mild and benign, presumably because they could not possibly compete with the true feelings Jews held toward him. During the war, for example, an American soldiers' magazine sponsored a contest: What would be the best punishment for Hitler when he was captured? The prize was won by a Jewish soldier with the American army in Italy, who responded: "He should live with my in-laws in the Bronx!"

In *Jewish Wit,* Theodor Reik recalls a joke from pre-Hitler Austria. At that time, newspapers were often read in coffeehouses, and a customer sometimes had to wait a long time until the paper he wanted was available. In this story, Hitler approaches the table of a Jew who has taken a pile of newspapers, putting aside each one after reading it. "Please," says Hitler, "is the *Wiener Journal* free?"

"Not for you, Herr Hitler," replies the Jew. The point, observes Reik, is that "the Jew cannot imagine a more cruel and more exquisite torment than the withholding of the desired newspaper and the suffering of agonizing suspense of the loathed enemy."

There were even jokes about Hitler in the Warsaw ghetto, where he was given the code name Horowitz.

When a Jew is right, he is beaten twice as hard.

IN the early 1940s, an elderly Jew in New York decided to surprise his wife on her birthday with a gift of intimate apparel. He went to Macy's, and began looking through the lingerie section. Finally, he settled on a display of brassieres.

"Can I help you, sir?" asked a young salesgirl, but the old man was so embarrassed he could hardly talk.

"Do you know your wife's bra size?" she asked. The old man merely shook his head.

"Well, then," she said softly, "tell me this: are they big?"

With an obvious sense of relief, the man replied, "Hoo boy, are they big! Hitler should have 'em for tonsils!"

This crude tale is more complex than it first appears. For one thing, it is unusual in that it lacks a direct response to the anti-Semitic provocation, and instead, defers the verbal response to a later time and a safer setting. Second, the degree of initial acquiescence on Freudenheim's part is rare in Jewish humor about anti-Semitism, although in real life it was all too necessary a response. Admittedly, this same joke might be enjoyed by an anti-Semite, but here, as always, it is the teller rather than the tale which determines the joke's real intent.

One can also imagine this joke being told by Eastern European or even Oriental Jews, for it makes fun of the German Jew's fondness for literalism, as well as his tendency to identify with the ruling establishment.

In a better-known joke in which discretion is placed before valor:

•

An elderly Jew in Berlin finds himself surrounded by a group of raucous Nazis, who knock him to the ground and ask him, derisively, "Jew, who is responsible for the war?"

The little Jew is no fool. "The Jews," he replies, "and the bicycle riders."

"Why the bicycle riders?" ask the Nazis.

"Why the Jews?" counters the old man.

•

FREUDENHEIM was walking down the street in Nazi Germany in 1934, when suddenly a large black limousine pulled up beside him. Freudenheim looked up in astonishment and terror as Hitler himself climbed out of the car.

Holding a gun to Freudenheim, Hitler ordered him to get down on his hands and knees. And pointing to a pile of excrement on the curb, Hitler ordered the Jew to eat it.

Freudenheim, putting discretion before valor, complied. Hitler began laughing so hard that he dropped the gun. Freudenheim picked it up, and ordered Hitler to undergo the same humiliation. As Hitler got down on the sidewalk, Freudenheim ran from the scene as fast as he could.

Later that day, when Freudenheim returned home, his wife asked him, "How was your day?"

"Oh, fine, dear," he answered. "By the way, you'll never guess who I had lunch with today!"

This story walks a tightrope between acquiescence and resistance. Far more common in Jewish humor, however, is another type of response to anti-Semitism: the witty retort that reflects not only on anti-Semitism but also on the anti-Semite. Frequently, this type of joke operates in a kind of judo-esque way, using the attacker's force against himself.

•

A classic example of this type of joke has the eighteenth-century philosopher Moses Mendelssohn, who looked very Jewish, walking down a busy street in Berlin, where he accidentally collides with a stout Prussian officer.

"Swine!" bellows the officer.

"Mendelssohn," replies the philosopher with a courteous bow.

•

This last joke (or a variation on it) appears in many collections of Jewish humor, and is often updated to a story about a similar collision on a street in Nazi Germany. Like many jokes about anti-Semitism, it is, alas, highly adaptable to different times and places, and it would not be surprising to learn that the Jews of fifteenth-century Spain told a similar tale about Torquemada.

ISRAEL ZANGWILL, the British-Jewish writer, once found himself at a fancy dinner party, seated next to a well-dressed matron. Zangwill was tired, and without thinking, he yawned—right in the face of the woman beside him. Taken aback by this rude behavior, she said to him, "Please mind your Jewish manners. I was afraid you were going to swallow me."

"Have no fear, madam," Zangwill replied. "My religion prohibits my doing that."

MOSES MONTEFIORE, the great nineteenth-century philanthropist, once found himself seated next to an anti-Semitic nobleman at a dinner party.

"I have just returned from Japan," the nobleman was saying, "and it's a most unusual country. Did you know that it has neither pigs nor Jews?"

"In that case," Montefiore replied, "you and I should go there, so it will have a sample of each."

A JEW from Kiev found himself on a train, sitting across from a Russian lieutenant with a dog. The officer made it a point to address the dog, loudly, by the name "Mendel."

"It's really a pity," the man finally said, "that your dog has a Jewish name."

"Why?" asked the officer.

"Otherwise," replied the Jew, "he could have become a lieutenant."

TRIEBWASSER, a twine merchant from New York, was trying desperately to sell some of his goods in Louisiana. But wherever he went, he kept encountering anti-Semitism. In one particular department store, the buyer taunted him: "All right, Jake, I'll buy some of your twine. As much as reaches from the top of your Jewish nose to the tip of your Jewish prick."

Two weeks later, the buyer was startled to receive a shipment containing eight hundred cartons of Grade A twine. Attached was a note: "Many thanks for your generous offer. Invoice to follow. [signed] Jacob Triebwasser—residing in New York, circumcised in Kiev."

> CAESAR SAID TO RABBI TANHUM, "COME, LET US
> BECOME ONE PEOPLE."
> RABBI TANHUM REPLIED,
> "BY MY LIFE, WE WHO ARE CIRCUMCISED CANNOT BE LIKE YOU.
> YOU, THEN, SHOULD BECOME CIRCUMCISED AND BE LIKE US."
> "A VERY GOOD ANSWER," CAESAR REPLIED.
> "UNFORTUNATELY, ANYONE WHO DEFEATS THE EMPEROR
> IN AN ARGUMENT MUST BE THROWN TO THE LIONS."
> SO THEY THREW RABBI TANHUM TO THE LIONS.
> BUT THE LIONS DID NOT EAT HIM.
> AN UNBELIEVER WHO WAS STANDING NEARBY SAID,
> "THE REASON THE LIONS DO NOT EAT HIM IS THAT THEY ARE NOT HUNGRY."
> TO TEST THIS THEORY, THEY THREW THE UNBELIEVER TO THE LIONS,
> WHO ATE HIM.
>
> TALMUD (SANHEDRIN 39a)

This bitter exchange about anti-Semitism brings to mind the story of two Jews walking in the street who are approached by a large dog, which is barking loudly.

"Let's run," says the first man.

"Don't be silly," his friend replies. "Don't you know that barking dogs don't bite?"

"Of course *I* know that," the first man says. "And *you* know that. *But do the dogs know that?*"

Dogs who bark (and even dogs who don't) are, in these stories, stand-ins for anti-Semites. To the people of the shtetl, dogs were not friendly household pets, but part of the enemy forces, guarding the enemy's estate, for example, or running wild with their peasant masters. During the Nazi period, dogs were used to seek out Jews in hiding.

But as times change, so do associations, and it is doubtful whether the image of the barking dog evokes the same emotional response in Jews as it once did.

In an American joke that is rapidly becoming outdated, a Jew who has long ago converted to Christianity confides to a friend: "In some ways I still feel Jewish. Every day I read *The New York Times,* every Sunday I have a pastrami sandwich, and I'm still afraid of dogs!"

TWO Jews were walking down the street in Nazi Germany when they came upon a public notice: "ESCAPED! A lion has escaped from the Berlin Zoo. The animal is to be shot on sight."

"That's it," said the first man. "I'm leaving town tonight."

"What are you talking about?" asked the second. "You're not a lion."

"No," said the first. "But try to tell them that after you've been shot!"

In a more elaborate story, General Patton assembles his troops on the eve of a great battle. "We need the best spy we can find," he says, "in order to scout the enemy position." Everyone agrees that Siegel is the best spy, and Siegel is sent ahead, and told to return by five the next afternoon.

At four o'clock, there is no sign of Siegel. Four-thirty—nothing. Finally, at ten minutes to five, Siegel returns, shaking and quivering.

"Siegel," says the general, "what did you find?"

"On the right flank, General, they have hundreds and hundreds of tanks."

"That's terrible!"

"No, sir. We have artillery, and we'll destroy their tanks and send in our infantry."

"Brilliant, Siegel, but what about the left flank?"

"On the left flank, sir, they have thousands of troops and hundreds of cannons."

"That's terrible!"

"No, sir. We'll send in our tanks to overrun them."

"Brilliant, Siegel, but what about the center?"

"Oy, sir, don't even ask."

"Siegel, what do you mean?"

"It's horrible. I can't even talk about it."

"So what are we going to do?"

"We'll stage a pincers movement and destroy them on both flanks."

"All right, but tell me—I have to know—what did you see in the center?"

"Oy, sir, in the center they've got *such a big dog!*"

SAMUELSON, a traveling salesman, lost his suitcase on the way to Chicago. When the train arrived at the station, he went into the public men's room to wash up. Approaching the man at the next sink, he asked, "Excuse me, mister, but can I borrow your soap?"

"Certainly," the man replied, handing Samuelson his bar of soap.

A moment later, Samuelson turned to the man and said, "Excuse me, friend, but I've lost my baggage. Would you mind if I borrowed your razor and some shaving cream?"

"That happened to me once," the man said. "Here, help yourself."

Five minutes later, Samuelson turned to him and said, "Could I borrow your towel?"

"Sure," came the reply.

A moment later, Samuelson turned to the man once more and said, "Would you mind if I borrowed your toothbrush?"

"I'm sorry, fella," the man replied, "but I'll have to draw the line here. Why don't you buy one at the corner drugstore?" "

"Anti-Semite!"

Two Jews meet on the street.
"Dave, how have you been?"
"N-n-not so good. I was just turned down for a j-j-job."
"Where?"
"At a r-r-radio s-s-station. D-d-damn anti-S-S-Semites!"

The self-deprecatory element in Jewish humor has been identified by many observers. The psychiatrist Martin Grotjahn writes: "One can almost see how a witty Jewish man carefully and cautiously takes a sharp dagger out of his enemy's hands, sharpens it so that it can split a hair in midair, polishes it until it shines brightly, stabs himself with it, then returns it gallantly to the anti-Semite with the silent reproach: Now see whether you can do it half as well."

Self-demeaning witticisms of this type have been echoed through the generations by various Jewish figures, especially those who have been successful in the non-Jewish world. Woody Allen, for example, begins his film *Annie Hall* by quoting the most famous of these quips, Groucho Marx's remark: "I wouldn't join any club that would have me as a member."

© 1981 S. Gross

"All I can say is the Lord works in mysterious ways."

Dick Codor © 1981

This exchange is a classic in the literature of humor about anti-Semitism, and it appears in all the older collections, each time in a slightly different setting and with a slightly different medical condition. Earlier versions of this joke make mention of the need to exercise after visiting the Carlsbad Spa, or after taking mineral oil. More recently, the same joke has been told about a Jew in Hitler's Germany.

•

A Jewish tailor walks by a czarist police inspector in the street. The inspector is furious that the Jew has neglected to doff his hat in the required manner.

"Jew!" he cries out. "What do you mean by this insolence? Where are you from?"

"From Minsk," replies the Jew meekly.

"And what about your hat?" the inspector demands.

"Also from Minsk," replies the Jew.

•

IN the days when residency permits were required of all Jews living in St. Petersburg, Lieberman was entertaining his cousin from the provinces. The cousin, lacking a permit, was constantly worried about being apprehended by the authorities. One day, while strolling through the main thoroughfare of the city, the two men noticed a policeman stopping passersby and asking to see their permits.

"Here's what we'll do," said Lieberman. "If he approaches us, I'll run away. He'll chase me, and you'll be able to escape."

A moment later the policeman looked their way, and Lieberman began to run, with the officer immediately giving chase. When his cousin was safely out of sight, Lieberman slowed down and was seized by the officer, who demanded to see his papers. Seeing that the documents were in perfect order, the officer asked:

"What is the meaning of this? Why did you run away when I came toward you?"

"Run away?" replied Lieberman. "I didn't run away. It's just that my doctor told me to run a mile after each meal in order to aid my digestion."

"But didn't you see that I was running after you?" asked the policeman.

"Certainly," replied Lieberman. "I assumed your doctor told you the same thing!"

COHEN and Katz used to play cards every day in a coffee-house. One day they quarreled, and Katz called out, "What kind of guy can you be if you sit down every day to play cards with a guy who sits down to play cards with a guy like you?"

A GALICIAN Jew, traveling on a train, finds himself in an empty compartment. He goes about making himself comfortable by unbuttoning his coat, opening a newspaper, and putting his feet up on one of the empty seats.

A few minutes later, the door opens and a gentleman in modern dress comes in and sits down. The Jew immediately pulls himself together, takes his feet off the seat, and assumes a proper pose. The stranger sits in silence, looking through his notebook and apparently making some calculations. "Excuse me," he says suddenly. "Do you know when Yom Kippur is this year?"

"Aha!" says the Jew, and puts his feet back up.

Some observers see this story as the quintessential Jewish anti-Semitic joke. It appears, for example, in a novel by the Viennese writer Arthur Schnitzler, in which the character who tells it goes on to comment: "It expresses the eternal truth that no Jew has any real respect for his fellow Jew, ever. As little as prisoners in a hostile country have any real respect for each other, particularly when they are hopeless. Envy, hate, yes, frequently admiration, even love; all that there can be between them, but never respect, for the play of all their emotional life takes place in an atmosphere of familiarity, so to speak, in which respect cannot help being stifled."

Heinrich Heine, the nineteenth-century German-Jewish writer who was himself a convert of convenience, used to say that he was suspicious of the sincerity of Jewish converts to Christianity because, he thought, no Jew could believe in the divinity of another Jew.

But Freud, who cites the same joke, sees it as an expression of Jewish democratic instincts, and uses it as an opportunity to point to the difference between anti-Semitic jokes made by Jews and by Gentiles. When made by Jews, he observes, these jokes serve as a kind of self-criticism; when made by Gentiles, they are "nearly all brutal buffooneries in which the wit is spoiled by the fact that the Jew appears as a comic figure to the foreigner." When Jews makes these same jokes, however, they are also aware of their own good qualities. "Incidentally," Freud concludes, "I do not know whether there are many other instances of a people making fun to such a degree of its own character."

Dick Codor © 1981

There are many versions of this joke, which is an old favorite, and is based upon the many Disputations which took place between Christians and Jews (and sometimes between Moslems and Jews) in medieval Europe. In one version, sent to us by a man compiling a collection of jokes for deaf Jews, Yankele is deaf, and so his use of sign language has as much to do with survival as with wit.

A Disputation in Paris in 1240 ended with twenty-five cartloads of copies of the Talmud being burned by the Christian authorities; the Talmud, however, continued to be taught in Paris, as some rabbis knew it by heart.

The Talmud ascribes Disputations even to Biblical figures, and the Mishnah reports that in a Disputation between Romans and Jews, the Jews were asked: If God does not desire idolatry, why does he not destroy it? The Jews answered: If mankind had been worshiping objects unnecessary to the cosmos, He would have destroyed them. But as they worship the sun and moon and stars and planets, should He destroy His world because of such foolishness?

IN a small town in Italy during the Middle Ages, there lived a notorious priest who hated the Jews. As was the custom of those times, the priest announced that there would be a disputation between the Jews and the Catholics. But this disputation was not merely for the sake of God and truth, for if the Jews lost, they would be banished from the town. If they won, they would be allowed to remain in peace.

The debate, the priest announced, would take place in one week's time, and would be conducted entirely in sign language. The Jews were to appoint a member of their community to debate against the priest, who would, of course, represent the Catholics.

The Jews in the town were greatly distressed. Even the rabbi was reluctant to debate against the priest, for although he was a learned man, what did he know of sign language?

In the entire community only one man stood willing to debate against the priest, and that was Yankele the poultry dealer. "Are you a fool?" his wife asked. "What do you know of theological matters? Wiser men than you have declined this dubious honor."

"My dear woman," replied Yankele, "there is simply no choice. Who else is willing to perform this task? And if nobody comes forward, we will be banished at once."

Mark Podwal © 1978

This is certain: That whichever
Shall at last be overthrown,
Must acknowledge the religion
Of the victor as his own.

That the Jew with holy water
Shall be sprinkled and baptized,
While the Christian, vice versa,
Shall be duly circumcised.

From Heinrich Heine's
The Disputation

On the afternoon of the disputation, the entire town gathered in the marketplace. The Catholics stood on one side, the Jews on the other. In the middle of the town square stood the priest, with Yankele beside him. The priest was dressed in white robes, while Yankele was wearing blue overalls.

Finally, the disputation began. The priest stepped forward and in the air he drew a large, lofty circle. When he had finished, Yankele stepped forward and stamped his foot on the ground. The priest looked worried, and the Catholics began to murmur that all was not well.

A moment later, the priest had recovered his calm, and mumbling a few words to himself, he stepped forward and held three fingers in the air. Yankele then stepped forward and held up one finger.

Once again, looking disturbed, the priest hesitated. Then he fumbled in his garments and drew out a chalice of wine and a loaf of bread. He bit off a piece of bread from the loaf, took a sip of wine from the cup, and then stepped back, smug and satisfied.

When he had finished, Yankele stepped forward. In his hand was an apple, and he took a big bite from it. At this point the priest threw up his arms in despair. "I give up," he cried. "Let the Jews live here in peace!"

There was great rejoicing among the Jews, and great amazement and consternation among the Catholics, who crowded around their leader. "O Holy Father," they said, "tell us the meaning of these symbols."

"My children," said the priest, "I began by describing an arc, reminding the Jew that God is everywhere. Then he stamped on the ground, reminding me that God was not in hell. Then I raised three fingers to indicate the Holy Trinity; he raised one finger to show that God was One and indivisible. Finally, I took out the holy bread of eternal life and the cup of everlasting salvation, representing the body and the blood of our Savior. But then the Jew brought out the apple, reminding me of original sin, and I knew that our argument had ended."

Meanwhile, on the other side of town, Yankele was surrounded by a delirious mob. "You are truly a great and wise man," the rabbi said. "And now tell us the meaning of what we have witnessed."

"Certainly," said Yankele. "First the priest pointed far away, meaning that the Jews had to leave this town and find another place to live. No, I replied, stepping on the ground, we were going to stay right here! Then he tried to tell me that we had three days in which to leave; I held up one finger, meaning that not a single one of us was leaving. Finally, I guess he gave up, because he took out his lunch—and so I took out mine!"

© 1973 Kirschen

A Jew who serves on the board of education in a southern town discovers that he is the lone proponent of desegregation laws.

"Don't you have a daughter?" asks a fellow board member.

"Yes," the Jew replies. "You know that I do."

"And would you let her go to school with the nigras?"

"I certainly intend to follow the law."

"And would you let her *marry* a nigra?"

"Frankly, gentlemen, I don't believe I'd let her marry *any* of you goyim!"

IN 1936, before the outbreak of war made such visits impossible, a New Yorker returned to his hometown shtetl in Poland. Upon arriving, he was greeted by the town's leading citizen, who led him on a grand tour. The town had grown rapidly since the visitor had left it twenty years earlier, and he asked his host and guide how many Jews resided there.

"Now, *baruch Hashem*—thank God—we have two thousand Jews."

"Really?" asked the visitor. "That's very impressive. When I left, there were only seven hundred Jews here. And how many goyim?"

"Oh, about six hundred families. It works out well—very well, in fact. Almost every Jewish household has its own *Shabbas goy,* so the fires remain burning through the entire day. And where you come from, in New York, how many Jews are there?"

"About two million."

"Two *million?* That's quite a town! And how many goyim?"

"Oh, around five million."

"Five million! What do you need so many goyim for?"

Let's put the **oy** back in goy

Philip Roth, *Portnoy's Complaint*

ON a train in czarist Russia, a Jew is eating a whitefish, wrapped in paper. A Gentile, sitting across the aisle, begins to taunt him with various anti-Semitic epithets. Finally, he asks the Jew, "What makes you Jews so smart?"

"All right," replies the Jew. "I guess I'll have to tell you. It's because we eat the head of the whitefish."

"Well, if that's the secret," says the Gentile, "then I can be as smart as you are."

"That's right," says the Jew. "And in fact, I happen to have an extra whitefish head with me. You can have it for five kopecks."

The Gentile pays for the fish head and begins to eat it. An hour later the train stops at a station for a few minutes. The Gentile leaves the train and comes back. "Listen, Jew," he says. "You sold me that whitefish head for five kopecks. But I just saw a whole whitefish at the market for three kopecks."

"See," replies the Jew. "You're getting smarter already!"

Not surprisingly, anti-goyism is rarely stressed in public discussions of Judaism. But it does exist, of course, although at no point in Jewish history does it surface in any authoritative way. True, it can be found in some places in the Talmud, but such references are generally to heathens rather than Christians, and many folk sayings about goyim predate Christianity. But centuries of hostility between Gentiles and Jews have led to a large body of aggressive and unpleasant feelings on both sides.

Floods Give Us Pleasure

Wallace Markfield is the author of numerous short stories and three novels: *To an Early Grave* (which was made into the film *Bye Bye Braverman*), *Teitlebaum's Window,* and *You Could Live if They Let You.*

You Could Live if They Let You is the story of Jules Farber, a Jewish comedian who incorporates parts of Lenny Bruce and Don Rickles; Van Horton is his Gentile interviewer.

A major theme in this novel, as well as in Philip Roth's *Portnoy's Complaint,* is that the Jewish attitude toward Gentiles is subtle and complex. Condescension is one part of the picture, but operating simultaneously is an opposite force: a kind of reverence, a fawning over those aspects of routine American culture which are in fact most mundane. To the foreigner and the outsider, the very epitome of American blandness still retains an aura of mysterious fascination.

•

Q. Why did God make goyim?
A. *Somebody* has to buy retail.

•

VAN HORTON: Is this, then, your point? That the sufferings of Jews are different from and deeper than the sufferings of all others?

FARBER: Not different, not deeper. I would say . . . here's what I'd say: You *goyim* don't, simply don't know how to suffer. Am I blaming you? How can I blame you? It's a question of basic training. Your God, He feels for you, *He's* all the time suffering for you. Our God, you tell Him, "It hurts, it hurts!" He'll answer, "I know, I know, and in a minute you're going to hear me with some yell!" . . .

VAN HORTON: Jung—I suspect it was Jung—makes somewhere the point that each race covets, unconsciously covets the disasters suffered by other races.

FARBER: Oh, I enjoy your forest fires, I love a nice blizzard, a dry spell is also good, that's if you people don't overdo it with the parched earth and the *kvetching* of the skinny farmers —I don't like a skinny farmer when he *kvetches:* "Look ter me lak we need rain, airp. . . ."

But a flood!

If I wasn't so mean-spirited, I would ask God to send your people only good floods.

VAN HORTON: Good floods . . .

FARBER: Not that they deserve the pleasure.

VAN HORTON: Floods give us pleasure. . . .

FARBER: I see already you don't know how to look at a flood. All right, never mind the advanced stuff. Forget the floating station wagon with the cat on top. And I won't talk variations—where in the current swirls a TV set, the set can be sixteen inches, it can be twenty inches. Or the guy paddling his boat—and the paddle could be a shutter, the paddle could be a storm window.

But back in that gym . . . that town hall!

They pick to interview some bone of a crone . . . a hundred and nineteen.

And what does she say?

With the IV tubes sticking out her . . . lying on a government-surplus cot, covered with a factory-reject blanket . . . gumming a day-old doughnut . . .

What does she say?

"Um real happy, um real glad; um real glad, um real happy."

Why is she so glad and why is she so happy?

"Wal, the real spirit of a town—t'ain't in yur greenbean snap-offs. It's frayns an naybees I ain't seen since the last barn-burnin' sharin' their pin-curlers. . . . It's the new young pastor stoppin' by and sayin', 'Hi, we sure missed you at our antifluoride rally.' . . . It's the chance to talk 'bout all them thay-ngs our town's been puttin' off, lak a statue of J. C. Penney, mebbe a new ink pad for Mayor Flang's notary public seal, maybe repaintin' the McDonald's golden arch. . . . Oh, mebbe it's jes plain belongin' . . . sayin', 'This yere's the leech field m' daddy dug.' . . . 'That there's the window fan he won in the Baptist Grand Raffle.' . . . 'The tire chain he used ter teach me right from wrong.' "

VAN HORTON: I take away the impression . . . In my America, amongst my people . . . Such woefully small expectations.

FARBER: Except—and it's a big except—when you deal with your storekeepers.

There you people shine and in that area I acknowledge your superiority.

For your quarter-pound chopped horseneck . . . your filet of fatback . . . your Ma Joad maggot mix . . .

This sixty-seven-cent order . . . it's bagged by a bagger, the bagger throws into the bag five calendars, a copy of *Great Dishes of the Delaware Water Gap,* an ice scraper for the windshield, a bus schedule, and a toilet plunger. The stapler staples it with Swedish steel staples, the manager carries it to the car, he apologizes that he can't give your exhaust system a six-point inspection but he just had a couple of disks fused . . . and before he leaves he puts on a little record, the record is John Gielgud going, "Yes, ah, yes, we gladly accept government food stamps. . . ."

VAN HORTON: Marx *did* speak of the idiocy of rural life. . . .

FARBER: Believe me, it's too good for those idiots. And the street is too good for the man in the street.

VAN HORTON: I am at this time tempted—no, compelled—I am compelled to say, along with Harry Stack Sullivan, that "most men are much more simply human than anything else."

FARBER: Yeah, yeah.

Sure, sure.

Most men . . . most men are much more simply schmucks than anything else.

VAN HORTON: Then what—I put to you Tolstoy's question—what shall a man live by?

FARBER: If he can afford it—by the seashore.

●

Throughout Jewish history, converts have been viewed with a range of feeling, from skepticism to contempt.

•

An Orthodox Jew converts to Catholicism and is invited to preach the Sunday sermon. He stands up proudly and begins: "Fellow goyim . . ."

•

"Mrs. Gottlieb, a widow, wanted to visit an expensive and restricted resort. Registering under an assumed name, she took a suite of rooms on the seventh floor. The next morning at breakfast she was seated with seven midwestern Gentile women.

In her best mock-English accent, Mrs. Gottlieb said, "My dear, would you please pass the butter?"

But as the butter was passed, it fell into Mrs. Gottlieb's lap. "Oy vey," she yelled, and then, composing herself, she added sweetly, "Whatever *that* means."

•

IT was a long and difficult struggle, but Shimon Fogelberg had finally become a financial success. Success brought with it new pressures, however, and Fogelberg, under advice from his doctor, began jogging several miles a day in the neighborhood of his New York apartment.

One morning, after a particularly strenuous workout, Fogelberg grew faint and collapsed outside the posh and restricted New York Athletic Club. The doorman studiously ignored Fogelberg's repeated requests for a glass of water and a place to sit. "This club is for members only," he haughtily announced.

Over the next few months, Fogelberg was obsessed by the New York Athletic Club and its restrictive policies. "Business is great," he announced to his partner one day, "and so I'm taking some time off to improve myself."

The next day, Fogelberg set off for Oxford University to be tutored in the niceties of social graces and manners. In time, his accent became that of a country gentleman. His clothes were tailored on London's Savile Row. He became something of an educated man. And he officially changed his name to Chauncey Fumpelroy III.

One day, almost two years after he had left, Fogelberg/Fumpelroy returned to New York. He got off the plane and took a taxi straight to the New York Athletic Club. He set down his luggage and, dressed to the teeth, approached the clerk.

"Good afternoon," he said. "I should like to apply for admission to this grand institution."

"Certainly, sir," said the clerk, taking out a printed form. "And may I ask your name?"

"Chauncey Fumpelroy the Third."

"Very good, Mr. Fumpelroy. And may I ask your occupation?"

"I deal in stocks and bonds."

"Very good, sir," said the clerk once more. "And I hope you won't mind, sir, but it is our policy to ask about your religion as well."

"Religion?" said Fumpelroy. "I'm of the goyish persuasion."

"God, I know we are your chosen people, but couldn't you choose somebody else for a change?"

Sholom Aleichem

A WEALTHY Boston Brahmin was on his deathbed. The end was near, and he asked his three business partners, a Catholic, a Protestant, and a Jew, to come to the hospital to discuss some matters pertaining to his estate.

"You boys know I have no family," he began, "so I'm dividing my wealth among the three of you, in three equal shares. As a sign of your good friendship, however, I would like each of you to make a token gesture after I'm gone, by putting a thousand dollars into my coffin before it is lowered into the ground."

Several days later, the funeral was conducted according to the wishes of the deceased. At the appropriate time, the Catholic friend walked up to the coffin and placed in it an envelope containing one thousand dollars. The Protestant friend came forward and did likewise. Finally, the Jew walked up to the coffin, took out the two envelopes, and replaced them with a check for three thousand dollars.

This is one of many jokes that can be viewed either as anti-Jewish or pro-Jewish, depending on who is telling it. It is a favorite, and is found in most collections of Jewish humor.

•

A minister, a rabbi, and a priest were discussing how they made use of the funds in the collection plate. The minister said, "I draw a line on the floor, and I throw the money into the air. Everything that lands to the right of the line is for God; everything on the left is for me."

"That's pretty much what I do," said the priest. "But instead of a line, I draw a circle. Everything in the circle is for God; everything outside the circle I keep for myself."

"I, too, have a system," said the rabbi. "I take the money and throw it up in the air, and whatever God catches He can keep!"

This is, of course, an assimilated joke, as Jews do not make use of a collection plate.

THREE Jews who had recently converted to Christianity were having a drink together in a posh WASP country club. They started talking about the reasons for their conversions.

"I converted out of love," said the first, and noticing the dubious looks on his friends' faces, he continued: "Not for Christianity, mind you, but for a Christian girl. As you both know, my wife insisted that I convert."

"And I," said the second, "I converted in order to rise in the legal system. You probably know that my recent appointment as a federal judge may have had something to do with my new religion."

The third man spoke up: "I converted because I think that the teachings of Christianity are superior to those of Judaism."

"Are you kidding?" said the first man, spitting out his drink. "What do you take us for, a couple of goyim?"

This joke is sometimes told with the punch-line: "Oh, yeah? Tell that to your Gentile friends!"

•

Three recent converts to Christianity were being tested.

"What is Easter?" the first man was asked.

"Easter is when Jesus was born."

"Go back and study," they said to him. "Next!"

"What is Easter?"

"Easter," said the second man, "was when Jesus split the Red Sea."

"I'm sorry," he was told. "You'll have to do some more studying. Next!"

"What is Easter?" the third man was asked.

"Easter," he said tentatively, "was when Christ was reborn."

"Excellent. Please continue."

"Well," the man said cautiously, "he was in the grave for three days. . . ."

"Very good; and then?"

"And then he came out, saw his shadow—and went back in!"

•

A RABBI and a minister were sitting together on a plane. The stewardess came up to them and asked, "Would you care for a cocktail?"

"Sure," said the rabbi. "Please bring me a Manhattan."

"Fine, sir," said the stewardess. "And you, Reverend?"

"Young lady," he said, "before I touch strong drink, I'd just as soon commit adultery."

"Oh, miss," said the rabbi. "As long as there's a choice, I'll have what he's having."

Jokes about ministers, priests, and rabbis (or, in lay terms, a Protestant, a Catholic, and a Jew) reflect the recent American tendency toward ecumenism, and the public ascendancy of Judaism to the trinity of official American religions. These have come to replace earlier jokes about conversion and assimilation.

A Catholic boy was bragging to his Jewish friend: "My priest knows more than your rabbi!"

"Of course he does," said the Jewish boy. "You *tell* him everything."

A RABBI and a priest were discussing their professions.

"Do you ever get ambitious?" asked the priest.

"Well," said the rabbi, "I suppose I could always move to a larger congregation. What about you?"

"Well, I suppose I could become a Cardinal."

"And then?"

"Well, it's theoretically possible that I could become the Pope."

"And then?" asked the rabbi.

"And then?" repeated the priest. "Isn't that enough? Do you want me to become God?"

"Well," said the rabbi softly, "one of *our* boys made it."

T WO poor and elderly Jews, looking for a warm place on a cold day, made their way into a Catholic church. They found seats at the back of the sanctuary and looked around in astonishment at the ornate fixtures. In the front, a ceremony was taking place as a hundred white-robed nuns were being inducted into the order.

Noticing the unusual visitors, a young priest went over to the men. "Excuse me, gentlemen," he said, "but what exactly brings you here today?"

"Not to worry," said one of the visitors. "We're from the groom's side."

Traditional Jews had little contact with any Christians, but nuns were especially distant and inaccessible figures. "Here's how my mother felt about nuns," recalls the narrator of Max Shulman's novel *Potatoes Are Cheaper.* "If she happened to see one on the street, she made a circle three times, said *Shma Yisrael* and ran to kill a chicken."

An old Jew was admitted to a Catholic hospital for an operation. A nun asked him who would be responsible for the bill, and the old man replied, "My only living relative is my sister, but she is an old maid who converted to Catholicism and became a nun."

"Just a minute," said the nun. "I'll have you know that we are not old maids—we are married to Jesus Christ."

"Fine," said the old man. "In that case, send the bill to my brother-in-law!"

M ENDEL KRAVITZ, eighty-four years old, was hit by a car and lay bleeding on the sidewalk. A policeman arrived on the scene and, glancing at the victim, immediately called for an ambulance and a priest.

The priest arrived first, and bending over Kravitz, he asked, "Do you believe in the Father, the Son, and the Holy Ghost?"

Kravitz lifted up his head, opened his eyes wide, and turned to the crowd that had gathered round him. "I'm laying here dying and he's asking me riddles!"

It was a dark and stormy night, and Mendelson, an old man, knew that the end was near. "Call the priest," he said to his wife, "and tell him to come right away."

"The priest? Max, you're delirious. You mean the rabbi!"

"No," said Mendelson, "I mean the priest. Why disturb the rabbi on a night like this?"

Mendelson is dying. "Call the priest," he says to his wife, "and tell him I want to convert."

"But, Max, you've been an Orthodox Jew all your life. What are you talking about, you want to convert?"

"Better one of them should die than one of us."

BERNSTEIN, retired, is resting peacefully on the porch of his small hotel outside Miami when he sees a cloud of dust up the road. He walks out to see who could be approaching: It is a southern farmer with a wagon.

"Good afternoon," says Bernstein.

"Afternoon," says the farmer.

"Where you headed?" asks Bernstein.

"Town."

"What do you have in the wagon?"

"Manure."

"Manure, eh? What do you do with it?"

"I spread it over the strawberries."

"Well," says Bernstein, "you should come over here for lunch someday. We use sour cream."

Gottlieb, a veteran lingerie salesman from New York, went on the road two or three times each year. One day he found himself in a small town in rural Alabama. Tired and hungry, and unable to find a restaurant, he walked into the general store on Main Street.

"And what can I do for you, sir?" asked the proprietor.

"You handle maybe fertilizer?" asked Gottlieb.

"Sure do," the man replied.

"Good," said Gottlieb. "So wash your hands and go make me a grilled cheese sandwich."

PHILIP ROTH

Shikses and Other Goyim

Just before he was drafted into the Army in 1943, Heshie decided to become engaged to a girl named Alice Dembosky, the head drum majorette of the high school band. It was Alice's genius to be able to twirl not just one but two silver batons simultaneously—to pass them over her shoulders, glide them snakily between her legs, and then toss them fifteen and twenty feet into the air, catching one, then the other, behind her back. Only rarely did she drop a baton to the turf, and then she had a habit of shaking her head petulantly and crying out in a little voice, "Oh, Alice!" that only could have made Heshie love her the more; it surely had that effect upon me. Oh-Alice, with that long blond hair leaping up her back and about her face! cavorting with such exuberance half the length of the playing field! Oh-Alice, in her tiny white skirt with the white satin bloomers, and the white boots that come midway up the muscle of her lean, strong calves! Oh Jesus, "Legs" Dembosky, in all her dumb, blond *goyishe* beauty! Another icon!

That Alice was so blatantly a *shikse* caused no end of grief in Heshie's household, and even in my own; as for the community at large, I believe there was actually a kind of civic pride taken in the fact that a Gentile could have assumed a position of such high visibility in our high school, whose faculty and student body were about ninety-five percent Jewish. On the other hand, when Alice performed what the loudspeaker described as her "piece de resistance"—twirling a baton that had been wrapped at either end in oil-soaked rags and then set afire

A major theme in *Portnoy's Complaint* is the hero's division of the entire world into Jews and Others, which is the most prominent theme in recent American-Jewish humor. Portnoy holds forth frequently on this topic, and it is difficult to know which group comes off worse: "The Jews I despise for their narrow-mindedness, their self-righteousness, the incredibly bizarre sense that these cave men who are my parents and relatives have somehow gotten of their own superiority—but when it comes to tawdriness and cheapness, to beliefs that would shame even a gorilla, you simply cannot top the *goyim*."

Surely one of the most controversial aspects of *Portnoy's Complaint* is that the novel brings to the surface some of the feelings and ideas that Jews have secretly held about their Gentile neighbors.

Just after the abdication of Prince Edward, two Jewish women went to watch the changing of the guard at Buckingham Palace.

"Who lives here now?" one of them asked.

"The Queen and the Duke."

"But what about the Prince of Wales?"

"Oh, didn't you hear? He went to America and married a *shikse*."

Drawing by David Levine. Copyright © 1977 by Nyrev, Inc.
By permission of *The New York Review of Books.*

—despite all the solemn applause delivered by the Weequahic fans in tribute to the girl's daring and concentration, despite the grave *boom boom boom* of our bass drum and the gasps and shrieks that went up when she seemed about to set ablaze her two adorable breasts—despite this genuine display of admiration and concern, I think there was still a certain comic detachment experienced on our side of the field, grounded in the belief that this was precisely the kind of talent that only a *goy* would think to develop in the first place.

Which was more or less the prevailing attitude toward athletics in general, and football in particular, among the parents in the neighborhood: it was for the *goyim.* Let them knock their heads together for "glory," for victory in a ball game! As my Aunt Clara put it, in that taut, violinstring voice of hers, "Heshie! Please! I do not need *goyishe naches!*" Didn't need, didn't want such ridiculous pleasures and satisfactions as made the Gentiles happy. . . . At football our Jewish high school was notoriously hopeless (though the band, may I say, was always winning prizes and commendations); our pathetic record was of course a disappointment to the young, no matter what the parents might feel, and yet even as a child one was able to understand that for us to lose at football was not exactly the ultimate catastrophe. Here, in fact, was a cheer that my cousin and his buddies used to send up from the stands at the end of a game in which Weequahic had once again met with seeming disaster. I used to chant it with them.

> Ikey, Mikey, Jake, and Sam,
> We're the boys who eat no ham,
> We play football, we play soccer—
> And we keep matzohs in our locker!
> Aye, aye, aye, Weequahic High!

So what if we had lost? It turned out we had other things to be proud of. We ate no ham. We kept matzohs in our lockers. Not really, of course, but if we wanted to *we could, and we weren't ashamed to say that we actually did!* We were Jews—and we weren't ashamed to say it! We were Jews—and not only were we not inferior to the *goyim* who beat us at football, but the chances were that because we could not commit our hearts to victory in such a thuggish game, we were superior! We were Jews—*and we were superior!*

> White bread, rye bread,
> Pumpernickel, challah,
> All those for Weequahic,
> Stand up and hollah!

Another cheer I learned from Cousin Hesh, four more lines of poetry to deepen my understanding of the injustices we suffered . . . The outrage, the disgust inspired in my parents by the Gentiles was beginning to make some sense: the *goyim* pretended to be something special, while *we* were actually *their* moral superiors. And what made us superior was precisely the hatred and the disrespect they lavished so willingly upon us!

Shikses

Shikses! In winter, when the polio germs are hibernating and I can bank upon surviving outside an iron lung until the end of the school year, I ice-skate on the lake in Irvington Park. In the last light of the weekday afternoons, then all day long on crisply shining Saturdays and Sundays, I skate round and round in circles behind the *shikses* who live in Irvington, the town across the city line from the streets and houses of my safe and friendly Jewish quarter. I know where the *shikses* live from the kinds of curtains their mothers hang in the windows. Also, the *goyim* hang a little white cloth with a star in the front window, in honor of themselves and their boys away in the service—a blue star if the son is living, a gold star if he is dead. "A Gold Star Mom," says Ralph Edwards, solemnly introducing a contestant on *Truth or Consequences,* who in just two minutes is going to get a bottle of seltzer squirted at her snatch, followed by a brand-new refrigerator for her kitchen. . . . A Gold

Star Mom is what my Aunt Clara upstairs is too, except here is the difference—she has no gold star in her window, for a dead son doesn't leave her feeling proud or noble, or feeling anything, for that matter. It seems instead to have turned her, in my father's words, into "a nervous case" for life. Not a day has passed since Heshie was killed in the Normandy invasion that Aunt Clara has not spent most of it in bed, and sobbing so badly that Doctor Izzie has sometimes to come and give her a shot to calm her hysteria down. . . . But the curtains—the curtains are embroidered with lace, or "fancy" in some other way that my mother describes derisively as *"goyishe* taste." At Christmastime, when I have no school and can go off to ice-skate at night under the lights, I see the trees blinking on and off behind the Gentile curtains. Not on our block—God forbid!—or on Leslie Street, or Schley Street, or even Fabian Place, but as I approach the Irvington line, here is a *goy,* and there is a *goy,* and there still another—and then I am into Irvington and it is simply awful: not only is there a tree conspicuously ablaze in every parlor, but the houses themselves are outlined with colored bulbs advertising Christianity, and phonographs are pumping "Silent Night" out into the street as though—as though?—it were the national anthem, and on the snowy lawns are set up little cut-out models of the scene in the manger—really, it's enough to make you sick. How can they possibly *believe* this shit? Not just children but grownups, too, stand around on the snowy lawns smiling down at pieces of wood six inches high that are called Mary and Joseph and little Jesus—and the little cut-out cows and horses are smiling too! God! The idiocy of the Jews all year long, and then the idiocy of the *goyim* on these holidays! What a country! Is it any wonder we're all of us half nuts?

But the *shikses,* ah, the *shikses* are something else again. Between the smell of damp sawdust and wet wool in the overheated boathouse, and the sight of their fresh cold blond hair spilling out of their kerchiefs and caps, I am ecstatic. Amidst these flushed and giggling girls, I lace up my skates with weak, trembling fingers, and then out into the cold and after them I move, down the wooden gangplank on my toes and off onto the ice behind a fluttering covey of them—a nosegay of *shikses,* a garland of Gentile girls. I am so awed that I am in a state of desire *beyond a hard-on.* My circumcised little dong is simply shriveled up with veneration. Maybe it's dread. How do they get so gorgeous, so healthy, so *blond?* My contempt for what they believe in is more than neutralized by my adoration of the way they look, the way they move and laugh and speak—the lives they must lead behind those *goyishe* curtains! Maybe a pride of *shikses* is more like it—or is it a pride of *shkotzim?* For these are the girls whose older brothers are the engaging, good-natured, confident, clean, swift, and powerful halfbacks for the college football teams called *Northwestern* and *Texas Christian* and *UCLA*. Their fathers are men with white hair and deep voices who never use double negatives, and their mothers the ladies with the kindly smiles and the wonderful manners who say things like: "I do believe, Mary, that we sold thirty-five cakes at the Bake Sale." "Don't be too late, dear," they sing out sweetly to their little tulips as they go bouncing off in their bouffant taffeta dresses to the Junior Prom with boys whose names are right out of the grade-school reader, not Aaron and Arnold and Marvin, but Johnny and Billy and Jimmy and Tod. Not Portnoy or Pincus, but Smith and Jones and Brown! These people are the *Americans,* Doctor—like Henry Aldrich and Homer, like the Great Gildersleeve and his nephew LeRoy, like Corliss and Veronica, like Oogie Pringle, who gets to sing beneath Jane Powell's window in *A Date with Judy*—these are the people for whom Nat "King" Cole sings, every Christmastime, "Chestnuts roasting on an open fire, Jack Frost nipping at your nose . . ." An open fire, in *my* house? No, no, theirs are the noses whereof he speaks. Not his flat black one or my long bumpy one, but those tiny bridgeless wonders whose nostrils point northward automatically at birth. And stay that way for life! These are the children from the coloring books come to life, the children they mean on the signs we pass in Union, New Jersey, that say CHILDREN AT PLAY and DRIVE CAREFULLY, WE LOVE OUR CHILDREN—these are the girls and boys who live "next door," the kids who are always asking for "the jalopy" and getting into "jams" and then out of them again in time for the final commercial—the kids whose neighbors aren't the Silversteins and the Landaus, but Fibber McGee and Molly, and Ozzie and Harriet, and Ethel and Albert, and Lorenzo Jones and his wife Belle, and Jack Armstrong! Jack Armstrong, the All-American *Goy!*—and Jack as in John, not Jack as in Jake, like my father . . . Look, we ate our meals with that radio blaring away right through to the dessert, the glow of the yellow station band is the last light I see each night before sleep—so don't tell me we're just as good as anybody else, don't tell me we're Americans just like they are. No, no, these blond-haired Christians are the legitimate residents and owners of this place, and they can pump any song they want into the streets and no one is going to stop them, either. O America! America! It may have been gold in the streets to my grandparents, it may have been a chicken in every pot to my father and mother, but to me, a child whose earliest movie memories are of Ann Rutherford and Alice Faye, America is a *shikse* nestling under your arm whispering love love love love love!

AMERICA • DIVISIONS • ISRAEL • COMMUNICATION

MORT DRUCKER / FRANK JACOBS • ALLAN SHERMAN • "AN ELDER OF ZION" (ELLIOT E. COHEN) • G. B. TRUDEAU • ELAN DRESHER / NORBERT HORNSTEIN / J. LIPA ROTH • RALPH SCHOENSTEIN • ABRAHAM SHULMAN • GERALD SUSSMAN • PAUL JACOBS • DICK CODOR • DIANA BRYAN • GARY EPSTEIN • DAN BEN-AMOTZ • MARK PODWAL • YORAM MATMOR • CHAIM BERMANT • KIRSCHEN • GARY ROSENBLATT • EDWARD FIELD • MILT GROSS • LEO ROSTEN • S. GROSS • NEIL SIMON • LOU MYERS

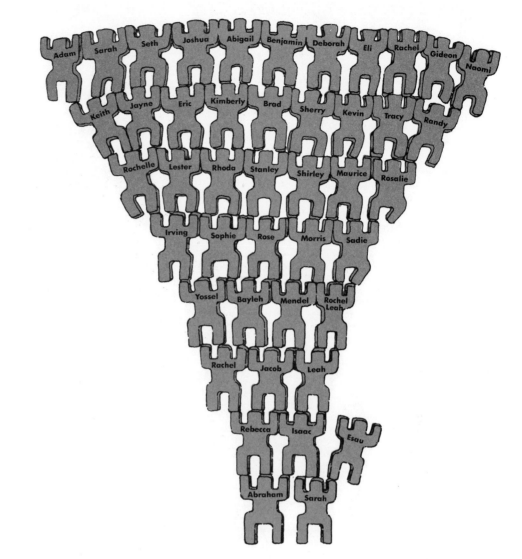

PART THREE

PROMISED LANDS

FIDDLER MADE A GOOF DEPT.

Practically everyone has seen the prize-winning musical about the lovable people in that little village in Old Russia called Anetevka. Well, as far as we're concerned, *Fiddler* made a *goof!* Because a show like that is very sentimental and touching until we think about the *descendants* of those oppressed people who fled Europe so many years ago, and how those descendants have almost destroyed a Dream. Which is why *Mad* now takes this famous musical about the problems of people who had *nothing,* and updates it with a version about the problems of people who have *everything*—mainly America's Upper Middle Class. Here, then, is our sing-along rendition, retitled . . .

ARTIST: MORT DRUC[K]

An antenna on the roof! What's so strange about **that?** Nothing much . . . except that **this** antenna is on the roof of our **kennel!**

You see, here in our $150,000 home in the suburbs, even our **dog** is spoiled rotten!

You may ask: Why do I work so hard to provide such luxuries as a **Zenith Color TV Console** for our **dog?** Why not just a simple **Black-and-White Emerson Portable?**

Because here in the **suburbs,** a family is measured by **one yardstick— POSSESSIONS!**

Possessions are what earn us the **respect** and **admiration** of the people who mean the **most** to us! And who are they . . . ? **THE NEIGHBORS!!**

Still, it's not so **easy** being prosperous! Even **WE** have our problems! And what a[re] our **biggest ones** . . . **OUR DAUGHTERS!**

POSSESSIONS! **THE NEIGHBORS!** **OUR DAUGHTERS!**

*Dum-dum of dum-dums!
Imbecile of Imbeciles!
God led us to the U.S.A.!
Said, "You are free," and,
Imbecile of imbeciles,
Look at what we find today!

Dum-dum of dum-dums!
Imbecile of Imbeciles!
God made a modern Cam-e-lot;
Now that we've seen the
Mess you've made,
We're afraid
God wants back his melting pot!

When Yippies tear the flag to shreds—
They act like imbeciles;
When hard-hats go crazy and start busting heads—
They act like imbeciles, too;

But though God's seen imbeciles great and small,
The most incredible thing of all
Is that God might as well say he is through—
None . . . will . . . e-ver . . . e-qual . . . you!

Dum-dum of dum-dums!
Imbecile of imbeciles!
Long years we suffered by the score;
Then we looked *here*, you
Imbecile of imbeciles;
Now . . . we . . . suf-fer . . . e-ven . . . more!

When in-dus-tries pollute the land,
They act like imbeciles;
When un-ions keep striking till they're out of hand,
They act like imbeciles, too;

INDUSTRY
STRIKE
WE WANT MORE
STRIKE
HIGHER WAGES
LOCAL 705 IS ON STRIKE

But though God's made imbeciles great and small,
The thing that bothers us most of all
Is that we fear that God may make a fuss
And . . . some . . . how . . . blame . . . you . . . on . . . us!

*Reprise to the tune of *"Miracle of Miracles"*

To the tune of "Seventy-six Trombones":

Seventy-six Sol Cohens in the country club,

And a hundred and ten nice men named Levine!

And there's more than a thousand Finks

Who parade around the links—

It's a sight that really must be seen!

ALLAN SHERMAN

"AN ELDER OF ZION"
The Man Who Exploded

Last Thursday evening about eleven-thirty o'clock I was walking down Jefferson Davis Avenue, the fashionable residential street of Bienville, swinging my cane and looking at the constellation Orion.

Suddenly down the quiet deserted street I saw a man striding along furiously through the shadows of the trees. When he came up to me, he peered hard into my face and stopped. I stopped too, and the man stood glaring at me with the most intense hatred. I was, I confess, somewhat taken aback. I had never seen the man before. He was a young man, about thirty or forty years old. He wore a black coat with a brown fur collar, tan gloves, and an ascot tie. He was, I should say, about five or six feet tall.

"Look here," he said, in a loud voice, "I won't be a Jew. There's no sense in it. I'm sick of it. I won't be a Jew and that's the end of it. Leave me alone!"

"All right," I said, and began to walk off.

"Look here," he said still more loudly, coming after me.

Parodies of Jewish life in America have been popular for at least a century. During the period of great immigration to the United States a hundred years ago, a number of parodies appeared in the form of classical Jewish texts. One writer, for example, expressed himself in the style of *Pirkei Avot* (Ethics of the Fathers):

The New World stands on three things: money and money and again money. All the people of this country worship the Golden Calf. . . .

No sinfearer will accumulate wealth, and no pious man will prosper, nor is the shamefaced apt to get rich; but he who does much traffic will grow wise, for his wealth will make him appear so.

The basis of all law and religion is: "Thou shalt love thy wealth with all thy heart and with all thy soul," and the rest is based on this principle.

Another parodist, writing in the style of the Talmud:

Akabiah the son of Charlie said: Consider three things and you will be able to exist in America: Forget who you are, wear a mask before those who know you, and do anything you can. He used to say, if you were an informer at home, become here a public busybody; if you taught children the alphabet, become here a preacher in an Orthodox syna-

---

Mad magazine published its first issue in 1952; the original title was *Tales Calculated to Drive You MAD: Humor in a Jugular Vein.* Harvey Kurtzman, the founding editor, had a special fondness for Yiddish words, and used them in almost every issue; his favorite was *furshlugginer* (beat up, decrepit), which was used more for

sound than for sense. The first issue included a story about a ghost named Melvin—Melvin soon became a running gag, evolving into the character of Alfred E. Neuman— and a crime story called "Gonifs."

The magazine has never had any pretensions, and has eagerly admitted its trashiness, which in turn

has led its many youthful readers (as many as two million copies are sold of the summer issues) to regard it as a publication that tells the truth. And *Mad* is probably the only magazine that includes the name of its attorney on the masthead, so that offended readers will know whom to contact.

gogue; if you were a masseur, become here a physician; if you were a drummer in the army, become a professor of music; if you were a clown at home, become here an actor; if you were a beadle, take to politics; and if you are simply an impudent fellow, become the president of a society.

"An Elder of Zion" was the pseudonym of Elliot E. Cohen, whose witty comments on American-Jewish life appeared regularly in *The Menorah Journal,* of which Cohen was managing editor. Cohen, who came from Alabama and who graduated from Yale at the age of eighteen, was the founder and first editor of *Commentary,* where he worked until his death in 1959.

Jokes about assimilation are, for obvious reasons, overwhelmingly American. In what may be the best-known joke on this topic:

A young Talmud scholar who left Poland for America returns several years later to visit his family.

"But where is your beard?" asks his mother.

"Mama, in America nobody wears a beard."

"But at least you keep the Sabbath?"

"Mama, business is business. In America people work on the Sabbath."

"But kosher food you still eat?"

"Mama, it's very difficult to keep kosher in America."

The old lady hesitates for a moment, and then, in a hoarse whisper, she says, "Shloime, tell me one thing. Are you still circumcised?"

After a visit to Hollywood, the Scottish director John Grierson is said to have remarked, "After a few years in this place, your foreskin falls away."

This reversal of the previous joke is a reminder that while American Jews were becoming increasingly assimilated, the rest of the country—or so it often seemed—was becoming increasingly Jewish.

For several decades, the most popular jokes about assimilation were about Jews who changed their names—a fairly common practice earlier in this century.

"I've got enough of it. My hair is blond and straight." He took off his hat. "My nose is straight. My shoulders are square. I play football, baseball, soccer, and squash. There's no sense in it."

"All right," I said, and began to walk off.

"Look here," he said, clutching my coat lapel. "I won't be bulldozed. I am an American. I pay my income tax. I serve on the jury. I vote for sheriff, alderman, mayor, and President. I was over there fighting with the Rainbow Division in the Great War. I am a Democrat."

"All right," I said.

"I studied anthropology," he said, shaking his fist in my face. "I've got Ethiopian blood in my veins, Aramaic blood, Babylonian blood, Assyrian blood, Canaanitish blood, Egyptian blood, Greek blood, Moorish blood, Tartar blood, Dutch blood, Spanish blood, Polish blood, and what-all not. It's a farce."

"All right," I said.

"I don't know a word of Hebrew," he said, stamping his feet. "I don't know ten words of Yiddish. I speak English with a Harvard accent. I read Shakespeare and Milton and Dryden and Pope and Tennyson and Browning and Alfred Noyes and what-all not. I listen to Brahms and Beethoven and Bach. I subscribe to the *American Mercury* and the *Atlantic Monthly.* I own the sixteenth edition of the *Encyclopaedia Britannica.*"

"All right," I said.

"My house is no different from anyone else's house," he said, banging his fist violently in his palm. "I own a Buick, a Frigidaire, an Atwater Kent. I have a bridge set, a gateleg table, and a sun parlor. There are hooked rugs on my floor and a colonial knocker on my door."

"All right," I said.

"I don't believe in God," he shouted punching me in the ribs. "I don't believe in the Bible. I don't believe in the Ten Commandments. I eat oysters, I eat ham and eggs, I don't fast, I don't keep the Sabbath, I don't go to Temple, I'm an agnostic. I'm a skeptic. I don't believe in sects. I'm an internationalist. I'm a universalist. I'm a modern man with twentieth-century ideas. I'm just a plain human being."

"All right," I said.

"I am vice-president of a Gentile bank," he said, jumping up and down on the sidewalk. "My partners are Gentiles. I make my money in lumber, no honester, no crookeder than anybody else. I'm on the membership committee of the Allstyne Luncheon Club, I'm on the greens committee of the Bienville Country Club, I'm on the house committee of the Corinthian Sodality. My wife is a Gentile and a DAR. My children have blue eyes. My son is going to St. Mark's, my daughter is going to Rosemary Hall. It's nonsense. I can read Greek at sight. I'm an excellent trapshot. I can play the mandolin. What's Jewish about that? I don't wear a beard. My manners are flawless. There's no point in it. I'm an Elk, I'm a Mason, I'm a Moose. It's sheer idiocy. How am I a Jew? There's no sense to it. I won't be a Jew and that settles it. Leave me alone."

"All right," I said.

"I'm not a Jew, I'm not a Jew, I'm not a Jew," he shouted, swinging his arms wildly. "Do you hear me? I'm not a Jew! What do you say to that?"

"All right," I said, and began to walk off.

He leaped after me and seized me by both shoulders.

"Who are you to tell me what I am?" he yelled, shaking me violently, his face white with passion. "Who are you to tell me what I am and what I am not? . . . Just because you have a long white beard, you think . . . Look here, I could be a Jew if I wanted to. . . . Listen here, goddamn you, listen to this . . . I'm every bit as good a Jew as you are right this minute, I bet. . . ."

"All right," I said.

He danced about me in a frenzy, broken words and strange gurglings in his throat, his head bobbing up and down, his eyes popping, his cheeks puffed out like toy balloons with rage. I did not know what the man wanted, and I was frightened.

I wrenched myself away, and began to run down the street.

I had not taken three steps when I heard a loud report behind me. I turned around. The street was empty. I saw something that looked like a cloud or a wisp of smoke disappearing over the top of the sycamore tree above me. Evidently he had exploded.

The street was quite deserted. I looked at my watch. It was two minutes past twelve.

So I continued my walk down Jefferson Davis Avenue, swinging my cane and looking at the constellation Orion.

Four salesmen who had met in a train began to play cards. "Let's introduce ourselves," said one man. "My name's Cole."

"I'm Kent," said the second salesman.

"Carleton," said the third.

"Also Cohen," added the fourth.

In *The Joys of Yiddish*, Leo Rosten tells of a young priest on Houston Street who sees a large sign over a store: "Pincus & O'Toole." The priest goes in and is greeted by a man with a beard and yarmulke.

The priest is delighted: "It does my heart glad to see how your people and mine have come together in friendship and in business. That's a pleasant surprise."

"Well," the man replies, "I've got a bigger surprise for you. I'm O'Toole!"

In Woody Allen's story "No Kaddish for Weinstein," there is an intellectual who "suffered untold injustices and persecutions because of his religion, mostly from his parents." Even though they are Jewish, "they could never accept the fact that their son was Jewish."

Doonesbury

ELAN DRESHER
NORBERT HORNSTEIN
J. LIPA ROTH

A Montrealer Seder

"A Montrealer Seder" appeared originally in *Strobe*, a publication of the Hillel Foundation of McGill University. Since this piece was written, however, the National Hockey League has undergone an expansion similar to those of other sports, and so the Stanley Cup Finals are no longer played during Passover. But for Canadian Jews, the former coexistence of hockey playoffs and Passover Seders was similar to the occurrence of the World Series during the High Holidays. Because of the prolonged baseball season, this conflict no longer occurs.

Everyone is familiar with the many colorful customs and special rituals associated with the Passover Seder. The Four Questions, Elijah's Cup, and the *afikomen* are a standard part of the traditional Passover feast for the forty million Jews in Israel today.

In addition to the usual customs of the holiday, however, many Jewish families have incorporated into the Seder the heritage of their respective Diaspora communities. Among the most colorful Seders are those held in the homes of the Montrealer Jews—those Jews whose ancestors lived for many years in a Canadian community which rose to prominence in the second half of the twentieth century.

On the eve of the Seder, the men of the household attend services just like everyone else. But midway through the evening prayers they leave the synagogue and silently say the rest of the prayers on their way home—a practice which gave rise to the idiom "to pray as fast as a Montrealer."

At home, one member of the family keeps watch at the window, anxiously awaiting the arrival of the father, the other men of the family, and the guests. When the shul-goers come into view, the mother blows a special whistle and all drop what they are doing, run to the door, and line up in single file.

As the men approach the house, their final strides become long and graceful. They walk without lifting their shoes, and they swing their arms vigorously. They enter the house one by one and consecutively shake the hands of all those who await them. The last to enter is the father. After going down the line,

he leads the Seder party around the table three times and is then warmly surrounded by the rest of the party and is vigorously slapped on the back. The mother blows the whistle again, the party cheers, a matzoh is dropped, and the Seder is under way.

The rest of the Seder is conducted in the traditional manner, except for certain customs which are unique to "Minhag Montreal." In most Jewish homes, for example, the Seder is conducted at a leisurely, relaxed pace, often not ending before midnight. Montrealers, however, take seriously the idea of *chipazon* (haste) traditionally associated with the Exodus, "because they were thrust out of Egypt and could not tarry." They therefore begin the Seder almost two hours earlier than their neighbors and conduct it at a greatly accelerated pace, often omitting passages from the Haggadah and progressively quickening the tempo of the Seder songs.

But in spite of this apparent haste, no major ceremonies are omitted. In fact, the Montrealers have elaborated on several traditional practices. Just before the youngest child asks the Four Questions, the head of the household asks the mother's brother (or if he is not present, another male member of the household) what time it is. The answer is always given with relation to eight o'clock. If the time is six-thirty, for example, the answer will be: "It is ninety minutes to eight."

At this point the father says, "Then let us proceed," and signals to the youngest child to begin. If it is already past eight o'clock, however, a special selection is read. These verses are found nowhere else in Jewish liturgy, although some scholars are reminded of the Yom Kippur passage which describes how blood was sprinkled on the outer altar of the Temple. The inserted passage begins: "What is the count? One and nil. One and one. Two and one. Three and one."

This section is followed by an even more obscure passage;

contemporary scholars believe it refers to the plagues and was inserted at a time when the Jewish community was threatened by harsh economic conditions. The "plague theorists" believe that the passage calls upon the Lord to smite the enemies of Israel just as He had done in Egypt. They cite the frequently recurring yet cryptic word "haki," which they claim to be a popular corruption of the Hebrew *hakeh,* which means to smite.

Another unique Montrealer custom concerns the *afikomen.* The father sends the youngest child to search for it, and upon finding it, the child runs back to the table and whispers in his father's ear. The father then jumps to his feet, raises his hands skyward, and shouts "Agol, Agol!" The rest of the males then rise with their arms raised and respond, "Hahllo Hahbs, Ahwei-Ahwei."

A highlight of the second half of the Seder has to do with Elijah's Cup. This is a large bowl with the names of the participants of past Seders engraved around the base. All through the Seder the cup has been standing in the center of the table filled to the brim with wine. Montrealer tradition is the only one which allows every member of the family to partake of the wine with Elijah. When the time comes for Elijah to "enter," all the men pull off their jerseys, while the head of the household lifts the cup above his head and deliberately allows some of the wine to spill. He drinks from the cup and passes it around the table, where each of the men spills some of the wine over the head of the man next to him. The Seder is then rapidly brought to a conclusion. The final songs are sung with the participants standing, and as they end, all the men rush from the room and leave the women to clean up.

The rest of the evening is spent in animated conversation, which usually lasts well into the night.

●

A Jew who has been shipwrecked on a deserted island for three years is finally reached by rescuers. Proudly, he shows them around the island, pointing out the irrigation system, the pastures and orchards, the barn, the house, and all his other constructions. At the end of the island are two small buildings. "And those," he announces, "are the synagogues."

"Two of them?" he is asked. "But you're alone here!"

"Well," he says, "this is the one I pray in—and the other one I wouldn't go in if you *paid* me!"

"AND what is your occupation, sir?" the judge asked the witness, an elderly Jew.

"Well, Your Honor, I'm a *minyan* man."

"What's a *minyan* man?" asked the judge.

"Well, Your Honor, when there are nine men in a synagogue, and I join them, they become ten."

"What are you talking about?" asked the judge. "When there are nine people and I join them, there are also ten!"

The Jew broke into a wide grin, and leaning toward the judge, he inquired, "Also a Jew?"

RALPH SCHOENSTEIN
Let Us Now Claim Famous Men

Joe Flaherty recently wrote that Roone Arledge has changed the mentality of America by presenting Howard Cosell, "the first Jew to play in Peoria." How I wish my grandfather were alive to see this particular player, for my grandfather happened to be the Scorekeeper of Zion. The happiest day of his life was either the day he got married or the day I told him that Dinah Shore was Jewish.

"Dinah *Shore?*" he said with rising delight. "The *blond* one with the *southern accent* . . . she's one of *my* kind?"

By "my kind" he didn't mean an unemployed florist: he meant a famous person who surreptitiously was giving him glory by passing as a Protestant. I collected many things as a boy, from trolley transfers to baseball cards, but nothing was more fun than helping my grandfather build his collection of surprising Jews, that tinseled Hebraic underground whose infiltration of the establishment allowed him to poke a passing Methodist and proudly say, "You know that Leslie Howard? The blond movie star with the fancy accent and the ruler for a nose? Well, he couldn't care less about Bethlehem."

Leonard Bernstein and Baron Rothschild also couldn't care, of course, but they were *known* to be Jewish and therefore no more collectable than Sid Luckman or Isaac Stern. My grandfather couldn't toss such men like glittering hand grenades, the way he tossed Dinah Shore when he casually said to an Irish teacher of mine, "I wonder if Dinah Shore has a recording of 'Kol Nidre' in the stores."

It was the secretly kindred celebrities that he loved to use for oneupmanship against the Christian foe; but they were as scarce as purey marbles or Vince DiMaggio cards. Just as Herbert Lehman, Eddie Cantor, and J. Robert Oppenheimer lacked punch, the foe was unimpressed by other obvious biggies too: Einstein, Disraeli, Sid Gordon, and Jesus Christ; Robert Moses, Meyer Lansky, Benny Leonard, and Mendelssohn. And so it became my job to find for my grandfather the most surprising Jews. I was, in short, the only boy in America who shared a mission with the Third Reich.

I can still remember the first great find that I brought to him: Jake Pitler, a Brooklyn Dodger coach. The entire world, of course, knew where Sandy Koufax went to pray, but Pitler was a Hebrew in the hole, a weapon my grandfather used for an inspired sneak attack in a crowded store one September day.

"If the World Series starts on Yom Kippur," he loudly said, "the Dodgers will be two men short."

Ralph Schoenstein, born in 1933, has worked as a radio and newspaper writer. He is the author of nine books, including *Citizen Paul,* the story of his father, who was editor of the old *New York Journal-American.*

Heads turned with puzzled looks as people counted Koufax and then wondered if Hank Greenberg had come out of retirement.

My grandfather took a long count, smiled triumphantly at me, and said, "Jake Pitler can't flash a sign on his solemn holiday."

When one year the series did have a Yom Kippur opening, my grandfather was exhilarated enough to take on the Arab Legion, the commander of which I had mentioned as an offbeat candidate for the collection.

"We could open it up to all Semites," I said, "and then we'd have Ibn-Saud too."

"Bring me more like Dinah Shore," he replied.

And so I did. Collecting for this proud son of David became even more fun than collecting new baseball cards—unless, of course, the card was Al Rosen or Moe Berg.

"Gramp, here's a beauty!" I told him breathlessly one day. "The American Revolution was financed by a guy whose first name was *Israel!*"

"No good," he said. "We've got too many money men."

"What are we short on?" I asked.

"Tennis players, princes, and secretaries of state."

Just a few days after, I brought him Nancy Walker, and soon after that, a prize to place even higher than Nancy Walker or Dinah Shore.

"Gramp!" I cried, "I got another Israel, but wait till you hear: It's *Mel Allen—he's Jewish!*"

He gasped and then he smiled and then I thought he might start to cry.

"Oh, that one comes right from God," he said. "We've been short on sportscasters . . . but the voice of *the Yankees . . . our kind* . . . Go look up all the *other* Allens—my God, what we could get!"

Within hours, I had checked out Fred Allen, Steve Allen, Gracie Allen, and Ethan too.

"No luck," I sadly told him. "Three Catholics and a Protestant."

Equally heartbreaking was our attempt to gain a second seat on the United States Supreme Court. In 1949, we had collected Melvyn Douglas and two years later we collected Kirk.

"Gramp, it just *hit* me," I told him one morning in the spring of 1952. "Melvyn Douglas, Kirk Douglas, . . . what about *Justice William O.?*"

His eyes took on the glow that I had seen the day I told him that Dwight D. Eisenhower's West Point nickname had been "The Swedish Jew."

"Justice William O. Douglas," he said softly, as if in prayer.

★★★★★★★★★★★★★★★★★★★★★★★★

The time is at hand when the wearing of prayer

shawl and skullcap will not bar a man from the

White House—unless, of course, the man is Jewish.

★★★★★★★★★★★★★★★★★★★★★★★★

Jules Farber, in Wallace Markfield's
You Could Live If They Let You

"Do I deserve such pleasure? It would be too much to hope."

It was; we had to settle for Felix Frankfurter, whose faith was just as unclassified as Henry Morgenthau's.

My grandfather then retreated into his favorite dream.

"If only we could prove that rumor about Roosevelt," he said.

Because he was Jehovah's fiercely competitive chauvinist, my grandfather was always vulnerable to the dashing of his hopes, the way they were dashed when he learned that there had been no bar mitzvah for Ike, and when he learned that he had mistakenly been counting Danny Thomas as part of our team.

One day shortly after we had picked up Edward G. Robinson, I came running to him and said, "Gramp, I just saw Mayor Wagner in a *yarmulke!* It was on the *news!*"

"Mayor *Wagner?*" he said. "One of *our . . .*" And then he suddenly remembered and smiled indulgently, the way Audubon must have looked when one of his students called a red-eyed vireo a wren. "No, he's a Gentile, I'm afraid. But La Guardia was *half.*"

"Nuts," I said. "I was ready for a Wagner run, maybe even to Honus. We need more than Greenberg in the Hall of Fame."

"Runs come hard," he said. "Remember when you thought that Richard Rodgers would give us Roy?"

Our collection wasn't involved in trades, but we did have a loss from time to time. My grandfather managed to sustain several days of gloom after Leonard Warren, the great baritone, had converted to Christianity. Luckily it wasn't long before our team got Elizabeth Taylor.

"We picked up a ton of beauty," I said to him when Liz signed on, "but we're still short a baritone."

"It's okay," he said, "we're deep in tenors."

He meant that splendid combination of Tucker and Peerce; and I knew it wouldn't be long before we drafted a baritone—not a richly Judaic Al Jolson, of course, but someone with a name like Laurence Witherspoon, who went to synagogue on the sly.

My desire to please my grandfather by building the collection was so intense that there was a moment when I almost ran a check on Cardinal Spellman because I met a Herbie Spellman and I found out he was Jewish.

"Wouldn't that have been something," my grandfather dreamily said. "But keep aiming high, Ralphie, because you never can tell. We have the Lord Mayor of Dublin, you know."

He died a few years ago, too soon to see the glory of Cosell or Kissinger, or the conversion of Rod Carew, who turned Jewish while leading the league. At the time of his death, I had just begun to check out something that might have kept him alive forever. I had heard that Christopher Columbus sometimes used Hebrew to sign his name.

●

Fresh from Europe, a Jew sees another Jew reading the Yiddish paper on a park bench, on the Sabbath, smoking a cigar. "America is wonderful," he says. "Here even the goyim can read Yiddish!"

●

Stein, who knew no English, opened a bank account and signed with two X's, as was the custom in those days. A few years later, having prospered, he came to the bank to make a large deposit. This time he signed with three X's.

"Mr. Stein," said the teller. "Why do you now use three X's?"

Stein blushed. "Oh, you know women," he said. "Now that we're rich, my wife wants me to take on a middle name."

●

ON his first day in America, the new immigrant went straight to the Automat, where he was seen feeding one nickel after another into the cherry pie slot.

"Are you crazy?" his cousin asked him. "You already have a dozen pieces of pie!"

The greenhorn replied, "What's it to you if I keep winning?"

The eye is small—but it sees the world.

ABRAHAM SHULMAN

The Lecture

The lecture was a calamity from the very beginning. I arrived by train in this remote town and nobody was waiting at the station as previously arranged. This was in itself aggravating. I called the secretary and his tone was cool and unfriendly. He advised me to get a cab and go to a hotel where the executive committee had reserved a room. He said he would come and pick me up shortly before the lecture.

The hotel was a dilapidated affair. The bellboy was an elderly half-blind and completely deaf gentleman who took me to my sixth-floor room in an antiquated elevator operated by a rope. The room was small. The walls were covered with black wallpaper, and the floor was waxed with some black shiny wax. There were only three pieces of furniture: a black wardrobe, a black rocking chair, and a huge bed covered with a black spread.

My mood was already gloomy, and was further depressed by the arrival of the secretary, a silent and irritable man, who didn't even try to suppress his impatience. He took me in his car —a black limousine—to the hall, which was half filled with a few dozen elderly people. The chairman introduced me briefly and then sat back, already bored. The subject of my lecture, "The Magic of Jewish Folklore," required a different setting. I must have looked miserable, because the majority of the listeners sat fidgeting in their seats. Before the lecture, which dragged hopelessly, was over, a part of the audience began to sneak out through a back door. One of them was the secretary. After I finished, the chairman waited until everybody had gone. He then put out the lights, led me out through the front door into a completely deserted street, advised me to get a cab, and disappeared.

I returned to the hotel room in a black mood, lay down in the black bed (what gave my wife the idea of putting a black pair of pajamas into the suitcase?), and as soon as I closed my eyes, I sank into a series of black nightmares.

It must have been no more than six in the morning when my telephone rang. I grabbed the black receiver. "Genosse Shulman?" "Yes." "This is the chairman." "Yes?" "The chairman of your last night's lecture." "What happened?" "Nothing special. I just wanted to tell you that your lecture was a catastrophe."

"And to tell me this you wake me at six in the morning? You couldn't wait till later?"

"I could," he said, "but I wanted to be the first."

●

Abraham Shulman, formerly the editor of a Jewish daily newspaper in Paris, is currently a columnist for the New York *Jewish Daily Forward*. This selection is from his *Adventures of a Yiddish Lecturer*.

FRANKLIN DELANO ROOSEVELT, JEWISH HUMANITARIAN

Franklin Delano Roosevelt was the greatest humanitarian President in our history. He was virtually born to it. Ever since he could remember, the Roosevelt home was the great gathering place for the Jewish show business humanitarians of the day. The hostess and guiding force of this unusual salon was his warm and wonderful mother, Eleanor, a woman who later was often mistaken for his wife.

As a boy, young Franklin hobnobbed with George Jessel, Sophie Tucker, and Al Jolson. He learned his craft from these greats and near-greats. He learned that you have to have heart. He learned that if everyone just gave a little bit, someday a little child might walk again. He learned that money isn't everything. But he knew how to ask people to give and give till it hurts.

He studied Eulogy with Jessel. Sophie Tucker gave him lessons in Farewell Performances. Jolson taught him to speak with a tear in his voice. By the time he was elected President, he was a master humanitarian at the moment when his country needed him desperately.

During Roosevelt's reign the White House was like a borscht-belt hotel on a Labor Day weekend. Humanitarians were everywhere, including the young Dannys—Danny Kaye and Danny Thomas—Jerry Lewis, and elder statesman Jean Hersholt. The air was always full of eulogies, tributes, toasts, songs, and dances.

These were the days of the famous Roosevelt Brain Trust, the team that helped launch the legislation of the New Deal. But behind the Brain Trust was Roosevelt's inner inner circle, the Borscht Belt Trust—or "Truss," as they called it—a small group of advisers who developed many of Roosevelt's greatest humanitarian ideas.

This group included comedian Jackie Joey, eccentric dancer Monte Mark, ex-boxer and restaurateur Tony Rocky, and Negro cantor Jesse Wayne. (Roosevelt used to say, "If you want to see a grown man cry and really shell out for a charity, ask Jesse to sing Kol Nidre. Every Jew is a sucker for a Negro cantor.")

The Borscht Belt Trust was largely responsible for such projects as the TVA, CCC, Social Security, and the Lend-Lease Act; and after World War II they laid the groundwork for Point Four and the Marshall Plan (an idea of Morty Marshall, a young ventriloquist Roosevelt adored, who died of throat cancer).

And behind everything was the persistent influence of Eleanor, who traveled around the world bearing small gifts, getting new humanitarian ideas, and never letting her son forget that "politics is like show business, and show business is people giving to people. And that's what great humanitarianism is all about."

"She was a real matzoh ball," FDR once said. "But she had a heart as big as a Seder table."

The day before his tragic death, Franklin Roosevelt was still dreaming up new humanitarian projects. He had an idea for one of his favorite causes, a polio foundation. It would be a twenty-four-hour radiothon that would be organized and produced by a young, eager Jerry Lewis. Lewis was one of the last men to see and work with FDR.

●

☆☆☆☆☆☆☆☆☆☆☆☆☆☆☆☆☆☆☆☆☆☆☆☆☆☆☆☆☆☆☆☆☆☆

I can understand why we can't have a Jewish President. It would

be embarrassing to hear the President's mother screaming at the

grandchildren: "Who's Grandma's baby! Who's Grandma's baby!"

". . . And this is Chet Huntley in New York. The First Lady's mother

opened the Macy's Day Parade screaming, *'Oy, zeishint minemine lieber'*

and furiously pinching young Stanley's cheeks . . ."

    Actually, she bit his ass,

    going, "Oom, yum yum,

    is this a tush,

    whose tushy is that?"

☆☆☆☆☆☆☆☆☆☆☆☆☆☆☆☆☆☆☆☆☆☆☆☆☆☆☆☆☆☆☆☆☆☆

Lenny Bruce, *How to Talk Dirty and Influence People*

"Screw the Jews"

Paul Jacobs, who died in 1978 at the age of sixty, functioned in a variety of roles: union organizer, staff member of the American Jewish Committee, writer, editor, speaker, and general political activist. He was an early opponent of nuclear energy, and was involved in the founding of both *Ramparts* and *Mother Jones* magazines. This selection is from his memoir *Is Curly Jewish?*

What does the American Jewish Committee do? And what about all those other Jewish organizations—the Anti-Defamation League, the American Jewish Congress, the American Council for Judaism, the Jewish Labor Committee, and the American Zionist Council—what do they do?

A fanciful way of describing the work of these groups is that some guy walks into the toilet of a gin mill on Third Avenue, New York, and while he's standing at the urinal, he notices that someone has written "Screw the Jews" on the toilet wall. He goes outside and immediately calls up the Anti-Defamation League of B'nai B'rith and the other organizations. An ADL man rushes down to the bar, carefully dusts the wall with fingerprint powder, photographs the prints, and goes back to the ADL office to check them against the two million prints of known anti-Semites. Thereupon the ADL publishes a photo of the slogan in its bulletin, proving that anti-Semitism is on the increase in the United States and, therefore, everybody should join B'nai B'rith.

When the man from the American Jewish Committee arrives at the bar, he purses his lips, studies the slogan from all angles, and leaves quietly. Shortly thereafter, the Committee announces that it is making a large grant to a social science research center at Columbia University to do a survey of anti-Semitic wall writing since the burial of Pompeii. At the same time, its own staff writes a pamphlet proving that Jews invented the martini. This pamphlet is then exhaustively pre-tested and tested for its effect by the AJC's research department. After all the bugs in the pamphlet are taken out and all possible "boomerang" effects eliminated, it is distributed by all the liquor dealers in the country, to be put in bars where drinkers can pick it up to read while they are getting stoned. The AJC also announces that at its next annual meeting, a distinguished medical authority will address the members on "Alcoholism and Anti-Semitism: A Clinical View," to be followed by a workshop discussion.

The American Jewish Congress representative shows up at the bar, and while he is inside the toilet looking at the writing, two dozen pickets from the organization are already marching up and down outside, carrying signs that say "Tear Down the Wall!" and "We Demand Action by the UN!" Back at the Congress's national office, the legal staff is busily preparing a brief, to be taken to the Supreme Court the next morning, requesting the Court to issue an order forbidding the sale of liquor to anyone making an anti-Semitic remark.

Meanwhile the Jewish Labor Committee is arranging a

whole series of weekend institutes for members of the bartenders union. At these institutes, speakers will discuss the history of the AFL-CIO, pointing out that Samuel Gompers, its founder and first president, was Jewish, and that Arthur Goldberg began his notable career as a CIO attorney. In the weeks that follow, every state AFL-CIO convention will pass a resolution, sponsored by the JLC, calling on union members not to pee in anti-Semitic urinals.

The American Council for Judaism calls a press conference in a fancy New York hotel, where its spokesman, flanked by two Arabs representing the American Friends of the Middle East, make a statesmanlike statement which has already been delivered to the U.S. Secretary of State. In the statement the Council denies that anyone could have written "Screw the Jews" on the toilet wall because in America there is no such thing as a Jew, but only Americans of Jewish descent, and pretty vague descent at that. The Council, therefore, calls upon the Secretary of State, the President, and all the governors in the country to condemn strongly the efforts of Israel and the Zionists to identify Israel with American Jews.

Finally, the American Zionist Council steps into the picture. Its operation is the simplest and easiest to understand. It simply borrows the photo of the slogan taken from the ADL and reprints it in the AZC bulletin under the caption: "If you [not us, of course] emigrate to Israel, you can write 'Screw the Christians' on the toilet walls there."

●

A STRANGER once came to town to look for Rubenstein, president of the synagogue.

"Which Rubenstein are you looking for?" he was asked. "Oh, *that* Rubenstein, who had the episode with the servant girl, the one who mumbles all the time. You'll find him downtown, living near the synagogue."

Finding his way downtown, the stranger asked again. "Ah, yes, Rubenstein," said the storekeeper. "Never pays his bills. Always in debt, that man. Don't sit down to play cards with him, either. Sure, you'll find Rubenstein living on Main Street."

When he got to Main Street, the stranger knocked on the door of the first house he came to. "Ah, Rubenstein," said the woman who answered the door. "He lives at the end of the block. Treats his wife terribly, by the way. You'll know the house because it's falling apart and needs a paint job."

Finally, the stranger caught up with Rubenstein. "It wasn't so easy to find you," he said. "Tell me, why are you president of the synagogue? What could it possibly do for you?"

"Not much," conceded Rubenstein. "But you know how it is. Every man likes a little *kavod.*"

Kavod (honor, glory, respect) has traditionally operated as the coin of the realm in Jewish organizational life. Often awarded in lieu of money for volunteer work, it can also be purchased—for the price of a new building, which entitles the buyer to a plaque and to name the building.

In a variant of this joke:

Rubenstein is slandered at great length by one man. "How do you know so much about him?" asks the stranger.

"Rubenstein?" the man replies. "We've been best friends for years!"

Light bulb jokes swept the country in 1980, as this book was being completed. They are thought to be spin-offs of Polish jokes:

How many Poles does it take to change a light bulb?

Three—one to hold the bulb and two to turn the ladder.

How many WASPs does it take to change a light bulb?

Two—one to call the electrician and one to mix the drinks.

How many Californians does it take to change a light bulb?

Four—one to change the bulb and three to share the experience.

How many psychiatrists does it take to change a light bulb?

Only one—but the bulb has to *want* to change.

How many graduate students does it take to change a light bulb?

Only one—but it takes nine years.

How many Jewish mothers does it take to change a light bulb?

None. "It's all right—I'll sit in the dark!"

The Jewish versions of the light bulb joke, by Don Cashman, appeared in the magazine *Shma.*

HOW many Lubavichers does it take to replace a light bulb? Three—one to screw it in and two to convince everyone else to do it too.

HOW many Satmarers does it take to replace a light bulb? Two—one to screw it in and another to denounce it as a Zionist plot.

HOW many Bratzlavers does it take to replace a light bulb? Bratzlavers don't replace light bulbs, because they know they'll never find one as good as the old one.

HOW many Zionists does it take to replace a light bulb? Four—one to stay home and convince someone else to do it, a second to donate the bulb, a third to screw it in, and a fourth to proclaim that the entire Jewish people stands behind their actions.

HOW many Jewish American Princesses does it take to replace a light bulb?
Two—one to pour the Tab, the other to call Daddy.

Dick Codor © 1980

Jacob's Dream

REFORM

A REFORM rabbi was so compulsive a golfer that once, on Yom Kippur, he left the house early and went out for a quick nine holes by himself. An angel who happened to be looking on immediately notified his superiors that a grievous sin was being committed on earth.

On the sixth hole, God caused a mighty wind to take the ball directly from the tee to the cup for a miraculous and dramatic hole in one.

The angel was horrified. "Lord," he said, "you call this a punishment?"

"Sure," answered God with a smile. "Who can he *tell?*"

Dick Codor © 1981

A SUBURBAN family bought a new Mercedes and wanted a rabbi to bless it. They called the Orthodox rabbi.

"Rabbi, would you make a *bracha* over our Mercedes?"

"How can I do that?" he replied. "I don't even know what a Mercedes is."

Next they called a Conservative rabbi.

"Rabbi, would you make a *bracha* over our Mercedes?"

"I'm sorry," he replied. "I don't know if I can or not."

Finally, they called a Reform rabbi.

"Rabbi, would you make a *bracha* over our Mercedes?"

"Sure," he replied. "But what's a *bracha?*"

T HREE Reform rabbis are bragging over who has the most progressive temple. "In our temple," says the first, "we have ashtrays in the pews so that our congregants can smoke during the Torah reading."

"That's nothing," says the second rabbi. "In our temple we serve a special snack during Yom Kippur—ham sandwiches."

"Not bad," says the third rabbi, "but in our temple, when Rosh Hashanah and Yom Kippur come around, we simply put up a big sign: 'Closed for the Holidays.' "

It is those at the far ends of the religious spectrum who are most often —and most easily—satirized: Hasidim, for their belief in miracle workers, and Reform Jews, who are routinely depicted as though they were not Jewish at all.

Reform Judaism has been attacked by more observant Jews ever since it began, in nineteenth-century Germany. In an early parody, taking off on a rabbinical conference held in Frankfurt in 1845, the writer imagines conversations between the attendant at the convention hall and various Jewish celebrities, both living and dead, who seek in vain to gain entrance. One of them is Judah Ha-Nasi, editor of the Mishnah, who proposes a new edition of that work, which now includes *Seder Kela-lot*—the order of curses—a catalog of terms of abuse against more traditional Jews, as well as *Massechet Sonntag*—a treatise on the observance of Sunday instead of Saturday.

Off-the-cuff quips about Conservative Jews are made all the time, but very few of these exist as actual jokes. The same is true for Reconstructionists, although it is sometimes said that for Reconstructionists, there is no God, and Mordecai Kaplan is His prophet, or that Reconstructionists address their prayers "to whom it may concern."

Mel Brooks Is God

Gerald Sussman is the editor of *National Lampoon,* where this piece first appeared.

His religion is simply called *The Mel Brooks Religion.* His houses of worship are called *Houses of Brooks.* They are actually perfect replicas of the old neighborhood movie theaters Brooks used to attend as a child, the Saturday matinee temples where we all used to worship our screen gods. The Houses of Brooks hold Saturday matinee services, complete with prayers, litanies, blessings, and hymns, all derived from the Works of Brooks—jokes, shticks, skits, and pieces of business from his movies, records, and TV shows.

Brooks designed every detail of his temples. Admission charge is eleven cents. All candy costs five cents; popcorn is ten cents. The Houses emit strange, musty odors with undertones of urine. The carpeting is a hideous brownish maroon, and is covered with Pepsi-Cola stains. Some of the seats are ripped. Others have broken springs. The usherettes are stern-faced women in their fifties who wear white uniforms and are called "matrons." Paper clips and rubber bands, essential weapons of Brooks's youth, are available for shooting at friends and at the screen. The decor is imitation Art Deco.

Some of the highlights of the Brooks service: After Horseplay (shooting paper clips, kicking and punching your friends, screaming and yelling, etc.), the head of the congregation, called a *Bernie,* leads the opening blessing, "Blessed Art Thou, O Brooks Our God, Creator of the Comic Universe and the nectarine." The Bernie shouts at the congregation, "I love your face!" The congregation shouts back, "You're so pretty!" The Bernie replies, "Chocolate is terrible for your teeth!" The congregation answers, "Are teeth so good for chocolate?" And so it goes for another few minutes, the group exchanging Brooksisms, *bons mots* they have picked up from Brooks's regular interviews and public appearances.

Among other items, the Houses of Brooks sell Mel Brooks T-shirts (he likes the one where he looks like Fred Astaire, in white tie and tails, dancing on a piano, in what looks like heaven); the Mel Brooks candy bar, called an *Embee,* after his initials, M.B.—a combination of Raisinettes, Milky Ways, Hersheys with almonds, and O'Henrys; the M.B. Jewish Jesse Owens sneakers, and the M.B. Spaldeens, the pink rubber ball used for street games in the Brooklyn of his youth.

Mel Brooks in Chopped Liver

Tales of the American Masters

SUCCESSION

Gary Epstein is a writer living in Iowa. These tales, which at first appear anti-Hasidic, are actually a parody of American Jews from an Orthodox perspective. They appeared originally in *Moment* and *Response* magazines.

Buber reports that no successor was found in Berditchev after the death of Levi Yizchak; there was no one who could take his place. Remarkably, after the death of Rabbi Swift in Sitka, Alaska, a similar situation prevailed.

Dick Codor © 1981

A TZADDIK

Dick Codor © 1981

We have all heard of the famous Berditchever Rebbe's refusal to blow the shofar on Rosh Hashanah until God showed the same degree of kindness toward His own people that he showed toward the Gentiles. *"Loz* Ivan *Blozen Shoifer!"* he cried. "Let Ivan the Gentile blow the shofar, for You have treated him as Your very own."

But how many of us have heard of Rabbi Jackson in Tallahassee, who not only had a Gentile blow the shofar, but also had a female choir and a Lutheran cantor?

That is a *tzaddik.*

Dick Codor © 1981

ACCOUNTABILITY

It is told of the famous Reb Isaac of Houston that he was once approached by a former disciple who had abandoned strict observance of the traditions after becoming a successful and prosperous businessman.

"Rabbi," said the man, for he always called him that, "I know that I have sinned, but now I am in dire need of help and there is no one else to whom I can turn."

Reb Isaac smiled. "By coming to me you have shown that your faith has never truly left you. Tell me, my son, what your problem is."

The businessman explained that he was heavily in debt, and that unless his upcoming annual sale was a great success, he would be ruined.

After pondering for a brief moment, the rabbi responded: "Your sale will be more of a success than you could ever have hoped for. But there is one condition."

"Anything," breathed the merchant.

"You must sign this pledge to donate half the profits from your sale to the shul."

The merchant agreed and, in high spirits, left the rabbi. For weeks he prepared for the event, and sure enough, it was a huge success, more than doubling the volume of the previous year's sale. After his initial joy wore off, though, the merchant again became troubled and again sought out the rabbi, who, with a benign smile on his saintly, shining face, was eagerly awaiting him.

"Have you brought your donation, my son?"

"Yes, Rabbi, here it is. And the sale was a great success. But, Rabbi, if I give you this money, all the extra profits will be gone!"

The rabbi, who was also a CPA, snatched the check and grinned, his eyes sparkling. "Ah, my son," he explained, "but this is deductible."

And so it was.

MESSIAH

A disciple once jokingly asked Rabbi Brown, Jr., of Fresno, a Reform rabbi, whether the Messiah would be Orthodox, Conservative, or Reform.

The rabbi thought a brief moment and answered, "Orthodox. That way everyone will eat in his house."

Dick Codor © 1981

EXODUS

After the summer riots in Newark, his beleaguered students approached Reb Gavriel the Wise and exclaimed, "Rabbi, what shall we do? Our homes are threatened, our stores gutted by fire, and our very persons endangered."

The rabbi thought for a brief moment, looking up from his books.

"Let us move to South Orange," he intoned.

And the congregation blushed.

TRADITION

When the great Rabbi Israel Baal Shem-Tov saw misfortune threatening the Jews, it was his custom to go into a certain part of the forest to meditate. There he would light a fire, say a special prayer, and the miracle would be accomplished and the misfortune averted.

When the great Maggid of Montana saw misfortune threatening the Jews, it was his custom to go off into the woods and smoke some grass. The misfortunes came and went, but the Maggid was averted.

PROPOSITION

It is said that the *tzaddik* of Concord, a man of great charm and physical beauty, was once propositioned by a beautiful member of the DAR.

The rabbi looked at her for a moment, smiled, and said, "Sure."

TEMPTATION

The St. Paul *tzaddik* used to confuse the Evil Urge by giving in without a struggle.

Dick Codor © 1981

DAN BEN-AMOTZ
There's More Ways Than One to Kill a Joke

THE PRELIMINARY QUESTION TECHNIQUE

You must have heard the one about the Jew who comes to Haifa port trying to smuggle two sacks of coffee and when they ask him, "What've you got in the sacks?" he says, "Bird feed." And then when they ask him, "Since when do birds eat coffee?" he says, "They'll eat if they want; if they don't, they won't." Don't you know that one? Okay, so listen: There was this Jew at Haifa port with two sacks of coffee . . .

Dan Ben-Amotz, an Israeli humorist and satirist, was born in Poland in 1924 and came to Palestine in 1938. He is the author of two collections of essays and several novels, and has edited an anthology of Israeli humor and *The World Dictionary of Hebrew Slang.*

THE QUESTION TECHNIQUE

Do you know the one about the guy who said, they'll eat if they want; if they don't, they won't?

THE PERSONAL STORY TECHNIQUE

About two months ago, when I came home from a trip to Italy, I got off the ship at Haifa port and was waiting for them to inspect my luggage at customs. I was standing there and in front of me was this man with two big sacks and some sort of suitcase in his hand. I didn't notice anything special about him; you know, I didn't expect anything to happen. Anyway, this customs officer comes over and asks him very politely, "What have you got in those sacks, sir?" and the man says to him, "Bird

feed." That was when I figured there was something funny going on. Then the officer says to him, "Would you mind opening the sacks, sir?" So the man opens the sacks, and what do you think they are full of? Coffee! So the officer says to him, "Why did you tell me bird feed when it's coffee? Since when do birds eat coffee?" I felt like butting in right then and there, but this man in front of me said . . .

THE SURPLUS DETAILS TECHNIQUE

There was this man whose name was, I think, Rabinowitz, who'd been living in France all his life. Well, one day he got a letter from his sister in Tel Aviv, and she wrote to him that she had a headache and she hadn't been feeling at all well recently and things weren't so great with her in general. It doesn't matter. Anyway, she wrote him: It's getting close to Passover, maybe you come to Israel to visit for a while. We'll take a tour to Galilee, there's a lot of beautiful flowers up there now. . . . The man liked the idea and decided to take the trip.

But he must bring his sister some sort of present. Now, what sort of present do you bring to Israel? So he went to the *pletzl* in Paris and asked around what's worthwhile to take to Israel these days. And they told him, "You can bring all sorts of things. You can bring wristwatches in sardine cans; diamonds on your person, radio sets inside a steam roller. It depends what you want. Tell us what you want." So he said, "I don't want to fool around with anything really black market; I'd like something simple, something to eat or drink. . . ."

So they told him, "To eat or drink? Take coffee!" So Rabinowitz asked them, "What sort of coffee is it worthwhile to take?" and they told him, "There's Turkish coffee, and there's Brazilian coffee, and there's this kind of coffee and there's that kind of coffee. . . . It all depends what you want."

So he bought two sacks of fine Argentinian coffee and started out on his trip to Israel. Now, he was, what'll I tell you, about forty-five years old at the time and on arriving in Haifa . . .

THE NEGLECTED CRUCIAL FACTS TECHNIQUE

A Jew once came to Haifa, got off the ship and went to customs. The officer asked him, "What've you got here?" and he said, "Bird feed." Oh, oh—just a minute. I forgot to tell you he was trying to smuggle in two sacks of coffee. So the officer saw the coffee and asked, "What's this?" and the man told him, "It's bird feed. . . ."

THE CULTURAL JOURNAL TECHNIQUE

Customs Official: What have we here?

The Jew: Nourishment for our feathered friends.

Customs Official: How now? Do our feathered friends consume coffee?

The Jew: If they so wish, they may consume as much as is their hearts' desire.

THE LITERAL-MINDED TECHNIQUE

A literal-minded gentleman heard the joke and said to himself: That's a good idea. He traveled abroad, bought two sacks of coffee, and came back with them to Haifa and customs. The customs officer asked him, "What have you got in those sacks?" The literal-minded gentleman promptly replied, "What I've got here is coffee for the birds."

Quoth the customs officer: "But, sir, birds don't eat coffee!" Quoth the literal-minded gentleman: "What do you mean, they don't eat coffee? There is one bird of the Litesrobucolo genus, of the Red Ribucoli family, that eats coffee when it has nothing else to eat."

THE MORAL OF THE STORY TECHNIQUE

A Jew comes up to customs in the Haifa port. The official asks him, "What have you got here in these sacks?" and the Jew answers him, "Where there's a will, there's a way." The official asks him, "What's that meant to mean?" and the Jew explains, "You'll see right away. These sacks of mine contain bird food." "Now open the sacks." The official sees that it's coffee, and says, "How's that? Since when do birds eat coffee?" The Jew shrugs his shoulders and says, "Didn't I tell you: Where there's a will, there's a way."

THE LACK OF CONFIDENCE TECHNIQUE

—Izzy, tell the joke about the coffee and the birds.

—Everybody knows that one.

—Tell it, Izzy, tell it.

—All right, all right. This here Jew came to Haifa. . . . He wanted to smuggle in two sacks of . . . You know the joke!

—We don't know it. Tell it, tell it!

—There's no point in telling a story everybody knows.

—Go ahead, tell it. We don't know it.

—All right. He wanted to smuggle in these two sacks of coffee. So the customs official asks him, "What have you got in these sacks?" So he says . . . You know the joke. Look, you're laughing already. . . . There's no point telling something everybody knows. . . .

Wife: Abie, tell that joke about the Jew who was smuggling coffee.

Husband: There's no point. Everybody knows the story.

Wife: Tell it, tell it. You tell it so nicely.

Husband: All right, I'll tell it. This Jew once brings two sacks of coffee to Haifa. When he goes into customs, the officer says to him . . .

Wife: It wasn't in Haifa. It was in Lydda.

Husband: It doesn't matter. What difference does it make? So this officer says to him, Open the sacks . . .

Wife: But it does make a difference. The whole thing is that he brought the sacks by plane and it cost him a small fortune. Why, that's the whole point of the story. . . .

●

AFTER an hour of standing in line at the bank, Chaim was furious. "I hate all this waiting!" he shouted to his wife. "I'm leaving. I'm going to kill Ben-Gurion."

An hour later, he returned to the bank. "What happened?" asked his wife, who was still waiting in line.

"Nothing," said the unhappy man. "There was a longer line over there."

AN Israeli dies and is greeted by Ben-Gurion, who offers to guide him through both heaven and hell, so that he can make up his own mind about where to spend eternity.

He goes first of all to heaven, which is filled with clouds, angels with harps, heavenly choruses, sweetness and light. Then he decides to look at hell—and hell turns out to be something else again. Wonderful parties, wild gambling, terrific bargains, outrageous food. The man doesn't hesitate. "Send me to hell," he says.

But a moment later he is shaking his head in disbelief. Suddenly there are demons with pitchforks, and hot fires, and people being flogged. "Wait!" he cries out at the departing figure of his guide. "What happened? The hell that you showed me looked so good!"

"No," Ben-Gurion responds, "it just seemed that way. The first time you went, you were only a tourist. But now you're a permanent resident."

Mark Podwal © 1978

TEL AVIV *& Jerusalem*

So, one afternoon I found myself in Tel Aviv, after the completion of all due formalities, with about one thousand pounds in my pocket. Not that a thousand pounds is a lot of money, objectively speaking, but it was ten times as much as I'd ever had before. So I wasn't objective. It called for a party. In Jerusalem all you had to do was say out loud, "I want a party!" and you had a party. Tel Aviv was different—probably because it is built on sand and not on rock, as the queen of cities is, and no matter what you do, you can't leave your mark on the sand; you have a feeling in Tel Aviv that nothing, neither love nor life, nor any other form of art, has any permanence. It drives company directors to make love to their secretaries, and serious writers to publish weekly articles in the newspapers. Of course, people lay their secretaries in Jerusalem too, and there are even some writers there who deliver themselves of occasional utterances in the prophetic vein, but it is all done with a difference. There's a feeling of perspective about it, a sense of History, of the thousands of secretaries who came before, and of the thousands who will come after, of a broad river of words, an Amazon of printed matter, rolling leisurely toward the horizon. When you make love in Jerusalem you can hear the beating of the wings of Time which gives the fleeting moment its sweet sadness. All I ever heard in Tel Aviv when making love was the creaking of the bedsprings. Of course, I may be prejudiced.
Yoram Matmor

CHAIM BERMANT

Covering the Yom Kippur War

Chaim Bermant, who was born in Glasgow and lives in England, is the author of several books, including *The Jews,* and *The Patriarch,* a novel.

The main anxiety of troops at the front seemed to be the worry they were causing at home, and every correspondent who moved among them was piled high with telephone numbers. Could I phone a wife, a mother, a girl friend, and tell her everything was all right? It proved to be a more difficult undertaking than I imagined, for apart from anything else, it is a good deal easier to phone London from Tel Aviv than to phone Jerusalem, or even another part of Tel Aviv; then, when one finally did get through, it was not all that easy to keep the conversation brief. One sometimes got the impression that the entire population was sitting by the phone hoping for, and yet dreading, a call. The receiver was snatched as soon as the phone rang, and there came an anxious, troubled voice: "Yes, yes, who's that? What is it?" And the grateful relief when one finally delivered the greeting. There was one exchange in particular which I noted down, for it summed up for me the Jewish capacity to shore up real fears with imaginary ones:

"Hullo," I began.

"Hullo? Who's that? What's that? Who are you?"

"My name is Bermant. I'm a journalist and I've just met your son."

"My son? How is he? Where is he? Is he all right? Nothing's the matter?"

"Not a thing. He's in fine spirits, fine shape."

"And?"

"And he asked me to give you his regards, and to tell you not to worry."

"Not to worry? If you had a son at the front, wouldn't you worry?"

"Of course I would, and he knew you would; that's why he asked me to tell you he's fine."

"He asked you to tell me?"

"Yes."

"You mean he's not fine, but he wants me to think he is?"

"No, he is fine; I saw him myself."

"Fine?"

"Perfectly."

"Then why didn't he phone himself?"

"Because he's in the middle of the desert."

"My neighbor's son is in the middle of the desert, and he phoned."

"Maybe he was near a telephone."

"If my neighbor's son could get to a telephone, why couldn't he? I've been going crazy with worry."

"Look, I saw him with my own eyes, and I can tell you you've nothing, but nothing, to worry about."

"You sure?"

"I'm sure."

"You're not just saying it to cheer me up?"

"I'm not just saying it to cheer you up."

"Because if there's something wrong I want to know it. People treat us like children; we're not children, you know."

"He's in perfect shape."

"Perfect?"

"Perfect."

"When did you see him?"

"Yesterday."

"And he was all right?"

"Fine."

"You speak Hebrew with an odd accent. Who are you?"

"I'm a foreign correspondent."

"If you're a foreign correspondent, how come you speak Hebrew?"

"Because I was interested in knowing Hebrew."

"You don't speak it very good."

"I'm a bad learner."

"What did you say your name was?"

"Chaim Bermant."

"Chaim?"

"Bermant."

"Any relation to the Bermans of Pardess Hannah?"

"Not that I know of."

"Like it here?"

"Very much."

"It's even nicer in peacetime."

"I'm sure it is."

"Why don't you come and settle?"

AN Israeli visiting Paris goes to a brothel and insists on the services of a certain Michelle. He is told that Michelle is unavailable, but when he offers a thousand dollars, she is brought to him, and they spend the night together. The next night the Israeli returns and repeats his generous offer—and again the third night.

Finally, on the third night, Michelle asks why she has been singled out for all this flattering attention.

"Well," says the man, "you see, I'm from Israel—"

"Why, so am I!" says Michelle.

"Yes, I know," the Israeli replies. "It turns out that your grandmother lives in the same building as my parents, and when she heard I was going to Paris, she asked me to give you the three thousand dollars you had asked for!"

ARABBI is walking down the street in Israel on the Sabbath, when a fifty-shekel note falls out of his pocket. Horrified, one of his disciples asks him, "Rabbi, how can you violate the commandment against carrying money on *Shabbas?*"

The rabbi replies, as he bends to pick up the cash, "Oh, this? You call this money?"

ATEXAN is visiting Israel, and feeling thirsty, he stops at a house along the road. "Can you give me a drink of water?" asks the Texan.

"Of course," says the Israeli, and invites the Texan to come in.

"What do you do?" says the Texan.

"I raise a few chickens," says the Israeli.

"Really?" says the Texan. "I'm also a farmer. How much land do you have?"

"Well," says the Israeli, "out front it's fifty meters, as you can see, and in the back we have close to a hundred meters of property. And what about your place?"

"Well," says the Texan, "on my ranch, I have breakfast and get into the car, and I drive and drive—and I don't reach the end of the ranch until dinnertime."

"*Really,*" replies the Israeli. "I once had a car like that."

This joke was said to be a favorite in diplomatic circles, and was well received when told by Israeli delegates to their Egyptian counterparts at the initial round of peace negotiations in 1978.

In general, sex is mostly absent in Israeli jokes, and even in this joke the subject is not really sex, but money. For a nation that has yet to achieve solvency, money is the chief topic of humor:

How do you make a small fortune in Israel?
Come with a large one.

God asked Moses to choose whatever promised land he wished. After weighing several factors, Moses settled on California. But Moses, according to legend, had a speech impediment, and he began to answer, "Ca-Ca-" whereupon God said, "Canaan, that wasteland? Well, okay, Mo. If you want it, you got it!"

There are a number of jokes about the dedication of UJA workers.

•

Goldberg, skiing in the Alps, loses his way. A search party is sent out, and on the third day, Goldberg hears his name echoing through the mountains: "Goldberg . . . Goldberg . . . Where are you?!"

A feeble voice reaches the search party: "If this is the UJA, I gave at the office!"

•

Meyer Weisgal, the famous Zionist leader, was known as a master fund raiser, a man who knew how to talk to the rich. Apparently, Weisgal had invited a miserly but exceedingly rich man to lunch; when the meal was over, the man took out his checkbook and wrote out a check for twenty-five thousand dollars.

"Thanks a lot," said Weisgal disdainfully as he tore up the check, "but the meal has already been paid for."

•

This is one of several traditional Jewish jokes that are occasionally dramatized (usually by Bert and Ernie) on *Sesame Street*.

•

The afternoon was drawing to a close, and the guests were getting ready to leave. "Mrs. Goldberg," said one of the ladies, "I just wanted to tell you that your cookies were so delicious I ate four of them."

"You ate five," replied the hostess. "But who's counting?"

•

ONE day the UJA solicitor came to the home of John McLaughlin.

"We have you down for a five-hundred-dollar pledge," said the solicitor.

"But that's impossible," said John McLaughlin. "I didn't make a pledge, and besides, I'm not even Jewish."

"I'm very sorry," said the man from UJA, "but the UJA never makes a mistake. Are you sure you're not Jewish?"

"How can I prove it to you?" said John McLaughlin. "As you can see, I have a crucifix on the wall. And my mother, a piano teacher, used to direct the Christmas play at school every year. And even my father, *alav hashalom,* is buried in a Catholic cemetery."

REB ISAAC and Reb Jacob were fund raisers for competing yeshivas. Finding themselves having tea together at the home of a wealthy benefactor, they soon became involved in an intricate discussion of Talmudic law, and were interrupted only by the arrival of the hostess, who brought their tea. A moment later she returned with a platter containing two cookies. Both cookies were substantial, but one was considerably larger than the other.

Observing the rules of etiquette, both men continued talking, and did their best to ignore the cookies. But before long Reb Isaac reached over and grabbed the larger cookie, devouring it in three swift bites.

Reb Jacob looked on in astonishment. "I can't understand this," he said. "How can a great scholar like you be so ignorant of table manners?"

Reb Isaac looked surprised. "Wait a minute," he said. "What would you have done in my place?"

"What *any* gentleman would have done," sniffed Reb Jacob. "I would have taken the smaller cookie."

"So what are you getting excited about?" replied Reb Isaac with a grin. "Isn't that what you got?"

Gary Rosenblatt, who prematurely prepared this special tribute on the occasion of Israel's 100th anniversary, is the editor of the weekly *Baltimore Jewish Times*. His work has appeared in *Moment* magazine.

Iyar 4, 5808
May 14, 2048

THE JERUSALEM ROAST

Remember the Arabs?

A disappointingly small crowd turned out at Hebrew University last night to hear Professor Chaim Schwartz discuss what he called the "extinct but still intriguing Arab people."

Scholars who were present unanimously deplored the poor showing as Professor Schwartz declaimed detail after detail concerning the quaint people who once inhabited the vast area of the Middle East now used primarily for depositing oil-spills (with the Arabs no longer there, it was easy to gather momentum for a campaign advocating "Drop the gunk back where it came from.")

Professor Schwartz revealed that only 60 years ago more than a hundred million Arabs lived in some 21 Arab nations, all hostile to the Jewish state. But after the Israel-Arab peace agreement of 1979, when under strong U.S. pressure Israel agreed to give up all territory except for a section of Tel Aviv known as the Yarkon River, there was peace in the Mid-East for a short time. "Actually, only a very short time," said Professor Schwartz, checking his notes, "about twenty minutes."

"The Arabs felt they had gotten a raw deal and they waged war to reclaim the river area, which they said was the exact spot of their true and historic homeland. However, at that moment Israel discovered a vast oil reservoir under the Yarkon. The Americans immediately came to Israel's aid and together they defeated the Arabs, whose survivors reportedly moved en masse to Argentina, where many are still thought to be living under assumed names."

Knesset Debates Treatment of West Bank Inhabitants

The Knesset today debated the question of what to do about the so-called "second-class citizens" of the West Bank.

"They are our brethren, after all, and we should treat them with compassion," a member of the Breira party said. But a member of the Sternstein party countered that the West Bank inhabitants are "different from us and not to be trusted—they are security risks, even if they do make up the vast majority of the population of Israel."

The West Bank has of course been the home for many years of Conservative and Reform Jews who have been critical of Israel's Orthodox control, and though they make up 94 percent of the Israeli population, they are prohibited from a variety of activities such as marrying, dying, giving birth, or mentioning the word "Seminary" in a public place.

News Briefs

Cannes, France—The Secretary-General of Histadrut issued another statement today praising the high level of Histadrut employee morale. The Secretary-General has been in Cannes at his villa for the past sixty days, investigating advanced health care concepts and studying new developments in actuarial theory.

London—The Royal Military Society gave this year's posthumous award for military genius to the late Ariel Sharon, in a ceremony held in Albert Hall. Previous winners of the award have been General George S. Patton and Attila the Hun.

Des Moines, Iowa—The Iowa chapter of Gush Emunim has set up civilian settlements in Des Moines, Cedar Rapids, and Ames as part of its plan to liberate "Biblical Iowa."

Jerusalem—The Minister of Finance refused again today to float the pound on the open market against the German Mark or the Japanese Yen. "Perhaps someday we shall float the pound against the mark," he said in an exclusive interview, "but never a yen."

Beersheva—Menachem Begin's great-grandson today obtained a long-sought ruling in probate court changing his name to Menachem Conclusion... "It was a hard fight," he said, "but I've finally shaken off this life-long embarrassment." Conclusion refused to reveal where he plans to take up residence, stating only that he will remain as anonymous as possible.

New York—An 800 page task force report issued today concluded that "Unless the present deplorable religious trend among American Jews is reversed, Judaism as we know it in America will cease to exist."

The report continues, "Unless Jews confront the threat of traditional Judaism which is attracting so many of our young people, no one will be left in future generations to concern him/herself with such major concerns as boycotting celery, tuna and marmalade, playing a bad game of tennis, or fostering participation in Ivy League language *ulpanim*, to name only a few potentially disastrous possibilities.

Anti-Aliyah Department Formed

The Jewish Agency has issued an urgent appeal to Jews from all over the world asking them to stay where they are.

"There are simply too many Jews living in Israel now," said a spokesman for the newly-formed Anti-Aliyah Department. He explained that the new department's predecessor, the original Aliyah Department, had been so successful over the years through its smoothly run, professionally staffed operation that Israel was filled to capacity.

The spokesman said that the new department plans to send *shlichim* (emissaries) all over Israel to promote the benefits of life in the Diaspora. "We're simply going to point to Jewish history and tell people, 'look, the Diaspora was our home for thousands of years and now it can be yours.'" He displayed a huge poster to be used in advertising campaigns which shows a crowded room of Talmudic scholars hovering over their texts. The large-sized caption reads: "This year in Babylonia—Renew Our Days As Of Old."

Yiddish Still Dying

New York—An urgent appeal has gone out to Jews all over the world to save the daily Yiddish newspaper, *The Forwards*, now in its 200th year of continuous publication.

A *Forwards* staffer deplored the fact that the Yiddish language is dying and cited as proof the fact that 42 books, 67 magazine articles and 2,800 doctoral dissertations have been published this year alone on the tragic theme that Yiddish is a forgotten language.

U.S.-Israel Peace Talks

Jerusalem—U.S. President George Barnett and Israeli Prime Minister Shoshana Vohu met here today regarding on-again off-again peace negotiations and though, as expected, no breakthroughs were announced, the two leaders pledged their commitment to the long-standing "special relationship" between the U.S. and Israel.

Talks focused on the role of an objective mediator, pressure for concessions, the need for secure borders, and the possibility of reassessment.

But the Jerusalem government asserted that it will continue to supply the U.S. with the sophisticated weapons Washington needs even if the U.S. and Canada are unable to resolve their bitter territorial dispute. Israel has also been aiding Canada.

Yesterday marked the ninth anniversary of America's attack on her northern neighbor. (Washington still insists on the term "defensive maneuver.") Israel has sought to act as an honest broker in the dispute, offering arms to the U.S. if it will agree to return Toronto to the Canadians, and lawyers to Canada if it will agree to withdraw its army from the Bronx. Israel's expanding law schools, already turning out enough lawyers to maintain 700 battle-ready regiments of military attorneys, anticipate no difficulty in fulfilling Canada's need for barristers.

"We do not expect peace overnight," an Israeli spokesman said, "but we are talking to both sides and will remain even-handed."

He rejected an American charge that Israel was tilting toward the Canadians in the dispute. The charge, which first appeared in America's most prestigious newspaper, the *National Inquirer*, asserted that since Israel received most of her lox from Canada, the Jerusalem government was bowing to Canadian lox pressure. The Canadian government recently limited the semi-annual price increase to eighteen percent in spite of increasing pressure from Nova Scotia separatists.

The Canadian Prime Minister is expected to follow President Barnett to Jerusalem in hopes of reviving the stalled Melbourne peace conference, and (continued on page 53)

Milky Way Kashrut Questioned

The religious controversy among Earth Jewry (Am Ha-Aretz) continues to rage on numerous fronts. The Rabbinical Council of Israel, meeting for thirty-nine hours last night, was no closer to resolving the question "What is a Jew?" at meeting's end.

Liberal rabbis argued that a Jewish Earth woman may marry a non-Jewish alien as long as the couple agrees to raise their children as human Jews (although some rabbis held out for the phrase "Jewish humans").

The council could not agree on whether to extend recognition to allegedly Jewish communities on Mercury, Venus, and Mars. The Jews of Mercury say they received a Pentateuch that includes among its Ten Commandments, "Thou shalt not covet thy neighbor's air-conditioner." The chief discrepancy found between the Venutian Torah and the Earth version is that rather than a great flood, the aquatic planet suffered a great drying-up, and the Venutian Noah is said to have constructed an enormous aquarium for the preservation of two of every Venutian species.

On Mars the Jews are divided between those who observe the lunar calendar keyed to Phobos, and those who follow a version based on Demos. The Demotic Jews persecute the Phobic sect as bitterly as both groups are persecuted by the Martian gentile majority.

Committees have invited Martian Jews to emigrate to Earth, but many who escape are making their homes on more attractive spheres such as Jupiter and Saturn, where the streets are allegedly lined with uranium.

On Earth, the powerful Reconstructionist branch is reported near schism over the problem of how to apply the term "humanism" to aliens, while the Lubavitcher Rebbe told a hastily convened press conference at his Waikiki home that Mitzvah-mobiles have landed on Pluto and Astro-Chassidim have successfully introduced *tallitot* and *t'fillin*. (The Rebbe issued an urgent plea for extra t'fillin, noting that Plutonians have three heads and eleven tentacles each).

The topic of interplanetary Yiddishkeit will be addressed at a Symposium here next week entitled, "Is the Milky Way Kosher?" Dynamic young Rabbi Gordon Glanz, author of *Chavurot in Space* and *Federation-Synagogue Tension on Uranus, A Case Study*, (continued on page 19)

Mark Twain and Sholom Aleichem

When Sholom Aleichem visited America in 1906, he was greeted with a host of parties and receptions. At one reception, Mark Twain was the special guest. Sholom Aleichem, so the story goes, was introduced to the American humorist as the "Jewish Mark Twain," to which Twain responded graciously, "Please tell him that I am the American Sholom Aleichem." Edward Field, born in 1924, is the author of *Stand Up, Friend, with Me; Stars in My Eyes; Variety Photoplays;* and *A Full Heart.*

Mark Twain and Sholom Aleichem went one day to Coney
    Island—
Mark wearing a prison-striped bathing costume and straw hat,
Sholom in greenish-black suit, starched collar, beard,
Steel-rimmed schoolmaster glasses, the whole works,
And an umbrella that he flourished like an actor,
Using it sometimes to hurry along the cows
As he described scenes of childhood in the village in Poland,
Or to spear a Jew on a sword like a cossack.

Sitting together on the sand among food wrappers and lost
    coins,
They went through that famous dialogue
Like the vaudeville routine After-you-Gaston:
"They tell me you are called the Yiddish Mark Twain."
"Nu? The way I heard it, you are the American Sholom Alei-
    chem."
And in this way passed a pleasant day admiring each other,
The voice of the old world and the voice of the new.

"Shall we risk the parachute jump, Sholom?"
"Well, Markele, am I properly dressed for it?
Better we should go in the water a little maybe?"
So Sholom Aleichem took off shoes and socks (with holes—a
    shame),
Rolled up stiff-serge pants, showing his varicose veins;
And Mark Twain, his bathing suit moth-eaten and gaping
In important places, lit up a big cigar,
And put on a pair of waterwings like an angel.

The two great writers went down where the poor
Were playing at the water's edge
Like a sewer full of garbage, warm as piss.
Around them shapeless mothers and brutal fathers
Were giving yellow, brown, white, and black children
Lessons in life that the ignorant are specially qualified to give:
Slaps and scoldings, mixed with food and kisses.

Mark Twain, impetuous goy, dived right in,
And who could resist splashing a little the good-natured Jew?
Pretty soon they were both floundering in the sea

The serge suit ruined that a loving daughter darned and
    pressed,
The straw hat floating off on the proletarian waters.

They had both spent their lives trying to make the world a
    better place
And both had gently faced their failure.
If humor and love had failed, what next?
They were both drowning and enjoying it now,
Two old men of the two worlds, the old and the new,
Splashing about in the sea like crazy monks.

YIDDISH

BERNSTEIN visits a kosher Chinese restaurant on the
Lower East Side, and to his great surprise, the Chinese
waiter addresses him in Yiddish.

On the way out, as he is paying the check, he says to the
proprietor, "You run a nice restaurant. And a Chinese waiter
who speaks Yiddish—what a wonderful gimmick that is."

"Not so loud," says the proprietor. "He thinks we're teaching him English."

BEFORE the war, there was a great international Esperanto
convention in Geneva. Esperanto scholars came from all
over the world to give papers about and to praise the idea of an
international language. Every country on earth was represented at the convention, and all the papers were given in Esperanto.

After the long meeting was finally concluded, the great
scholars wandered amiably along the corridors, and at last they
felt free to talk casually among themselves in their international language: *Nu, vos macht a yid?*

AFTER the war, a funeral procession was moving slowly
down a narrow street on the Lower East Side. Their route
took them past the offices of the last Yiddish newspaper left in
the city. One of the editors, looking out the window, saw the
funeral procession passing by and called to his colleague; "Hey,
Mottel, print one less!"

THE PASKEN & RABBIS ICE CREAM MENU

Pasken & Rabbis ice creams are available in cohens, frozen on a shtick, or in a plastic Yid-dish. In addition to their up-to-the-mitzvah selections of ice cream flavors, P. & R.'s also offers such taste treats as Tosefloats, Saturdaes, Madua-lo-diet freezes, the tantalizing Bamid-Bar, as well as traditional ice cream Sotahs in a variety of delicious flavors—the latter, of course, made with Korban-ated water and, if you wish, an extra pshat of seltzer.

And while our competitors may offer a multilayered Goyishe Cup, remember that only Pasken & Rabbis features a free sample of any flavor—which we call Bameh Madlickin'.

We are proud to continue our old and sacred tradition of serving a multitude of flavors, a custom which began with the sainted Ga'on of V'nila (may his memory be a dressing), who first claimed the mitzvah of Hachnassat ice cream.

His disciples, known as the Eggnogdim, carried on for generations a debate with the followers of the Baal Shempaigne over which scoop to put on top. Today, we abide by the decisions of the Ga'on's school, and we have adopted his famous slogan, "Talmond Tort K'neggnog Cool-lime."

Maccabean	Rhubarbanel	Af Al Pecan
Leviticustard	Chazalnut	Mi Kamocha
Olive Hashalom	Pear V'Chavod	Mizrachi Road
L'chu Vanillcha	Citrus D'Achra	Tora Shebe'al Pear
Oy Gemalt	Halva-Chomer	Chuppapaya
Wailing Walnut	Oy Vey Iz Mirachino Cherry	M'lo Kol Ha'aretz Avocado
Cherry Bim	Rashi Road	Butter Shkotz
Yasher Cocoach	Balak Berry	Prune Ur'voon
Bubble Gumora	Buberry	Brand Ice
Lemontations	Lubavicher Resberre	Olime Habah
Chocolitvak	Shulamit Spumoni	Asseret Yummy Chewvah
Hanava Bananot	Zalmond Schachter	Mi Kamarshmallow
Meshuganougat	Abba Ebanana	Berry P'ri Hagafen
Soda & Gomorra	Bernard Malamint	Britishman Date
Manishta Nut	Molly Pecan	Rav Kooconut
Rachma Nut	Cin'm'n Toff & Mazel Toff-ee	Weizmann Institutti-Frutti
Tisha B'Avarian Cream	Cashew LePesach	Carmel Shake
Moishmallow	Lehitra Oats	ChocEilat Chip
Maimonidip (Rumbomb)	Tzur Marshmalo	S. Y. Agnog
	Kol HakaVodka	

A MAN asks a passerby, "Do you speak Yiddish?" The man shakes his head. He asks a second man, but gets no answer. He stops a third man: "Do you speak Yiddish?"

"Of course."

"Please, vat time is it?"

A NEWCOMER to America took his pregnant wife to the hospital, but during the delivery of the twin babies, he fainted. His brother had to be brought in to name them.

"My brother named the kids?" he asked. "My brother is an idiot, a numskull. What did he call the girl?"

"He named the girl Denise."

"Denise? Well, that's not such a bad name. I kind of like it. And what did he call the little boy?"

"De Nephew."

AN elderly Jewish couple, on their way to a vacation in Hawaii, got into an argument about the correct pronunciation of Hawaii: he was sure it was Ha*v*aii, but she maintained it was Ha*w*aii.

As soon as they got off the plane, they ran over to the first person they saw. "Hi there," said the husband. "Would you mind telling me how you pronounce the name of this island?"

"Ha*v*aii," the man replied.

"Thank you," said the husband, gloating.

"You're velcome," the man replied.

A traditional background—or at least a working knowledge of Hebrew—is essential to understanding many of these puns, and we won't even try to explain them. To those whose tastes run in these directions, we offer several questions.

1. **Who are the three cowboys in Adon Olam?**

   BILLY REYSHEET, BILLY TACHLEET, and KID RUCHI.

2. **What did the robbers say when they held up a Lubavicher bank?**

   GIMMEE LOOT, HASIDIM!

3. **And what did they get away with?**

   LOOT OF THE FRUM.

This selection of ice cream flavors was compiled by the readers and editors of *Response,* a quarterly magazine of new and dissenting voices in the Jewish community.

Ferry Tale from Romplesealskin
for Nize Baby Wot Ate Opp
All de Crembarry Suss

Milt Gross (1895–1953) was a well-known cartoonist and author. He began his career by writing a satirical piece in dialect for the New York *World* to fill an empty space in that paper. He was the author of five books: *Nize Baby, Dunt Esk, De Night in de Front from Chreesmas, Famous Fimmales,* and *Dear Dollink.*

Oohoo, nize baby, itt opp all de crembarry suss so momma'll gonna tell you a ferry tale from Romplesealskin. Wance oppon a time was a werry, werry poor fommer wot he dicited wot he'll gonna go witt a weesit to de Keeng. So in horder he should make a imprassion on de Keeng wot he was a somebody so he cocknocted a skim witt a bloff. Wot he sad, he hed it a dudder, wot she could speen straw in a speening whill it should come out gold. Of cuss, she didn't rilly could, it was jost a hux on de pot from de fommer. (Nize baby, take anodder spoon crembarry suss.)

POT II

So de Keeng was all agrog from excitamment wot it stodded in to hitch by heem de palm. (He was a werry griddy micer.) So he lad her in a room wot it was full from straw, so he sad, "Nu, speen!" Und he locked de door und went away.

So de poor dudder was full from griff wot she deedn't know ivvin how to monopolate a speening whill. So she was seeting witt tears in de heyes, so all from a sodden it stood in de front from her a leedle Dwuff, witt beeg wheeskers, wot he sad:

"Why you wipping, leedle goil?"

So she oxplained heem de rizzon, so he sad, "Hm! Und soppose wot I do dees for you, wot you'll gonna geeve me?"

So she sad: "Mine ganuine poil nacklaze from hunbreakable poils."

So he sad: "Is a boggain!!" So he set don, so in fife meenits he spon de whole straw wot it was a room full from 14 kerrot gold!!

POT TREE

So de naxt monnink de Keeng was extrimmingly jubilious, wot he robbed gliffully de hends. Bot instat he should be setisfite, dot apparitious crichure, he lad her in de grend ballroom wot it was feeled witt straw, witt hay, witt hoats yat, so he sad: "Eef you'll gonna speen all dees stoff it should be gold so tomorrow, we'll gat gredually merried wot you'll be de Quinn. . . . Eef not — Hm, you gatting pale, ha? So take hidd!!!!"

POT FUR

So it came agan de Dwuff wot he sad, "Steel cryink, ha? So eef I'll gonna do for you dees job ulso, so you'll promise me wot de foist baby wot you'll gonna have so I could take heem away??"

So she tut: "Hm, who knows wot'll gonna be? Could be ivvin maybe tweens, wot nidder one is foist, so he'll gat it in de nack, dot dope." So she sad: "Ho K, is agribble by me!!" So he set don to speen, so de straw witt de hoats became solit gold.

POT FIFE

So she bicame gredually de Quinn wot she hed it a leedle baby —so wan day she was seeting so it came in all from a sodden de Dwuff wot he sad, "Ha, goot monnink, mine prout byooty!! You rimamber me, ha?? De keed himsalf!! Nu, so punny opp!! Come acruss witt de bret!!!"

So she stodded in to cry und to plid witt heem und to cux heem wot he took gredually compression on her, so he sad:

"I'll make you a preposition. In tree days time eef you'll gass by me de name, so you could kip de baby!"

POT SEEX

So a hull night long she was wrecking de brains she should tink from hodd names wot she put yat in de paper wot annyone wit a treek name so dey should sand it to de Quinn, so it came de naxt day de Dwuff wot he sad:

"Nu, geeve a gass!!"

So she sad: "Meetchel??"

So he sad: "Nup!!"

"Fillix??"

"Nup!!"

"Chake??"

"Nup (ha, ha)!!!"

"Hichabod??"

"Gatting warm, try agan!!!"

"Rastus??"

"Nup!!"

"Choolius??"

"N—n—nnn—"

"Helphonse??"

"Nup!!"

"Zik??"

"Nup!! It sims wot you heving a hod time, ha? So I'll be beck tomorrow und in de minntime you could lat me know where I could gat chip a goot creeb for de baby, ulso you'll geeve me a leest deeference tings wot I could fidd heem (ha, ha). Goot night!!"

THE VOCABULARY OF YINGLISH

A select listing of English words that sound as if they ought to be Yiddish

bedraggled	far-fetched	ladle	poised	box kite	fear-laden
lentil	seminal vesicle	cardigan	filch	melt	shush
conniption	fiscal	mental	shyster	coil	foible
mishmash	smuggle	dental	garnish	ploy	svelte

So de poor Quinn was at de weets-hend from dasparation, so jost den it came in a massanger wot he sad: "Hm! I was tooning in by de radio so it came in all from a sodden a strange wafe-lengt wot I hoid so a song in a werry piccooler woice wot it seng:

Today I brew, tomorrow I bake,
Naxt day de Quinn's keed I shell take.
Hm! I'm heppy! No one knows
Wot mine name is Romplesealskin!!!' "

So de Quinn was overjoined witt de noose, so it came in gredually de naxt day de Dwuff, so he sad: "Wal, wal, goot monnink. I was looking on some fine boggains from baby ker-riages!! Ulso I saw werry chip some nize neeples!! Is batter for de baby Grate Hay odder Grate Bee meelk?? Heh, ha, ha!! Nu, lat's gat don alrady to bress tecks!! Geeve anodder gass!!"

So she sad: "Is you name maybe Mex?"

"Nup!!"

"Dave??"

"Nup!!"

So she sad: "Could be maybe—Romplesealskin??"

YI YI YI YI YI YI YI—deed he geeve a jomp witt a lipp witt a bond hout from de chair wot he stodded in to scrim witt shrick, "Is a jeep!! Is a frame-opp!!! A fake!!! It teeped you huff a weetch!! A weetch!!! A WEETCH!!!!!!"

So he gave a stemp witt de foot so hod wot it stock in de grond.

So he trite he should pool himsalf hout so he gave sotch a pool de odder lag wot he turr himsalf in a heff!!!

(Hm! Sotch a dollink baby, ate opp all de crembarry suss!!)

> The novelist, what's his name, Markfield, has written in a story somewhere that until he was fourteen he believed "aggrava-tion" to be a Jewish word. Well, this was what I thought about "tumult" and "bedlam," two favorite nouns of my mother's. Also "spatula." I was already the darling of the first grade, and in every schoolroom competition expected to win hands down, when I was asked by the teacher one day to identify a picture of what I knew perfectly well my mother referred to as a "spatula." But for the life of me I could not think of the word in English.
>
> *Philip Roth,* Portnoy's Complaint

CURSES

May a child be named after you soon.

May you be known for your hospitality to God's creatures: lice, rats, bedbugs, fleas, worms, and maggots.

May your blood turn to whiskey, so that a hundred bedbugs get drunk on it and dance the mazurka in your belly button.

May the worms hold a wedding in your belly and invite all their relatives from Yehupetz to Slobodka.

May a trolley car grow in your stomach.

May your stomach churn like a music box.

May you be caught between a heifer and a bull who thinks he's Thomashefsky.

May onions grow in your navel.

May you lie in the earth and bake bagels.

May you be seized by a nine-year convulsion.

May all your teeth fall out—except one, so you can have a toothache.

May you turn into a *lulav,* so I can shake you for seven days and put you away for the rest of the year.

May your teeth get angry and chew off your head.

It is in the Yiddish curse that traditional Jewish humor expressed its aggressive and earthy side, and while these colorful phrases do lose something in translation, the imaginative energy in their hostility remains vivid and clear. Curses were especially useful to the *schnorrer;* the man who refused to give a donation might have this wished upon him: "May every kopeck in your pocket turn into a bomb and hurl your stingy flesh where even the Messiah can't find you!"

May God answer all your prayers—and then may He
mistake your worst enemy for you.

May Gypsies camp out in your belly and steal your guts
one by one.

May the heartburn after one of your meals be strong
enough to heat the Czar's palace.

May your corns grow higher than Mount Sinai.

May your bones be broken as often as the Ten
Commandments.

May your husband's father marry three times so you'll
have three mothers-in-law.

May the dybbuks of all King Solomon's mothers-in-law
settle in your mother-in-law and may they all nag you
at the same time.

May you fall into the outhouse just as a regiment of
Ukrainians is finishing a prune stew and twelve
barrels of beer.

May your enemies get cramps in their legs when they
dance on your grave.

May you back into a pitchfork and grab a hot stove for
support.

May you grow like an onion—with your head in the
ground.

I wish you everything you wish me, and everything
you'll regret not having wished me after I've wished you
everything I wish you.

Contemporary curses: May your neighborhood change!   May your son meet a nice Jewish
                                                                      doctor!

Mr. K ★ A ★ P ★ L ★ A ★ N's White Banner

The Education of H ★ Y ★ M ★ A ★ N ★ K ★ A ★ P ★ L ★ A ★ N by Leonard Q. Ross (Leo Rosten) was first published in book form in 1937, after the individual stories about a memorable participant in an immigrant night class in New York had appeared in *The New Yorker*. The book was such a huge success that Mr. Kaplan eventually made a triumphant return in a second volume of stories.

There was a period when dialect formed the backbone of popular Jewish humor in America, and even today there are joke tellers who would not dream of telling a Jewish joke without it. At the same time, the public use of dialect has always been a source of some discomfort and even controversy in a community obsessed with its image in the larger society. Nathan Ausubel, who used no dialect jokes in his collection, insisted that "Jewish dialect jokes are not Jewish at all, but the confections of anti-Semites who delight in ridiculing and slandering Jews." And indeed, reports folklorist Dan Ben Amos, who rejects this view, there was a period following World War II when dialect jokes were so closely associated with anti-Semitism that Jewish comedians were forced to retire from radio appearances under public pressure, or at least, to impose self-censorship.

"The issue," writes Ben Amos in "The 'Myth' of Jewish Humor," "was directly related to self-ridicule as a distinctive mark of Jewish humor." Those who opposed the use of dialect, Ben Amos continues, "violently objected to any ridicule of a trait to which Jews, as any other immigrants, are very sensitive, namely speech." But Ben Amos's own research, and that of the folklorist Richard Dorson, makes clear that Jews themselves are generally fond of dialect stories. Such jokes, he maintains, are "part of the repertoire only of second generation immigrants, whose own English is normative and who at the same time heard at home the accented speech of their parents."

It was only logical that, having drilled the class before the holidays on the writing of personal letters, Mr. Parkhill should now take up the business form with the beginners' grade. Business letters, indeed, might be even more practical from the students' point of view. They might want to apply for a job, or answer an advertisement, or things of that sort.

"The general structure of the business letter follows that of the personal letter," Mr. Parkhill had said. "It, too, requires the address, the date, a salutation, a final greeting or 'complimentary close.'" Then he had gone on to explain that the business letter was more formal in mood and content; that the address of the person or company to whom you were writing had to be included in the form of the letter itself, on the left-hand side, above the salutation; that both the salutation and final greeting were formalized: "Dear Sir," "Dear Sirs," or "Gentlemen," and "Yours truly," "Yours very truly," "Very truly yours." Mr. Parkhill was a conscientious teacher, and aware of the queer things some of the students had done with previous exercises, he was careful to introduce the beginners' grade to business letters with particular care.

All had gone well—very well. So much had Mr. Parkhill been pleased by his success that, for homework, he had assigned a composition entitled "A Short Business Letter."

And now the students were presenting their homework on the blackboard for class analysis. Mrs. Tomasic, anticipating some halcyon day in the future, was applying for a position as private secretary to the President of the Good English Club. Mr. George Weinstein was ordering "a dozen assoted colors sox size 12 silk" from a well-known department store. Mr. Norman Bloom, ever the soul of business, was inscribing a polite but firm note reminding "S. Levin—Inc.—Jobbers" that they still owed him $17.75 for merchandise taken "on assignment." Miss Schneiderman described a hat, coat, and "pair gloffs" she wished delivered "C.O.T." Mr. Hyman Kaplan was copying his letter on the blackboard in the right-hand corner of the room, near the door. There was a serenity in Mr. Kaplan's ubiquitous smile as he put the finishing touches to his creation. This night there was something luminous about that smile. Mr. Parkhill, always uneasy about the form Mr. Kaplan's genius might give to any assignment, found himself reading Mr. Kaplan's letter with unconscious curiosity and quite conscious anxiety. This was the letter Mr. Kaplan had written:

Bus. Let.

459 E. 3. Street
New York
Janu. 8

Joseph   Mandelbaum
A-I Furniture Comp. N.Y.

Dear Sir Mandelbaum—

Sarah and me want to buy refrigimator. Sarah wants bad. Always she
is saying "Hymie, the eyes-box is terrible. Leeking." Is true. So I answer "Sarah, by me is O.K. refrigimator."

Because you are in furniture so I'm writing about. How much will
cost refrigimator? Is axpensif, maybe by you is more cheap a little. But
it *must not* have short circus. If your eye falls on a bargain please pick
it up.

Very Truly Your Customer

H ⋆ Y ⋆ M ⋆ A ⋆ N   K ⋆ A ⋆ P ⋆ L ⋆ A ⋆ N
(Address on Top)

Best regards Sarah and me.

Affectionately,
H ⋆ Y ⋆ M ⋆ I ⋆ E

Mr. Parkhill frowned several times during his reading of
this document, sighed when he had finished his examination
of it, and resigned himself to another tortuous excursion into
the strange linguistic universe of his most remarkable student.
As for Mr. Kaplan, he reread his handiwork several times lovingly, his eyes half closed in what was supposed to be a self-
critical attitude. He kept shaking his head happily as he read,
smiling, as if delighted by the miracle of what he had brought
into being. Mr. Kaplan was an appreciative soul.

When the last student had finished, Mr. Parkhill said
quickly, "I think we'll take your composition *first,* Mr. Kaplan."
He wasn't quite sure why he had said that. Generally he started
with the exercise in the *left*-hand corner of the blackboard.

"Me *foist?*" asked Mr. Kaplan.

"Er—yes." Mr. Parkhill almost wavered at the last minute.

Mr. Kaplan's smile widened. "My!" he said, getting up from
his seat. "Is awreddy *foist* I'm makink rasitations!" By the time
he reached the blackboard his smile had become positively
celestial.

Mr. Kaplan faced the class, as if it were an exercise in
Recitation and Speech rather than composition.

"Ladies an' gantleman," he began, "in dis lasson I falt a
fonny kind problem. A problem abot how—"

"Er—Mr. Kaplan," Mr. Parkhill broke in, "please *read* your
letter."

Only Mr. Kaplan's delight in being first carried him over
this cruel frustration. "Podden me," he said softly. He began to
read the letter. " 'Dear Sir Mendelbum.' " He read slowly, with
dignity, with feeling. His smile struggled between pride and

modesty. When he came to the last words, there was a tinge of melancholy in his voice. " 'Affectionately, Hymie.' " Mr. Kaplan sighed. "Dat's de and."

"Mr. Kaplan," began Mr. Parkhill cautiously, "do you think that's strictly a *business* letter?"

Mr. Kaplan considered this challenge by closing his eyes and whispering to himself. "Business ladder? *Streectly* business ladder? Is?"

Mr. Parkhill waited. The years had taught Mr. Parkhill patience.

"It's *abot* business," suggested Mr. Kaplan tentatively.

Mr. Parkhill shook his head. "But the content, Mr. Kaplan. The tone. The final—er—well—" Mr. Parkhill caught *himself* on the verge of an oration. "I'll let the class begin the corrections. There are *many* mistakes, Mr. Kaplan."

Mr. Kaplan's grave nod indicated that even the wisest of men knew what it was to err.

"Corrections, class. First, let us consider the basic question. Is this a business letter?"

The hand of Rose Mitnick went up with a menacing resolution. When the work of Mr. Kaplan was under consideration, Miss Mitnick functioned with devastating efficiency.

"I think this isn't," she said. "Because in business letter you don't tell your wife's *first* name. And you don't send 'best regards.' All that's for *personal* letters like we had before."

"An' vat if I vanted to wride a *poisonal* business ladder?" asked Mr. Kaplan with diabolic logic.

Miss Mitnick paid no attention to this casuistry. "It's wrong to give family facts in business letter," she insisted. "It's no business from the company what is a wife saying to a husband."

"Aha!" cried Mr. Kaplan. "Mitnick, you too axcited. You forgeddink to *who* is dis ladder!"

Mr. Parkhill cleared his throat. "Er—Mr. Kaplan, Miss Mitnick is quite right. One doesn't discuss personal or family details, or give one's wife's first name, in a business letter—which is, after all, to a stranger."

Mr. Kaplan waited until the last echo of Mr. Parkhill's voice had died away. Then, when the classroom was very quiet, he spoke. "Mendelbum," he said, "is mine oncle."

There was a collective gasp. Miss Mitnick flushed. Mr. Marcus's eyes opened very wide. Mrs. Friedman blinked blankly.

"But, Mr. Kaplan," said Mr. Parkhill quickly, realizing that in such a mood there were no limits to Mr. Kaplan's audacity, "if the letter *is* addressed to your uncle"—he pronounced "uncle" suspiciously, but Mr. Kaplan's firm nod convinced him that there was no subterfuge here—"then it shouldn't be a business letter in the first place!"

To this Miss Mitnick nodded, with hope.

"Dat pozzled me, too," said Mr. Kaplan graciously. "An' dat's vy I vas goink to axplain abot de fonny kind problem I falt, in de few voids before I rad de ladder." His tone was one of righteousness. "I figgered: buyink a refrigima—"

"Refrig*erator!* *R,* not *m.*"

"Buyink a refrig*erator* is business. Also de axercise you givink for homevork is about business. So I must kipp in business *atmosvere.* So in de foist pot I wrote mine oncle a real business ladder—cold, formal. You know, stock-op!" Mr. Kaplan wrinkled his nose into a pictorialization of "stock-op." "But den, by de and, I falt is awreddy time to have mit family fillink. Becawss *is,* efter all, mine oncle. So I put don 'Affectionately, Hymie.'"

"And is 'Affectionately' right for a business letter?" asked Miss Mitnick, trying to conceal the triumph in her voice.

"It's *spalled* right!" Mr. Kaplan cried with feeling.

Mr. Parkhill felt old and weary; he began to realize the heights yet to be scaled. "Mr. Kaplan," he said softly, "we are not concerned with the spelling of 'affectionately' at the moment. 'Affectionately' is *not* proper in a business letter, nor is 'Very truly yours' in a personal letter." He spent a few minutes analyzing the impasse. "You cannot combine the two forms, Mr. Kaplan. Either you write a business letter *or* a personal letter." He suggested that in the future Mr. Kaplan write personal letters to his uncle, but choose absolute strangers for his business communications. "Let us go on with the corrections, please."

Mr. Bloom's hand went up.

"Mistakes is terrible," he said. "Where's the address from the company? How is abbreviated 'Company'? Where's colon or comma after 'Dear Sir'? And 'Dear Sir Mandelbaum'! What kind combination is this? Is maybe Mr. Kaplan's uncle in English House Lords?"

Mr. Kaplan smiled bravely through this fusillade. Even the sarcasm about his titled lineage did no perceptible damage to that smile.

"'Sarah and me' should be 'Sarah and I,'" Mr. Bloom went on. "And 'eyes-box'! Phooey! I-c-e means 'ice'; e-y-e-s means 'eyes.' One is for seeing, the other for freezing!"

Mr. Bloom was in faultless form. The class listened breathlessly to his dissection of Mr. Kaplan's business letter. His recitation filled them with confidence. When he finished, a forest of hands went up. With new courage the beginners' grade leaped into the critical fray. It was pointed out that "leaking" was spelled wrong, and "expensive." Mr. Pinsky remarked pointedly that there should be no capitals after "Very" in "Very truly" and cast doubts on the legitimacy of "Very Truly Your Customer." Miss Caravello suggested that Mr. Mandelbaum might be wise enough to read Mr. Kaplan's address without being told where to look for it, in the phrase "Address on Top." Even Mrs. Moskowitz, simple, uninspired Mrs. Moskowitz, added her bit to the autopsy.

"I only know vun ting," she said. "I know vat is a circus. Dat's mit hanimals, clons, tricks, horses. An' you ken't put a circus in icebox—even a *'short* circus'!"

"You don' know about laktric!" cried Mr. Kaplan, desperate to strike back at this united front. "Ufcawss, you a voman."

"Laktric—gas—even *candles!"* retorted Mrs. Moskowitz. "Circus ken't go in icebox!"

"Maybe de kind *you* minn," said Mr. Kaplan hotly. "But in laktricity is alvays denger havink short coicus. Becawss—"

Mr. Parkhill intervened, conscious that here was the making of a feud to take its place beside the Mitnick-Kaplan *affaire.* "You don't mean 'short circus,' Mr. Kaplan. You mean 'short cir-*cuit!'* C-i-r-c-u-i-t."

From the expression on Mr. Kaplan's face it was clear that even this approximation to "circus" was a victory for him and a rebuff to Mrs. Moskowitz and the forces she had, for the moment, led into battle.

"Another mistake," said Miss Mitnick suddenly. There was a glow in her cheeks; evidently Miss Mitnick had discovered something very important. Mr. Kaplan's eyes turned to narrow slits. "In the letter is: 'If your eye falls on a bargain please pick it up.'" Miss Mitnick read the sentence slowly. "'If your *eye* falls on a bargain pick *it* up'?"

The class burst into laughter. It was a masterly stroke. Everyone laughed. Even Mr. Parkhill, feeling a bit sorry for Mr. Kaplan, permitted himself a dignified smile.

And suddenly Mr. Kaplan joined in the merriment. He didn't laugh; he merely smiled. But his smile was grandiose, invincible, cosmic.

"An' vat's wronk dere, plizz?" he asked, his tone the epitome of confidence.

Mr. Bloom should have known that he was treading on ground mined with dynamite. But so complete had been the rout of Hyman Kaplan that Mr. Bloom threw caution to the winds. "Miss Mitnick's right! 'If your *eye* falls on a bargain please pick *it* up'? Som English, Mr. Kaplan!"

Then Mr. Kaplan struck.

"Mine oncle," he said, "has a gless eye."

The effect was incredible. The laughter came to a convulsive stop. Mr. Bloom's mouth fell open. Miss Mitnick dropped her pencil. Mrs. Moskowitz looked at Mr. Kaplan as if she had seen a vision; she wondered how she had dared criticize such a man. And Mr. Kaplan's smile was that of a child, deep in some lovely and imperishable sleep. He was like a man who had redeemed himself, a man whose honor, unsmirched, was before him like a dazzling banner.

★　　★　　★

The Straight Man and the Jew

STRAIGHT MAN *enters and sings a song. After the song, shots are heard offstage and* JEW COMIC *(with hat over ears, short beard, and misfit suit) comes running out.*

S.M.: Mr. Cohen, what are you running for?

COHEN: I'm trying to keep two fellows from fighting.

S.M.: Who are the fellows?

COHEN: An Irishman and me. *(After laugh is over)* Say, why don't you pay me for that suit you got on?

S.M.: Well, really, Mr. Cohen, I would pay you, only I haven't the money.

COHEN: *(Mocking* STRAIGHT MAN*)* Yeh, I'd be a rich man, only I ain't got the money. Can't you pay me something on the bill?

S.M.: How much do you want?

COHEN: I'd like enough to hire a lawyer to sue you for the balance.

S.M.: You're a pretty smart fellow. Are you good at spelling?

COHEN: You betcha my life I'm a good speller.

S.M.: I'll bet you that you can't spell "needle."

COHEN: I'll bet you my life I can spell it.

S.M.: I won't bet you that.

COHEN: I'll bet you my whole family's life.

S.M.: No, I won't bet you that, but I'll tell you what I will do; I'll bet you ten dollars that you can't spell "needle."

COHEN: No siree. When it comes to betting money, that's another matter.

S.M.: I'll try you anyway. How do you spell "needle"?

COHEN: N-i-e-d-l-e.

S.M.: You're wrong.

COHEN: I'm right.

Vaudeville was the side door through which Jews became an integral part of American show business. Most of the older Jewish entertainers had their start in vaudeville, and vaudeville featured Jewish characters even before it featured Jewish entertainers. In this sketch, for example, "Cohen" would normally be played by a Gentile.

S.M.: We will leave that to the leader. He looks like an intelligent person. (*Goes over to* LEADER *of the orchestra*) You heard the argument, George. Who is right?

LEADER: Why, you are, of course.

S.M.: (*To* COHEN) You see? (*To* LEADER) Do you smoke?

LEADER: Why, of course.

S.M.: (*Takes cigar out of pocket*) Well, here's a cigar. Try spelling it again, Mr. Cohen.

COHEN: (*Looks at* LEADER *through the business of* S.M. *giving* LEADER *cigar, etc. Is disgusted with* LEADER *when he says that* S.M. *is right, after tries in vain with motions behind* S.M.*'s back to make the* LEADER *say that he is right*) All right, here I go again. N-e-e-d-l. (*Triumphantly*) Now, *that's* right.

S.M.: (*Laughing heartily*) Why, no, that's worse than your first attempt.

COHEN: No, that's spelt right.

S.M.: We'll ask George. (*Goes to* LEADER *again*) Who was right that time, George?

GEORGE: (*Paying no attention to* COHEN, *who is again trying to make motions behind* S.M.*'s back to make* GEORGE *say he is right*) Why, you are right.

S.M.: Have another cigar. (*Gives* LEADER *cigar*) Well, Cohen, I will give you one more chance.

COHEN: Needle. Is that the word?

S.M.: Yes.

COHEN: Why didn't you say so? N-i-d-l-e.

S.M.: Wrong again.

COHEN: I'm right.

S.M.: We will ask . . .

COHEN: I will ask him this time. Mr. Musiker, who is right this time?

LEADER: Why, you are, Mr. Cohen.

COHEN: (*Very happy, making faces at* S.M.) See? (*To* LEADER) Do you smoke?

LEADER: Why, yes.

COHEN: (*Hand in pocket as if to take out cigar*) Here's a *match*.

S.M.: (*Laughs*) Mr. Cohen, you are a card. Say, Cohen, I was reading the papers this morning and I see that (*Local town*) has three saloons to one policeman.

COHEN: That gives you three guesses as to where the policeman is.

S.M.: By the way, where is your boy?

COHEN: You mean my boy Abie? He is an eye doctor.

S.M.: (*Surprised*) Why, I thought he was a chiropodist.

COHEN: He *was* a chiropodist. You see, he began at the foot and worked himself up.

Drawing by S. Gross; © 1978 National Lampoon, Inc.

S.M.: Are you still happily married?

COHEN: Yeh, I don't live with my wife.

S.M.: You know, I've been married since I saw you last. I married
    a sharpshooter from the Buffalo Bill Show.

COHEN: A shipshopper, eh?

S.M.: Yes, sir. My wife's a very good shot. Why, she can hit a
    silver dollar at a hundred yards.

COHEN: Dot's nothing. My wife goes through my pockets and
    never misses a dime. You know, I got a great idea how to
    get along with my wife.

S.M.: I'd like to hear it; it may come in handy sometime.

COHEN: When I come home I throw things around the house, I
    put cigar ashes on the floor.

S.M.: Why, what's the idea of that?

COHEN: I get my wife so mad she won't speak to me. Then we get
    along fine.

S.M.: A woman that doesn't speak—why, that's a miracle. Of course you know what a miracle is?

COHEN: Sure I know what a miracle is.

S.M.: Well, tell me, what is a miracle?

COHEN: Well, if you see a bull in the field . . .

S.M.: Yes, if you see a bull in the field?

COHEN: Dot ain't no miracle.

S.M.: Of course not.

COHEN: If you see a thistle in a field, dot ain't no miracle.

S.M.: Of course a thistle in a field is no miracle.

COHEN: And if you hear a lark singing, dot ain't no miracle.

S.M.: Of course hearing a lark sing is no miracle.

COHEN: But if you see a bull sitting on a thistle singing like a lark, *dot's a miracle.*

S.M.: *(Laughs)* You're a card, Cohen. Will you have dinner at my house tonight?

COHEN: Say, that was a nice dinner we had at your house last week. The salmon was wonderful.

S.M.: Why, that wasn't salmon, that was *ham.*

COHEN: *(Makes funny face)* Who asked you?

S.M.: Say, are you still playing the horses?

COHEN: I played a horse yesterday twenty to one.

S.M.: And did he win?

COHEN: He didn't come in until a quarter past six.

S.M.: By the way, how is your uncle, the one that was so sick?

COHEN: My sick uncle? You know the Board of Health wouldn't let me bury him?

S.M.: *(Indignantly)* Why, I never heard of such a thing. Why wouldn't they let you bury him?

COHEN: Because he ain't dead yet.

S.M.: *(Laughs)* You're a card, Cohen.

COHEN: I'm a whole deck. I'm going to get a drink.

S.M.: What's the idea?

COHEN: Then I'll be a *full* deck.

S.M.: You're incorrigible.

COHEN: Why bring religion into this? I'm going now.

S.M.: Where are you going?

COHEN: I'm going to get my wife a nice dog. He must be able to swim.

S.M.: Why must he be able to swim?

COHEN: You see, my wife holds him on her lap, and she has water on the knee.

S.M.: *(Laughs)* I think we better sing.

(STRAIGHT MAN *sings a popular song. Then* COHEN *sings a parody on it. Then they both Exit.)*

NEIL SIMON

Dr. Klockenmeyer

(The curtain rises, and the set is fully lit. The frail man in the hat is sitting on the chair as WILLIE, *the doctor, dressed in a floor-length white doctor's jacket, a mirror attached to his head and a stethoscope around his neck, is looking into the* PATIENT's *mouth, holding his tongue down with an "ahh" stick.)*

WILLIE: Open wider and say "Ahh."

PATIENT: Ahh.

WILLIE: Wider.

PATIENT: *Ahhh!*

WILLIE: *(Moves with his back to the audience)* A little wider.

PATIENT: Ahhh!

WILLIE: *(Steps away)* Your throat is all right, but you're gonna have some trouble with your stomach.

PATIENT: How come?

WILLIE: You just swallowed the stick.

(The PATIENT *feels his stomach.)*

PATIENT: Is that bad?

WILLIE: It's terrible. I only got two left.

PATIENT: What about getting the stick out?

WILLIE: What am I, a tree surgeon? . . . All right; for another ten dollars, I'll take it out.

PATIENT: That's robbery.

WILLIE: Then forget it. Keep the stick.

PATIENT: No, no. I'll pay. Take the stick out.

WILLIE: Come back tomorrow. On Thursdays I do woodwork.

(The PATIENT *gets up and crosses to the door, then exits.* WILLIE *calls out)* Oh, Nurse! Nursey!

(The NURSE *enters. She is a tall, voluptuous, and overstacked blonde in a tight dress.)*

NURSE: Did you want me, Doctor?

WILLIE: *(He looks at her, knowingly)* Why do you think I hired you? . . . What's your name again?

NURSE: Miss MacKintosh. You know, like the apples.

WILLIE: *(Nods)* The name I forgot, the apples I remembered. . . . Look in my appointment book, see who's next.

NURSE: It's a Mr. Kornheiser.

WILLIE: Maybe you're wrong. Look in the book. It's better that way.

Neil Simon, born in 1927, is the author of many comic plays, including *Promises, Promises; The Odd Couple; The Prisoner of Second Avenue;* and *Plaza Suite. The Sunshine Boys,* from which this selection is taken, is the story of two old vaudeville stars, formerly a team, who have been feuding for years, and who are brought together for a reunion on television. After a great deal of bickering, they finally re-enact their most famous skit, which takes place in a doctor's office.

The story is clearly based on the famous vaudeville team of (Joe) Smith and (Charlie) Dale, who began their partnership at the turn of the century. Their most famous routine was "Dr. Kronkhite," with Smith playing the aggressive patient and Dale as the doctor.

In a book entitled *The Vaudevillians,* Joe Smith recalled the act that made them famous:

The Dr. Kronkhite bit—I'll tell you how it came to be Dr. Kronkhite. We used to do a school act in one and then I did a series of imitations. One was an imitation of a friend of mine going into a delicatessen store to buy something. I'd be the friend and Charlie would be the proprietor. I'd say, "Good morning." He'd say, "Good afternoon." I'd say, "Good evening," and he'd say, "Good night—make a day of it." I'd say, "I've only got five minutes to spend a nickel. Gimme five cents' worth of that salmon." Charlie would say, "That's not salmon, that's ham." And I'd say, "Did I ask you what it was?"

Then I'd do more imitations and finally I had one on going into a doctor's office. This one began in 1906 at Hammerstein's Victoria. One of our boys would say offstage, "Oh you butcher." And I would look and he would come out with a handkerchief over his eye. And I'd say, "Did you holler inside?" and he'd say, "Yes." "Did the doctor pull out your eye?" He said, "No, five dollars is what he pulled out of me." "Five dollars? What does he charge for a visit?" "Five dollars for the first visit, three dollars for the second, and one dollar for the third." Charlie would come out and I'd say, "Well, doctor, here I am again, for the fifth time. If I come again, you'll owe me eight cents." He would say, "Continue on the same medicine." That's how it took off.

One time I said, "Well, doctor, I'm here for the fifth time," and Charlie broke in with, "What's the trouble with you?" I was flabbergasted. Finally I ad-libbed. I said, "I don't know but every time I eat a heavy meal I don't feel so hungry after." He said, "What do you

eat? What kind of dishes do you eat?"
And I said, "What do you mean, dishes?
What am I, a crocodile?"

So we kept adding. One time I ad-libbed, "Are you a doctor?" and when he said he was, I said, "I'm dubious," and he said, "How do you do, Mr. Dubious." Then we called it "Dr. Kronkhite" and we had a sign on the drop that said, "Dr. Kronkhite, M.D.," and that's how it was established. Later we used a nurse.

We did a Dr. Kronkhite for TV, using Barbra Streisand as the nurse. But for some reason they never put it on. The nurse bit went like this: I walk into the doctor's office and I'm greeted by the nurse. I say, "Excuse me, is this the doctor's office?" She says, "Yes, I'm his nurse." "His nurse? Is the doctor sick too?" She says, "No, I'm a trained nurse." "Oh, you do tricks?" Then I ask, "What are the doctor's office hours?" She answers, "Twelve to three, three to six, six to nine, nine to twelve, twelve to three." I say, "With such hours he must be a horse doctor."

Charlie would come out with a funny little walk. One time I said, "You walk like you're in the State Department." When we played Washington we were told not to use that line. So instead I said, "You look like a new congressman looking for a seat," and that got a big laugh.

We changed around in vaudeville. For example, in Pittsburgh, a very tough town, we were careful of what lines we used. When we first did the "Hungarian Rhapsody" there was a line where one of the waiters used to say, "I'd like to have some corn." I'd say, "We don't have any corn." Charlie would come right out and say, "I have two—one on each foot." We had to cut that out in Philadelphia. We also had to cut it out at the Palace. In fact, we had to cut it out in so many places that we finally dropped it.

Occasionally we would add this to the doctor bit: I would say I had the Asiatic flu and I took so much medicine that I was sick for a long time after I got well. Charlie would say, "Who recommended you?" I'd say, "A friend, Jacob T. Sonnevitch." "Sonnevitch?" I'd say, "Yes." Charlie would say, "I had a patient—Sonnevitch—he lost me twenty-five dollars."

If we had to lengthen the doctor sketch we would put in an insurance routine: "Are you insured? No? Well, you should be insured." "What do I get in your company?" "Well, for two dollars a week, if you lose your head, two hands, or three legs, you can get seventy-five dollars a week for the rest of your natural life." "Two hands, three legs—what am I, an octopus? I could pay two dollars a week for a whole year and never get hurt." "Well, maybe the following year you'll have better luck. And they've got their own cemetery—and it's wonderful, it's right near the golf course." "A cemetery next to a golf course? That must be the last hole."

(She crosses to the desk and bends way over as she looks through the appointment book. Her firm, round rear end faces us and WILLIE. WILLIE *shakes his head from side to side in wonderful contemplation.)*

NURSE: *(Still down)* No, I was right.

WILLIE: So was I.

NURSE: *(Straightens up and turns around)* It's Mr. Kornheiser.

WILLIE: Are you sure? Spell it.

NURSE: *(Turns, bends, and gives us the same wonderful view again)* K-o-r-n-h-e-i-s-e-r!

(She turns and straightens up.)

WILLIE: *(Nods)* What's the first name?

NURSE: *(Turns, bends)* Walter.

WILLIE: Stay down for the middle name.

NURSE: *(Remains down)* Benjamin.

WILLIE: Don't move and give me the whole thing.

NURSE: *(Still rear end up, reading)* Walter Benjamin Kornheiser.

(She turns and straightens up.)

WILLIE: Oh, boy. From now on I only want to see patients with long names.

NURSE: Is there anything else you want?

WILLIE: Yeah. Call a carpenter and have him make my desk lower.

(The NURSE *walks sexily right up to* WILLIE *and stands with her chest practically on his, breathing and heaving.)*

NURSE: *(Pouting)* Yes, Doctor.

WILLIE: *(Wipes his brow)* Whew, it's hot in here. Did you turn the steam on?

NURSE: *(Sexily)* No, Doctor.

WILLIE: In that case, take a five-dollar raise. Send in the next patient before *I'm* the next patient.

NURSE: Yes, Doctor. *(She coughs)* Excuse me, I think I have a chest cold.

WILLIE: Looks more like an epidemic to me.

NURSE: Yes, Doctor. *(She wriggles her way to the door)* Is there anything else you can think of?

WILLIE: I can *think* of it, but I'm not so sure I can *do* it.

NURSE: Well, if I *can* help you, Doctor, that's what the nurse is for.

(She exits and closes the door with an enticing look.)

WILLIE: I'm glad I didn't go to law school. *(Then we hear three knocks on the door. "Knock, knock, knock")* Aha. That must be my next patient. *(Calls out)* Come in! *(The door starts to open)*—and *enter!*

(AL steps in and glares angrily at WILLIE. *He is in a business suit, wears a wig, and carries a cheap attaché case.)*

AL: I'm looking for the doctor.

WILLIE: Are you sick?

AL: Are *you* the doctor?

WILLIE: Yes.

AL: I'm not *that* sick.

WILLIE: What's your name, please?

AL: Kornheiser. Walter Benjamin Kornheiser. You want me to spell it?

WILLIE: Never mind. I got a better speller than you. . . . *(Takes a tongue depressor from his pocket)* Sit down and open your mouth, please.

AL: There's nothing wrong with my mouth.

WILLIE: Then just sit down.

AL: There's nothing wrong with that, either.

WILLIE: Then what are you doing here?

AL: I came to examine you.

WILLIE: I think you got everything backwards.

AL: It's possible. I dressed in a hurry this morning.

WILLIE: You mean you came here for me to examine *you.*

AL: No, I came here for me to examine *you.* I'm a tax collector.

WILLIE: *(Nods)* That's nice. I'm a stamp collector. What do you do for a living?

AL: I find out how much money people make.

WILLIE: Oh, a busybody. Make an appointment with the nurse.

AL: I did. I'm seeing her Friday night. . . .

WILLIE: *(Jumps up and down angrily)* Don't fool around with my nurse. DON'T FOOL AROUND WITH MY NURSE! She's a nice girl. She's a *Virginian!*

AL: A what?

WILLIE: A *Virginian.* That's where she's from.

AL: Well, she ain't going *back,* I can tell you that. *(He sits, opens the attaché case)* I got some questions to ask you.

WILLIE: I'm too busy to answer questions. I'm a doctor. If you wanna see me, you gotta be a patient.

AL: But I'm not sick.

WILLIE: Don't worry. We'll find something.

AL: All right, you examine me and I'll examine you. . . . *(Takes out a tax form as* WILLIE *wields the tongue depressor)* The first question is, How much money did you make last year?

WILLIE: Last year I made . . .

(He moves his lips mouthing a sum, but it's not audible.)

AL: I didn't hear that.

WILLIE: Oh. Hard of hearing. I knew we'd find something. Did you ever have any childhood diseases?

AL: Not lately.

WILLIE: Father living or deceased?

AL: Both.

WILLIE: What do you mean, both?

AL: First he was living, now he's deceased.

WILLIE: What did your father die from?

AL: My mother . . . Now it's my turn. Are you married?

WILLIE: I'm looking.

AL: Looking to get married?

WILLIE: No, looking to get out.

(He looks in AL's ear with a flashlight.)

AL: What are you doing?

WILLIE: I'm examining your lower intestines.

AL: So why do you look in the ear?

WILLIE: If I got a choice of two places to look, I'll take this one.

AL: *(Consulting his form)* Never mind. Do you own a car?

WILLIE: Certainly I own a car. Why?

AL: If you use it for medical purposes, you can deduct it from your taxes. What kind of car do you own?

By permission of the artist.

WILLIE: An ambulance.

AL: Do you own a house?

WILLIE: Can I deduct it?

AL: Only if you use it for medical purposes. Where do you live?

WILLIE: In Mount Sinai Hospital. . . . Open your shirt. I want to listen to your heartbeat.

AL: *(Unbuttons two buttons on his shirt)* Will this take long?

WILLIE: Not if I hear something. *(He puts his ear to* AL*'s chest and listens)* Uh-huh. I hear something. . . . You're all right.

AL: Aren't you going to listen with the stethoscope?

WILLIE: Oh, sure. I didn't know you wanted a thorough examination. *(Puts the stethoscope to his ears and listens to* AL*'s chest)* Oh, boy. Ohhh, boyyyy! You know what you got?

AL: What?

WILLIE: A filthy undershirt.

AL: Never mind that. Am I in good health?

WILLIE: Not unless you change your undershirt.

AL: What is this, a doctor's office or a laundry? I bet you never went to medical school.

WILLIE: *(Jumping up and down again)* What are you talkin'? . . . WHAT ARE YOU TALKIN'? . . . I went to Columbia Medical School.

AL: Did you pass?

WILLIE: Certainly.

AL: Well, you should have gone *in!*

WILLIE: Never mind. . . . I'm gonna examine your eyes now.

AL: They're perfect. I got twenty-twenty eyes.

WILLIE: That's too much. All you need is one and one. Look at that chart on the wall. Now put your left hand over your left eye and your right hand over your right eye. *(AL does so)* Now tell me what you see.

AL: I don't see nothing.

WILLIE: Don't panic, I can cure you. . . . Take your hands away. *(AL does)* Can you see now?

AL: Certainly I can see now.

WILLIE: You know, I fixed over two thousand people like that.

AL: It's a miracle.

WILLIE: Thank you.

AL: A miracle you're not in jail. . . . What do you charge for a visit?

WILLIE: A dollar.

AL: A dollar? That's very cheap for an examination.

WILLIE: It's not an examination. It's just a visit: "Hello and Goodbye." "Hello and How Are You?" is ten dollars.

AL: If you ask me, you're a quack.

WILLIE: If I was a duck I would ask you. . . . Now roll up your sleeve. I wanna take some blood.

AL: I can't do it.

WILLIE: Why not?

AL: If I see blood, I get sick.

WILLIE: Do what I do. Don't look.

AL: I'm sorry. I'm not giving blood. I'm anemic.

WILLIE: What's anemic?

AL: You're a doctor and you don't know what anemic means?

WILLIE: That's because I'm a specialist.

AL: What do you specialize in?

WILLIE: Everything but anemic.

AL: Listen, can I continue my examination?

WILLIE: You continue yours, and I'll continue mine. All right, cross your legs. *(He hits* AL*'s knee with a small hammer)* Does it hurt if I hit you with the hammer?

AL: Yes.

WILLIE: Good. From now on, try not to get hit with a hammer. *(He throws the hammer over his shoulder. He takes a specimen bottle from the cabinet and returns)* You see this bottle?

AL: Yes.

WILLIE: You know what you're supposed to do with this bottle?

AL: I think so.

WILLIE: You *think* so or you *know* so? If you're not sure, let me know. The girl doesn't come in to clean today.

AL: What do you want me to do?

WILLIE: I want you to go in this bottle.

AL: I haven't got time. I have to go over your books.

WILLIE: *The hell you will!*

AL: If I don't go over your books, the *government* will come in here and go over your books.

© 1973 Kirschen

WILLIE: Don't they have a place in Washington?

AL: Certainly, but they have to go where the books are.

WILLIE: The whole government?

AL: No, just the Treasury Department.

WILLIE: That's a relief.

AL: I'm glad you're relieved.

WILLIE: I wish *you* were before you came in here.

(The door opens and the big-chested NURSE *steps in.)*

NURSE: Oh, Doctor. Doctor Klockenmeyer.

WILLIE: Yes.

NURSE: Mrs. Kolodny is on the phone. She wants you to rush right over and deliver her baby.

WILLIE: I'm busy now. Tell her I'll mail it to her in the morning.

NURSE: Yes, Doctor.

(She exits and closes the door.)

AL: Where did you find a couple of nurses like that?

WILLIE: She was standing on Forty-third and Forty-fourth Street. . . . Let me see your tongue, please.

AL: I don't want to.

*(*WILLIE *squeezes* AL*'s throat, and his tongue comes out.)*

WILLIE: Open the mouth. . . . How long have you had that white coat on your tongue?

AL: Since January. In the spring I put on a gray sports jacket.

WILLIE: Now hold your tongue with your fingers and say "shish-kabob."

GIVE AND TAKE • SCHNORRERS • BUSINESS • RABBIS • DOCTORS

DAVID LEVINE • GEORGE S. KAUFMAN / MORRIE RYSKIND • DICK CODOR • S. J. PERELMAN • ISRAEL ZANGWILL • JOHN CALDWELL • GEORGE PRICE • ALLAN SHERMAN • SAM LEVENSON • MOISHE NADIR • MAX SHULMAN • MARK PODWAL • WOODY ALLEN • SHOLOM ALEICHEM • KIRSCHEN

PART FOUR

MAKING A LIVING

GEORGE S. KAUFMAN
MORRIE RYSKIND

Groucho and Chico Make a Deal

Throughout their movies, the Marx Brothers personified the *luftmenschen* (literally, men of air) who appear frequently in Jewish jokes. Part huckster, part *schnorrer*, the *luftmensch* lives by his wits, disdaining the professionalism he can never attain. In their various films, the Marx Brothers ridiculed the respected professions of the day: impresarios, doctors, college presidents, and the like.

Groucho, more than his brothers, retained the flavor of the Jewish vaudeville wiseacre. When the chorus in *Animal Crackers* sings "Hooray for Captain Spaulding, the African Explorer!" Groucho mutters: "Did someone call me *schnorrer*?" And indeed, his favorite way to make a living—was to *schnorr* from various well-endowed matrons, usually played by Margaret Dumont.

Albert Goldman has observed that the comedy of the Marx Brothers brings into focus "the anarchic mockery of conventions and values, which crumble to dust at the touch of a rudely irreverent jest. 'Subversive' was the word for the Marx Brothers, as it has been the word often since employed both as condemnation of and tribute to the work of Jewish humorists who refuse to be trammeled by the conventional pieties, delighting instead in demonstrating the fragility and preposterousness of much that passes as social law and order."

And Philip Roth has fantasized about a movie that could be made of Kafka's *The Castle*, with Groucho Marx as K. and Chico and Harpo as the two "assistants": "I thought about Groucho walking into the village over which the Castle looms, announcing he was the Land Surveyor; of *course* no one would believe him. Of *course* they would drive him up the wall. They had to—because of that cigar."

GROUCHO: Two beers, bartender.

CHICO: I'll take two beers too.

GROUCHO: (*Drifting right into that barroom conversation*) Well, things seem to be getting better around the country.

CHICO: I don't know—I'm a stranger here myself.

GROUCHO: (*Looking at him curiously*) Stranger? Aren't you an Italian?

CHICO: No, no. I just look that way because my mother and father are Italian.

GROUCHO: I just remembered—I came back here looking for somebody. You don't know who it is, do you?

CHICO: Funny—it just slipped my mind.

GROUCHO: (*Snapping his fingers*) I remember now—the greatest tenor in the world, that's what I'm after!

CHICO: That's funny. I am his manager.

GROUCHO: Whose manager?

CHICO: The greatest tenor in the world.

GROUCHO: The fellow that sings at the opera here?

CHICO: Sure!

GROUCHO: What's his name?

CHICO: What do you care? Some Italian name—I can't pronounce it. What you want with him?

GROUCHO: Well, I'd like to offer him a job. Would he be interested?

CHICO: I don't know, but *I'm* interested. That's the main thing. What sort of job?

GROUCHO: With the New York Opera. America is waiting to hear him sing.

CHICO: Well, he can sing loud, but he can't sing that loud.

GROUCHO: Well, I think we can get America to meet him halfway. The main thing is, can he sail tomorrow night?

CHICO: If you pay him enough money, he can sail *last* night. How much you pay him?

GROUCHO: (*Aside*) Let's see—a thousand dollars a night. I'm entitled to a little profit. (*To* CHICO) How about ten dollars a night?

CHICO *laughs scornfully.*

CHICO: Ten dollars! . . . (*A quick change of mood*) All right. I'll take it.

GROUCHO: That's fine. Of course, I want a ten percent commission for putting the deal over.

CHICO: And I get ten percent as his manager.

GROUCHO: Well, that leaves eight dollars. Say he sings once a week—that's eight dollars a week clear profit for him.

CHICO: *(Considering a week)* He sends five dollars home to his mother.

GROUCHO: Well, that still leaves him three dollars.

CHICO: Three dollars. Can he live in New York on that?

GROUCHO: Like a prince—of course, he won't be able to eat, but he can live like a prince. Oh, I forgot to tell you. He'll have to pay income tax on that three dollars.

CHICO: Income tax?

GROUCHO: Yes, there's a federal tax and the state tax and there may be a city tax. And, naturally, a sales tax.

CHICO: How much does that all come to?

GROUCHO: Well, I figure if he doesn't sing too often, he can break even.

CHICO: All right. We'll take it.

GROUCHO: Fine! *(He pulls out two contracts)* Now, just his name there and you sign on the bottom. You don't have to read yours because it's a duplicate.

CHICO: What?

GROUCHO: A duplicate. *(*CHICO *looks at him)* Don't you know what duplicates are?

CHICO: Oh, sure! Those five kids up in Canada.

GROUCHO: Well, I wouldn't know about that. I haven't been in Canada for years.

CHICO: Wait a minute. Before I sign anything, what does it say?

GROUCHO: Go ahead and read it.

CHICO: *(A little reluctantly)* Well—er—you read it. I don't like to read anything unless I know what it says.

GROUCHO: *(Catching on)* I see. All right, *I'll* read it to you. Can you hear?

CHICO: I haven't heard anything yet. Did you say anything?

GROUCHO: Well, I haven't said anything worth hearing.

CHICO: I guess that's why I didn't hear anything.

GROUCHO: *(Having the last word)* Well, that's why I didn't say anything.

(He scans the contract, holding it near him and then far away. CHICO *watches him suspiciously.)*

CHICO: Wait a minute. Can *you* read?

GROUCHO: *(Holding contract farther and farther away)* I can read, but I can't see it. If my arms were a little longer, I could read it. . . . Ah, here we are. Now pay attention to this first clause. *(Reads)* "The party of the first part shall be

The Wise Son

The Dumb Son

The Bad Son

Dick Codor © 1981

The Simple Son

known in this contract as the party of the first part." How do you like that? Pretty neat, eh?

CHICO: No, that'sa no good.

GROUCHO: *(Indignantly)* What's the matter with it?

CHICO: *(Conciliatorily)* I don't know—let's hear it again.

GROUCHO: "The party of the first part shall be known in this contract as the party of the first part."

CHICO: It sounds a little better this time.

GROUCHO: Well, it grows on you. Want to hear it once more?

CHICO: Only the first part.

GROUCHO: The *party* of the first part?

CHICO: No. The *first part* of the party of the first part.

GROUCHO: Well, it says, "The first part of the party of the first part shall be known in this contract—" Look! Why should we quarrel about a thing like that? *(He tears off the offending clause)* We'll take it right out.

CHICO: *(Tearing the same clause out of his contract)* Sure, it's too long anyhow. Now what have we got left?

GROUCHO: Well, I've got about a foot and a half. . . . Now, then:

"The party of the second part shall be known in this contract as the party of the second part."

CHICO: Well, I don't know. I don't like the second party, either.

GROUCHO: You should have come to the first party. We didn't get home till around four in the morning. *(Slight pause)* I was blind for three days.

CHICO: Look, couldn't the first part of the second party be the second part of the first party? Then we got something.

GROUCHO: Look! Rather than go through all that again, what do you say?

(He indicates a willingness to tear further.)

CHICO: Fine. *(They both tear off another piece.)*

GROUCHO: Now, I've got something here you're *bound* to like. You'll be crazy about it.

CHICO: No, I don't like it.

GROUCHO: You don't like what?

CHICO: Whatever it is.

GROUCHO: All right. Why should we break up an old friendship over a thing like this? Ready?

CHICO: Okay. *(They both tear)* Now, the next part I don't think you're going to like.

GROUCHO: All right—your word's good enough for me. *(They both tear)* Now then, is my word good enough for *you*?

CHICO: I should say not.

GROUCHO: All right—let's go. *(They both tear.* GROUCHO, *looking at the contract)* The party of the eighth part—

CHICO: No. *(They tear)*

GROUCHO: The party of the ninth part—

CHICO: No. *(They tear)* Say, how is it I got a skinnier contract than you?

GROUCHO: I don't know. You must have been out on a tear last night. Anyhow, now we're all set. Now sign right here. *(He produces a fountain pen)*

CHICO: I forgot to tell you. I can't write.

GROUCHO: That's all right. There's no ink in the pen, anyway. But listen, it's a bargain, isn't it? We've got a contract, no matter how small it is.

CHICO: *(Extending hand.* GROUCHO *clasps it)* You betcha! Only one thing I want to know: what does this say? *(Showing last piece of contract left)*

GROUCHO: Oh, that's nothing. That's the usual clause in every contract. It says if any of the parties participating in the contract are shown not to be in their right mind, the contract is nullified.

CHICO: What do you call it?

GROUCHO: That's what they call a sanity clause.

CHICO: You can't fool me. There ain't no sanity clause!

●

S. J. PERELMAN
(With a Bow to Mr. Clifford Odets)

Waiting for Santy

SCENE: *The sweatshop of S. Claus, a manufacturer of children's toys, on North Pole Street. Time: The night before Christmas.*

At rise, seven gnomes, Rankin, Panken, Rivkin, Riskin, Ruskin, Briskin, and Praskin, are discovered working furiously to fill orders piling up at stage right. The whir of lathes, the hum of motors, and the hiss of drying lacquer are so deafening that at times the dialogue cannot be heard, which is very vexing if you vex easily. (Note: The parts of Rankin, Panken, Rivkin, Riskin, Ruskin, Briskin, and Praskin are interchangeable, and may be secured directly from your dealer or the factory.)

RISKIN: *(Filing a Meccano girder, bitterly)* A parasite, a leech, a bloodsucker—altogether a five-star nogoodnik! Starvation wages we get so he can ride around in a red team with reindeers!

RUSKIN: *(Jeering)* Hey, Karl Marx, whyn'tcha hire a hall?

RISKIN: *(Sneering)* Scab! Stool pigeon! Company spy! *(They tangle and rain blows on each other. While waiting for these to dry, each returns to his respective task.)*

BRISKIN: *(Sadly, to Panken)* All day long I'm painting "Snow Queen" on these Flexible Flyers and my little Irving lays in a cold tenement with the gout.

PANKEN: You said before it was the mumps.

BRISKIN: *(With a fatalistic shrug)* The mumps . . . the gout—go argue with City Hall.

PANKEN: *(Kindly, passing him a bowl)* Here, take a piece fruit.

BRISKIN: *(Chewing)* It ain't bad, for wax fruit.

PANKEN: *(With pride)* I painted it myself.

BRISKIN: *(Rejecting the fruit)* Ptoo! Slave psychology!

RIVKIN: *(Suddenly, half to himself, half to the party)* I got a belly full of stars, baby. You make me feel like I swallowed a Roman candle.

PRASKIN: *(Curiously)* What's wrong with the kid?

RISKIN: What's wrong with all of us? The system! Two years he and Claus's daughter's been making googoo eyes behind the old man's back.

PRASKIN: So what?

RISKIN: *(Scornfully)* So what? Economic determinism! What do you think the kid's name is—J. Pierpont Rivkin? He ain't even got for a bottle Dr. Brown's Celery Tonic. I tell you, it's like gall in my mouth two young people shouldn't have a room where they could make great music.

S. J. Perelman (1904–1979)—the initials stood for Sidney Joseph—was often said to be the funniest author of his time. A *New Yorker* writer through five decades, Perelman was a master parodist who loved using wild puns and mocking contemporary clichés.

He wrote numerous plays and screenplays, including the Marx Brothers films *Monkey Business* and *Horse Feathers.* "Humor is purely a point of view," he once said, "and only the pedants try to classify it. For me its chief merit is the use of the unexpected, the glancing allusion, the deflation of pomposity, the constant repetition of one's helplessness in a majority of situations. One doesn't consciously start out wanting to be a social satirist. You find something absurd enough to make you want to push a couple of anti-personnel bombs under it. If it then seems to have another element of meaning, that's lagniappe. But the main obligation is to amuse yourself."

When asked about the frequency of Yiddish words in his writing, Perelman responded that he liked Yiddish words "for their invective content. There are nineteen words in Yiddish that convey gradations of disparagement from a mild, fluttery helplessness to a state of downright, irreconcilable brutishness. All of them can be usefully employed to pin-point the kind of individuals I write about."

RANKIN: *(Warningly)* Shhh! Here she comes now! *(Stella Claus enters, carrying a portable phonograph. She and Rivkin embrace, place a record on the turntable, and begin a very slow waltz, unmindful that the phonograph is playing "Cohen on the Telephone.")*

STELLA: *(Dreamily)* Love me, sugar?

RIVKIN: I can't sleep, I can't eat, that's how I love you. You're a double malted with two scoops of whipped cream; you're the moon rising over Mosholu Parkway; you're a two weeks' vacation at Camp Nitgedaiget! I'd pull down the Chrysler Building to make a bobby pin for your hair!

STELLA: I've got a stomach full of anguish. Oh, Rivvy, what'll we do?

PANKEN: *(Sympathetically)* Here, try a piece fruit.

RIVKIN: *(Fiercely)* Wax fruit—that's been my whole life! Imitations! Substitutes! Well, I'm through! Stella, tonight I'm telling your old man. He can't play mumblety-peg with two human beings! *(The tinkle of sleigh bells is heard offstage, followed by a voice shouting, "Whoa, Dasher! Whoa, Dancer!" A moment later, S. Claus enters in a gust of mock snow. He is a pompous bourgeois of sixty-five who affects a white beard and a false air of benevolence. But tonight the ruddy color is missing from his cheeks, his step falters, and he moves heavily. The gnomes hastily replace the marzipan they have been filching.)*

Dick Codor © 1979

STELLA: *(Anxiously)* Papa! What did the specialist say to you?

CLAUS: *(Brokenly)* The biggest professor in the country . . . the best cardiac man that money could buy . . . I tell you I was like a wild man.

STELLA: Pull yourself together, Sam!

CLAUS: It's no use. Adhesions, diabetes, sleeping sickness, decalcomania—oh, my God! I got to cut out climbing in chimneys, he says—me, Sanford Claus, the biggest toy concern in the world!

STELLA: *(Soothingly)* After all, it's only one man's opinion.

CLAUS: No, no, he cooked my goose. I'm like a broken uke after a Yosian picnic. Rivkin!

RIVKIN: Yes, Sam.

CLAUS: My boy, I had my eye on you for a long time. You and Stella thought you were too foxy for an old man, didn't you? Well, let bygones be bygones. Stella, do you love this gnome?

STELLA: (*Simply*) He's the whole stage show at the Music Hall, Papa; he's Toscanini conducting Beethoven's Fifth; he's—

CLAUS: (*Curtly*) Enough already. Take him. From now on he's a partner in the firm. (*As all exclaim, Claus holds up his hand for silence*) And tonight he can take my route and make the deliveries. It's the least I could do for my own flesh and blood. (*As the happy couple kiss, Claus wipes away a suspicious moisture and turns to the other gnomes*) Boys, do you know what day tomorrow is?

GNOMES: (*Crowding around expectantly*) Christmas!

CLAUS: Correct. When you look in your envelopes tonight, you'll find a little present from me—a forty percent pay cut. And the first one who opens his trap—gets this. (*As he holds up a tear-gas bomb and beams at them, the gnomes utter cries of joy, join hands, and dance around him, shouting exultantly. All except Riskin and Briskin, that is, who exchange a quick glance and go underground.*)

●

The *schnorrer*, perhaps the richest character in all Jewish humor, is often described as a Jewish beggar with *chutzpah*. He does not actually solicit help; he *demands* it, and considers it his right.

Through vaudeville, the character of the *schnorrer* was translated into the American idiom as the proud panhandler. He has been especially well portrayed in cartoons and drawings, and a recent example depicts a panhandler approaching a businessman and asking, "Can I have a dime to call my answering service?"

But there is more to it than that. The *schnorrer* is actually a poor Jew with middle-class values. Perhaps better than anyone else in the community, he understands the true intention of *tzdakkah* (literally, righteousness, but generally translated as charity), which holds that sharing one's wealth with those less fortunate is not a favor or an act of grace for Jews, but an *obligation*. And so it is not simply *chutzpah* that motivates the *schnorrer*—although he is seldom lacking in it—but rather a different set of expectations and values than those generally held to by the rest of the community.

For this reason, the *schnorrer* has traditionally been regarded with a curious ambivalence; at times he is the successful underdog, while at other times the joke is at his expense. Were the *schnorrer* of no status or importance, such jokes would not exist, as Jewish humor does not normally attack the weak.

MRS. KRASNOV, feeling sorry for a *schnorrer* who appeared at her door, invited him in and gave him a substantial meal: chicken, *kugel*, wine, and two kinds of bread: black bread and challah.

The *schnorrer* devoured everything he was given, except the black bread. "The challah was wonderful," he said. "Do you have any more?"

"My dear man," said Mrs. Krasnov, "we have plenty of black bread, but challah is very expensive."

"I know," said the *schnorrer*. "But believe me, lady, it's worth it!"

Sometimes the lady of the house gets the last word:

●

Mrs. Krasnov once opened the door of her house and found a *schnorrer* standing there.

"Please, lady," he said. "I haven't eaten in three days."

"You should force yourself."

●

A poor man once dreamed he was frying dung.

He went to a dream interpreter and asked for an explanation.

"I'll interpret your dream for a zuza," said the soothsayer.

"If I had a zuza would I be frying dung?" responded the poor

man angrily. "I'd buy me a fish and fry that!"

medieval Jewish folktale

A SCHNORRER once wangled an appointment with Rothschild by insisting that he had a foolproof way for the banker to make half a million rubles.

"So let me hear your great idea," said the skeptical Rothschild.

"It's very simple," replied the *schnorrer*. "I understand that when your daughter gets married you're planning to give her a dowry of a million rubles."

"Nu?"

"So I've come to tell you that I'll marry her for half that amount!"

There are countless stories about Rothschild in Jewish lore, especially in connection with *schnorrers,* who flocked in droves to the handful of Jewish millionaires in Europe—who were regarded almost as fantasy figures by their impoverished countrymen. In perhaps the most famous of the Rothschild-*schnorrer* jokes:

•

A *schnorrer* tells his friend, "If I were Rothschild, I'd be richer than Rothschild."

"How can that be?" asks his friend.

"Simple—I'd do a little teaching on the side."

•

A *schnorrer* used to visit Rothschild every month with his brother, and each would be given a handout of fifty marks. The brother died, and the following month the *schnorrer* came alone. Upon seeing him, Rothschild's secretary handed the man fifty marks.

"Just a minute," protested the *schnorrer*. "I'm entitled to a hundred marks."

"But your brother is dead," replied the secretary. "And so his handout is canceled."

"What do you mean, canceled?" asked the *schnorrer* angrily. "Am I my brother's heir—or is Rothschild?!"

Rothschild is traveling through Minsk, and stops for breakfast in a small Jewish café. When he is finished, the waiter brings him the bill.

"Twenty rubles for two eggs!" shouts Rothschild. "That's impossible. Are eggs so rare in these parts?"

"No," replies the waiter. "But Rothschilds are."

•

A *schnorrer* tries without success to get an appointment with Rothschild. Finally, he stands outside the family mansion and shouts: "My family is starving to death and the baron refuses to see me!"

Rothschild acquiesces and gives the *schnorrer* thirty rubles. "Here you are," he says. "And let me tell you that if you hadn't caused such a scene, I would have given you sixty rubles."

"My dear Baron," replies the *schnorrer.* "You're a banker, and I don't give you banking advice. I'm a *schnorrer,* so please—don't give me *schnorring* advice."

•

This may be the quintessential *schnorrer* story; Freud tells it in his book on humor, and comments: "What these jokes whisper may be said aloud: that the wishes and desires of men have a right to make themselves acceptable alongside of exacting and ruthless morality."

Elsewhere in the book, Freud explains the psychology of the *schnorrer* "who in his thoughts treats the rich man's money as his own," and who "has actually, according to the sacred ordinances of the Jews, almost a right to make this confusion."

A *SCHNORRER* came to visit a rich man, who was so moved by the man's story that he gave him twenty dollars. An hour later, walking on the street, the rich man wandered into a restaurant and was astonished to see the *schnorrer* feasting on bagels and lox.

"What *chutzpah!*" said the rich man. "Is this why I gave you twenty dollars—so you could go out and eat bagels and lox?"

"Now just a minute," replied the *schnorrer*. "Before I came to you, when I didn't have any money at all, I couldn't *afford* to eat bagels and lox. Now, with God's help, I can finally pay for this nice breakfast, and you come in here and tell me I *shouldn't* eat bagels and lox. So tell me, *when can I eat bagels and lox?*"

•

A row of houses is destroyed by fire, and the community provides a fund for the victims. As the money is being disbursed, a poor man whose house was untouched by the fire comes for a handout.

"What do you mean by this?" he is asked. "Did you suffer from the fire?"

"Suffer?" he replies. "Believe me, I was scared to death!"

•

A DESTITUTE man went from door to door asking for alms because his house was destroyed in a fire.

"Have you a document from your rabbi affirming that your story is true?" he was asked.

"Oy," he replied. "That, too, was destroyed in the fire!"

This same joke appeared in *Fiddler on the Roof,* where the *schnorrer* listened to the rich man's woes, and said, "So, if you had a bad week, should *I* suffer?"

THE *schnorrer* comes to Kugelman for his monthly handout. He knocks on the door, but there is no reply. He knocks again, and a disheveled-looking Kugelman answers the door.

"What's the matter?" asks the *schnorrer*. "Is something wrong?"

"I've gone bankrupt, haven't you heard?"

"Certainly I've heard."

"Then what do you want from me?"

"Ten cents on the dollar."

A classic.

•

A poor man is observed staring in admiration at the large and ornate tombstone of the richest man in town. He shakes his head slowly and mutters, "Now, *that's* what I call living!"

•

AT the funeral of the richest man in town, a stranger was observed crying louder than any of the other mourners. One of the townspeople approached him. "Are you a relative of the deceased?"

"No."

"Then why are you crying?"

"That's why!"

ISRAEL ZANGWILL

The *Schnorrer's* Apprentice
How Yankele, the Polish *Schnorrer,*
Wins the Hand of the Daughter of Manasseh,
King of the *Schnorrers* (a Sephardi),
by Finagling a Sabbath Meal from the
Miserly Rabbi Remorse Red-herring

The rabbi drained the glass of schnapps, smacked his lips, and resumed his knife and fork. Manasseh reached for the unoffered bottle, and helped himself liberally. The rabbi unostentatiously withdrew it beyond his easy reach, looking at Yankele the while.

"How long have you been in England?" he asked the Pole.

"Not long," said Yankele.

"Ha! Does Gabriel the cantor still suffer from neuralgia?"

Yankele looked sad. "No—he is dead," he said.

"Dear me! Well, he was tottering when I knew him. His blowing of the ram's horn got wheezier every year. And how is his young brother, Samuel?"

"He is dead!" said Yankele.

"What—he, too! Tut, tut! He was so robust. Has Mendelssohn the stonemason got many more girls?"

"He is dead!" said Yankele.

"Nonsense!" gasped the rabbi, dropping his knife and fork. "Why, I heard from him only a few months ago."

"He is dead!" said Yankele.

"Good gracious me! Mendelssohn dead!" After a moment of emotion, he resumed his meal. "But his sons and daughters are all doing well, I hope. The eldest, Solomon, was a most pious youth, and his third girl, Neshamah, promised to be a rare beauty."

"They are dead!" said Yankele.

This time the rabbi turned pale as a corpse himself. He laid down his knife and fork automatically.

"D-dead," he breathed in an awestruck whisper. "All?"

"Every one. De same cholera took all de family."

The rabbi covered his face with his hands. "Then poor Solomon's wife is a widow. I hope he left her enough to live upon."

"No, but it doesn't matter," said Yankele.

"It matters a great deal," cried the Rabbi.

"She is dead," said Yankele.

"Rebecca Schwartz dead!" screamed the rabbi, for he had

Israel Zangwill (1864–1926) was England's most prominent Jewish writer. Aside from his prolific literary output (which included novels, stories, plays, poems, essays, and polemics), he devoted his life to a number of causes, including Zionism, the rights of women, pacifism, and the brotherhood of man. Today he is known mostly for his more serious works, such as *Children of the Ghetto, Ghetto Tragedies,* and his influential *The Melting Pot.*

But Zangwill was also a fine humorist, as *The King of Schnorrers* makes clear. First published in 1894, the novel is about masterly *schnorrer* Manasseh Bueno Barzilai Azevedo da Costa and his confrontation with Grobstock, a wealthy London philanthropist and Manasseh's reluctant benefactor.

The second half of the book concerns Manasseh's relationship with his apprentice, Yankele, an Ashkenazi *schnorrer* who must contend not only with poverty but with the haughtiness of his mentor's Sephardic elitism. In this selection, Yankele is put to the supreme test: to win the hand of Manasseh's daughter, he must successfully *schnorr* a Sabbath dinner from the notorious miser, Rabbi Remorse Red-herring. To add to Yankele's difficulties, he finds the King of the Schnorrers seated at the rabbi's table, having arrived a few minutes earlier.

once loved the maiden himself, and not having married her, had still a tenderness for her.

"Rebecca Schwartz," repeated Yankele inexorably.

"Was it the cholera?" faltered the rabbi.

"No, she vas heartbroke."

Rabbi Remorse Red-herring silently pushed his plate away, and leaned his elbows upon the table and his face upon his palms, and his chin upon the bottle of schnapps in mournful meditation.

"You are not eating, Rabbi," said Yankele insinuatingly.

"I have lost my appetite," said the rabbi.

"Vat a pity to let food get cold and spoil! You'd better eat it."

The rabbi shook his head querulously.

"Den I vill eat it," cried Yankele indignantly. "Good hot food like dat!"

"As you like," said the rabbi wearily. And Yankele began to eat at lightning speed, pausing only to wink at the inscrutable Manasseh; and to cast yearning glances at the inaccessible schnapps that supported the rabbi's chin.

Presently the rabbi looked up. "You're quite sure all these people are dead?" he asked with a dawning suspicion.

"May my blood be poured out like this schnapps," protested Yankele, dislodging the bottle, and vehemently pouring the spirit into a tumbler, "if dey be not."

The rabbi relapsed into his moody attitude, and retained it till his wife brought in a big willow-pattern china dish of stewed prunes and pippins. She produced four plates for these, and so Yankele finished his meal in the unquestionable status of a first-class guest. The rabbi was by this time sufficiently recovered to toy with two platefuls in a melancholy silence which he did not break till his mouth opened involuntarily to intone the grace.

When grace was over he turned to Manasseh and said, "And what was this way you were suggesting to me of getting a profitable Sephardic connection?"

"I did, indeed, wonder why you did not extend your practice as consolation preacher among the Spanish Jews," replied Manasseh gravely. "But after what we have just heard of the death rate of Jews in Grodno, I should seriously advise you to go back there."

"No, they cannot forget that I was once a boy," replied the rabbi with equal gravity. "I prefer the Spanish Jews. They are all well-to-do. They may not die so often as the Russians, but they die better, so to speak. You will give me introductions, you will speak of me to your illustrious friends, I understand."

"You understand!" repeated Manasseh in dignified astonishment. "You do not understand. I shall do no such thing."

"But you yourself suggested it!" cried the rabbi excitedly.

"I? Nothing of the kind. I had heard of you and your ministrations to mourners, and meeting you in the street this afternoon for the first time, it struck me to inquire why you did not carry your consolations into the bosom of my community, where so much more money is to be made. I said I wondered you had not done so from the first. And you—invited me to dinner. I still wonder. That is all, my good man." He rose to go.

The haughty rebuke silenced the rabbi, though his heart was hot with a vague sense of injury.

"Do you come my way, Yankele?" said Manasseh carelessly.

The rabbi turned hastily to his second guest.

"When do you want me to marry you?" he asked.

"You have married me," replied Yankele.

"I?" gasped the rabbi. It was the last straw.

"Yes," reiterated Yankele. "Hasn't he, Mr. da Costa?"

His heart went pit-a-pit as he put the question.

"Certainly," said Manasseh without hesitation.

Yankele's face was made glorious summer. Only two of the quartet knew the secret of his radiance.

"There, Rabbi," he cried exultantly. "Good Sabbath!"

"How do I know you won't spend it on a massage?"

"Good Sabbath!" added Manasseh.

"Good Sabbath," dazedly murmured the rabbi.

"Good Sabbath," added his wife.

"Congratulate me!" cried Yankele when they got outside.

"On what?" asked Manasseh.

"On being your future son-in-law, of course."

"Oh, on *that?* Certainly, I congratulate you most heartily." The two *schnorrers* shook hands. "I thought you were asking for compliments on your maneuvering."

"Vy, doesn't it deserve dem?"

"No," said Manasseh magisterially.

"No?" queried Yankele, his heart sinking again. "Vy not?"

"Why did you kill so many people?"

"Somebody must die dat I may live."

"You said that before," said Manasseh severely. "A good *schnorrer* would not have slaughtered so many for his dinner. It is a waste of good material. And then you told lies!"

"How do you know they are not dead?" pleaded Yankele.

The king shook his head reprovingly. "A first-class *schnorrer* never lies," he laid down.

"I might have made truth go as far as a lie—if you hadn't come to dinner yourself."

"What is that you say? Why, I came to encourage you by showing you how easy your task was."

"On de contrary, you made it much harder for me. Dere vas no dinner left."

"But against that you must reckon that since the rabbi had already invited one person, he couldn't be so hard to tackle as I had fancied."

"Oh, but you must not judge from yourself," protested Yankele. "You be not a *schnorrer*—you be a miracle."

"But I should like a miracle for my son-in-law also," grumbled the king.

"And if you had to *schnorr* a son-in-law, you vould get a miracle," said Yankele soothingly. "As he has to *schnorr* you, *he* gets the miracle."

"True," observed Manasseh musingly, "and I think you might therefore be very well content without the dowry."

"So I might," admitted Yankele, "only *you* vould not be content to break your promise. I suppose I shall have some of de dowry on de marriage morning."

"On that morning you shall get my daughter—without fail. Surely that will be enough for one day!"

"Vell, ven do I get de money your daughter gets from de synagogue?"

"When she gets it from the synagogue, of course."

"How much vill it be?"

"It may be a hundred and fifty pounds," said Manasseh pompously.

Yankele's eyes sparkled.

"And it may be less," added Manasseh as an afterthought.

"How much less?" inquired Yankele anxiously.

"One hundred and fifty pounds," repeated Manasseh pompously.

"D'you mean to say I may get not'ing?"

"Certainly, if she gets nothing. What I promised you was the money she gets from the synagogue. Should she be fortunate enough in the *sorteo—*"

"De *sorteo!* Vat is dat?"

"The dowry I told you of. It is accorded by lot. My daughter has as good a chance as any other maiden. By winning her you stand to win a hundred and fifty pounds. It is a handsome amount. There are not many fathers who would do as much for their daughters," concluded Manasseh with conscious magnanimity.

"But about de Jerusalem estate!" said Yankele, shifting his standpoint. "I don't vant to go and live dere. De Messiah is not yet come."

"No, you will hardly be able to live on it," admitted Manasseh.

"You do not object to my selling it, den?"

"Oh, no! If you are so sordid, if you have no true Jewish sentiment!"

"Ven can I come into possession?"

"On the wedding day, if you like."

"One may as vell get it over," said Yankele, suppressing a desire to rub his hands in glee. "As de Talmud says, 'One peppercorn today is better dan a basketful of pumpkins tomorrow.' "

"All right! I will bring it to the synagogue."

"Bring it to de synagogue!" repeated Yankele in amazement. "Oh, you mean de deed of transfer."

"The deed of transfer! Do you think I waste my substance on solicitors? No, I will bring the property itself."

"But how can you do dat?"

"Where is the difficulty?" demanded Manasseh with withering contempt. "Surely a child could carry a casket of Jerusalem earth to synagogue!"

"A casket of earth! Is your property in Jerusalem only a casket of earth?"

"What then?' You didn't expect it would be a casket of diamonds?" retorted Manasseh, with gathering wrath. "To a true Jew, a casket of Jerusalem earth is worth all the diamonds in the world."

"But your Jerusalem property is a fraud!" gasped Yankele.

"Oh, no; you may be easy on that point. It's quite genuine. I know there is a good deal of spurious Palestine earth in circulation, and that many a dead man who has clods of it thrown into his tomb is nevertheless buried in unholy soil. But this casket I was careful to obtain from a rabbi of extreme sanctity. It was the only thing he had worth *schnorring.*"

"I don't suppose I shall get more dan a crown for it," said Yankele, with irrepressible indignation.

"That's what I say," returned Manasseh. "And never did I think a son-in-law of mine would meditate selling my holy soil for a paltry five shillings! I will not withdraw my promise, but I am disappointed in you—bitterly disappointed. Had I known this earth was not to cover your bones, it should have gone down to the grave with me, as enjoined in my last will and testament, by the side of which it stands in my safe."

"Very vell, I von't sell it," said Yankele sulkily.

"You relieve my soul. As the Mishnah says, 'He who marries a wife for money begets forward children.'"

"And vat about de province in England?" asked Yankele, in low, despondent tones. He had never believed in *that,* but now, behind all his despair and incredulity, was a vague hope that something might yet be saved from the crash.

"Oh, you shall choose your own," replied Manasseh graciously. "We will get a large map of London, and I will mark off in red pencil the domain in which I *schnorr.* You will then choose any district in this—say, two main streets and a dozen byways and alleys—which shall be marked off in blue pencil, and whatever province of my kingdom you pick, I undertake not to *schnorr* in, from your wedding day onwards. I need not tell you how valuable such a province already is; under careful administration, such as you would be able to give it, the revenue from it might be doubled, trebled. I do not think your tribute to me need be more than ten percent."

Yankele walked along mesmerized, reduced to somnambulism by his magnificently masterful patron.

"Oh, here we are!" said Manasseh, stopping short. "Won't you come in and see the bride, and wish her joy?"

A flash of joy came into Yankele's own face, dissipating his gloom. After all, there was always da Costa's beautiful daughter—a solid, substantial satisfaction. He was glad she was not an item of the dowry.

The unconscious bride opened the door.

"Ah, ha, Yankele!" said Manasseh, his paternal heart aglow at the sight of her loveliness. "You will be not only a king, but a rich king. As it is written, 'Who is rich? He who hath a beautiful wife.'"

Drawing by George Price; © 1938 The New Yorker Magazine, Inc.

I'm singing you a ballad of a great man of the cloth.

His name was Harry Lewis and he worked for Irving Roth.

He died while cutting velvet on a hot July the Fourth,

But his cloth goes shining on!

> Glory glory Harry Lewis.
>> Glory glory Harry Lewis.
>>> Glory glory Harry Lewis,
>>>> His cloth goes shining on!

Oh, Harry Lewis perished in the service of the Lord.

He was trampling through the warehouse where the drapes of Roth are stored.

He had the finest funeral the union could afford,

But his cloth goes shining on.

ALLAN SHERMAN

"The Drapes of Roth," sung to the tune of "The Battle Hymn of the Republic," was part of the enormously successful hit album of 1963 *My Son the Folksinger.* The album was recorded one night in Hollywood, in a party setting, with several noted "real" songwriters in attendance. The audience was delighted, but Sherman, who had been performing his material at Hollywood parties for years, recalls in his autobiography that he left the recording session thinking: "Well, that came out nice; tomorrow I'd better start looking for work again."

The album was so popular that at Sam Goody's in New York there was a sign next to the pile: "Limit: 12 to a Customer." The title of the album entered the language. *Time* magazine did a story on Rose Kennedy called "My Son, the President." El Al took a full-page ad, "My Son, the Pilot." And Paul Krassner's magazine, *The Realist,* published a drawing of the Madonna and Child, captioned "My Son, the Savior."

The characters who appear in traditional Jewish humor tend to be either very poor or very rich. Jewish humor in America reflects the rise of the Jewish middle class—especially a business-oriented middle class. Part of its success follows from the Jewish art of *hondling* (Yiddish for "bargaining"); more than a way to save money, *hondling* came to represent a social process by which both buyer and seller were satisfied that the best possible deal had been made.

* * *

A merchant who is known to be remiss in paying his bills is seen haggling with a wholesaler.

"Why bother?" he is asked. "You won't pay the guy anyway, so why all the bargaining?"

"I like him," the merchant answers, "and I want to help keep down his losses."

•

"My son," Blumberg was saying upon his early retirement from the garment business, "it's all yours now. I've made a good living because of two principles: honesty and wisdom. Honesty is very important. If you promise the goods by the first of April, *no matter what happens in the shop* you've got to deliver them by the first of April."

"Sure, Pop. But what about wisdom?"

"Wisdom means: Dummy, who said you should *promise?*"

•

Manoff and Siskind met one day for lunch in the garment district. It was hard to tell which of them was more depressed. Manoff began: "Siskind, my friend, life is treating me badly. June was a disaster. Never in my entire career have I seen a June like the one I had. I felt miserable—until July. July made June look good. I didn't make a single sale all month! You had to see it to believe it. In fact—"

"Just a minute," said Siskind. "You think you've got problems? Listen to this. My wife has cancer. My brother is getting divorced. And my son, my only son, came to tell me yesterday that he was getting married: to somebody named *Harold.* You understand? He wants to marry a *boy!* My son is a *fairy.* Nu, I ask you, what can be worse than that?"

"I'll tell you," said Manoff. "August."

•

An emperor once called in his business adviser, who was a Jew. "Here are twenty gold pieces," said the emperor. "I want you to go out and buy me a dachshund."

"Your Excellency," replied the Jew, "where do you think I can get a good dachshund for twenty gold pieces? It will take at least forty gold pieces, and that way I can find you a really *good* dachshund."

"Very well," said the emperor, handing over twenty more coins. "But it must be a very fine dachshund."

"Have no fear, Your Excellency," replied the Jew. "I promise it will be the finest dachshund that money can buy. But there is just one small thing, if it please Your Excellency."

"And what is that?"

"A thousand pardons, Your Excellency, but what exactly *is* a dachshund?"

SHAPIRO walks into work one day at nine, half an hour late. The boss is furious. "You should have been here at eight-thirty!" he shouts.

"Why?" says Shapiro. "What happened at eight-thirty?"

RACKMAN and Fleisher, partners in the garment industry, had just suffered through their worst season ever. Ten thousand madras sports coats were hanging on the rack unsold, and bankruptcy was looming closer.

Out of the blue, in walked a buyer from Australia. "I say there," he began. "You boys wouldn't have any madras sports coats, would you? I've been looking for them everywhere!"

Rackman allowed as how there just might be a few left, and soon a deal was made whereby the ten thousand jackets would be shipped to Australia at a handsome profit. "There is one thing, though," said the buyer. "For an order this large, I'll have to get a confirmation from my home office. I don't anticipate any problem, and unless I send you a cable by the end of the week, the deal goes through."

Tuesday, Wednesday, and Thursday passed slowly, with the partners nervously waiting to see if the Australian would change his mind. Friday morning went by without incident. Rackman and Fleisher were closing up shop when, at ten minutes to five, there was a knock on the door: "Telegram!"

The partners froze. Trembling, Fleisher grabbed the cable and opened it. Suddenly his face lit up: "Benny, great news! Your sister died!"

A WOMAN walked into Rosenfeld's bakery and asked, "How much are bagels?"

"Three twenty-five a dozen," came the reply.

"That's pretty high," said the woman. "Eagerman sells them for two-seventy."

"So buy from Eagerman."

"I can't," said the woman. "He's out of bagels."

"Aha!" said Rosenfeld. "When I'm out of bagels, I also sell for two-seventy."

PUTTERMAN went into a small grocery store to buy salt. "What kind of salt would you like?" asked the owner.

"What *kind?*" replied Putterman. "You mean there are different kinds?"

"Hoo-boy!" said the owner. "There sure are. Come with me into the back room." And there, in the back of the store, Putterman saw three dozen barrels of salt. "And what's more," said the owner, "each kind is different."

"Good Lord," said Putterman. "You turn out to be quite a specialist. Boy, you really must know how to sell salt."

"Not me," said the owner. "I'm not so good at it. But the guy I bought it from—boy, can *he* sell salt!"

ROMBERG, on a business trip, found himself having to use a pay toilet in a public building. He had just made himself comfortable when he noticed that the toilet paper roll was empty. Seeing a pair of shoes in the next booth, he called out, "Excuse me, friend, but do you have any toilet paper in there?"

"No, I'm afraid there doesn't seem to be any here, either."

Romberg paused for a moment. "Listen," he said, "do you happen to have a newspaper or magazine with you?"

"Sorry, I don't."

Romberg paused again, and then said, "How about two fives for a ten?"

A DRY-GOODS merchant from Lublin orders a consignment of goods from Warsaw. Instead of the goods, he receives a cable: "Sorry, cannot fill order until previous order is paid for."

Regretfully, the merchant wires back: "Please cancel order. Can't wait that long."

Old Mrs. Morgenbesser had been looking over every paper fan in the pushcart, feeling them, holding them, waving them back and forth. Finally, she made a selection.

The next day she returned, holding the fan, which was ripped down the middle.

"Look what happened," she said to the peddler. "I want my money back."

"Lady, how much did I charge you for this fan?"

"A penny."

"And what did you do with it?"

"What else? I waved it back and forth in front of my face."

"Well," said the peddler, "that's your problem. That's what you do with a *nickel* fan. With a penny fan, you hold the fan still and you wave your *head!*"

"How much is this fan?" says Mrs. Morgenbesser.

"One cent," replies the peddler.

"Too much," says Mrs. Morgenbesser.

"Okay, lady," says the peddler. "So make me an offer."

The young optometrist had just been hired at a new job. "Here's how we work," said Feinberg, the boss. "A customer comes in for a new pair of glasses. First you examine him. Then you start to show him some frames."

"But the prices aren't marked," said the young man.

"Exactly," said Feinberg. "When the customer selects a frame that he likes, he'll ask you how much they cost. You say, 'Eighty dollars.' If he doesn't object, then you add, 'And the lenses, of course, are twenty dollars.' And if he still doesn't object, you say 'each'!"

Ginsberg lost his wallet at a testimonial dinner. He went to the microphone and announced: "Ladies and gentlemen, I've lost my wallet, with eight hundred dollars in it. Whoever finds it will get a reward of fifty dollars."

A voice from the back of the room yelled: "I'll give seventy-five!"

SAM LEVENSON

Bargaining

Sam Levenson (1911–1980) was a true product of postwar American Judaism. A liberal and a universalist, he worked as a schoolteacher (teaching Spanish) in Brooklyn before going into show business, and he drew upon his teaching career as the basis for his early routines.

During the late 1940s and early 1950s, when he was establishing himself as a Jewish humorist—as opposed to a Jewish comic—Levenson represented a particular style of Jewish humor: warm and sweet, without sharp edges, and unsophisticated—a Jewish humor that easily ingratiated itself with the newly emerging Jewish middle class, and well beyond.

By studiously avoiding dialect humor, and anything that smacked of vaudeville, Levenson differentiated himself from the comic styles of most of his contemporaries. By the 1960s, as he achieved national prominence, Levenson adjusted his material still further. His nostalgia grew increasingly *pareve;* by now Levenson represented the antithesis of the vibrant energy of the newly emerging "sick" comics (like Shelley Berman and Lenny Bruce), who reflected in their work the tension and anxiety of the contemporary American and Jewish experience.

•

"Good morning. I came to this store because I don't like to bargain."

"Well, you've come to the right place. We're strictly a one-price outfit."

"Excellent. I like that blue suit over there. What will it cost?"

"Like I said, I don't fool around with bargaining. So I'm not going to ask two-fifty for this suit, or even two thirty-five. I'm going to give you my best price: two hundred and twenty dollars."

"Well, you're my kind of businessman, and that's why I'm here. I won't fool around and offer you one-sixty for that suit, or even one seventy-five. I'll give you two hundred dollars for that suit."

"You can have it for two hundred and ten."

"I'll take it."

•

Our mamas did not hesitate to bargain. Questioning a price was standard procedure.

"How much are these cucumbers?"

"Two for five."

The mama pushed one aside. "And how much is this one?"

"Three cents."

"Okay. I'll take the other one."

Fair trade meant that you never paid the asking price. All deals were negotiable, a custom that in America goes at least as far back as the purchase of Manhattan Island.

When one mama was caught shoplifting, the butcher naturally did not press charges. "Just pay for the chicken and we'll forget what happened."

Tears of gratitude running down her face, she kissed his, sobbing, "I don't know why I did it, and I swear to you I'll never do it again. I'll be glad to pay for it, but not at your prices, you crook, you!"

Making a good deal called for every known technique and stratagem of logic and pseudologic deduction, induction, seduction, abduction, thesis, hypothesis, and antithesis. Rich people could afford logical reasoning: Parker sells good suits. This is a Parker suit. Therefore this is a good suit.

People like Mama, however, who could not risk spending an extra penny, questioned everything: "Parker sells good suits? This is a good suit? Who said so—Parker?"

When I was about to be graduated from elementary school, Mama took me to the pushcart market to buy me a tie. I was the last of her kids, and she was going to treat me to my first brand-new, never-handed-down tie.

The tie man asked fifty cents and, to my utter astonishment, Mama paid it—no counteroffer, no debate, no dissent, just fifty cents paid politely in cash, without comment, and, "Thank you," yet, to close the deal.

I didn't dare ask. As we walked home Mama read my mind. "Sammy, you are wondering why your mother paid the fifty cents without a word. Well, you are young yet. Some day you'll understand. I never liked that man. I'm getting even. Tonight he will kill himself because he didn't ask me a dollar."

•

"NAME?"

"Rabinowitz."

"Wait a minute, Mr. Rabinowitz. You really don't look like you're cut out for this job. Are you sure you're a lumberjack?"

"Yes."

"It's just that you're such a little man. Well, let's see what you can do. Can you chop down that tree over there? Hm, not bad. How about that big one behind it? In one stroke? This I want to see. Hm. Very impressive, Mr. Rabinowitz. Really, I apologize for doubting your ability. I mean, you really don't *look* like a lumberjack, but you sure can cut trees! Say, where did you learn your trade?"

"Well, for many years I worked in the Sahara Forest."

"Surely you must mean the Sahara Desert?"

"Sure. *Now* it's a desert!"

This is a favorite of comedian Myron Cohen. Jokes almost always have *some* basis in reality, and in Eastern Europe, Jews were said to be especially adept at logging—as well as at certain other unlikely occupations, including teamsters, porters, blacksmiths, drivers, innkeepers, and dairymen.

•

During the Nazi period, Lefkowitz walks into a German police station, carrying a newspaper with a job advertisement circled in red.

"You've come about this job?" asks the desk sergeant. "You must be kidding. Can't you read? We need a young man, strong and hardy, a man who doesn't wear glasses. And look—the ad specifically mentions that we want an Aryan. You're obviously a Jew. So what are you doing here?"

"I've just come to tell you," says Lefkowitz, "that on me you shouldn't count."

•

Dick Codor © 1979

MOISHE NADIR

Thoughts About Forty Cents

With the fish course, my wife also served me a bit of news about a town called Roosevelt, where they had shot into a crowd of strikers without any rhyme or reason. I felt my blood begin to boil, seethe, spill over. Picking carefully at the bones of my carp, I chewed the delicious fish and talked to myself.

"Those vile capitalists! We ought to twist their heads off! Such swinish cannibals! Such cannibalistic swine!"

When my wife handed me the plate of soup, and I saw amidst the noodles the kind of marrow bone I love to chew on,

Moishe Nadir (Isaac Reiss; 1885–1943) was a celebrated humorist, an American-Yiddish writer of verse and short essays. He delighted in inventing new words, in mixing the contemporary American idiom into his Yiddish, thus making his work a challenge to translators. Much of his humor was topical, and appealed to a specialized audience, so his work is not widely known today. "Others write clever things for foolish people," he once observed. "I write foolish things for clever people."

my wrath cooled down somewhat, and blowing on the tasty soup I murmured to myself:

"Who knows, after all, which side is guilty? It's impossible that they would just go and shoot innocent people for nothing. For instance—has anyone shot at *you* lately?" (I said to myself.)

This logical argument pleased me immensely and I considered myself a thoughtful individual, a wise man, a radical thinker, and so on.

When my wife brought the meat to the table and I saw the two chicken wings and a sweet chicken liver and a splendid chicken leg, I began to see the situation in a completely new light. Munching on the white wing and washing it down with a glass of good wine, I began to see that the whole thing was not so terrible as it had appeared during the fish course, and that you have to give the other side a chance to tell its story too.

"Who knows!" I asked myself as I chewed on the chicken leg. "Who knows whether those strikers aren't really dangerous? And why (I thought further) should poor people strike, anyway? Who asked them to? If the Law (I said) *ordered* them to strike, well, that would be a different story. But as long as the Law allows you to live on a dollar and sixty cents a day, and doesn't bother you—then why should you go out and strike for a lousy forty pennies a day? Really! It's ridiculous!"

When my wife brought me the wonderful apple compote and a piece of fresh strudel, I took another look at the piece of news about the shooting of the strikers in the town of Roosevelt, and sipping the last of my Turkish demitasse, I said to myself (and I could feel my blood starting to boil again):

"What the hell is the matter with those strikers, anyway! What are they making such a fuss about! They must have exactly two dollars a day? In the first place, how do they know the bosses can afford two dollars a day? Maybe they don't have it. Maybe they don't want to. Maybe they don't have any time to bother with the whole thing.

"And in the second place, if they *do* go out on strike—why *not* shoot them? If (I said to myself as I cleaned my teeth with a toothpick)—if in Europe they are shooting thousands of people who are *not* striking, then why shouldn't we here be allowed to shoot a couple dozen foolish workers who are striking for a lousy forty cents a day? It's ridiculous, that's what it is!"

And only at this point (when I lit up my fine Havana cigar and made myself comfortable on my soft easy chair) did I see with brilliant clarity how silly, how trivial those workers are. For a measly forty cents a day, to make all that commotion and even risk their necks!

I couldn't help laughing, really I couldn't.

THREE clothing manufacturers are having lunch together, and they get into an argument about which of them is the most important. Katz brags about how much he gives to charity. Gold boasts about how much income tax he pays. Dorfman describes the clothing empire he is building.

Finally, Katz begins to tell a story: "A few months ago I had to go to Washington. I'm walking down the street and suddenly a black limousine pulls up beside me. And who do you think is inside? President Reagan, that's who. 'Katz,' he yells out the window. 'What brings you to Washington?' I tell him I'm there on business. 'Where are you staying?' he asks. I tell him I'm staying at the Mayflower Hotel. 'No you aren't,' says the President. 'Get in the car and stay with me at the White House.' And that's how important I am."

Gold and Dorfman are listening patiently. "Big deal," says Gold when Katz is finished. 'It reminds me of when I was in London. There I am, walking down the street, when who should stroll by but Queen Elizabeth. 'Hello there, Gold,' she says. 'What brings you to London?' I tell her I'm there on business. 'And you're probably staying at some hotel?' she asks me. So I tell her where I'm staying. 'Don't be silly, Gold,' she says. 'When you're in London you'll stay with us at the palace.' And that's how important I am."

Dorfman says nothing, but three days later, Katz and Gold receive first-class airplane tickets to Rome. They go to the airport, where Dorfman is waiting for them. "There's something I want to show you," he says.

When the plane lands in Rome, the men take a taxi to the Vatican. Dorfman brings them into a large courtyard, filled with thousands of tourists. "Now wait here, boys," he says, and then disappears.

A few minutes later the crowd breaks into a cheer. People are pointing to a balcony, and when Katz and Gold look up, they notice two figures waving to the crowd. An American tourist taps them on the shoulder. "Excuse me, gentlemen," he says, "but some of us were wondering: Who's that fellow in the white robes standing next to Dorfman?"

•

Stein, a clothing manufacturer, returns from three weeks in Italy.

"How was your trip?" asks his partner.

"Terrific," replies Stein.

"Did you get to see the Pope?"

"Certainly."

"Nu?"

"I figure a thirty-nine short."

•

Cohen returns from Rome and is asked by his partner, "Did you see the Pope?"

"Certainly. We had lunch together."

"Nu?"

"He's all right. Her I didn't care for!"

•

In a possibly apocryphal story, when the Pope visited Israel a few years ago and was photographed with a government official, an Israeli newspaper ran the photograph with a caption reading: "The Pope is the one with the yarmulke."

To sell something you have
to someone who wants it—
that is not business.
But to sell something you don't have
to someone who doesn't want it—
that is business.

FOGELMAN needs a job, and has no qualms about inventing the necessary qualifications. He reasons that once he finds work, he will impress the boss so much that everything will be forgiven.

After a successful initial interview with the *Encyclopedia of American History,* he is called back to meet the sales manager.

"You say you have experience selling books?"

"Lots of it," replies Fogelman.

"And you have a master's in American history from the University of Michigan?"

"Correct," replies Fogelman. "History is my field of study."

"Well, then," says the sales manager. "As soon as I can complete this form, we can get you started in our firm."

While the sales manager is making a few notations, Fogelman, obviously pleased with himself, begins to whistle. Looking around the room, he notices pictures of Washington and Lincoln on the walls. Pointing to the portraits, he turns to the sales manager and says, "Fine-looking men. Your partners?"

BERGER, a newly rich businessman, is told to invest in paintings for tax purposes.

"What do I know about art?" he asks.

"Never mind that," says the adviser. "Go to a reputable gallery and buy whatever you like."

Berger visits a fancy little gallery on Madison Avenue, where he is shown a huge canvas that is completely black except for a round spot of red in the lower-right-hand corner. The size of the painting and the shock of the red spot captivate Berger, and he asks the gallery owner about the meaning of the work, and its price.

"My, my," says the owner. "You obviously have an eye for good art. This is one of our finest pieces. It's by Rothkofsky, and it sells for fifty-five thousand dollars."

"I don't want to sound naive," says Berger, "but it doesn't seem to be *about* anything."

"On the contrary," says the art dealer. "It's about *everything,* although of course it's all symbolic. The black background represents the vastness of the universe, and the red spot stands for the finite nature of man adrift in it."

Berger is duly impressed, and writes out a check. The painting is delivered and hung in his home the next day.

The following winter, his investment adviser tells him it's time to invest in a second piece of art. Again he goes to the gallery on Madison Avenue. "Is there anything else by Roth-kofsky?" he asks.

"You're in luck, Mr. Berger," says the owner, leading him into a back room, where a canvas covers an entire wall. The canvas is painted black, except for two yellow spots in the low-er-right-hand corner.

"Well," says the owner. "What do you think? Amazing, isn't it?"

"It's pretty," concedes Berger. "But *tsu feel ungepatchket* [too busy]!"

Rava said: "A man should get so drunk on Purim that he can't distinguish between 'Cursed is Haman' and 'Blessed is Mordecai.'"

Rabbah and Rabbi Zeira once made a Purim feast together. They got drunk, and Rabbah went and cut Rabbi Zeira's throat. In the morning, Rabbah prayed to God, and brought Rabbi Zeira to life again.

The next year, Rabbah again invited Rabbi Zeira to join him for a Purim feast.

"No, thank you," said Rabbi Zeira. "A miracle may not happen every time!"

—Talmud (Megillah 7b)

IT was Yom Kippur, and the cantor was chanting the *Hineni*, the self-deprecatory supplication that begins the Musaf Ser-vice. Coming to the end of the prayer, the cantor added his personal cry: "Dear God, Lord of the Universe, I am nothing, nothing, nothing at all!"

Hearing this heartfelt plea, the rabbi added a similar prayer: "I am nothing, Lord, nothing, even less than nothing."

And then a third voice joined in, from the back of the room. It was the *shammes,* the sexton, who had thrown himself on the floor and was proclaiming: "I, too, am nothing, O Lord, nothing, nothing at all."

Whereupon the rabbi turned to the cantor with a sniff and whispered, "Look who thinks he's a nothing!"

One day a wealthy but ignorant man came into the synagogue. The *shammes,* impressed by the man's attire, led him to the seat of honor, next to the rabbi.

Searching for some appropri-ate conversation, the wealthy man turned to the rabbi and said, "Rabbi, it says here in the prayer book that 'beast has been placed next to man.' Who is responsible for this strange order?"

The rabbi replied, "In the pre-sent case, the *shammes.*"

The naiveté of rabbis when it comes to financial matters is frequently commented on in jokes. Originally, rabbis were unpaid lay leaders who had their own professions. Hillel was a woodcutter and Shammai was a carpenter. Maimonides and Nachmanides were physicians. But over the centuries, the rabbinate has evolved into a profession of its own.

•

Two litigants came before the rabbi, and when the case was settled, they gave him fifteen rubles.
"What's this?" asked the rabbi.
"It's money," the men explained.
"What's money?" the rabbi asked.
"Money is the medium of exchange. It's how people do business."
"Nu, so what does a rabbi need with business?"
"You can give it to your wife."
"And what will my wife do with it?"
"Rabbi, she can use the money to buy fish, meat, potatoes, clothes —everything!"
"Really? Well, in that case, maybe you should let me have a little more!"

•

Max Shulman (born in 1919) is the author of many novels and screenplays, including *The Many Loves of Dobie Gillis* (as well as the scripts for the CBS television series of the same name, which ran from 1959 to 1962); *Rally Round the Flag, Boys; I was a Teen-Age Dwarf;* and *Potatoes Are Cheaper,* from which this selection is taken.

THE rabbi was distressed at the lack of generosity among his congregants, and he prayed that the rich should give more charity to the poor.

"And has your prayer been answered?" asked his wife.

"Half of it was," replied the rabbi. "The poor are willing to accept."

MAX SHULMAN

Rabbis

Next Ma went to hire a rabbi for the wedding. There were three synagogues in Saint Paul but one was Reform, so naturally to this one we didn't belong. The other two were Orthodox and at one time or another we'd been members of both.

First we belonged to the Sons of David, but that ended when Ma got into a fight with the rabbi—Rabbi Greenberg, his name was. What happened was Ma was cleaning a chicken one day and she found a little piece of something hard in the gizzard. According to the rules, if there's anything in the gizzard that's made out of metal, the chicken is not kosher. But if it's made out of sand or gravel, the chicken *is* kosher. But you're not allowed to decide by yourself; you got to take the chicken to a rabbi.

So off Ma went to Rabbi Greenberg and he took a look at the gizzard and he said, "Too bad, missus. That's a cuff link."

"What are you talking?" Ma said. "That's a piece gravel."

"With *initials?*" said the rabbi.

So of course Ma did what everybody does in those cases: you eat the chicken and join a different shul.

So we joined the Sons of Zion, and in fact we were still members, but Ma decided not to have the rabbi marry Libbie —Rabbi Sopkin, his name was. It wasn't that Ma didn't like Rabbi Sopkin; she did; everybody did. He was a nice easygoing old guy who was always willing to turn a blind eye when you showed up with a chicken who had metal in the gizzard, but the point was he *did* have a blind eye. He wore a black patch over it when he remembered, but generally he forgot. Also he had this bad stammer and there was a hunch on his back, not too big, but you could notice it all right, don't worry. And another thing: I don't mean any disrespect, but facts are facts. Rabbi Sopkin was a terrible farter. And not little sneaky ones, either;

great big rolling ones, and steady. My uncle Shimen, a veteran, said it reminded him of Château-Thierry.

Well, as I said, we all liked Rabbi Sopkin but here's how Ma figured and I think she was right: why spend a whole fortune to impress A. M. Zimmerman and then drag in a comedy rabbi to cock it up?

So Ma decided to call in Rabbi Pflaum of Temple Beth El, which surprised hell out of me because Beth El was the Reform shul, and Ma has always had only one word for Reform Jews: *goyim.*

Still and all, if class was what Ma was after, she couldn't have done better than Rabbi Pflaum. Class he had plenty, right down to the white piping on his vest. And what a fancy talker! He talked even fancier than Mr. Harwood, that prick adviser of mine at the university. "Esteemed lady," Rabbi Pflaum said to Ma, "I shall be happy to officiate, for is not marriage an honorable estate?"

Ma just gave him a look; she didn't understand a word.

"What stipend have you in mind?" he said.

This she understood. "Five dollars," she said.

"Surely you jest," he said.

"Take it or leave it," Ma said.

"Come, madam, haggling is not seemly," he said. "I'll take twenty dollars."

"Six," said Ma.

"Fifteen," he said. "The ball is in your court."

"Seven-fifty," she said.

"Where will this wedding occur?" he said.

"By the Lowry Hotel in the Grand Ballroom," she said.

"All right," he said. "Ten dollars plus supper."

"You got it," she said.

"Supper for my wife too," he said.

"But no kids," Ma said.

"Just the oldest boy," he said.

"How old?" she said.

"Fourteen," he said.

"Then knock off a dollar," Ma said.

"He's small for his age," he said.

"Nine dollars," said Ma. "There'll be cigars too."

"Done and done," said the rabbi.

"Wear a yarmulke," said Ma.

Mark Podwal © 1978

This well-known anti-Hasidic story has evoked a fair amount of interpretation. Freud comments on it with the proverb, "In great things it is enough to have wished." Theodor Reik, Freud's student, interprets the jokes to mean that the Cracrow Rabbi has expressed an unconscious desire to see his rival dead. The disciple's reply, according to Reik, is actually a warning: "Beware of me! I am a pupil of that rabbi who is so powerful in his hatred."

•

A Hasid comes to see his rabbi: "Rabbi, I have had a dream in which I am the leader of three hundred Hasidim."

The Rabbi replies: "Come back when three hundred Hasidim have a dream that you are their leader."

•

THE great Rabbi of Cracow was in the synagogue with his disciples when suddenly he let out a loud cry.

"Rabbi, what is the matter?" asked his disciples.

"A terrible thing has just happened," the rabbi replied. "I have just learned that the great Rabbi of Lemberg has died!"

The disciples of the Cracow Rabbi were amazed at this display of telepathic power, and they immediately went into mourning for the Lemberg Rabbi.

A few days later a delegation from Lemberg made its way to Cracow on business. The members of the Cracow community offered their condolences to the travelers, but were astonished to learn from them that the Lemberg Rabbi was alive and in excellent health.

It was soon verified that the Cracow Rabbi's "knowledge" was incorrect, and some of the skeptics in town began to ridicule him and tease his disciples. "Your rabbi is an impostor," they said. "The Rabbi of Lemberg is still alive!"

"That's not important," replied one of the Cracow Rabbi's disciples. "Isn't it enough that our rabbi was able to see all the way from Cracow to Lemberg?"

Dick Codor © 1981

A MAN was boasting about the piety of his rabbi. "My rabbi, may he live to be a hundred and twenty, is so pious that he fasts every day—except, of course, for Saturdays and holidays."

"How can that be true?" asked his friend. "Why, just this morning I saw your rabbi eating breakfast."

"That shows how much *you* know," replied the first man. "You see, my rabbi is very modest about his piety. If he eats, it is only to hide from others the fact that he is fasting."

TWO women were discussing their rabbis.

"Has your rabbi performed any miracles lately?" asked one.

"It depends what you mean," said her friend. "Is it a miracle if God does whatever the rabbi asks Him?"

"I would think so!"

"Well," said the first woman, "around here we consider it a miracle if our rabbi does whatever God asks *him!*"

As the obvious authority figures in Jewish life, rabbis come in for more than their fair share of abuse. Rabbi Nahman of Bratzlav, evidently no great fan of his colleagues, is quoted as having said that "it was difficult for Satan alone to mislead the entire world, so he appointed rabbis in various communities."

Dick Codor © 1981

THREE Hasidim were bragging about their rabbis.

"My rabbi is so pious," began the first man, "that day and night he trembles. When he goes to sleep he has to be strapped to the bed so that he doesn't fall out."

"Your rabbi may be pious," said the second man, "but my rabbi is so close to God that *God* trembles, and is afraid of displeasing him."

"Very well," said the third man. "But *my* rabbi has gone through both of those stages. At first, he used to tremble. Then it got to the point where God trembled. Finally, my rabbi said to God, "Look, why should we *both* tremble?"

Dick Codor © 1981

Treat him like a rabbi, but watch him like a thief.

Hasidic Tales, with a Guide to Their Interpretation by the Noted Scholar

These tales are clearly a parody of Martin Buber's famous rendition of Hasidic tales. Woody Allen is clearly fascinated with Hasidim, who make absurd, cameo appearances in several of his films (in *Annie Hall,* Allen turns into a Hasid when viewed by Annie's mother; in *Take the Money and Run,* Allen takes an experimental drug and turns into a Hasidic preacher); perhaps, like Kafka, he thinks of them as the *real* Jews.

Whether or not he is aware of it, Woody Allen is contributing here to a venerable strain of Jewish humor: parodies against Hasidim. The first major work in this tradition was *Megalleh Temirin* (Revealer of Secrets), published in 1819; it was so skillfully rendered that it was accepted as genuine—*even by Hasidim.* A similar fate has taken place with anti-Hasidic songs. The famous *"Un Az Der Rebbe Zingt"* ("When the Rebbe sings, so do all the Hasidim . . .") was composed as an attack on Hasidism and the way the disciples instinctively follow their leader. The song, however, endures as a piece of nostalgia, evoking a scene of warmth and good humor.

An anonymous parody from 1868 was more effective; it described a novice who encounters a group of Hasidim playing cards, and who explains:

"What shall I tell you, dear brother? The *Shechinah* [divine presence] actually revealed itself there, for the room was full of smoke from end to end, as from twenty pipes. But it was certainly no smoke, because it was Sabbath, and therefore must have been the *Shechinah* in full revelation. . . . Then I saw them take many pieces of paper that looked like tablets, bearing strange images of female servants, priests, butchers, each one with two heads. Some of these they held in their holy hands and some they threw at each other. I do not know what all this signified, but I am sure there is some sublime secret in these tablets. For I have seen how careful they were with them and how they counted them many times. . . ."

A man journeyed to Chelm in order to seek the advice of Rabbi Ben Kaddish, the holiest of all ninth-century rabbis and perhaps the greatest *noodge* of the medieval era.

"Rabbi," the man asked, "where can I find peace?"

The Hasid surveyed him and said, "Quick, look behind you!"

Dick Codor © 1981

The man turned around, and Rabbi Ben Kaddish smashed him in the back of the head with a candlestick. "Is that peaceful enough for you?" he chuckled, adjusting his yarmulke.

In this tale, a meaningless question is asked. Not only is the question meaningless but so is the man who journeys to Chelm to ask it. Not that he was so far away from Chelm to begin with, but why shouldn't he stay where he is? Why is he bothering Rabbi Ben Kaddish—the rabbi doesn't have enough trouble? The truth is, the rabbi's in over his head with gamblers, and he has also been named in a paternity case by a Mrs. Hecht. No, the point of this tale is that this man has nothing better to do with his time than journey around and get on people's nerves. For this, the rabbi bashes his head in, which, according to the Torah, is one of the most subtle methods of showing concern. In a similar version of this tale, the rabbi leaps on top of the man in a frenzy and carves the story of Ruth on his nose with a stylus.

A man who could not marry off his ugly daughter visited Rabbi Shimmel of Cracow. "My heart is heavy," he told the Reb, "because God has given me an ugly daughter."

"How ugly?" the seer asked.

"If she were lying on a plate with a herring, you wouldn't be able to tell the difference."

The Seer of Cracow thought for a long time and finally asked, "What kind of herring?"

The man, taken aback by the query, thought quickly and said, "Er—Bismarck."

"Too bad," the Rabbi said. "If it was matjes, she'd have a better chance."

Dick Codor © 1981

Here is a tale that illustrates the tragedy of transient qualities such as beauty. Does the girl actually resemble a herring? Why not? Have you seen some of the things walking around these days, particularly at resort areas? And even if she does, are not all creatures beautiful in God's eyes? Perhaps, but if a girl looks more at home in a jar of wine sauce than in an evening gown she's got big problems. Oddly enough, Rabbi Shimmel's own wife was said to resemble a squid, but this was only in the face, and she more than made up for it by her hacking cough—the point of which escapes me.

●

Rabbi Zwi Chaim Yisroel, an Orthodox scholar of the Torah and a man who developed whining to an art unheard of in the West, was unanimously hailed as the wisest man of the Renaissance by his fellow Hebrews, who totaled a sixteenth of one percent of the population. Once, while he was on his way to synagogue to celebrate the sacred Jewish holiday commemorating God's reneging on every promise, a woman stopped him and asked the following question: "Rabbi, why are we not allowed to eat pork?"

"We're *not?*" the Reb said incredulously. "Uh-oh."

Dick Codor © 1981

This is one of the few stories in all Hasidic literature that deals with Hebrew law. The rabbi knows he shouldn't eat pork; he doesn't care, though, because he *likes* pork. Not only does he like pork; he gets a kick out of rolling Easter eggs. In short, he cares very little about traditional Orthodoxy and regards God's covenant with Abraham as "just so much chin music." Why pork was proscribed by Hebraic law is still unclear, and some scholars believe that the Torah merely suggested not eating pork at certain restaurants.

●

Drawing by David Levine. Copyright © 1978 by Nyrev, Inc. By permission of *The New York Review of Books*.

SHOLOM ALEICHEM

What Kind of Rabbi We Have

All this happened to me a long time ago. I was still a young man and I was living not far from here, in a village near the railroad. I traded in this and that, I had a small tavern, made a living. A Rothschild I didn't become, but bread we had, and in time there were about ten Jewish families living close by—because, as you know, if one of us makes a living, others come around. They think you're shoveling up gold. . . . But that isn't the point. What I was getting at was that right in the midst of the busy season one year, when things were moving and traffic was heavy, my wife had to go and have a baby—our boy—our first son. What do you say to that? "Congratulations! Congratulations, everybody!" But that isn't all. You have to have a *bris,* the circumcision. I dropped everything, went into town, bought all the good things I could find, and came back with the *mohel* with all his instruments, and for good measure I also brought the *shammes* of the synagogue. I thought that with these two holy men and myself and the neighbors, we'd have the ten men that we needed, with one to spare. But what does God do? He has one of my neighbors get sick—he is sick in bed and can't come to the *bris,* you can't carry him. And another has to pack up and go off to the city. He can't wait another day! And here I am without the ten men. Go do something. Here it is—Friday! Of all days, my wife has to pick Friday to have the *bris*—the day before the Sabbath. The *mohel* is frantic—he has to go back right away. The *shammes* is actually in tears. "What did you ever drag us off here for?" they both want to know. And what can I do?

All I can think of is to run off to the railroad station. Who knows—so many people come through every day, maybe God will send someone. And that's just what happened. I come running up to the station—the agent has just called out that a train is about to leave. I look around—a little roly-poly man carrying a huge traveling bag comes flying by, all sweating and out of breath, straight toward the lunch counter. He looks over the dishes—what is there a good Jew can take in a country railroad station? A piece of herring—an egg. Poor fellow—you could see his mouth was watering. I grab him by the sleeve. "Uncle, are you looking for something to eat?" I ask him, and the look he gives me says: "How did you know that?" I keep on talking: "May you live to be a hundred—God himself must have sent you." He still doesn't understand, so I proceed: "Do you want to earn the blessings of eternity—and at the same time eat a beef roast that will melt in your mouth, with a fresh white loaf right out of the oven?" He still looks at me as if I'm crazy. "Who are you? What do you want?"

So I tell him the whole story. What a misfortune had overtaken us: here we are, all ready for the *bris,* the *mohel* is waiting, the food is ready—and such food!—and we need a tenth man! "What's that got to do with me?" he asks, and I tell him: "What's that got to do with you? Why, everything depends on you—you're the tenth man! I beg you—come with me. You will earn all the rewards of heaven—and have a delicious dinner in the bargain!" "Are you crazy," he asks me, "or are you just out of your head? My train is leaving in a few minutes, and it's Friday afternoon—almost sundown. Do you know what that means? In a few more hours the Sabbath will catch up with me, and I'll be stranded." "So what!" I tell him. "So you'll take the next train. And in the meantime you'll earn eternal life—and taste a soup, with fresh dumplings, that only my wife can make. . . ."

Well, why make the story long? I had my way. The roast and the hot soup with fresh dumplings did their work. You could see my customer licking his lips. So I grab the traveling bag and I lead him home, and we go through with the *bris.* It was a real pleasure! You could smell the roast all over the house, it had so much garlic in it. A roast like that, with fresh warm twist, is a delicacy from heaven. And when you consider that we had some fresh dill pickles, and a bottle of beer, and some cognac before the meal and cherry cider after the meal—you can imagine the state our guest was in! His cheeks shone and his forehead glistened. But what then? Before we knew it, the afternoon was gone. My guest jumps up, he looks around, sees what time it is, and almost has a stroke! He reaches for his traveling bag: "Where is it?" I say to him, "What's your hurry? In the first place, do you think we'll let you run off like that—before the Sabbath? And in the second place, who are you to leave on a journey an hour or two before the Sabbath? And if you're going to get caught out in the country somewhere, you might just as well stay here with us."

He groans and he sighs. How could I do a thing like that to him—keep him so late? What did I have against him? Why hadn't I reminded him earlier? He doesn't stop bothering me. So I say to him, "In the first place, did I have to tell you that it was Friday afternoon? Didn't you know it yourself? And in the second place, how do you know—maybe it's the way God wanted it? Maybe He wanted you to stay here for the Sabbath so you could taste some of my wife's fish? I can guarantee you, that as long as you've eaten fish, you haven't eaten fish like my wife's fish—not even in a dream!" Well, that ended the argument. We said our evening prayers, had a glass of wine, and my

Dick Codor © 1981

wife brings the fish to the table. My guest's nostrils swell out, a new light shines in his eyes, and he goes after that fish as if he hadn't eaten a thing all day. He can't get over it. He praises it to the skies. He fills a glass with brandy and drinks a toast to the fish. And then comes the soup, a specially rich Sabbath soup with noodles. And he likes that too, and the *tzimmes* also, and the meat that goes with the *tzimmes,* a nice, fat piece of brisket. I'm telling you, he just sat there licking his fingers! When we're finishing the last course, he turns to me: "Do you know what I'll tell you? Now that it's all over, I'm really glad that I stayed over for *Shabbas.* It's been a long time since I've enjoyed a Sabbath as I've enjoyed this one." "If that's how you feel, I'm happy," I tell him. "But wait. This is only a sample. Wait till tomorrow. Then you'll see what my wife can do."

And so it was. The next day, after services, we sit down at the table. Well, you should have seen the spread. First the appetizers: crisp wafers and chopped herring, and onions and chicken fat, with radishes and chopped liver and eggs and *gribbenes.* And after that the cold fish and the meat from yesterday's *tzimmes,* and then the jellied calf's foot, or *fisnoga* as you call it, with thin slices of garlic, and after that the potato *cholent* with the *kugel* that had been in the oven all night—and you know what that smells like when you take it out of the oven and take the cover off the pot. And what it tastes like. Our visitor could not find words to praise it. So I tell him: "This is still nothing. Wait until you have tasted our *borscht* tonight; then you'll know what good food is." At that he laughs out loud —a friendly laugh, it is true—and says to me: "Yes, but how far do you think I'll be from here by the time your *borscht* is ready?" So I laugh even louder than he does, and say, "You can forget that right now! Do you think you'll be going off tonight?"

And so it was. As soon as the lights were lit and we had a glass of wine to start off the new week, my friend begins to pack his things again. So I call out to him: "Are you crazy? Do you think we'll let you go off, the Lord knows where, at night? And besides, where's your train?" "What?" he yells at me. "No train? Why, you're murdering me! You know I have to leave!" But I say, "May this be the greatest misfortune in your life. Your train will come, if all is well, around dawn tomorrow. In the meantime I hope your appetite and digestion are good, because I can smell the *borscht* already! All I ask," I say, "is just tell me the truth. Tell me if you've ever touched a *borscht* like this before. But I want the absolute truth!" What's the use of talking —he had to admit it: never before in all his life had he tasted a *borscht* like this. Never. He even started to ask how you made the *borscht,* what you put into it, and how long you cooked it. Everything. And I say, "Don't worry about that! Here, taste this wine and tell me what you think of *it*. After all, you're an expert. But the truth! Remember—nothing but the truth! Because if there is anything I hate, it's flattery. . . ."

So we took a glass, and then another glass, and we went to bed. And what do you think happened? My traveler overslept, and missed the early morning train. When he wakes up he boils over! He jumps on me like a murderer. Wasn't it up to me, out of fairness and decency, to wake him up in time? Because of me he's going to have to take a loss, a heavy loss—he doesn't even know himself how heavy. It was all my fault. I ruined him. I! . . . So I let him talk. I listen, quietly, and when he's all through, I say, "Tell me yourself, aren't you a queer sort of person? In the first place, what's your hurry? What are you rushing for? How long is a person's life altogether? Does he have to spoil that little with rushing and hurrying? And in the second place, have you forgotten that today is the third day since the *bris?* Doesn't that mean a thing to you? Where we come from, on the third day we're in the habit of putting on a feast better than the one at the *bris* itself. The third day—it's something to celebrate! You're not going to spoil the celebration, are you?"

What can he do? He can't control himself anymore, and he starts laughing—a hysterical laugh. "What good does it do to talk?" he says. "You're a real leech!" "Just as you say," I tell him, "but after all, you're a visitor, aren't you?"

At the dinner table, after we've had a drink or two, I call out to him. "Look," I say, "it may not be proper—after all, we're Jews—to talk about milk and such things while we're eating meat, but I'd like to know your honest opinion: what do you think of *kreplach* with cheese?" He looks at me with distrust. "How did we get around to that?" he asks. "Just like this," I explain to him. "I'd like to have you try the cheese *kreplach* that my wife makes—because tonight, you see, we're going to have a dairy supper. . . ." This is too much for him, and he comes right back at me with, "Not this time! You're trying to keep me here another day, I can see that. But you can't do it. It isn't right! It isn't right!" And from the way he fusses and fumes, it's easy to see that I won't have to coax him too long, or fight with him either, because what is he but a man with an appetite, who has only one philosophy, which he practices at the table? So I say this to him: "I give you my word of honor, and if that isn't enough, I'll give you my hand as well—here, shake —that tomorrow I'll wake you up in time for the earliest train. I promise it, even if the world turns upside down. If I don't, may I—you know what!" At this he softens and says to me, "Remember, we're shaking hands on that!" And I: "A promise is a promise." And my wife makes a dairy supper—how can I describe it to you? With such *kreplach* that my traveler has to admit that

Mark Podwal © 1978

it was all true: he has a wife too, and she makes *kreplach* too, but how can you compare hers with these? It's like night to day!

And I kept my word, because a promise is a promise. I woke him when it was still dark, and started the *samovar*. He finished packing and began to say goodbye to me and the rest of the household in a very handsome, friendly style. You could see he was a gentleman. But I interrupt him: "We'll say goodbye a little later. First, we have to settle up." "What do you mean, settle up?" "Settle up," I say, "means to add up the figures. That's what I'm going to do now. I'll add them up, let you know what it comes to, and you will be so kind as to pay me."

His face flames red. "Pay you?" he shouts. "Pay you for what?" "For what?" I repeat. "You want to know for what? For everything. The food, the drink, the lodging." This time he becomes white—not red—and he says to me: "I don't understand you at all. You came and invited me to the *bris*. You stopped me at the train. You took my bag away from me. You promised me eternal life." "That's right," I interrupt him. "That's right. But what's one thing got to do with the other? When you came to the *bris* you earned your reward in heaven. But food and drink and lodging—do I have to give you these things for nothing? After all, you're a businessman, aren't you? You should understand that fish costs money, and that the wine you drank was the very best, and the beer too, and the cherry cider. And you remember how you praised the *tzimmes* and the puddings and the *borscht*. You remember how you licked your fingers. And the cheese *kreplach* smelled pretty good to you too. Now, I'm glad you enjoyed these things: I don't begrudge you that in the least. But certainly you wouldn't expect that just because you earned a reward in heaven, and enjoyed yourself in the bargain, that *I* should pay for it?" My traveling friend was really sweating; he looked as if he'd have a stroke. He began to throw himself around, yell, scream, call for help. "This is Sodom!" he cried. "Worse than Sodom! It's the worst outrage the world has ever heard of! How much do you want?" Calmly I took a piece of paper and a pencil and began to add it up. I itemized everything, I gave him an inventory of everything he ate, of every hour he spent in my place. All in all it added up to something like thirty-odd *rubles* and some *kopecks* —I don't remember it exactly.

When he saw the total, my good man went green and yellow, his hands shook, and his eyes almost popped out, and again he let out a yell, louder than before. "What did I fall into—a nest of thieves? Isn't there a single human being here? Is there a God anywhere?" So I say to him, "Look, sir, do you know what? Do you know what you're yelling about? Do you have to eat your heart out? Here is my suggestion: let's ride into town together —it's not far from here—and we'll find some people. There's a rabbiner there—let's ask the rabbi. And we'll abide by what he says." When he heard me talk like that, he quieted down a little. And—don't worry—we hired a horse and wagon, climbed in, and rode off to town, the two of us, and went straight to the rabbi.

When we got to the rabbi's house, we found him just finishing his morning prayers. He folded up his prayer shawl and put his phylacteries away. "Good morning," we said to him, and he: "What's the news today?" The news? My friend tears loose and lets him have the whole story—everything from A to Z. He doesn't leave a word out. He tells how he stopped at the station, and so on and so on, and when he's through he whips out the bill I had given him and hands it to the rabbi. And when the rabbi had heard everything, he says, "Having heard one side,

I should now like to hear the other." And turning to me, he asks, "What do you have to say to all that?" I answer, "Everything he says is true. There's not a word I can add. Only one thing I'd like to have him tell you—on his word of honor: did he eat the fish, and did he drink the beer and the cognac and the cider, and did he smack his lips over the borscht that my wife made?" At this the man becomes almost frantic, he jumps and he thrashes about like an apoplectic. The rabbi begs him not to boil like that, not to be so angry, because anger is a grave sin. And he asks him again about the fish and the borscht and the *kreplach,* and if it was true that he had drunk not only the wine, but beer and cognac and cider as well. Then the rabbi puts on his spectacles, looks the bill over from top to bottom, checks every line, and finds it correct! Thirty-odd rubles and some kopecks, and he makes his judgment brief: he tells the man to pay the whole thing, and for the wagon back and forth, and a judgment fee for the rabbi himself. . . .

The man stumbles out of the rabbi's house looking as if he'd been in a steam bath too long, takes out his purse, pulls out two twenty-fives, and snaps at me, "Give me the change." "What change?" I ask, and he says, "For the thirty you charged me—for that bill you gave me." "Bill? What bill? What thirty are you talking about? What do you think I am, a highwayman? Do you expect me to take money from you? I see a man at the railroad station, a total stranger; I take his bag away from him, and drag him off almost by force to our own *bris,* and spend a wonderful *Shabbas* with him. So am I going to charge him for the favor he did me, and for the pleasure I had?" Now he looks at me as if I really am crazy, and says, "Then why did you carry on like this? Why did you drag me to the rabbi?" "Why this? Why that?" I say to him. "You're a queer sort of person, you are! I wanted to show you what kind of man our rabbi was, that's all!"

Some of Sholom Aleichem's readers attacked his early humorous stories, protesting that a Jewish writer should not waste his energy on such trivia. But the author persisted, and one of his celebrated literary gifts was his ability to take a standard joke—admittedly, in this case, a reasonably complex one—and turn it into a shaggy dog story without losing his audience along the way.

The joke that is the kernel of this story goes as follows:

•

A wealthy skeptic once came to visit a wonder-working rabbi. "Peace be with you, Rabbi," he said, handing the rabbi a five-dollar bill.

The rabbi accepted the gift without a word. "And peace be with you, my good man," he replied. "Have you come to see me on a family matter? Does it have to do with having children?"

"No, Rabbi," the man replied, handing him another five-dollar bill. "Nothing like that; I'm not married."

"Then perhaps you have come to inquire about some fine point in Jewish law?" the rabbi asked.

"Not at all, Rabbi," the man replied, handing him another five dollars. "You see, I can't even read Hebrew."

"Then you have come to ask me to bless your business, perhaps?"

"No, Rabbi," the man replied, handing over another five dollars. "I'm having a good year, and I only hope that every year will be this good."

"Well, my friend," said the rabbi, "I don't understand. What is it you wish? You must have had a reason for coming to see me."

"Oh, yes," the man replied. "I was curious to know how long a man could go on accepting money for nothing."

•

Dick Codor © 1981

This subtle tale demonstrates the difficult challenge that rabbis have traditionally faced in interpreting the law for their congregants. Because the laws of the Torah were not always clear in themselves, the ancient sages, to prevent their being easily transgressed, developed the idea of a metaphorical "fence" around the Torah, consisting of supplementary regulations and prohibitions which provided for a certain margin of error.

Over time, these laws, many of which were codified in the Talmud, became integrated into the larger body of Jewish law, which ceased to distinguish the original source of each rule and regulation. While the rabbi did not have the authority to tamper with basic Jewish law, he was permitted to lower the fence, as it were. Among respected *halachic* (Jewish legal) authorities, the tradition, at least until our own time, was always to be lenient in interpreting Jewish law for others, especially when strictness might cause hardship—even if the rabbi chose to be more stringent in his own personal conduct.

REB MEYER was a small-time merchant in Poland. He was also a pious man, from a distinguished Hasidic family, and he went nowhere without his black coat and fur hat. Over the years, Meyer had grown increasingly successful in his business, and he began to expand into increasingly higher levels of trade.

Finally, Meyer began to feel uneasy about the way he looked. He still wore *peyes*, earlocks, and these, together with his Hasidic dress, made him feel uneasy in the presence of modern businessmen. He began to suspect that the way he looked might be hindering his success in business. At the same time, Meyer felt highly ashamed of these thoughts. God had been good to him, and he had no wish to give offense. Still, he decided to speak to the rabbi.

The rabbi was a good and understanding man. "God," he explained, "is not so much interested in physical appearances as He is in inner qualities. If you were to increase your contributions to the poor, it would be permissible for you to dress in the modern way for your business trips."

After a long discussion, Meyer left the rabbi's house walking on air. A great heaviness had been lifted from his heart. He walked quickly, thinking: It's all right! I can do it! Suddenly a look of resentment crossed his face. Oy, he thought, those rabbis, thieves that they are. What else do they know and don't tell the rest of us!

© 1973 Kirschen

A MAN goes to consult a famous specialist about his medical problem.

"How much do I owe you?"

"My fee is fifty rubles," replies the physician.

"Fifty rubles? That's impossible."

"In your case," the doctor replies, "I suppose I could adjust my fee to thirty rubles."

"Thirty rubles for one visit? Ridiculous."

"Well, then, can you afford twenty rubles?"

"Who has so much money?"

"Look," replies the doctor, growing irritated. "Just give me five rubles and be gone."

"I can give you two rubles," says the man. "Take it or leave it."

"I don't understand you," says the doctor. "Why did you come to the most expensive doctor in Warsaw?"

"Listen, Doctor," replies the patient. "When it comes to my health, nothing is too expensive!"

The Jewish interest in matters of health comes close to being an obsession, and many Jews have found it necessary to respond to the question "How are you?" as though it were meant literally. Indeed, the traditional Jewish greeting of farewell is *"Zei gezunt,"* which means "Stay well," and which recalls the old line, "Cancer shmancer; as long as you're healthy."

How do you feel?
> **How should I feel?**

What hurts you?
> **What doesn't hurt me?**

When do you feel bad?
> **When don't I feel bad?**

When did it start?
> **When will it end, better!**

TWO immigrants meet on the street.

"How's by you?" asks one.

"Could be worse. And you?"

"Surviving. But I've been sick a lot this year, and it's costing me a fortune. In the past five months I've spent over three hundred dollars on doctors and medicine."

"Ach, back home on that kind of money you could be sick for *two years."*

"How do you feel today?" asks the doctor. "Sort of sluggish?"

"Sluggish?" repeats the weary patient. "If I felt that good I wouldn't be here!"

•

"Doctor, I hope I really *am* sick. I'd hate to feel this way if I were healthy."

•

Weinstein visits a specialist. "You seem fine to me," says the doctor.

"But what about my headaches?" asks Weinstein.

"I'm not worried about your headaches," says the doctor.

"Listen, Doctor," replies Weinstein, "if you had my headaches, I wouldn't worry about them either."

•

AT his wife's insistence, Gold finally went for a checkup. "You look terrible," said the doctor. "Do you drink?"

"Why, yes," said Gold. "I start every day with a bottle of schnapps."

"And with that cough," the doctor continued, "you probably are a smoker."

"You bet," said Gold. "Three packs a day for me."

"Look, Mr. Gold," the doctor said. "You're not a healthy man. You're going to have to give up smoking and drinking right away, and that's an order. And before you go, that'll be forty dollars for my advice."

Replied Gold: "Who's taking it?"

GOD • ANIMALS • BAR MITZVAH •
MEN AND WOMEN • FAMILY • FOOD •
DEATH • STEADY WORK

JOHN CALDWELL • LENNY BRUCE • JACK
ZIEGLER • WOODY ALLEN • JULES
FEIFFER • SHEL SILVERSTEIN • DICK
CODOR • RICHTER • MORDECAI RICHLER
• S. GROSS • RALPH STEADMAN •
ISAAC ROSENFELD • D. REILLY •
STANLEY ELKIN • HENNY YOUNGMAN •
BRUCE JAY FRIEDMAN • JUDITH VIORST •
DAN GREENBURG • ROBERT MEZEY •
PHILIP ROTH • SAM LEVENSON • JOEL
ROSENBERG • JOSEPH HELLER • SAUL
BELLOW • HOWARD WEISS • SEYMOUR
CHWAST • ROBERT GROSSMAN • I. L.
PERETZ • ALLAN SHERMAN

From *Running A Muck,* copyright © 1978 by John Caldwell. By permission of Writer's Digest Books.

PART FIVE

FIRST THINGS LAST

God Talk

Lenny Bruce died in 1966, but already it is difficult to appreciate who he was and what he did. He performed in an era when a comedian could be arrested for what he said onstage, and yet that was only a few years ago. Appreciating Lenny Bruce is not made any easier by the cult of beatification standing guard over his reputation, which in turn has been enhanced by his sordid and ignoble death. As Mordecai Richler has quipped, "He didn't die for *my* sins."

And yet Bruce's contribution to Jewish humor was most significant. "People should be taught what is, not what should be," he said. "All my humor is based on destruction and despair. If the whole world were tranquil, without disease and violence, I'd be standing in the bread line—right back of J. Edgar Hoover."

Jewish humor has always dealt with the real world, warts and all, but Bruce was important for carrying a Jewish sensibility forward into a new era; he was a pioneer in the rediscovery of a publicly articulated Jewish sensibility.

He grew up in an entirely assimilated household on Long Island; his Jewish education, such as it was, and his knowledge of Yiddish words were both acquired in his mid-twenties from fellow comic Joe Ancis, a legendary New Yorker who is said to be too shy to perform publicly, but who has influenced many successful comedians.

Appearing before mixed audiences, Bruce played with and upon Jewish symbols, to listeners who were mostly unaware of a Jewish spirit alive in the world. Rather than disguise his own origins, like so many of his contemporaries, Bruce continually emphasized his Jewishness, and was clearly fascinated by the condition of Jewishness in America. True, he changed his name, but as he would often remind his audiences, it was still Leonard Schneider who was addressing them, the new name being the price he had to pay for success.

•

Before they teamed up to produce "The Two Thousand Year-Old Man," Mel Brooks and Carl Reiner used to perform comic routines at parties. In one of these improvized scenes, Reiner opened with:

•

"You're a little storekeeper in Nazareth, and I would like to know what happened the day when they crucified Christ on the mountain. Did you know Christ?"

Now the reason, perhaps, for my irreverence is that I have no knowledge of the god, because the Jews lost their god. Really. Before I was born the god was going away.

Because to have a god you have to know something about him, and as a child I didn't speak the same language as the Jewish god.

To have a god you have to love him and know about him as kids—early instruction—and I didn't know what he looked like. Our god has no mother, no father, no manger in the five-and-ten, on cereal boxes, and on television shows. The Jewish God—what's-his-face? Moses? Ah, he's a friend of god's: "I dunno. Moses, he's, I dunno, his uncle, I dunno. . . ." He has no true identity. Is he a strong God? Are there little stories? Are there Bible tales about god, that one god, our faceless god?

The Christian god, you're lucky in that way, because you've got Mary, a mother, a father, a beginning, the five-and-ten little mangers—identity. Your god, the Christian god, is all over. He's on rocks, he saves you, he's dying on bank buildings—he's been in three films. He's on crucifixes all over. It's a story you can follow. Constant identification.

The Jewish God—where's the Jewish God? He's on a little box nailed to the doorjamb. In a *mezuzah.* There he is, in there. He's standing on a slant, god. And all the Jews are looking at him, and kissing him on the way into the house:

"I told the super *don't paint god!* Hey, super! C'mere. What the hell's the matter with you? I told you twenty times, that's *god* there. What're you painting god for? My old lady kissed the doorbell three times this week. You paint here, here, but don't paint there, all right? Never mind it's dirty, we'll take care of it. All right.

"Wait a minute. . . . Maybe he's not in there anymore . . . maybe the Puerto Ricans stole him—they probably would, to make more garbage. That's it. . . . I dunno what to do. . . . You wanna open it up? . . . Yeah? . . . We'll pry it open, if he's in there. . . . *Gevalt!* They stashed a joint!"

Now there's a curtain line for great Jewish theater.

Brooks: "Yes; thin, thin, nervous—wore sandals. Came in the store, didn't buy much, mainly water, wanted water—so I gave him water. Look! You have a business. You can't always make a sale. So when people want water, you give them water. But one thing I have to admit. He was a bit of a troublemaker. He beat up a couple of *rovs* on the steps of the shul—and *you know you can't do that!* But they didn't have to nail him up. They could have given him a severe lecture. I didn't agree with such a severe punishment. Oh, such a terrible day! All that yelling and screaming up on the mountain. I tell you it was very upsetting. In fact, it got so bad, I had to close up the store."

•

By permission of the artist.

"Oh, nothing ... I guess I just expected you to be a bit larger, that's all!"

Christ and Moses

Every day people are straying away from the church
And going back to God.
Really.
But I know that Christ and Moses are in heaven,
And they're saying:
"What the hell are they doing with the Book?
They're shoving it in motel drawers?
Let's make Earth!"

Come on down, Christ and Moses!
Come on down!
Come on down!

And they're going to come down,
They're going to come down.
And they're going to make you pay some dues,
You people who believe.

Christ and Moses
Standing in the back of Saint Pat's,
Looking around.

Confused, Christ is,
At the grandeur of the interior,
The baroque interior,

The rocoque baroque interior.
Because his route took him through Spanish Harlem
And he was wondering
What the hell fifty Puerto Ricans were doing
Living in one room
When that stained-glass window
Is worth ten G's a square foot
And this guy had a ring worth ten grand.
Why weren't the Puerto Ricans living here?
That was the purpose of the church—
For the people.

Spellman is up on the lectern—
Played by Ed Begley—
Telling about giving to the people
And loving.
Love,
Christian Love
That is nothing but forgiveness and no hostility.

Bishop Sheen—
Played by Hugh Herbert—
Spots Christ and Moses standing in the back,

Arguing back and forth,
And runs up to Spellman on the lectern:

Sheen:
Psst! Spellman!
C'mon down here!
I gotta talk to you!
They're here!

Spellman:
Get back to the blackboard, dum-dum.
And stop bugging me.

Sheen:
Dum-dum, your ass!
You better get down here.

Spellman:
Okay, put the choir on for ten minutes. . . .
Hey, putzo!
Whaddaya mean running up here
In the middle of a bit like that?

Sheen:
Oh, it's terrible, terrible, terrible!
They're here, they're here!

Ohhh, owwww!
They're *here,* they're *here,*
They're really *here!*

Spellman:
Who's here?

Sheen:
Who's here?
I'm here, *you're* here . . .

Spellman:
You're not all *there.*

Sheen:
Hoo-hoo!
It's here, it's here!

Spellman:
Who's here?

Sheen:
You better sit down, you're gonna faint!
Ready for a shocker?
Christ and *Moses,* schmuck,
That's who's here!

Drawing by Ziegler; © 1974 The New Yorker Magazine, Inc.

"Hello? 'Beasts of the Field'? This is Lou, over in 'Birds of the Air.'
Anything funny going on at your end?"

Spellman:
Oh, bullshit!
Are you putting me on, now?
Where?

Sheen:
They're standing in the back—
Don't look now, you idiot!
They can see us.

Spellman:
Which ones are they?

Sheen:
The ones that're *glowing.*
Hoo! Glowing! Terrible!

Spellman:
Are you sure it's them?

Sheen:
I've just seen 'em in pictures,
But I'm pretty sure—
Moses is a ringer for Charlton Heston.

Spellman:
Are they armed?

Sheen:
I dunno.

Spellman:
Poorbox locked?

Sheen:
Yeah.
I'll grab the box
And meet you round the back!

Spellman:
No, we better just cool it.
You better get me Rome, quickly.
Now what the hell do they want here?

Sheen:
Maybe they want to audit the books?

Spellman:
No, I don't think so.
Well, we're in for it now, goddammit!
Did Christ bring the family with him?
What's the mother's name? . . .
Mary Hale, Hail Mary? . . .
Hurry up with Rome!
If we just cool it,
Maybe we can talk to them. . . .
Don't tell anyone they're here. . . .
Oh, shit!
Who copped out they're here?

Sheen:
Why?

Spellman:
Why?
Schmuck, look at the front door!

Sheen:
What's the matter?

Spellman:
What's the *matter?*
Putz!
Here come the lepers!

Sheen:
Where the hell do they live around here?
Oh, Christ!

Spellman:
Phew!
All right, get me Rome!
Hurry up!
(Cheerful, loud voice)
Hello, lepers!
How are you?
Hello, lepers, hello, lepers.
"Hello, young lepers,
Wherever you are . . ."
How are ya?
Look, ah, nuttin' personal,
But, ah, don't touch anything, okay?
Heh-heh, that's right.
No offense,
But what the hell,
You can pick up anything.
You might get something from *us!*
Heh-heh, right?
So, ah, why don't you all get outside
And get some air, okay?
Pick up your nose, your foot, and your arm
And split.
That's right. . . .

Now look, whaddaya doing?
You're waiting for Saint Francis?
Look,
I'm gonna level with you right now—
That's a bullshit story.
He never kissed any lepers!
He just danced with two merchant marines
And we kicked him the hell
Out of the parish.
That's all.

What the hell you wanna kiss a leper for?
Put yourself in our place.
Would *you* kiss a leper?
What the hell you gonna get out of that?
Awright?
That's a lotta bullshit.
You try to kiss 'em
And they fall apart.

Kissing lepers . . .
You know how
Ben Hur's mother and sister
Got leprosy, don't ya?
They didn't put paper on the seats,
That's all.
Now come on, haul ass!
Can't you be nice, you people?
Just get the hell outta here!

THEY WERE WONDERING IF YOU'D LIKE TO BE IN THEIR PARADE?

From *Running A Muck*, copyright © 1978 by John Caldwell. By permission of Writer's Digest Books.

(Talking into the phone)
Hullo, John? . . .
Fran, New York.
Listen, a coupla the kids dropped in. . . .
You bet your ass you know them! . . .
Ah, well, I can't really talk now,
There's a lotta people.
It's really filling up here. . . .
Well, one kid is like:
"With the cross of blank-blank . . ."
No, not *Zorro!*
Yes, *him!*
Yeah . . . I'm not kidding you.
Yes, he brought
A very attractive Jewish boy
With him.
Excuse me . . .

(Off phone)
What is it?

   Reporters:
Ah, we're from *Life* magazine

And we want to know if that's really them.

   Spellman:
Ah, just a moment—
Sonny, will you get off my hem here?
Yes, that is them. . . .
No, I don't know
If they're gonna do any tricks.

(Back to phone)

Hello? . . .
They're standing in back,
Way in the back. . . .
Course they're *white!*
Look, this is New York City, mister!
Puerto Ricans stand in the back. . . .
Look, I don't wanna hear that!
The place is filling up!
What're we paying protection for? . . .
I dunno. . . .
Look, all I know's that I'm up to my ass
In crutches and wheelchairs here!

One Who Killed Our Lord

I am of a Semitic background—I *assume* I'm Jewish. A lot of Jews who think they're Jewish are not—they're switched babies.

Now, a Jew, in the dictionary, is one who is descended from the ancient tribe of Judea, or one who is regarded as descended from that tribe. That's what it says in the dictionary; but you and I know what a Jew is—*One Who Killed Our Lord.* I don't know if we got much press on that in Illinois—we did this about two thousand years ago—two thousand years of Polack kids whacking the shit out of us coming home from school. Dear, dear. And although there should be a statute of limitations for that crime, it seems that those who neither have the actions nor the gait of the Christians, pagan or not, will bust us out, unrelenting dues, for another deuce.

And I really searched it out, why we pay the dues. Why do you keep breaking our balls for this crime?

"Why, Jew, because you skirt the issue. You blame it on Roman soldiers."

All right. I'll clear the air once and for all, and confess. Yes, we did it. I did it, my family. I found a note in my basement. It said:

"We killed him.
        "signed,
              "Morty."

And a lot of people say to me, "Why did you kill Christ?"

"I dunno. . . . It was one of those parties—got out of hand, you know."

We killed him because he didn't want to become a doctor, that's why we killed him.

●

Jews are frequently misinformed not only about Christianity but about their own religion as well. In Woody Allen's *Annie Hall:*

●

Alvie Singer, a Jew, is visiting Annie's very WASPish family when suddenly the screen is divided and we see each family at its own dinner table. Across the two cultures, the two mothers have a brief and telling conversation, which Annie's mother initiates:
"How do you plan to spend the holidays, Mrs. Singer?"
"We fast."
"Fast?"
"No food. To atone for our sins."
"What sins? I don't understand."
"To tell you the truth, neither do we."

God loves the poor and helps the rich.

AN elderly Jewish man walks into a jewelry store to buy his wife a present. "How much is this?" he asks the clerk, pointing to a sterling silver crucifix.

"That's six hundred dollars, sir," replies the clerk.

"Nice," says the man. "And without the acrobat?"

The Sacrifice of Isaac

The process of embellishing upon the Biblical text, which is often spare in its use of detail, is known as midrash. This folk process of reading between the lines to make characters and situations come alive was formalized by the Talmudic sages, but it is an ongoing process, and it is today enjoying a rejuvenation.

Bill Cosby has a famous midrashic routine about Noah:

•

Hey, you up there!" calls Noah's neighbor.

"Whadya want?"

"What is this?"

"It's an ark."

"Uh-huh. Wanna get it out of my driveway? I gotta get to work. What's this thing for, anyway?"

"I can't tell you, ha-ha-ha-ha-ha!"

"Can't you give me a little hint?"

"You want a hint?"

"Yes, please."

"How long can you tread water?"

•

In another of Cosby's routines, Noah is talking with God.

"NOAH!"

"What? Whadya want?"

"YOU GOTTA TAKE ONE OF THOSE HIPPOS OUT AND BRING IN ANOTHER ONE."

"What *for?*"

"'CAUSE YOU GOT TWO MALES DOWN THERE AND YOU NEED TO BRING IN A FEMALE."

"I'm not bringing *nothing* in! You *change* one of 'em!"

"COME ON, YOU KNOW I DON'T WORK LIKE THAT."

"Well, I'm sick and tired; I've had enough of this stuff. I've been working all day, working for days, I'm sick and tired of this. . . ."

"NOAH?"

"Yeah?"

"HOW LONG CAN YOU TREAD WATER?"

•

. . . And Abraham awoke in the middle of the night and said to his only son, Isaac, "I have had a dream where the voice of the Lord sayeth that I must sacrifice my only son, so put your pants on." And Isaac trembled and said, "So what did you say? I mean when He brought this whole thing up?"

"What am I going to say?" Abraham said. "I'm standing there at two A.M. in my underwear with the Creator of the Universe. Should I argue?"

"Well, did he say why he wants me sacrificed?" Isaac asked his father.

But Abraham said, "The faithful do not question. Now let's go because I have a heavy day tomorrow."

And Sarah who heard Abraham's plan grew vexed and said, "How doth thou know it was the Lord and not, say, thy friend who loveth practical jokes, for the Lord hateth practical jokes and whosoever shall pull one shall be delivered into the hands of his enemies whether they can pay the delivery charge or not." And Abraham answered, "Because I know it was the Lord. It was a deep, resonant voice, well-modulated, and nobody in the desert can get a rumble in it like that."

And Sarah said, "And thou art willing to carry out this senseless act?" But Abraham told her, "Frankly, yes, for to question the Lord's word is one of the worst things a person can do, particularly with the economy in the state it's in."

And so he took Isaac to a certain place and prepared to sacrifice him but at the last minute the Lord stayed Abraham's hand and said, "How could thou doest such a thing?"

And Abraham said, "But thou said—"

"Never mind what I said," the Lord spake. "Doth thou listen to every crazy idea that comes thy way?" And Abraham grew ashamed. "Er—not really . . . no."

"I jokingly suggest thou sacrifice Isaac and thou immediately runs out to do it."

And Abraham fell to his knees. "See, I never know when you're kidding."

And the Lord thundered, "No sense of humor. I can't believe it."

"But doth this not prove I love thee, that I was willing to donate mine only son on thy whim?"

And the Lord said, "It proves that some men will follow any order no matter how asinine as long as it comes from a resonant, well-modulated voice."

And with that, the Lord bid Abraham get some rest and check with him tomorrow.

the Deluge
by Jules Feiffer

One night as Harvey W. Noah government worker was asleep

he was visited by an angel

YOU DON'T KNOW ME HARVEY W. NOAH BUT I'M HERE FROM HEAVEN WHERE SOMEBODY GAVE ME YOUR NAME AND TOLD ME TO GIVE YOU THIS MESSAGE OF SPECIAL INTEREST.

Whereupon the angel proceeded to explain that soon the Earth would be deluged with 40 days and 40 nights of atomic rainfall, at the end of which period there would be left no living creature on the land or in the sea and that Harvey W Noah had been chosen to gather from over the world two of every kind of living thing and that he was to build an ark on which these creatures would live and that they would be the sole survivors of the deluge.

"What a screwy dream" thought Harvey W. Noah

and he went back to sleep

Only to be awakened the next morning by a telegram being slipped under the door.

This is to confirm your hallucination of last night. Proceed as directed re conversation pertaining to deluge etc.

So Harvey W. Noah now had a mission. "But what can one man do?" he asked himself

Private

So he took the problem to his government supervisor—

who said: This is all very interesting Mr. Noah, but deluges do not fall under the jurisdiction of our department. I suggest we send this over to the navy.

and the navy said:

Well, Mr. Noah, atomic rainfall is not actually the legitimate concern of the Navy Department. Why don't we kick this over to the Atomic Energy Commission

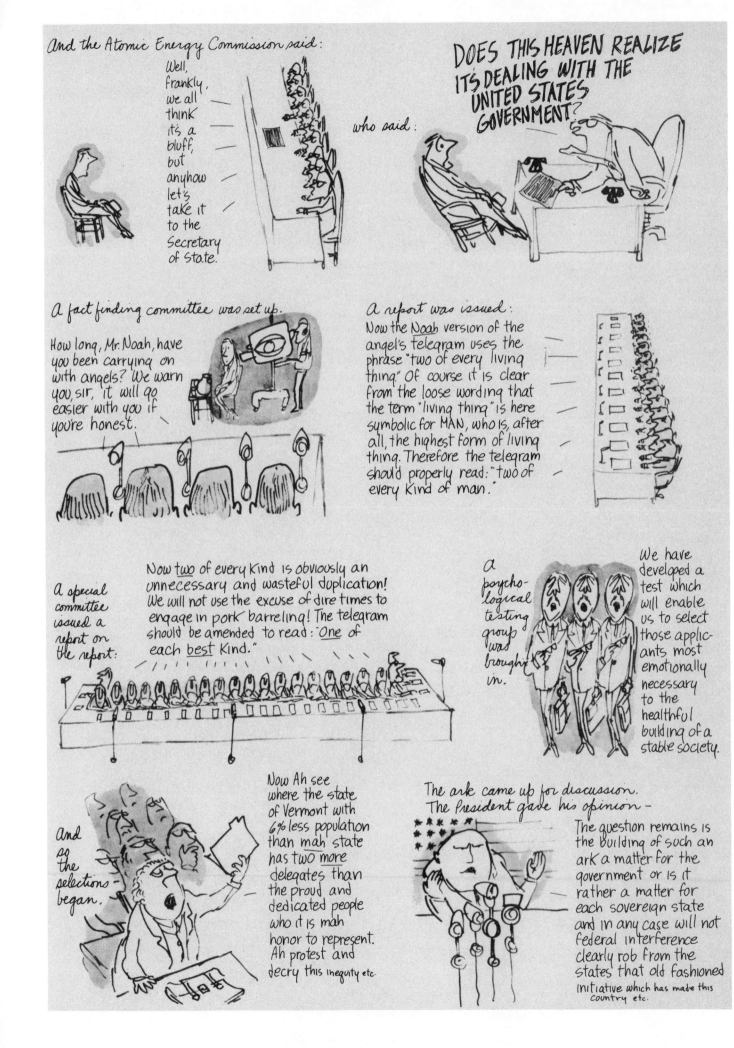

Generally understood to mean doubter, scoffer, or denier, *apikoros* (the word exists in both Hebrew and Yiddish) comes from the Greek Epicurean, meaning a pragmatic sensualist, somebody who is this-worldly. The term resists easy translation, and the common English equivalents, like apostate or atheist, are not quite right.

As the joke makes clear, the *apikoros* must *earn* his skepticism. Becoming an *apikoros* involves a long process of study, for the *apikoros* is neither an ignoramus nor a conventional renegade. He functions as a kind of critic from within, although his skepticism and cynicism about Jewish belief and Jewish institutions do not undermine his allegiance to the community. In modern times, the learned *apikoros* has become an alternative model of a committed Jew, especially in secular Jewish national movements like Bundism and Zionism.

A SMALL-TOWN *apikoros,* after trying unsuccessfully to spread enlightenment to his coreligionists, decided to travel to Warsaw to seek counsel and encouragement from the Great Apikoros of Warsaw. Arriving on a Friday afternoon, he was told that the Great Apikoros had gone to visit the *mikvah,* the ritual bath.

The small-town *apikoros* was amazed at the bravery of the Great Apikoros of Warsaw, who was evidently not afraid to enter into the midst of Jewish ritual observance. Arriving at the *mikvah,* the small-town *apikoros* almost collided with the Apikoros of Warsaw, who was just leaving.

"O Great Apikoros," he said, "I have come all the way from Shklov to learn from you." But the Great Apikoros of Warsaw resisted his introduction. "Not now," he insisted. "We'll talk later. Come to my house for Sabbath dinner. Right now I'm going to the synagogue."

Again the small-town *apikoros* was amazed at the courage of his hero, and followed him to the main synagogue, where, to his astonishment, the Great Apikoros himself ascended the pulpit to lead the congregation in prayer. The small-town *apikoros* was flabbergasted. Never in his life had he even considered such an act. What a marvelous way to sway the congregation from its superstitious ways! He was certain that the Great Apikoros would insert modern, enlightened prayers in the place of the original texts, but no—the service was unchanged, and the small-town *apikoros,* puzzled and disappointed, followed the Great Apikoros to his home, hungry for an explanation.

After a sumptuous Sabbath meal, the Great Apikoros asked his guest to wait until the end of the Sabbath before discussing the details of his mission. The next day passed with its traditional peace and calm, and not before three stars appeared in the heavens, signaling the end of the Sabbath, would the Great Apikoros consent to discuss the younger man's agenda.

"I don't understand," the small-town *apikoros* began. "I come from a small town, and I observe absolutely nothing of Jewish ritual. I don't eat kosher food, I never visit the *mikvah,* and the idea of leading services in the synagogue is unthinkable. I openly desecrate the Sabbath and I lose no opportunity to influence young people away from the Torah and into the secular sciences. But you—Great Apikoros of Warsaw—you don't seem to violate any of the commandments. I just don't understand!"

The Great Apikoros of Warsaw thought for a while, and then looked over at the small-town *apikoros* from Shklov. "You're right," he said. "There *is* a difference between us. I'm an *apikoros*—but you're a goy!"

IT was a hot day at Jones Beach. Bessie Cohen was there with her three-year-old grandson; she had bought him a cute little sailor suit with a hat, and she watched with delight as he played with his toys at the edge of the water.

Suddenly a giant wave swept onto the shore and before Bessie could even move, the boy was swept out into the cold Atlantic.

Bessie was frantic. "I know I've never been religious," she screamed to the heavens. "But I implore You to save the boy! I'll never ask anything of You again!"

The boy disappeared from view, and Bessie was beside herself. He went under a second time, and Bessie began to wail. As he went under for the third time, she screamed mightily, appealing to God to save the boy's life.

Her final supplication was answered, as the sea suddenly threw the child onto the shore. He was badly shaken but clearly alive. Bessie picked him up and put him down gently on a blanket, far from the water. After looking him over, she turned her face toward the heavens, and complained loudly, "He had a *hat!*"

FDR told a version of this joke in response to the ingratitude of rich Republicans at his rescue of American capitalism. And in a secular version of the same joke, Bessie's exchange takes place not with God but with a lifeguard.

•

Sholom Aleichem's Tevye says to God: "You help complete strangers —why not me?"

•

THE TWENTY COMMANDMENTS

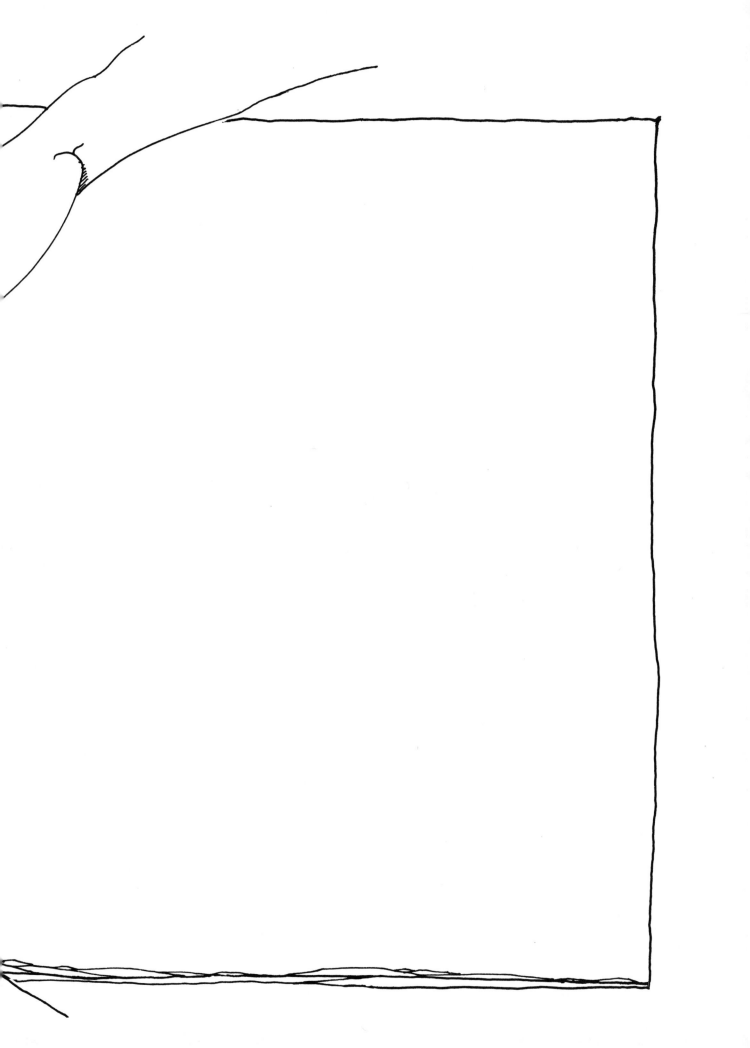

I T is the afternoon of Yom Kippur. The sun is low in the sky, and only a few prayers remain in the service. As the concluding *Ne'illah* service is about to begin, the cantor's voice gives out. The old man can barely utter a whisper, and it is clear to everyone in the synagogue that he won't be able to conclude the service.

The president of the congregation stands up: "Does anybody here know how to chant the service?" But nobody stands up to volunteer for the task. The president begins to plead with the congregation: "Surely *somebody* knows the service well enough to lead it?" But nobody steps forward.

Finally, in the back of the room, one man cautiously raises his hand. "Nu?" says the president. "Be so kind as to come up and finish the service."

"No, it's not me," the man replies. "It's my dog. He's at home now, but he knows the whole service. We went over it just the other day. I'm telling you that my dog can sing it beautifully."

After the laughter dies down, the call goes out again. But still there is nobody who can finish the service. Now the sun is sinking further, and unless somebody can be found to lead the rest of the service, the entire group may have to remain in its place without food or drink until a cantor can be brought from a far-off city to finish the task.

The man in the back stands up and says, once again, "I'm telling you, my dog knows the service!" This time some of the people are not laughing.

As more time passes, the man's offer is starting to sound more reasonable. An emergency meeting is called of the board of directors, and after a heated discussion, it is decided that if the dog will wear a tallith and a yarmulke, he will be permitted to ascend to the pulpit and lead the congregation in the concluding prayers of Yom Kippur.

It is almost dark when a medium-sized white-and-tan shaggy dog, wearing a tallith and a yarmulke, walks up to the podium. Nobody is prepared for what follows. The dog not only knows all the prayers and the melodies, but he sings them better than the *chazzan!* Never before has anyone in the congregation heard such beautiful melodies—and so piously rendered. One by one even the most skeptical members of the congregation are moved to tears as the dog's chant ascends to heaven. After a few minutes, after the dog has the feel of the room, he actually closes his prayer book, and many in the congregation will later claim that it was as though he were reading the prayers out of the very heavens.

And still the dog continues to sing. The room is filled with the spirit of repentance that is normally reserved for the sages of old. When the final shofar blast is sounded, and the dog's work completed, and Yom Kippur is finally brought to a close, nobody in the congregation is able to leave. Everyone is too excited about the dog, and they all gather around the man who had been sitting in the back of the room.

The president speaks for everyone. "Your dog is just wonderful," he says. "The service has been an inspiration to us all. This is just terrific, hearing such a talented dog. Why don't you get him to become a *chazzan?"*

"You talk to him," replies the owner. "He wants to be a doctor!"

Dick Codor © 1980

THERE once was a king, old and a little crazy, who summoned the Chief Rabbi of his kingdom. "Rabbi," he said, "there's one thing I'd like to see. I want you to teach my pet monkey how to doven."

"Your monkey should learn how to doven?"

"I'm giving you one year to do it, and if you fail, I'll have you put to death."

"Begging your pardon, sire," said the rabbi, "but that's a most difficult request. I'll need at least five years to accomplish the task."

"All right," said the king, softening a little. "You have exactly five years. Take the monkey and go home."

When the rabbi returned to his people, he told them of the king's command, and they were greatly distressed. "Rabbi," they asked, "what on earth will you do?"

"What on earth *can* I do?" replied the rabbi. "This is how I see it. A lot of things can happen in five years. First, the king is old, and he might die. Or I could die. Or the monkey could die. And besides, in five years, well, who knows? If I can teach your children their haftorahs, maybe I can teach that monkey how to doven!"

This is a case of a new joke created by adding a single line (about teaching the children their haftorahs) to an existing humorous folktale.

MANNY FELDMAN was a bachelor who lived alone. The hours that other men spent with their families, Manny spent with his friends at the racetrack. And when the track was closed, Manny would indulge in his favorite hobby—listening to his vast collection of cantorial records.

One day, feeling more lonely than usual, Manny decided to buy a parrot for companionship. He began to talk to the parrot as though it were human, and one evening Manny played one of his favorite cantorial records for the bird.

A few days later, Manny was astonished to hear the parrot

singing along with Richard Tucker on "Kol Nidre." This, in turn, was followed by the parrot's performance of other liturgical favorites, and within a few weeks, the parrot was singing many liturgical selections on his own—without the records.

Manny was surprised and delighted. He called the parrot "Yossele Rosenbird," and told his racetrack cronies about the wonderful talent his parrot had revealed. They were amused and skeptical, and when Manny offered even money that the bird could perform part of the Rosh Hashanah service the following week, they eagerly agreed to the wager.

Just prior to the holiday, Manny went out and bought the bird a tiny yarmulke and tallis, and with the pious parrot perched on his shoulder, Manny entered the synagogue. No sooner did he arrive than Manny began announcing to everyone within earshot that he had brought a wonderful addition to the service.

"This isn't a zoo, mister," said one of the officers of the congregation, attempting to restrain both man and bird from going any further. But Manny retorted that his parrot could sing better than the rabbi or the cantor, and once again offered even money to prove his case. Immediately a ruckus broke out, as members of the congregation, as well as Manny's friends, started making book on the parrot's potential. Even the rabbi came in for a piece of the action.

Finally, the room was quiet, and the parrot, dressed in his tiny yarmulke and tallis, took his precarious place on the podium. The congregation settled down anxiously to see what would happen, and Manny's friends could hardly refrain from snickering.

Their snickering grew louder when the bird failed to open its mouth, and when it became clear that Yossele Rosenbird was not going to be doing any praying. Manny nervously hummed the traditional theme of the High Holidays, and while there were scattered protests and shouts of "No coaching!" his efforts were in vain, as the parrot just stood there in silence.

Humiliated and furious, Manny grabbed the bird and stormed out of the synagogue. Upon arriving home, he picked up a carving knife and began to sharpen it. The bird, realizing his life was in danger, fled to the dining room and perched on the chandelier. "Manny, calm down!" said the parrot.

"So *now* you talk!" screamed Manny. "You humiliated me, not to mention the hours I spent working with you, the money I spent on your food and your cage. I'm going to have to kill you for double-crossing me like that!"

"Manny, who's double-crossing?" said Yossele Rosenbird. "Just think of the odds we can get for Yom Kippur!"

This is a favorite of many contemporary joke tellers, and is one of several Jewish jokes told well by Danny Thomas. That there is more than one joke about an animal who is also a cantor reflects the traditional Jewish view toward that profession by which a good cantor, even if he is dead—*especially* if he is dead—is revered; a bad cantor, on the other hand, is reviled.

•

There is a very old joke in which two members of a congregation are talking. "Our cantor is magnificent," says the first. "No big deal," says the second man. "If I had his voice, I'd sing just as well."

•

Happy Bar Mitzvah, Bernie!

Mordecai Richler, a Canadian-Jewish writer, is the author of several novels, including *The Apprenticeship of Duddy Kravitz, St. Urbain's Horseman,* and *Joshua Then and Now,* as well as numerous essays, reviews, and screenplays.

Duddy Kravitz is Richler's best-known work, mostly because of the successful film version of the novel. The movie, for which Richler himself wrote the screenplay, was a realistic but controversial portrayal of immigrant Jews in Montreal. Duddy Kravitz, played brilliantly by Richard Dreyfus, evoked mixed responses from audiences, who saw in him a Canadian Sammy Glick.

A highlight of both the novel and the film is Duddy's attempt to produce an artistic bar-mitzvah film under the direction of a down-and-out alcoholic filmmaker. In this scene, the finished product is screened for a group of family and friends.

THE SCREENING

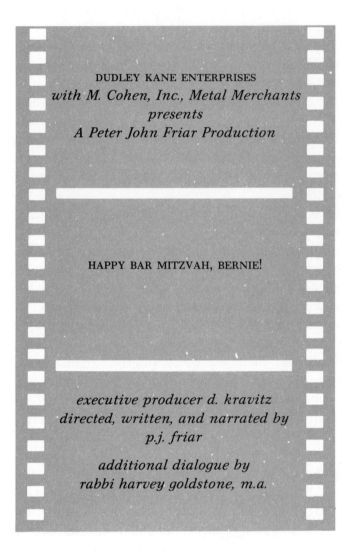

DUDLEY KANE ENTERPRISES
*with M. Cohen, Inc., Metal Merchants
presents
A Peter John Friar Production*

HAPPY BAR MITZVAH, BERNIE!

*executive producer d. kravitz
directed, written, and narrated by
p.j. friar*

*additional dialogue by
rabbi harvey goldstone, m.a.*

"So far so good."
"Would you mind taking off your hat please, Elsie?"
"Sh."

1. *A close shot of an aged finger leading a thirteen-year-old boy's hand over the Hebrew letters of a prayer book.*
2. *Grandfather Cohen is seated at the dining room table with Bernard, teaching him the tunes of the Torah.*

NARRATOR: *Older than the banks of the Nile, not so cruel as the circumcision rite of the Zulus, and even more intricate than a snowflake is the bar mitzvah. . . .*

"Hey, what's that he said about niggers being clipped? I thought—"

"—comparative religion. I take it at McGill."

"Comparative *what?* I'll give you such a *schoss.*"

---

3. *In the synagogue Bernard stands looking at the Holy Ark. His reaction.*

CHOIR: *Hear O Israel the Lord is Our God the Lord is One.*

4. *Grandfather Cohen, wearing a prayer shawl, hands the Torah to Mr. Cohen, who passes it to his son.*

NARRATOR: *From generation to generation, for years before the birth of Christ . . .*

"Hsssssss . . ."

"O.K., smart guy. Shettup!"

NARRATOR: *. . . the rule of law has been passed from hand to hand among the Chosen People. Something priceless, something cherished . . .*

"Like a chinchilla."

"One more crack out of you, Arnie," Mr. Cohen said, "and out you go."

In the darkness Duddy smiled, relieved.

NARRATOR: *. . . a thing of beauty and a joy forever.*

5. *The wrappings come off and Mr. Cohen holds the Torah aloft.*

CHOIR: (Recites in Hebrew) *In the beginning God created heaven and earth . . .*

6. *Camera closes in on Torah.*

NARRATOR: *. . . In the beginning there was the Word . . . There was Abraham, Isaac, and Jacob . . . There was Moses . . .*

(As CHOIR hums in background)

King David . . . Judas Maccabee . . .

(CHOIR to climax)

. . . and, in our own time, Leon Trotsky . . .

"What's that?"

"His bar mitzvah I would have liked to have seen. Trotsky!"

NARRATOR: *. . . in all those years, the Hebrews, whipped like sand by the cruel winds of oppression, have survived by the word . . . the law . . .*

7. *A close shot of a baby being circumcised.*

"Lock the doors. Here comes the dirty part."

"Shame on you."

"Awright, Sarah. O.K. You've seen one before. You don't have to pretend you're not looking."

NARRATOR: . . . *and through the centuries the eight-day-old Hebrew babe has been welcomed into the race with blood.*

(Tom-toms beat in background. Heightening)

8. (Montage) *Lightning. African tribal dance. Jungle fire. Stukas diving. A jitterbug contest speeded up. Slaughtering of a cow. Fireworks against a night sky. More African dancing. Torrents of rain. An advertisement for Maidenform bras, upside down. Blood splashing against glass. A lion roars.*

"Wow!"

"Are you all right, *Zeyda?*"

(Drums to climax. Out)

9. *A slow dissolve to close-up of Bernard Cohen's shining morning face.*

NARRATOR: *This is the story of one such Hebrew babe, and how at the age of thirteen he was at last accepted as an adult member of his tribe.*

"If you don't feel well, *Zeyda,* I'll get you a glass of water."

NARRATOR: *This is the story of the bar mitzvah of Bernard son of Moses. . . .*

10. *A smiling Rabbi Goldstone leads Bernard up the aisle of the Temple. In the background, second cousins and schoolmates wave and smile at the camera.*

"Good," Duddy said. "Excellent." He had asked Mr. Friar to work Rabbi Goldstone into every possible shot.

"Look, there I am! Did you see me, Mommy?"

"You see Harry there picking his nose? If he'd known the camera—"

"A big joke!"

---

11. *Bernard and Rabbi Goldstone reach the prayer stand.*

NARRATOR: *As solemn as the Aztec sacrifice, more mysterious than Helen's face, is the pregnant moment, the meeting of time past and time present, when the priest and his initiate each* ho'mat.

Rabbi Goldstone coughed. "That means priest in the figurative sense."

"He's gone too far," Duddy whispered to Yvette. "Jeez."

CHOIR: (Singing in Hebrew) *Blessed is the Lord our God, Father of Abraham, Isaac, and Jacob . . .*

"There, *Zeyda,* isn't that nice?"

"Oh, leave him alone, Henry."

"Leave him alone? I think he's had another stroke."

---

12. *As Bernard says his blessings over the Torah, the camera pans around the Temple. Aunt Sadie giggles shyly. Ten-year-old Manny Schwartz crosses his eyes and sticks out his tongue. Grandfather Cohen looks severe. Mr. Cohen wipes what just might be a tear from his eye. Uncle Ernie whispers into a man's ear. The man grins widely.*

13. *A close shot of Bernard saying his blessings. The camera moves in slowly on his eyes.*

(Bring in tom-toms again.)

"Today I am a man!"

14. *Cut to a close shot of circumcision again.*

"It's not me," Bernie shouted. "Honest, guys."

"Atta boy."

"Do you think this'll have a bad effect on the children?"

"Never mind the children. I've got such a pain there now you'd think it was me up there."

---

15. *Résumé shot of Bernard saying his haftorah.*

NARRATOR: *The young Hebrew, now a fully accepted member of his tribe, is instructed in the ways of the world by his religious adviser.*

16. *A two-shot of Rabbi Goldstone and Bernard.*

NARRATOR: *"Beginning today," the rabbi tells him, "you are old enough to be responsible for your own sins. Your father no longer takes them on his shoulders."*

(As CHOIR hums Elgar's "Pomp and Circumstance")

17. *Camera pans round Temple again. Cutting back again and again to Bernard and the rabbi.*

(Superimpose Kipling's "If" over the above.)

NARRATOR: *"Today you are a man, Bernard son of Moses."*

18. (Montage) *Lightning. Close shot of head of Michelangelo's statue of David. Cartoon of a Thurber husband. African tribal dance. Close shot of a venereal disease warning in a public urinal.*

"*Zeyda,* one minute."

"You'd better go with him, Henry."

Soldiers' marching speeded up. Circumcision close-up again. Upside-down shot of a hand on a woman's breast.

"Hey," Arnie shouted, "can you use a new casting director, Kravitz?"

"Haven't you any appreciation for the finer things?"

"Hoo-haw."

Duddy bit his hand. The sweat rolled down his forehead.

"This is meant to be serious, Arnie. Oh, he's such a fool."

A lion roars. Close shot of Bernard's left eye. A pair of black panties catch fire. Lightning. African tribal dance.

NARRATOR: *Today you are a man and your family and friends have come to celebrate.*

(Giuseppe di Stefano sings Drinking Song from *La Traviata.*)

19. *Close shot of hands pouring a large Scotch.*
20. *Cut to general shots of guests at Temple kiddush.*

"There I am!"

"Look at Sammy, stuffing his big fat face as usual."

"There I am *again!*"

"What took you so long, Henry?"

"Did I miss anything?"

"Aw. Where's the *Zeyda?*"

"He's sitting outside in the car. Hey, was that me?"

"I'd like to see this part again later, please."

"Second the motion."

NARRATOR: *Those who couldn't come sent telegrams.*

21. *Hold a shot of telegrams pinned against green background.*

(As CHOIR hums "Auld Lang Syne")

NARRATOR: "HAPPY BAR MITZVAH, BERNIE. BEST UNCLE HERBY." . . . "MAY YOUR LIFE BE HAPPY AND SUCCESSFUL. THE SHAPIRO BROTHERS AND MYRNA." . . . "BEST WISHES FOR HEALTH, HAPPINESS, AND SUCCESS FROM THE WINNIPEG BRANCH OF THE COHENS . . . SURPRISE PARCEL FOLLOWS." . . . "MY HEART GOES OUT TO YOU AND YOURS TODAY, MYER." . . .

"You notice Lou sent only a Greetings telegram? You get a special rate."

"He's had a bad year, that's all. Lay off, Molly."

"A bad year! He comes from your side of the family, you mean."

NARRATOR: *Those who came did not come empty-handed.*

"Try it sometime."

They came with tributes for the boy who had come of age.

22. *Camera pans over a table laden with gifts. Revealed are four Parker 51 sets, an electric razor, a portable record player . . .*

"Murray got the player wholesale through his brother-in-law."

. . . three toilet sets, two copies of Tom Sawyer, *five subscriptions to the* National Geographic *magazine, a movie projector, a fishing rod and other angling equipment, three cameras, a season's ticket to hockey games at the Forum, a set of phylacteries and a prayer shawl, a rubber dinghy, a*

savings account book open at a first deposit of five hundred dollars, six sport shirts, an elaborate chemistry set, a pile of fifty silver dollars in a velvet-lined box, at least ten credit slips (worth from twenty to a hundred dollars each) for Eaton's and Morgan's, two sets of H. G. Wells's Outline of History.

(As CHOIR sings "Happy Birthday, Bernie!")

23. *Hold a shot of numerous checks pinned to a board. Spin it.*

"Dave's check is only for twenty-five bucks. Do you know how much business he gets out of Cohen every year?"

"If it had been Lou you would have said he had a bad year. Admit it."

"Hey, Bernie," Arnie yelled, "how many of those checks bounced? You can tell us."

"I was grateful for all of them," Bernie said, "large or small. It's the thought that counts with me."

"Isn't he sweet?"

"Sure," Arnie said, "but he could have told me that before."

---

24. *A shot of Rabbi Goldstone's study. Bernard sits in an enormous leather chair and the rabbi paces up and down, talking to him.*

NARRATOR: *But that afternoon, in the good rabbi's study, the young Hebrew learns that there are more exalted things in this world besides material possessions; he is told something of the tragic history of his race, how they were exploited by the ancient Egyptian imperialists, how reactionary dictators from Nehru to Hitler persecuted them in order to divert the working classes from the true cause of their sorrows, he learns—like Candide—that all is not for the best in the best of all possible worlds.*

(As Al Jolson sings "Eli, Eli")

25. *Rabbi Goldstone leads Bernard to the window and stands behind him, his hands resting on the lad's shoulders.*

"Five'll get you ten that right now he's asking Bernie to remind his father that the Temple building campaign is lagging behind schedule."

Rabbi Goldstone coughed loudly.

NARRATOR: (Recites) *"I am a Jew: hath not a Jew eyes? Hath not a Jew hands, organs, dimensions, senses, affections, pas-*

sions, fed with the same food, hurt with the same weapons, subject to the same diseases, healed by the same oils, warmed and cooled by the same winter and summer as a Christian is? If you prick him does he not bleed?"

26. *Rabbi Goldstone autographs a copy of his book,* Why I'm Glad to Be a Jew, *and hands it to Bernard.*

27. *Hold a close shot of the book.*

From there the movie went on to record the merrymaking and odd touching interludes at the dinner and dance. Relatives and friends saw themselves eating, drinking, and dancing. Uncles and aunts at the tables waved at the camera, the kids made funny faces, and the old people sat stonily. Cuckoo Kaplan did a soft-shoe dance on the head table. As the camera closed in on the dancers, Henry pretended to be seducing Morrie Applebaum's wife. Mr. Cohen had a word with the bandleader and the first *kazatske* was played. Timidly the old people joined hands and began to dance around in a circle. Mr. Cohen and some spirited others joined in the second one. Duddy noticed some intruders at the sandwich table. He did not know them by name or sight, but remembering, he recognized that they were FFHS boys and he smiled a little. The camera panned lovingly about fish and jugs and animals modeled out of ice. It closed in and swallowed the bursting trumpeter. Guests were picked up again, some reeling and others bad-tempered, waiting for taxis and husbands to come round with the car outside the Temple.

And Mr. Cohen, sitting in the first row with his legs open like an inverted nutcracker to accommodate his sunken belly, thought, It's worth it, every last cent, or what's money for, it's cheap at any price to have captured my family and friends and foolish rabbi. He reached for Gertie's hand and thought, I'd better not kiss Bernie. It would embarrass him.

(As CHOIR sings "Hallelujah Chorus")

74. *Rear-view long shot. Mr. Cohen and Bernard standing before the offices of M. Cohen, Inc., Metal Merchants.*

FADE OUT

Nobody spoke. Duddy began to bite his fingernails and Yvette pulled his hand away and held it.

"A most edifying experience," Rabbi Goldstone said. "A work of art."

Everybody began to speak at once.

"Thank you very much, indeed," Mr. Friar said. "Unfortunately, the best parts were left on the cutting room floor."

"Play it again."

"Yeah!"

The *shadchan* (marriage broker) is not so old-fashioned a character as he may appear; it has been only two generations since he was highly visible, and in some circles, the profession continues to this day. There have always been matchmakers for those who care to look for them, and some are still practicing, advertising their services in Jewish newspapers.

Originally, the *shadchan* was a scholar, as matchmaking has traditionally been regarded as God's work. But at some point between the Middle Ages and modern times, the figure of the *shadchan* began to shift away from scholars and men of piety, and in favor of businessmen. A really skillful *shadchan,* it was said, could bring two walls together.

Even when the profession was dominated by some of the less pious members of society, an important principle endured: marriage was for everyone, which is clear from the many jokes that survive about prospective mates with various physical and personality flaws.

IT had been nine years since the *shadchan* had first visited the family and now, suddenly, he was back. The boy, now a young man, was still unmarried, and no wonder: he weighed close to three hundred pounds, he stammered, he lacked a sense of humor, and was something of an imbecile.

"I have finally found a match for your son," the *shadchan* began.

"Who is she?" asked the anxious parents.

"Wait," said the *shadchan.* "Before I tell you her name, let me say she is a woman of extremely high social position, of significant wealth, and from a refined background."

"For our son? That's wonderful. It's been worth the long wait. What's her name?"

"Princess Anne."

The family was speechless. After a moment, the mother reacted indignantly: "A *shikse?* For my son?"

It took the *shadchan* almost three hours to convince the family that they were in no position to be choosy. Finally, they agreed to the match, and signed the contract. The *shadchan* took the document, folded it carefully, and put it in his pocket. He walked out onto the street, took a deep breath, and said to himself, "Well, that's half the battle!"

"She looks terrible," the young man reported to the *shadchan.* "How could I marry a woman who looks like that?"

"Look," replied the *shadchan,* "either you like Picasso or you don't!"

A *SHADCHAN* was trying to arrange a match between a yeshiva *bocher* and a young woman. The girl had a rich father and a fine education, but she was far from a beauty. After meeting the girl, the boy went back to see the *shadchan.* "She's very nice," he reported, "and she is certainly smart. But I'm afraid that she's so ugly that if I marry her I'll be unhappy for the rest of my life!"

"Not so fast, my young friend," said the *shadchan,* who was relishing the idea of this lucrative alignment. "Now, let's look at the problem. All right, she's ugly. Nu? Think about it. When you're studying all day long, will you be looking at her? No! And when you come home for supper, will you be looking at her while you eat? No! And when you go to bed at night, will you be looking at her in the dark? Of course not! And when you're sleeping, will you be looking at her? Not at all! And in your free time, will you *want* to look at her? No; instead you'll go out for a walk with the children, God willing you'll have many of them. So I ask you, what's the problem? *When will you look at her?*"

THE *shadchan* approached a young man and suggested a match to him. The man, being far from wealthy and not at all brilliant, was delighted with the prospect, and listened eagerly.

"You know," said the *shadchan,* "I like you, and you're a nice fellow. So even before you meet this girl, I want to explain something about her. She's not a great cook. Nobody's ever died from her cooking, but even *schnorrers* don't come to her house."

"Well," the young man replied, "that's really not so important. What do I know about fancy eating, anyway?"

"I can see you're a very nice fellow," the *shadchan* said. "So I'll let you in on something else: this girl is no beauty. There's nothing exactly *wrong* with her looks, but she hasn't won any beauty prizes, either."

"To tell you the truth," the young man replied, "you may have noticed that I'm not exactly the Prince of Denmark. At least, if she's ugly, nobody will run off with her."

"My sentiments exactly," said the *shadchan,* excited that he had a live prospect. "Well, in that case, let me fill you in on one more thing. I can't say she's terribly bright. She gets along, but maybe she's a little on the slow side."

"Well," the young man said, "in a wife that can be a real advantage. I wouldn't want my wife to be smarter than me."

"I can see that you're pretty smart yourself," replied the *shadchan.* "And so I won't hide anything from you. I might as well tell you right now that this girl has a slight hunchback."

"A hunchback?" said the young man. "A hunchback? How *dare* you match me up with a hunchback?"

"Wait a minute," said the *shadchan.* "You're going to *marry* this girl. *What's one little thing?*"

•

The town *shadchan* was getting old, and could no longer get around as he used to. So he hired a young assistant who knew nothing about the business. He had to start from scratch with him, teaching him all the basic points of the trade.

"The most important thing is exaggeration," said the *shadchan.* "You have to lay it on thick."

"I understand," said the assistant.

One day the *shadchan* took his assistant along on a matchmaking visit to a rich family who had an only son.

"Don't forget," said the *shadchan.* "Be enthusiastic, and don't hesitate to exaggerate."

When they arrived, the *shadchan* began: "I've found the right girl for your son. She comes from a very good family."

"Good family!" exclaimed the assistant. "They are descendants of the Gaon of Vilna!"

"And rich too," said the *shadchan.*

"Practically millionaires," add-

"She's very pretty," said the *shadchan.*

"Pretty?" said the assistant. "She's gorgeous!"

"But I should tell you," added the *shadchan,* giving his assistant a stern look, "that she has a small handicap. There's a tiny wart on her back."

"What do you mean, a wart?" cried the assistant. "It's a regular hump!"

•

Freud was especially fond of *shadchan* jokes, which, he wrote, often "have something forbidden to say." He continued: "Anyone who has allowed the truth to slip out in an unguarded moment is in fact glad to be free of pretense. This is a correct and profound piece of psychological insight. . . . But this converts the laughable figure of the *shadchan* into a sympathetic one, deserving of pity. How happy the man must be to be able at last to throw off the burden of pretense, since he makes use of the first chance of shouting out the very last scrap of truth!"

To illustrate this point, Freud offered this joke:

•

A *shadchan* is trying to impress a young man with the wealth of the bride's family. The boy, however, is skeptical, and asks, "Don't you think they might have borrowed the silverware in order to make a good impression?"

"Nonsense," cries the *shadchan*. "Who would lend any silverware to such thieves?"

•

ONCE a *shadchan* came to a young man and said, "Son, I have just the girl for you. She's terrific!"

"I'm not interested," the young man replied. "I don't want to get married just now."

"What are you talking about?" said the *shadchan*. "How can a Jew live without a wife?"

"Why do I need a wife?" said the young man?

"Ach," replied the *shadchan*. "Now you're being foolish. Without a wife, my friend, you'll never be happy. You'll be lonely, like an island in the middle of the ocean. Imagine getting up in the morning, and she brings you a hot cup of tea. And after you come home from work, you eat together at the table. On Friday night, it's peaceful and serene, and when the Holy Sabbath arrives, the house is spotless, the candles are on the table, the meal is ready, the wine, the challah—all of this beauty is bound up in marriage.

"And there, opposite you, sits your wife, telling witty stories. She chatters, sweetly talking about this and that while you listen, just like *my* wife does. Oh, she talks and talks, and she goes on talking, and still she talks, and talks—oy, can that woman talk! *She's driving me crazy with her talk!*"

ISAAC ROSENFELD

The Queen of Sheba

Isaac Rosenfeld, essayist, reviewer, novelist, and literary personality during the 1940s and 1950s, died in 1956 of a heart attack at the age of thirty-eight. Saul Bellow remembers him as a "marvelous clown" who "loved hoaxes, mimicry, parody. . . . With Isaac, the gravest, the most characteristic, the most perfect strokes took on a comic slant."

From all over they have come, and they keep coming, though the King is now an old man. It may be owing to his age that he has grown lenient, admitting women to concubinage whom, the counselors swear, he would have sent packing in the old days. He has reached the years when anything young looks good to him. This may not be true, there may be other reasons; but the counselors have a point in saying that the standards have fallen, and they tell the story of the Queen of Sheba.

A letter came; it was the first application to be received by mail. From a foreign country, the woman signed herself The Queen. She flattered Solomon's wisdom, word of which had reached her from afar; her own ears longed to hear his discourse, her own eyes, to behold his person. An unorthodox application, written in a powerful, forward-rushing though feminine hand on strangely scented paper: the King said it reminded him of jungles. He inspected the postmark, clipped off the stamp, and pasted it on a page by itself in his album. His expression was hidden in his beard.

The woman meant it. Boxes began to arrive, plastered with travel stickers. They came on sand-choked, sneezing camels, in long trains, attended by drivers, natives of the Land of Sheba. The next day, more boxes, and again on the third. Gifts of all description, of money and goods, spangles and bangles for the entire court. It made an excellent impression, but Solomon, who distributed the gifts, did not seem pleased. . . . Here the counselors pretend to know the King's mind. First of all, they say, he was annoyed at having to put up so many camels, whole droves of them—his stables were crowded, and there was a shortage of feed for his own animals. Then the camel drivers, rough and barbarous men, were inflamed by the sight of Solomon's women, and the King had to double the guard and pay overtime; this killed him. But their greatest presumption lies in saying that Solomon thought, *"Adonai Elohenu!* Is she coming to stay?" No one knows what the King thought.

He may well have been glad that the Queen was coming. No queen had ever before asked to be his slave—and she was a queen for sure, and of a rich country: think of the gifts she had sent. Solomon put his economists to work and they submitted a report: the financial structure was sound, and the country led in the production of myrrh, pepper, and oil. Now, to be sure, the Queen's letter made no direct application; apart from the flattery, it merely said, "Coming for a visit," as an equal might say. But the interpretation was clear. An equal would not come uninvited, only one who meant to offer herself would do so—unless the Queen was rude; but the gifts she had sent took care of that. Yet as a queen, writing from her own palace, she could not have expressed the intention; it would have been treason to her own people. Nevertheless, she had every intention: otherwise, why would she have gone to the trouble? The fact is, there was rejoicing in the palace, Solomon himself led the dancing, and he declared a holiday when the Queen of Sheba arrived.

She came in a howdah, on a camel, preceded by troops of archers and trumpeters. Solomon helped her down, and washed and anointed her feet in the courtyard. This didn't come off so well. Sheba used coloring matter on her toenails and the soles of her feet, and the coloring ran; Solomon was out of practice, he tickled her feet a few times and made her laugh. The ceremony was supposed to be a solemn one, the people took it very seriously, and they were offended by her toenails—feet were supposed to be presented dusty: as for the giggling, it was unpardonable, and the priests took offense. A poor set of omens.

Besides, Sheba was not quite so young as the autographed picture, which she had sent in advance to Solomon, would have led one to expect. Her skin was nearly black, and her black hair, which she had apparently made some effort to straighten, had

From *Running A Muck*, copyright © 1978 by John Caldwell. By permission of Writer's Digest Books.

gone frizzled and kinky again in the heat of the desert crossing. She wore anklets of delicate chain, gold bracelets all over her arms, and jewels in both obvious and unexpected places, so that the eye was never done seeing them; their light was kept in constant agitation by the massive rhythm of her breathing, which involved her entire body. A sense of tremendous power and authenticity emanated from her breasts. Some thought she was beautiful, others not.

No one knows what the King thought; but he may well have felt what everyone else did who came to witness her arrival— drawn, and at the same time stunned.

But the King is glad in his heart as he leads Sheba to the table, where he has put on a great spread for her. He is attended by his court and surrounded by his women—and how lordly are his movements as he eats meat and rinses his mouth with wine! At the same time he is uneasy in the Queen's presence—after all, this is no maiden lurking in the garden to trip up to him and fold her hands upon his breast. The meal goes well enough: Sheba asks for seconds, and seems impressed with the napkins and silverware. But suddenly, right in the middle of dessert, she turns to him and demands, in front of everyone and that all may hear, that he show her his famous wisdom. This comes as something of a shock. The implication is twofold: that so far he has spoken commonplaces; and secondly, that he is to suffer no illusions, it was really for the sake of his wisdom that she made the difficult trip. The people turn their eyes on the King, who handles the awkward moment with skill; he clears his throat on schedule, and raises his hand in the usual gesture, admonishing silence. But nothing comes.

In the official account of the visit, which Solomon had written to order, he was supposed to have

. . . told her all questions: There was not anything . . . which he told her not. And when the Queen of Sheba had seen all Solomon's wisdom, and the house that he had built, and the meat of his table and the sitting of his servants . . .

etc.,

there was no more spirit in her. And she said to the King, It was a true report that I heard in mine own land, of thy acts and thy wisdom. Howbeit, I believed not the words, until I came and mine eyes had seen it; and behold, the half was not told me: Thy wisdom and prosperity exceedeth the fame which I heard. Happy are thy men . . . which stand continually before thee and that hear thy wisdom.

After which there was supposed to have been a further exchange of compliments and gifts.

Now, this is not only a bit thick; it gets round the question of Solomon's wisdom. What *did* the King say, when put to it by the Queen? That there were so many feet in a mile? That all circles were round? That the number of stars visible on a clear night from a point well out of town was neither more nor less than a certain number? Did he advise her what to take for colds, give her a recipe for salad dressing, or speak of building temples and ships? Just what does a man say under the circumstances?

Certainly, he hadn't the nerve, the gall, to repeat the abominable invention to her face of the two women who disputed motherhood of a child. She would have seen through it right away. And surely he knew this was not the time to quote his sayings; besides, he always had trouble remembering them. Then what did he say?

His economists had worked up a report on the Land of Sheba. He may have sent for a copy; more likely, he knew the essential facts cold, and spoke what came to mind: industry, agriculture, natural resources. Of the financial structure, the public debt, the condition of business. Of the production of pepper, myrrh, and oil, especially oil. Grant him his wisdom.

Certainly, the Queen was impressed, but one need not suppose that the spirit was knocked out of her or that she said, "It was a true report that I heard in mine own land . . ." etc. Chances are, she paid no attention to his words (except to note the drift) but watched him as he spoke, taking in the cut of his beard, the fit of his clothes, and wondering, betimes, what sort of man he was. She saw his initial uncertainty give way and his confidence grow as he reached the meaty part of his delivery. And all along, she observed how he drew on the admiring glances of his girls, soaked up their adoration, as they lay open-mouthed on couches and rugs at his feet, all criticism suspended, incapacitated by love. Love ringed him round, love sustained him, he was the splendid heart of their hearts. She must have forgotten the heat and sand images of the desert crossing, she, too, lapped from all sides and borne gently afloat. . . .

So much one may imagine. But the Queen spent a number of days or weeks, perhaps even a month or two in the King's company, and of what happened during the time of her stay, let alone the subsequent events of the first night, the official chronicles say nothing. A merciful omission, according to the counselors, who report that it went badly from the start. When the King had finished his discourse, they say the Queen felt called upon to answer. But words failed her, or she felt no need of words: she was the Queen. What she did was to lean forward and, in utter disregard of the company, take his head into her hands, gaze at him for a long time with a smile on her thick lips, and at last bestow on him a kiss, which landed somewhere in his beard.

Then she jumped onto the table, commanded music, and danced among the cups and bowls, the dishes and the crumpled napkins. The counselors were shocked, the girls smirked painfully, the servants held their breath. Nor was Sheba so slender as the autographed picture may have led one to believe. When she set her feet down, the table shook, and the carafes of wine and sweetened water swayed and threatened to topple. Solomon himself hastily cleared a way for her, pushing the dishes to one side; his hands were trembling. But she proceeded with the dance, the chain anklets tinkled, her fingers snapped, the many jewels she wore flashed wealthily. Her toes left marks on the tablecloth, as though animals had run there. And run she did, back and forth over the length of the table, bending over the counselors to tweak this one's nose and that one's ear. But always she glanced back to see if she had the King's eye.

She had it, darker than usual. To her, this meant that he was admiring her, gravely, as befits King and Queen, and her feet quickened. How stern she was! Already she felt the King's love, harder than any courtier's and so much more severe. She increased the tempo, the musicians scrambling to keep up with her, and whirled. Round and round she sped, drawing nearer the end of the table where the King sat. It was a dance in the style of her country, unknown in these parts, and she did it with

"If this stuff is retroactive to last weekend, we're in big trouble."

the abandon of a tribesgirl, though one must assume she was
conscious, in her abandonment, that it was she, the Queen,
none other than Sheba, who abandoned herself to King Solomon. That was the whole point of it, the mastery of the thing.
Pride did not leave her face, it entered her ecstasy and raised
it in degree. Already cries, guttural, impersonal, were barking
in her throat; then with a final whoop she spun round and
threw herself, arms outstretched and intertwined, like one
bound captive, to fall before him on the table where his meal
had been.

It was a terrible mistake. The women and the counselors
knew the King so much better than she, and their hearts went
out in pity. The Queen had offered herself in the only way she
knew—majesty, power, and reign implied—throwing herself
prone with a condescending crash for the King to rise and take
her. What presumption! He did not move. He sat infinitely
removed, almost sorrowing over this great embarrassment.
The music had stopped; there was an unbearable silence in the
banquet hall. The King rumbled something deep in his beard;
perhaps he was merely clearing his throat, preparatory to saying a few words (if only his wisdom did not fail him!). Some of
the servants took it to mean more wine, others, more meat, still
others, finger bowls. They ran in all directions. Sheba lowered
herself into her seat at the King's side. Her dark face burned.
. . . Somehow the time went by, and the evening was over.

Solomon led Sheba off to his chamber, as courtesy demanded. Even as she went with him, it was apparent that she still went in hope; even at the last moment. The older women wept.

Day by day, the strain mounted. Sheba was sometimes with the King, they played chess or listened to the radio, they bent their heads over maps, discussed politics, and played croquet. But there were no festivities and she did not dance again. She bore herself with dignity, but she had grown pale, and her smile, when she forgot herself, was cringing and meek. Sometimes, when she was alone, she was seen to run her finger over the tabletops and the woodwork, looking for dust. She could not bear the sight of her waiting women—lest the revival of her hope, as they did her toilet, become apparent to them—and would chase them out of the room, only to call them back to help her prepare for an audience with the King. Finally, she quarreled with some of the girls of the harem. And when this happened, Sheba knew that the day had come and she began to pack.

A pinochle game was in progress when the Queen of Sheba, unannounced and without knocking, came into the room to say she wanted a word with the King. He dismissed his counselors, but one of them swears he managed to hide behind the draperies, where he witnessed the scene.

The King was in his undershirt, smoking a cigar. He apologized for his dishevelment and offered to repair it. The affairs of state, he explained, were so trying lately, he found he worked better in dishabille. Had he been working? asked the Queen with a smile. She thought this was some sort of game, and she fingered the cards with pictures of kings and queens. Solomon, knowing that women do not play pinochle, told her the cabinet had been in extraordinary session, trying fortunes with the picture cards. The times were good, but one must look to the future, and he offered to show her how it was done.

"No, I don't want to keep you," said the Queen of Sheba. "I beg only a few words."

"Speak," said Solomon.

"Solomon, Solomon," said the Queen, "I am going away. No, don't answer me. You will say something polite and regretful, but my decision can only be a relief to you." She paused, taking on courage. "You must not allow this to be a disappointment to you, you must let me take the whole expense of our emotion upon myself. I did a foolish thing. I am a proud woman, being a Queen, and my pride carried me too far. I thought I would take pride in transcending pride, in offering myself to the King. But still that was pride, you did wisely to refuse me. Yes, you are wise, Solomon, let no one question your wisdom. Yours is the wisdom of love, which is the highest. But your love is love only of yourself; yet you share it with others by letting them love you—and this is next to the highest. Either way you look at it, Solomon is wise enough. Understand me—" She took a step forward, a dance step, as though she were again on the tabletop, but her eyes spoke a different meaning.

"I am not pleading with you that you love me or allow me to love you. For you are the King; your taking is your giving. But allow me to say, your power rests on despair. Yours is the power of drawing love, the like of which has not been seen. But you despair of loving with your own heart. I have come to tell the King he must not despair. Surely, Solomon who has built temples and made the desert flourish is a powerful king, and he has the power to do what the simplest slave girl or washerwoman of his harem can do—to love with his own heart. And if he does not have this power, it will come to him, he need only accept the love which it is his nature to call forth in everyone, especially in us poor women. This is his glory. Rejoice in it, O King, for you are the King!"

The counselor who hid behind the drapes said he regretted his action, to see how his King stood burdened before the Queen. His own heart filled with loving shame. Solomon looked lost, deprived of his power, as though the years in the palace and the garden had never been. He made an effort to stand dignified in his undershirt, he bore his head as though he were wearing the crown, but it was pitiful to see him.

"The Queen is wise," said he. Then he broke down, and the counselor did not hear his next words. He did hear him say that the Queen was magnificent, that she had the courage of lions and tigers . . . but by now his head was lowered. Suddenly, he clasped the Queen to his breast in an embrace of farewell, and the Queen smiled and stroked his curly beard. They did not immediately take leave of each other, but went on to speak of other matters. Before the Queen of Sheba left the country, King Solomon had leased her oil lands for ninety-nine years.

But on the day of her departure, he stood bareheaded in the crowded courtyard to watch her set out, with her trumpeters and archers mounted on supercilious camels. He extended his hand to help her up, and she, with her free hand, chucked him under the chin. Then she leaned out of the howdah to cry, "Long live the King!" King Solomon stood with bowed head to receive the ovation. Now more than ever they yearned for him.

When Sheba moved off, at the head of the procession, Solomon led the people onto the roof, to watch the camels file across the sand. He stood till evening fell, and the rump of the last plodding animal had twitched out of sight beyond the sand hills. Then he averted his face and wept silently lest the people see their King's tears.

Dick Codor © 1979

Transitory Love

From the story "Perlmutter at the East Pole." Morty Perlmutter, anthropologist and explorer, has been around the world looking for the meaning of life. He ends up in New York, riding the subways.

In the second year something happened to interrupt Morty's researches.

"I'm a scientist," Morty explained suddenly to the woman next to him.

This was his third day underground. "I'm trying to get the feel of the earth," he said. "Last night I was on the Broadway-Seventh Avenue local and I got out at Fourteenth Street and walked along the tracks through the tunnel to Eighth Street. Exhilarating, *marvelous.*" The train had broken from its tunnel and begun to climb The Bronx. He glanced casually along the woman's bosom and down at Jerome Avenue. He looked back at the woman. She was a blue-haired lady of about fifty-three, heavy, probably powerful. He had seen the type before, in London, in Buenos Aires, in Paris, in Chicago. He saw in her

WHAT'S HE DOING HERE? I THOUGHT I TOLD YOU TO COME ALONE!

S. GROSS

a sort of *bahlabustuh*-cum-duchess who would survive her husband by twenty years. Perlmutter was attracted to such women; something atavistic in him responded while his heart said no. He imagined them around bridge tables, or playing poker in their dining rooms. He saw them giving daughters away in hotel ballrooms, and ordering meat from the butcher over the telephone, and in girdles in the fitting rooms of department stores. He had seen thousands of these women since coming to New York, recognizing in them, from the days of some Ur-Morty (as if he had known them in the sea), old, vital aunts. She troubled him. He was responding, he supposed, to the *science* in her, to the solid certainty she gave off like a scent, to what he guessed might be in her an almost Newtonian *suspicion,* and to what he knew would be her fierce loyalty. Recognizing what he really wanted—it was to seduce one of these women—he had to laugh. The Morty Perlmutter who had known African Amazons and snuggled beneath arctic skins with Eskimo girls, who had loved queens of the circus and lady pearl divers—was this a Morty Perlmutter who could be stymied in The Bronx? (Because he understood that he would probably never make it with her, he sighed.) A scientist *tries,* he told himself, and tried.

"Excuse me, my dear," he said. "I'm very clumsy at this sort of thing, but I find myself extraordinarily attracted to you. Will you have a drink with me?"

The woman would have changed her seat right then, but she was by the window and Morty had her penned in.

"I'll call the guard," she said.

"Now, now," Morty said. "What's in the bag?" he said. "Some little pretty for yourself?" he asked brightly. "Or is it for your husband?"

"None of your business. Let me out, you pervert, or I'll yell."

Morty stood up quickly. She seemed genuinely frightened and he leaned down to reassure her. "I am no punk molester of women," he said. "I speak from respectable need. Of course, if you insist on making a scene I'll have to leave you alone, but yours is a rare type with a rarer appeal. It is precisely my perversion, as you call it, which makes you attractive to me. Don't knock success, lady. When was the last time someone not your husband wanted to have a drink with you? I do not count the one time in the Catskills ten years ago when the guests waited on the waiters and the band played on. This I write off. Or when you danced with the college busboy and he kissed you for the tip. *This* I write off."

She stared at him for a moment with an astonished respect, and Morty sat down again. He contemplated using the Haitian Sleep Stone but decided it would be immoral. "All right, I'm

Morton Perlmutter and I'm here in the final phase of my search for synthesis. More later over cocktails."

"I'm married," she said, out of breath.

"Of course you are. Don't I know that? You think your kind of character is possible otherwise? It's sacrifice and single-mindedness that does that. It's years of love love love. You'll have to tell me all about yourself. I'm dying to kiss you. Where does your boy intern?"

"We have no children," she said shyly.

He wanted to take her hand. It was unscientific, but there it was. He wondered, too, if he might not make a cozy confidante of this woman. He knew what it meant, of course. Why not? He knew everything. All that was nonsense about the vital aunts. Morty was King Oedipus. He shrugged. I am what I am. Nothing bothers me, he thought lightly. This is my finest hour. One of them. It's all been swell.

"Let me have your number," he told her.

She shook her head.

"Let me have your phone number."

"No," she said, frightened again.

He used the Sleep Stone.

"I . . . am . . . Rose . . . Gold. You . . . can . . . usually . . . reach . . . me . . . at Klondike 5- . . . 6 . . . 7 . . . 4 . . . 3. Tuesdays I . . . play . . . mah-jongg. Wednesdays I at . . . tend matinees."

He brought her out of it quickly. "Now, about that drink . . ." Morty said.

"No. Leave me alone. You're a strange man."

"I am what I am," he said.

"This is my stop," she said, getting up. "Don't try to follow me. You'll be arrested. I'm warning you."

When she had called him a strange man, she had meant something unpleasant. His shock value had worn off. That often happened to him now. He equated it with the dying sense of wonder in the world. TV has done that, he thought absently, mass communication has. It made him angry. He followed her to the platform.

She turned quickly and faced him. "I meant what I said."

"I've got *your* number, Rose Gold," he said passionately. She started to walk away and Morty ran after her. "Listen to Perlmutter's curse," he commanded darkly. "May your neighborhood change!" She was running along the platform now. "May the fares to Miami be trebled! May your chicken soup freeze over!" She was going down the stairs now and he rushed after her. *"May your fur coats explode!"* he roared.

●

Quickies

A NINETY-YEAR-OLD couple comes to see a divorce lawyer. The lawyer is shocked. "Why now?" he asks. "You've been together all this time. Why have you waited so long?"

The old woman replies, "We wanted to wait until the children died!"

A MAN walks into a store and says, "This is my wife's birthday, and I'd like to buy her a beautiful fountain pen."

The clerk looks up and says, "A little surprise, huh?"

"Right," says the man. "She's expecting a Cadillac!"

MY wife divorced me for religious reasons. She worshiped money and I didn't have any!

I'VE been married for thirty-four years and I'm still in love with the same woman. If my wife ever finds out, she'll kill me!

CAN that woman talk! She went to Miami, and when she got home her tongue was sunburned!

Henny Youngman's answering service picks up the phone and says: "Henny Youngman, King of the One-Liners." He has a unique approach to comedy. He doesn't waste a word, and never draws out a story. "Guy goes to a doctor," he will begin. "Doctor says, 'You're sick.' Guy says, 'I want another opinion.' 'Okay, you're ugly too.'"

Not surprisingly, according to a *New Yorker* profile of Youngman, done by Tony Hiss in 1977, he is still actively buying jokes: "He estimates that in forty years of buying jokes he's laid out at least a quarter of a million dollars to build his unbelievable four-hour joke repertoire: unbelievable because Henny can tell six or seven jokes a minute, which means that he knows over fifteen hundred jokes—and all of them guaranteed surefire, because jokes that falter are retired immediately. 'Jokes cost money,' he says. 'You don't get them that easy. Two pages of special material can cost fifteen hundred dollars, and that's only six minutes' worth of jokes. You gotta take care of your business, or you gotta worry. When you're on that stage, no one can help you. A stage is only thirty square feet. Any stage. So where the hell can you go? Cheap comedians never invest a nickel in the business. Nobody's paid his dues like I have.'"

I'm sure you know the views of Buber. It is wrong to turn a man (a subject) into a thing (an object). By means of spiritual dialogue, the I-It relationship becomes an I-Thou relationship. God comes and goes in man's soul. And men come and go in each other's souls. Sometimes they come and go in each other's beds, too. You have dialogue with a man. You have intercourse with his wife.

Saul Bellow, *Herzog*

Rosh Hashanah Interruptus

Bruce Jay Friedman was born in New York in 1930. He is the author of several novels, including *Stern, A Mother's Kisses, The Dick;* two collections of short stories: *Far from the City of Class* and *Black Angels;* and several plays and screenplays, including *Scuba Duba, Steambath, and Stir Crazy.*

Stern, his first novel, is the story of a *schlemiel* who lives mostly in fantasy—and in fear of anti-Semitism. The novel earned Friedman a reputation as a master of black humor.

In the Air Force, Stern, recently married and swiftly packing on hip fat, felt isolated, a nonflying officer in a flying service, at a time when the jets were coming in and there was no escaping them; the air was full of strange new jet sounds and the ground reverberated with the throb of them. Somehow Stern connected his nonflying status with his Jewishness, as though flying were a golden, crew-cut, gentile thing while Jewishness was a cautious and scholarly quality that crept into engines and prevented planes from lurching off the ground with recklessness. In truth, Stern feared the sky, the myriad buttons and switches on instrument panels. He was afraid of charts with grids on them, convinced he could never master anything called grids, and he was in deadly fear of phrases like "ultra high frequency" and "landing pattern." He had a recurring dream in which he was a fighter pilot, his plane attended to by a ground mechanic who resented Stern's profile for spoiling the golden, blue-eyed look of the squadron. Each day the mechanic would stand by, neutral-faced, arms folded, while Stern, able to check his plane only peremptorily, took off with heavy heart, convinced wires had been crossed and would split his aircraft in mid-flight. Stern, who traveled to distant bases to do administrative Air Force things, rode once to California as a guest on a general's luxury B-17, sitting alone in the bombardier's bubble and feeling over Grand Canyon that he had been put in a special Jewish seat and sealed off from the camaraderie in the plane's center. After eight hours of self-control, Stern felt the plane shudder and then hang uncertainly for a moment as it circled a West Coast Air Force base. He spread a thin layer of vomit around his bubble and then kneeled inside it as the plane landed, the pilots and other flying personnel filing by him in silence. Cowardly Jewish vomit staining a golden aircraft.

Stern lusted after the tiny silver wings that said you were a pilot, and once, in a Wyoming PX, he ducked his shoulders down and slipped on a pair, crouching as he did so that no one would see, holding his breath as though each second might be his last. Then he took them off and walked quickly out of the PX, feeling as though he'd looked under a skirt. A great eagle sat atop the cap of every Air Force officer, flying or nonflying, and there were those in small towns, ignorant of insignia, who thought each Air Force man was a pilot clearing the skies of Migs above Korea. One day on Rosh Hashanah, Stern, shipped for a two-week tour to Illinois, walked into a small-town synagogue, his khakis starched, his brass agleam, as though he had scored a dozen flying kills and now sought relaxation. He'd draped a tallith round his shoulders and stood, stooped with humility, in the last row of the temple, mouthing the prayer book words with all of his old speed. One by one, the congregation members, who seemed a race of Jewish midgets, turned and noticed him, and Stern, aware of their fond glances, sent forth some low groans and did several dipping knee bows he remembered from the old days. He did this to cheer them on further and to make it all the more marvelous that he, a man of the sky, took off precious flying time to pray in strange synagogues. Within minutes, the rabbi called him forward and began to heap honors upon his head. Not only was he allowed to read from the Torah but he got to kiss it, too, and then to escort it in a march around the synagogue. Ordinarily only one such honor was dealt out to a congregation member, and then only upon the occasion of a new grandson birth or wedding anniversary. The Torah back in its vault, Stern walked humbly to his seat, aware of the loving glances the tiny Jews kept shooting him. Wasn't it wonderful? A Jewish boy. A fighter. A man who had shot down planes. Yet when there's a holiday he puts on a tallith and with such sweetness comes to sit in synagogues. And did you see him pray? Even in a uniform he reads so beautifully. Stern loved it, and when they shot him glances, he responded with religious groans and dipping bows and as much humility as he could summon. When the shofar had blown, they clustered around him, touching him, telling him what a handsome Jewish boy he was, saying how wonderful it must be to fly. They knew Jewish boys did accounting for the Army. But Stern was the first they knew who flew in planes. Dinner invitations were flung at the savior, and Stern, silent on his nonflying status, his lips sealed on the subject of his new bride, chose an Orthodox watchmaker who did up timepieces for major league umpires and had a large and bovine unmarried daughter named Naomi. When Stern had finished dinner, he was left alone with the girl in a parlor that smelled of aged furniture, unchanged since it had been brought across from Albania after a pogrom. The light was subdued and Stern, belly bursting with chopped liver and noodle pudding, swiftly got her breasts out. They were large and comfortable ones, the nipples poorly placed, glancing out in opposite directions and giving her a strange, dizzying look. Stern fell upon them while the girl settled back in bovine defeat, as though she were able to tell from the sucks, greedy, anxious, and lacking in tenderness, that nothing of a permanent nature would come of this, just as nothing ever came of her father's synagogue dinner invitations. She curled a finger through Stern's hair and seemed to think of the procession of dark-skinned boys who had been at her chest, wondering when a serious one would appear and want to wrap them up forever.

Stern stayed at her breasts like a thief, dizzy with adulterous glee. They were large, his wife's were small, and he stored up each minute as though it were gold. For hours he stayed upon her, expecting an exotic perfume he'd dreamed about to cascade from her bosom. The off-balance arrangement of her nipples prevented him from plunging on further; he was afraid there would be equal strangeness beneath her skirts. Then, too, the room smelled old and religious and Stern imagined himself piercing her and thereby summoning up the wrath of ancient Hebraic gods, ones who would sleep benignly as long as he stayed above the waist. She lay beneath him with cowlike patience while the night went by, and then Stern rose, said, "I have to go back now," and flew out of the house, reeling with guilt, a day of flying heroism beneath his belt and four hours of capacious bosom-sucking engraved in his mind that no one could ever steal.

To a Jew f-u-c-k and s-h-i-t have the same value on the dirty-word graph. A Jew has no concept that f-u-c-k is worth 90 points, and s-h-i-t 10. And the reason for that—well, see, rabbis and priests both s-h-i-t, but only one f-u-c-ks.

You see, in Jewish culture, there's no merit badge for not doing that.

...And since the leaders of my tribe, rabbis, are schtuppers, perhaps that's why the words come freer to me.

Lenny Bruce

Jokes about sex were mostly absent from traditional Jewish humor, but in the twentieth-century American experience Jewish humor has adapted to the American preoccupation with sex. Still, Jewish humor rarely depicts sex for its own sake, and as in this joke, the desire for sexual gratification is often halfhearted and easily sublimated. Many of the jokes about sex focus on the naiveté of both men and women—a naiveté that was genuine enough among the immigrant generation.

ON the day of his retirement, Grossman, a manufacturer, decided to celebrate in style. He called in his messenger and said, "I want you to get me an ounce of the best marijuana, a gram of cocaine, and three call girls: a blonde, a tall black woman, and an Oriental virgin in a red dress with black boots."

Three hours later the messenger returned. "Mr. Grossman," he said, "I have the marijuana and the cocaine. I found a blonde, and I found a black woman, but I haven't been able to find an Oriental virgin in a red dress with black boots."

"I see," said Grossman. "Look, in that case, just cancel the order and get me a prune Danish and a coffee, all right?"

LIPOWITZ, a house painter, was nearing retirement, and only occasionally took on a new job.

While working in the Upper East Side apartment of Dr. and Mrs. Weisman, he saw that the job would take two or three days. After the first day's work, Mrs. Weisman was showing her husband the old man's handiwork, and the good doctor, a little nearsighted, smeared his hand on the wet paint of the bedroom wall.

The next morning, when the painter arrived to continue the job, Mrs. Weisman came up to him and said, "Before you start, come into the bedroom with me. I'd like to show you where my husband put his hand last night."

"Please, lady," the painter replied. "I'm not a young man anymore. Better just let me have a hot glass of tea with lemon!"

THREE older men were sitting together on a porch, each on his rocking chair. "When I die," said the first man, "I'd like to be buried next to George Washington. There will be a nice monument, and everyone will know that I was an important fellow."

"And when I die," said the second, "I want to be buried in Grant's tomb. I think it's a very dignified place, overlooking the Hudson. People will know that I, too, was a somebody."

"And I," said the third man, "I want they should lay me down next to Becky Rapoport."

"But, Sam," he was told, "Becky's not dead yet!"

"Neither am I!" replied Sam.

BORIS THOMASHEFSKY, a star of the Yiddish theater, was as famous for his romantic pursuits as for his acting, and there was always an attractive woman waiting for him at the stage door.

One night, the story goes, Thomashefsky went home with an alluring young lady. In the morning, he handed her a gift— two front-row tickets to that evening's performance.

The young lady was evidently disappointed, and she began to cry.

"What's wrong?" asked the actor in astonishment.

"Oh, Mr. Thomashefsky," she said. "I'm very poor. I don't need tickets. I need bread!"

"Bread?" cried Thomashefsky. "Thomashefsky gives tickets. You want bread? Sleep with a baker!"

In a mirror-image joke that plays upon similar themes:

An elderly man is told by his doctor that the only thing that will restore him to health is the milk of a nursing mother. A young mother is found, and the man begins to nurse at her breast. The woman grows excited, and says, "Tell me, is there anything else I can do for you?"

After a long pause, the old man replies: "I'm so glad you asked—I was so embarrassed—you got maybe a cookie?"

Two old men are sitting on a Miami beach in March.

"Morris, tell me, do you still have any interest in making love?"

"Well . . ."

"Come on, Morris, how often?"

"Well . . ."

"Every week?"

"No."

"Every month?"

"No, no."

"Nu, how often?"

"Once every winter."

"Morris, tell me the truth— have you made love yet this winter?"

"Sam, look around. The sun is shining. We're sitting here in our shirtsleeves. The water is calm and blue. Tell me, Sam, *you call this a winter?*"

"When [Thomashefsky] played King Solomon," writes Nahma Sandrow in *Vagabond Stars,* a history of the Yiddish theater, "the quip was that the only difference between Thomashefsky and the real king was that Solomon had to support his harem, whereas the actor's harem supported him. . . . For several decades respectable people worried about Thomashefsky's luscious thighs, which in flesh-colored tights were destroying the modesty of American Jewish womanhood."

"It's the only way I can get it to stay on."

ONCE there was an ordinary little Jewish man who worked in a factory. Every day he went to work and came home, and nothing exciting ever happened to him.

One day, however, on the way to work, he looked in a store window and saw a pair of red alligator shoes. The sign said: "Alligator shoes, $100." He decided he had to have those shoes, that he'd be somebody, really *somebody,* if only he had those shoes. After two months of saving, he went into the store and came out wearing the new shoes.

When he got home, his wife was cooking dinner. "Becky," he called to her. "Give a look on me!"

Becky looked him over and said, "Yeah?"

"No, Becky, really, give a good look on me!"

"I don't see anything."

He went into the bedroom and took off his hat, his coat, and his jacket. Then he came back in. "So, Becky, what do you see?"

"Nothing."

"Nothing different?"

"No, nothing different."

He returned to the bedroom, and this time he took off all his clothes except the new red alligator shoes. Walking back to the kitchen, he asked, "Nu, Becky, what do you notice?"

"Nothing. Same old *putz* hanging between your legs."

"Aha, Becky! That old *putz* is pointing to a pair of hundred-dollar shoes! What do you think of that?"

Becky looked him right in the eye and said, "I think—better you should have bought a hundred-dollar hat!"

THERE was an old man whose third wife had just died. He met a girl of eighteen and wanted to marry her, but his friends were skeptical. "Are you sure it's all right?" they asked. "Better go ask the rabbi."

He went to the rabbi and the rabbi said, "Well, it's an unusual question, but I can't find any reason to say no. But my advice is that you should also take in a boarder," said the rabbi with a wink.

The man agreed. Several months later he met the rabbi on the street.

"How are you getting along?" asked the rabbi.

"Very well, thank you, Rabbi."

"And how's your young wife?"

"She's pregnant, Rabbi."

"Aha," said the rabbi with a smile. "And how's the boarder?"

"Also pregnant!"

MILLIE SILVERMAN and her family had just moved to Denver, where Millie lost no time in joining the local chapter of Pioneer Women.

"Lou," she said to her husband one evening. "Can you give me two hundred dollars for our chapter benefit dinner?"

"Two hundred dollars?" replied Sam. "Do you have any idea how much this move cost me? What's your rush to start spending more money? We've just arrived in this town, and I'm not a rich man. You want two hundred dollars, you go out and earn it."

"That's just what I'm going to do," said Millie, as she left the house. She did not return until the fourth day. "I'm back," she finally announced as she walked through the door. "And I've raised the money on my own."

"Great," said Lou. "How did you do it?"

"I'm still an attractive woman," said Millie, "and I was able to raise two hundred and twelve dollars and twenty-five cents."

Sam was incredulous. "Wait a minute," he said. "Who gave you the quarter?"

"All of them!"

Dick Codor © 1979

GITTELMAN returned home from a business trip to discover that his wife had been unfaithful during his absence.

"Who was it?" he roared. "That bastard Freedman?"

"No," replied his wife. "It wasn't Freedman."

"Was it Lowenthal, that creep?"

"No, it wasn't him."

"I know—it must have been that idiot Fishman."

"No, it wasn't Fishman, either."

Gittelman was furious. "Whatsa matter?" he cried. "None of my friends good enough for you?"

At her daughter's urging, Mrs. Winchevsky agrees to visit a gynecologist for the first time in her seventy-three years. After taking her medical history, the nurse sends her into the examination room, where she is greeted by Dr. Ross.

"Would you please step behind the curtain and take off your clothes?"

"You want I should take off my clothes?"

"That's right."

"Listen, Doctor, does your mother know that from this you make a living?"

"YOU look fine to me, Mr. Saperstein. I'll see you again next year for another checkup. By the way, do you have any questions?"

"Just one, Doctor. But I'm a little embarrassed about it."

"Don't be silly, Mr. Saperstein, that's what I'm here for! I've known you for years. What is it you want to know?"

"Well, I was wondering: What is sodomy?"

"That's easy enough to answer. Sodomy is having sex with a sheep."

"This I've heard of. I can almost understand that a shepherd must sometimes get lonely at night, just like anybody else. So that's what sodomy is?"

"Sodomy is also having sex with a cow."

"Well, this, too, I've heard of. What else?"

"Sodomy is having sex with a horse."

"Nu, if there's nothing else around, I suppose . . ."

"Sodomy is having sex with a chicken," said the doctor.

"A chicken? Feh!"

A sexy young woman walks into a dinner party on the arm of a crusty old man. At dinner, the lady sitting to the woman's right turns to her and says, "My, that's a beautiful diamond you're wearing. In fact, I think it's the most beautiful diamond I've ever seen!"

"Thank you," the young woman replies. "This is the Plotnick diamond."

"The Plotnick diamond? Is there a story to it?"

"Oh, yes. This diamond comes with a curse."

"A curse?" asks the lady. "What's the curse?"

"Plotnick," comes the whispered reply.

ONE day Jake said to his wife, "Becky, there's something you should know. Like many other businessmen, I have a girl friend. She's called my mistress."

"All right," said Becky, who was very trusting. "If that's what people do, what can I say? You've always been a good husband to me."

A few weeks later they were sitting in a theater, and Becky said, "Jake, who's that woman who smiled at you?"

"Her?" said Jake. "That's my mistress, the one I told you about."

"And who's that woman sitting beside her?"

"Let me see—oh, that's Feinberg's mistress."

Becky considered the matter for a few moments, and then said, "You know, Jake, ours is prettier."

Rabbi
Johanan said:
"Rabbi Ishmael's penis
was like a wineskin of nine
kavs' capacity." Rav Pappa said:
"Rabbi Johanan's penis was like a
wineskin of five kavs' capacity." Some
report him as giving the measurement as
three kavs' capacity.

And what about Rav

Pappa himself?

His penis was like

a Harpanian jug.

Talmud (Bava Metsia 84a)

GREENBAUM, a traveling salesman, has been on the road all day. At night he pulls into a motel and goes up to the counter. Just then, a businesswoman comes into the motel, and they both arrive at the counter together. "I'm sorry," says the desk clerk, "but I have only one room left."

"Normally I'd let you have it," Greenbaum tells the woman, "but I've been traveling since early this morning, and I've just got to get some rest."

But the woman is equally determined to have the room, and after a long argument, she finally offers a compromise. "Mister," she says, "I don't know you, you don't know me. We don't know them, they don't know us. So we'll take the room together, and one of us will sleep on the chair."

Greenbaum agrees, and when they get to the room, he curls up on the chair. "Look, mister," says the woman from the bed. "I don't know you, you don't know me. We don't know them, they don't know us. So why don't you come over here, onto this big bed, and make yourself comfortable on the other side?"

Greenbaum agrees. "Boy, this feels much better," he says. "I really needed to stretch out like this."

"Look, mister," says the woman on the other side of the bed. "I don't know you, you don't know me. We don't know them, they don't know us. Why don't you get under the covers?"

"Under the covers?" says Greenbaum.

"Sure, why not?" And Greenbaum complies.

And then the woman says, "Look, mister. I don't know you, you don't know me. We don't know them, they don't know us. So why don't we have a party?"

At this Greenbaum sits up in the bed. "Oh, boy, lady," he says. "You sure are something. I don't know you, you don't know me. We don't know them, they don't know us. So tell me one thing: *who will we invite?*"

Most Jewish jokes about sex concern what used to be the very real naiveté of Jewish women.

•

This one is an amusing switch on that old theme, and it recalls a scene in Woody Allen's movie *Love and Death* when the most beautiful woman in Russia whispers to Allen, "My room at midnight."

"Great," he replies. "Will you be there too?"

•

Two blacks were walking past a synagogue on Rosh Hashanah when they heard the long, plaintive wail of the ram's horn.

"What's that?" asked the first man.

"Just the Jews blowing their shofar," said the second.

"Wow," said the first man. "Those people sure do know how to treat their help!"

IT was an especially hot and dry Yom Kippur afternoon, and the *chazzan* was finding it difficult to concentrate as the afternoon wore on. A nearby window offered more than a welcome breeze, for just as the concluding Ne'illah service was about to begin, the *chazzan* looked outside and noticed a curvaceous young woman dressed in a skimpy outfit. The *chazzan* stood transfixed as he watched her go by.

Suddenly the rabbi came over and nudged his colleague. "Sam," he whispered, "are you with us? And what are you looking at? Don't you know that this is Yom Kippur?"

"It may be Yom Kippur in here," the *chazzan* replied with a grin, "but it's Simchas Torah in my pants!"

By permission of the artist.

Leonard Fein, editor of *Moment* magazine, calls this "the first modern Jewish joke." Certainly it is one of the few that could have developed only in our own time.

Two attractive young Jewish women in their mid-twenties were waiting at the bus stop, comparing their weekends.

"On Saturday I pretended I was a Gentile nurse," said the first.

"How did you do that?" asked her friend.

"I slept with a Jewish doctor."

TWO women meet on the street.

"Molly, I understand you have a mazel tov coming to you."

"Oh, yes—my daughter is getting married."

"Isn't that wonderful! And who's the lucky man?"

"David is the chief surgical resident at Cedars-Sinai Hospital."

"Really? That's *wonderful*. But wait—I thought he was a professor."

"Oh, no. That was her previous husband, a law professor at Yale."

"My goodness, that's really something. Then why do I seem to remember a psychiatrist?"

"You must be thinking of Saul, her first husband. He was a very prominent analyst."

"Oh, Molly, you're a lucky woman. Imagine, to have so much *naches* from just one daughter!"

JUDITH VIORST
Family Reunion

The first full-fledged family reunion
Was held at the seashore
With 9 pounds of sturgeon
7 pounds of corned beef
1 nephew who got the highest mark on an intelligence test
    ever recorded in Hillside, New Jersey
4 aunts in pain taking pills
1 cousin in analysis taking notes
1 sister-in-law who makes a cherry cheesecake a person
    would be happy to pay to eat
5 uncles to whom what happened in the stock market
    shouldn't happen to their worst enemy
1 niece who is running away from home the minute the
    orthodontist removes her braces
1 cousin you wouldn't believe it to look at him only likes
    fellows
1 nephew involved with a person of a different racial
    persuasion which his parents are taking very well
1 brother-in-law with a house so big you could get lost and
    carpeting so thick you could suffocate and a mortgage so
    high you could go bankrupt
1 uncle whose wife is a saint to put up with him
1 cousin who has made such a name for himself he was
    almost Barbra Streisand's obstetrician
1 cousin who has made such a name for himself he was
    almost Jacob Javits' CPA
1 niece it wouldn't surprise anyone if next year she's playing
    at Carnegie Hall
1 nephew it wouldn't surprise anyone if next year he's
    sentenced to Leavenworth
2 aunts who go to the same butcher as Philip Roth's mother
And me wanting approval from all of them.

Judith Viorst is the author of several collections of verse, including *It's Hard to Be Hip Over Thirty, and Other Tragedies of Married Life; People and Other Aggravations;* and *Yes, Married: A Saga of Love and Complaint.*

Dick Codor © 1979

DAN GREENBURG

How to Be a Jewish Mother

Dan Greenburg, writer and journalist, is the author of many articles and books, including *How to Make Yourself Miserable.*

Jokes about the Jewish mother —the biggest cliché in contemporary Jewish humor—are a relatively recent phenomenon. Traditional Jewish humor had no such jokes, although mothers-in-law were quite another matter; they served as fine targets for scoffing and derision, probably because the son-in-law was frequently supported by the bride's parents for several years after the wedding—a kind of familiarity which breeds real contempt. Sholom Aleichem remarked that "Adam was the luckiest man to ever live, because he had no mother-in-law."

The vital economic role played by Jewish mothers in Eastern Europe is one explanation for the absence of jokes at their expense: one didn't joke about where one's next meal came from. Mother earned the bread, in many cases, while Father was occupied with prayer and study.

Jewish mothers have always been invested in the success of their children, but it was not until the mass arrival of Jewish immigrants to America that the Jewish mother was transformed into an object of humor —and even then, only after several decades.

A possible reason for this change may be the image of womanhood which confronted the new immigrants. One sign of financial success in America was the ability to earn enough money so that one's wife did not have to work. And so Jewish mothers gradually became removed from active participation in the economic survival of their families, and began to live vicariously through their children. This in turn led to certain neuroses and problems —and in their wake, a double helping of jokes.

HOW TO PAY A COMPLIMENT

Paying people compliments is really a lot of foolishness because it either embarrasses them or gives them a swelled head. It is permissible, however, to pay a compliment in an emergency:

"Florence, what have you done to your hair? It looks like you're wearing a wig!"

"I am. All my hair fell out."

"Oh. Listen, it looks so natural I'd never have known."

HOW TO ACCEPT A COMPLIMENT

Never accept a compliment:

"Irving, tell me how is the chopped liver?"

"Mmmm! Sylvia, it's delicious!"

"I don't know. First the chicken livers that the butcher gave me were dry. Then the timer on the oven didn't work. Then at the last minute I ran out of onions. Tell me, how could it be good?"

HOW TO TELL A FUNNY STORY

Your family and friends will expect you to be able to relate amusing stories which you have heard at the butcher shop, at a meeting of Hadassah, or which your husband has told at a previous gathering of these same people. Familiarize yourself with the following formula for successful storytelling and in no time at all you will have a widespread reputation as a raconteuse. To begin the telling of any story:

(1) *Ask whether anybody has heard it before.*

"Listen, you all know the story about the old Jewish man?"

It is important that this initial query be as general as possible, so that anybody who has heard the story before should not recognize it and hence have it spoiled for him. The next step is:

(2) *Ask someone else to tell it.*

"Listen, it's a very funny story. About an old Jewish man. Al, you tell it."

"I don't know the story you mean, Sylvia."

"Of course you know. Don't you? The story about the old Jewish man. Go ahead, you tell it, Al. You know I can't tell a story properly."

This modesty is very becoming to a performer and will

surely be countered with heartfelt cries of denial from your audience. You are now ready to:

(3) *Explain Where You Heard the Story.*

"All right. This story I heard originally from Rose Melnick. You all know Rose? No? Her husband is in dry goods. Melnick. You know the one? All right, it doesn't matter to the story, believe me. Anyway, Rose Melnick heard it from her son-in-law, Seymour, a lovely boy, really. A nose and throat man. Seymour Rosen—you know the name?"

Dick Codor © 1979

By now your audience has been sufficiently prepared for the story and will be anxious for you to begin. Go ahead and tell it, but be sure to:

(4) *Begin the Story at the Ending.*

Professional comedians call the end of the story "the punch line." Since this is usually the funniest part of the story, it is logically the best place to start: "Anyway, there's this old Jewish man who is trying to get into the synagogue during the Yom Kippur service, and the usher finally says to him, 'All right, go ahead in, but don't let me catch you praying.' *(Pause.)* Oh, did I mention that the old man just wants to go in and give a message to somebody in the synagogue? He doesn't actually want to go into the synagogue and *pray*, you see. *(Pause. Frown.)* Wait a minute. I don't know if I mentioned that the old man doesn't have a ticket for the service. You know how crowded it always is on Yom Kippur, and the old man doesn't have a ticket, and he explains to the usher that he has to go into the synagogue and tell somebody something, but the usher isn't going to let him in without a ticket. So the old man explains to him that it's a matter of life and death, so then the usher thinks it over and he says to the old man, 'All right, go ahead in, but don't let me catch you praying.' *(Pause. Frown. Stand and begin emptying ashtrays.)* Ach, I don't think I told it right. Al, *you* tell it."

●

This classic circulates in several versions. In some, it is the son who calls, often upon returning from military service, with news of the *shikse* he has met, and married, overseas.

In a related and equally well known joke:

•

The married daughter calls:
"Hello, Ma?"

"*Shirley darling*, what's the problem?"

"Oh, Ma, I don't know where to begin. Both of the kids are sick with the flu. The Frigidaire has just broken down. The sink is leaking. In two hours my Hadassah group is coming here for lunch. What am I going to do?"

"*Shirley darling, don't worry. I'm going to get on a bus and go into the city. Then I'll take the train out to Long Island. Then I'll walk the two miles from the station to your house. I'll take care of the kids, I'll cook a nice lunch for the Hadassah ladies, and I'll even make dinner for Barry.*"

"Barry, who's Barry?"

"*Barry—your husband!*"

"But, Ma, my husband's name is Steve. Is this 536-3530?"

"*No, this is 536-3035.*"

(Pause.) "Does that mean you're not coming?"

•

Carol, thirty-seven and unmarried, calls her mother. "Hello, Ma? It's Carol. Yes, I'm here in New York. Yes. Listen, Ma, I have news for you."

"*Carol, is that you? In New York? Are you healthy? What's the news?*"

"Well, Ma, it finally happened. I met him. I finally met him. It's going to be wonderful. I'm getting married!"

"*Carol! Wonderful, darling, wonderful. We were afraid you never would! This is wonderful news. We're so happy for you!*"

"Ma, before I bring my fiancé to visit, I want to tell you a few things about him. I know this may be hard for you, but he's not of our faith."

"*A goy? Nu, it's not so terrible. As we get older, it's important to find somebody, anybody, to build a life with.*"

"Ma, I knew you'd understand. It's great that we can talk openly to each other. There's another thing I want to tell you. He's not of our color, either."

"*A shvartze? Oh, color, shmolor. Doesn't matter. As long as you're happy, then we're happy.*"

"Ma? You're such a wonderful mother. I feel I can really share things with you. Richard doesn't have a job."

"*No job? Nu, you'll survive. Don't worry, a wife should stand by her husband, help him out. It'll work out fine, I'm sure.*"

"You're terrific, Ma. There's just one more thing: We don't have enough money to get a place to live, and when we get married we won't have a home."

"*No place to live? Don't worry, you'll live with us. You and Richard can sleep in the master bedroom. Pop will be fine on the couch.*"

"But, Ma, what about you? Where will *you* sleep?"

"*Honey, about me you shouldn't worry. As soon as I get off the phone I'm gonna stick my head in the oven!*"

My Mother

My mother writes from Trenton,
a comedian to the bone
but underneath serious
and all heart. "Honey," she says,
"be a mensch and Mary too,
it's no good, to worry, you
are doing the best you can
your Dad and everyone
thinks you turned out very well
as long as you pay your bills
nobody can say a word
you can tell them, to drop dead
to save a dollar it can't
hurt—remember Frank you went
to highschool with? he still lives
with his wife's mother, his wife
works while he writes his books and
did he ever sell a one
the four kids run around naked
36, and he's never had,
you'll forgive my expression
even a pot to piss in
or a window to throw it,
such a smart boy he couldnt
read the footprints on the wall
honey you think you know all
the answers you dont, please, try
to put some money away
believe me it wouldn't hurt
artist shmartist life's too short
for that kind, forgive me,
horseshit, I know what you want
better than you, all that counts
is to make a good living,
as Sholom Aleichem said,
he was a great writer did
you ever read his books dear,
you should make what he makes a year
anyway he says some place
Poverty is no disgrace
but its no honor either
that's what I say,
                    love,
                         Mother"

Robert Mezey, born in 1935, is the editor of *Poems from the Hebrew,* and the author of several books of poetry including *The Lovemaker* and *The Door Standing Open,* from which this poem is taken.

From *Running A Muck*, copyright © 1978 by John Caldwell. By permission of Writer's Digest Books.

PHILIP ROTH

My Mother

The conventional wisdom is that *Portnoy's Complaint* is a vitriolic attack on the Jewish Mother, but this is a gross distortion of the real feelings that are described in the book. These feelings are complicated, and include no small degree of admiration, as well as the tension—frequently comic, but painful as well—between a child's affection for his mother and that same child's difficulty in adapting to a more appropriate relationship as he grows into a man.

•

Mrs. Goldfarb takes her little boy to the beach, and as soon as she settles under an umbrella, the routine begins:

"Alan, come here. Don't go into the water, you'll drown!"

"Alan, don't play in the sand. It'll get in your eyes."

"Alan, come out of the sun. You'll get sunstroke!"

"Oy vey, such a nervous child!"

•

It was my mother who could accomplish anything, who herself had to admit that it might even be that she was actually too good. And could a small child with my intelligence, with my powers of observation, doubt that this was so? She could make jello, for instance, with sliced peaches *hanging* in it, peaches just *suspended* there, in defiance of the law of gravity. She could bake a cake that tasted like a banana. Weeping, suffering, she grated her own horseradish rather than buy the *pishachs* they sold in a bottle at the delicatessen. She watched the butcher, as she put it, "like a hawk," to be certain that he did not forget to put her chopped meat through the kosher grinder. She would telephone all the other women in the building drying clothes on the back lines—called even the divorced *goy* on the top floor one magnanimous day—to tell them rush, take in the laundry, a drop of rain had fallen on our windowpane. What radar on that woman! And this is *before* radar! The energy on her! The thoroughness! For mistakes she checked my sums; for holes, my socks; for dirt, my nails, my neck, every seam and crease of my body. She even dredges the furthest recesses of my ears by pouring cold peroxide into my head. It tingles and pops like an earful of ginger ale, and brings to the surface, in bits and pieces, the hidden stores of yellow wax, which can apparently endanger a person's hearing. A medical procedure like this (crackpot though it may be) takes time, of course; it takes effort, to be sure—but where health and cleanliness are concerned, germs and bodily secretions, she will not spare herself and sacrifice others. She lights candles for the dead—others invariably forget, she religiously remembers, and without even the aid of a notation on the calendar. Devotion is just in her blood. She seems to be the only one, she says, who when she goes to the cemetery has "the common sense," "the ordinary common decency," to clear the weeds from the graves of our relatives. The first bright day of spring, and she has mothproofed everything wool in the house, rolled and bound the rugs, and dragged them off to my father's trophy room. She is never ashamed of her house: a stranger could walk in and open any closet, any drawer, and she would have nothing to be ashamed of. You could even eat off her bathroom floor, if that should ever become necessary. When she loses at mah-jongg she takes it like a sport, not-like-the-others-whose-names-she-could-mention-but-she-won't-not-even-Tilly-Hochman-it's-too-petty-to-even-talk-about-let's-just-forget-she-even-brought-it-up. She sews, she knits, she darns—she irons better even than the *shvartze,* to whom, of all her friends who each possess a piece of this grinning childish black old lady's hide, she alone is good. "I'm the only one who's good to her. I'm the only one who gives her a whole can of tuna for lunch, and I'm not talking *dreck,* either. I'm talking Chicken of the Sea, Alex. I'm sorry, I can't be a stingy person. Excuse me, but I can't live like that, even if it is 2 for 49. Esther Wasserberg leaves twenty-five cents in nickels around the house when Dorothy comes, and counts up afterwards to see it's all there. Maybe I'm too good," she whispers to me, meanwhile running scalding water over the dish from which the cleaning lady has just eaten her lunch, alone like a leper, "but I couldn't do a thing like that." Once Dorothy chanced to come back into the kitchen while my mother was still standing over the faucet marked *H,* sending torrents down upon the knife and fork that had passed between the *shvartze*'s thick pink lips. "Oh, you know how hard it is to get mayonnaise off silverware these days, Dorothy," says my nimble-tongued mother—and thus, she tells me later, by her quick thinking, has managed to spare the colored woman's feelings.

●

Mama Goes Shopping

The Jewish housewife and her butcher have become stock characters and witty and worthy adversaries.

•

A woman goes to buy a chicken, and after rejecting several, she settles on one and begins to examine it carefully. First she lifts a wing and smells underneath; then she lifts the other wing and smells. Then she spreads apart the chicken's legs, and smells again. "Mister," she says to the butcher, "this chicken is no good. I want to see another one."

The butcher is not amused. "Lady," he replies, "can you pass a test like that?"

•

Against the vibrant smells of edibles there was a running counterpoint of audibles, the voices of the people.

Mr. Man's shop was a stronghold of democracy, an open forum in which the mamas and the owner engaged in what today is called a dialogue. At that time it was more like a heated *ad hominem* debate in which claims were refuted, allegations hurled, exceptions taken, motives impugned. Those confrontations were my first lessons in ideological warfare.

"I don't like the looks of this codfish."

"Lady"—when he called her "lady" he no longer thought she was—"for looks you don't buy codfish; you buy goldfish."

"Mister, this chicken has a broken leg."

"Look, lady, you gonna eat it or dance with it?"

"Yesterday in the dozen eggs you sold me was two stinkin' eggs. Shall I bring them back?"

"No, lady. Your word is as good as the eggs."

"Listen, my friend the butcher, before you weigh the meat, take out the bones."

"I buy with bones; you'll buy with bones."

"I don't pay with no bones."

"All right. No bones."

"Thank you. You're a gentleman. Now put the bones in a separate bag for soup. Thank you. Now, never mind the meat. I don't like your meat anyhow."

•

AN old Jewish woman, on her eightieth birthday, decides to prepare her last will and testament. She goes to the rabbi to show it to him and ask his advice on certain points. After all the monetary bequests are allotted, she tells the rabbi of two last requests. The first request is that upon her death, she is to be cremated. The rabbi strenuously tries to change her mind, explaining that Judaism does not permit such a practice, but the woman is adamant and cannot be swayed.

Seeing the futility of his arguments, the rabbi asks, "And what is your second request?"

"I want my ashes scattered over Bloomingdale's."

"Bloomingdale's? Why Bloomingdale's?"

"Then I'll be sure that my daughters will visit me twice a week!"

A HOLLYWOOD agent, "Monte" Steinberg, finally made his first million dollars, and celebrated by buying a yacht. To go with the boat, he also purchased a captain's uniform and a hat.

His parents still lived in Queens, and Steinberg invited them to Long Island to go sailing. As they boarded the boat, Monte turned to his mother and said, "Well, Mama, what do you think of me now? I'm a regular captain, right?"

Mrs. Steinberg said nothing, but she smiled and nodded. Finally, she said, "Very nice, dear, very nice."

"But, Mama," said her son, "really, you don't seem very excited. Look at me—I'm a *captain!*"

"Morris," said the old lady. "By your father here you're probably a captain. And by me you're a captain for sure. But tell me—are you a captain by the captains?"

Truman and the Uncles

Joel Rosenberg, a poet and essayist, teaches Hebrew Literature at Tufts University.

When Truman died a while back, I started thinking
back to when I was a kid and he was President.
Back to the men in baggy suits around the barbershops,
and me reading the headlines to the housepainters,
a skinny runt in saggy pants with flexing waistbands.
Hearing Benny on the radio on Sunday afternoons,
while crawling through the legs of grunty uncles,
at their pinochle with tea in striped glass cups
in wicker canisters my mother only used for guests.

I'd get my hair cut by my uncle Harry, a retired barber.
He would choke a pin-striped dropcloth to my throat,
and grind my neck up with the hand-pressed clippers,
while he'd tell me with a Yiddish accent to keep still.
It's possible my uncle Harry looked a lot like Truman.
Truman with a Yiddish accent. Uncle Harry Truman,
cutting hair. "I do this for you hundet tventy year,"
he'd say.

Evenings, the uncles would lean forward
to the radio and shush each other: Walter Winchell
saying "Good evening," to us and the ships at sea.
I'd squirm around between the creaking chair legs,
tugging at the gummy tags that said: ALL NEW MATERIAL,
while Winchell made his buzzy, beepy sounds,
and said a lot of things the uncles liked.
I wondered if he was an uncle. If he looked
like Truman. Or if Truman buzzed and beeped.
If Winchell could cut hair, or Benny read
the headlines, or the uncles paint the house.

Sometimes, I'd read my textbook from the Sunday
Hebrew school. My mother drove me there, complaining,
in our boxy, roomy '46 De Soto, even when it rained.
I learned how Jews must choose to die
instead of kneeling down to foreign gods.
I hoped that if it ever came to that,
that maybe I could work out something.
The textbook from Sunday school contained
a picture of the evil foreign king, the one
who made us bow to all the foreign gods.
He had a long, black, curly beard, thick brow,
a red hat like a 7-tiered fire hydrant.
He did not resemble Truman. Or an uncle.

I remember Truman talking. When he spoke,
he always sounded like he had a cold.
Or people with colds sounded like Truman.
Truman, one could say, was something of a way
one saw the world. Invoking him explained a lot.
They used to say: that Truman, dirty s. o. b.,
look what he's gone and done, goddammit,
now the world will never be the same.

But Sundays, long here, long gone Sundays,
it sure seemed like things would stay the same.
Good gosh. Here, Truman's dead. And here,
I've passed the age of thirty. What a haircut.
I sure hope I never have to kneel to foreign gods.

●

SCHWARTZ and his grandson were watching the circus in Madison Square Garden. A violinist calmly climbed into the mouth of the cannon, instrument in hand.

Suddenly there was a loud explosion, and the stunt man was hurled clear across the arena. While still in midair, he managed to fiddle a few notes.

As the crowd exploded in applause, Benjie turned to his unresponsive grandfather.

"Grandpa, Grandpa, wasn't that great? What did you think?"

After a moment, the old man said, "Not bad. But a Heifetz he ain't!"

"Of all the Jewish holidays," goes a contemporary witticism, "I observe only the Jascha Heifetz concerts."

Isaac Stern is said to have quipped that the nature of the American-Russian cultural exchange programs was: "They send us their Jews from Odessa, and we send them *our* Jews from Odessa."

If you insist too long that you're right, you're wrong.

A Visit from My Mother-in-Law

My mother-in-law
Comes to visit
With her own apron,
Her own jar of Nescafé,
And the latest news.

Uncle Leo,
She's sorry to say,
Is divorcing Aunt Pearl,
Whose sister Bernice
Is having
A nervous breakdown.
The week
That they spent in Miami
It rained every day,
And her health,
Though she isn't complaining,
Has never been worse.
The lady upstairs
With the limp
Was attacked in broad daylight,
And Seymour her nephew
Has cataracts, flu,
and no job.
My husband,
She thinks she should mention,
Looks thin as a rail,
And the children,
It hurts her to hear,
Are coughing again.
Belle's son,
Only forty years old,
Dropped dead Friday morning,
And don't even bother
To ask
About Cousin Rose.

I don't think I will.

JOSEPH HELLER
Gold's Stepmother

Gold's stepmother, who was from an old Southern Jewish family with branches in Richmond and Charleston, habitually made things difficult for him in a variety of peculiar ways. Frequently when he spoke to her she did not answer at all. Other times she said, "Don't talk to me." When he didn't talk to her, his father moved up beside him with a hard nudge and directed, "Go talk to her. You too good?" She was always knitting thick white wool. When he complimented her once on her knitting, she informed him with a flounce that she was crocheting. When he inquired next time how her crocheting was going she answered, "I don't crochet. I knit." Often she called him to her side just to tell him to move away. Sometimes she came up to him and said, "Cackle, cackle."

He had no idea what to reply.

Gold's stepmother was knitting an endless strip of something bulky that was too narrow to be a shawl and too wide and uniformly straight to be anything else. It was around six inches broad and conceivably thousands of miles long, for she had been working on that same strip of knitting even before her marriage to his father many years before. Gold had a swimming vision of that loosely woven strip of material flowing out the bottom of her straw bag to the residence Sid found for his father and her each summer in Brooklyn in Manhattan Beach and from there all the way down the coastline to Florida and into unmeasured regions beyond. She never wanted for wool or for depth inside her straw bag into which the finished product could fall. The yarn came twitching up through one end of the opening in her bag, and the manufactured product, whatever it was, descended, perhaps for eternity, into the other.

"What are you making?" he'd asked her one time out of curiosity that could no longer be borne in silence.

"You'll see," she replied mysteriously.

He consulted his father. "Pa, what's she making?"

"Mind your own business."

"I was only asking."

"Don't ask personal questions."

"Rose, what's she knitting?" he asked his sister.

"Wool," Belle answered.

"Belle, I know that. But what's she doing with it?"

"Knitting," said Esther.

Gold's stepmother was knitting knitting, and she was knitting it endlessly. Now she asked, "Do you like my wool?"

Joseph Heller, born in 1923, is the author of *Catch-22, Something Happened,* and *Good as Gold,* from which this selection is taken.

FIRST THE GOOD NEWS. I'M POSTPONING THE RAIN 3 MORE WEEKS...

CALDWELL

From *Running A Muck,* copyright © 1978 by John Caldwell. By permission of Writer's Digest Books.

"Pardon?"

"Do you like my wool?"

"Of course," he replied.

"You never say so," she pouted.

"I like your wool," said Gold, retreating in confusion to a leather armchair near the doorway.

"He told me he likes my wool," he heard her relating to his brothers-in-law Irv and Max. "But I think he's trying to pull it over my eyes."

"How was your trip?" his sister Esther asked dotingly.

"Fine."

"Where were you?" said Rose.

"Wilmington."

"Where?" asked Ida, passing with a serving tray.

"Washington," said Rose.

"Wilmington?"

"Wilmington."

"Washington."

"Washington?"

"Wilmington," he corrected them all. "In Delaware."

"Oh," said Rose, and looked crestfallen.

"How was your trip?" asked Ida, passing back.

Gold was going mad.

"He said it was fine," answered Esther before Rose could reply, and drifted toward a coffee table on which were platters holding loaves of chopped liver and chopped eggs and onions under attack by small knives spreading each or both onto round crackers or small sections of rye bread or very black pumpernickel.

"Meet any pretty girls there?" Muriel asked. The youngest of the sisters present, Muriel was ever under obligation to be up-to-date.

"Not this time," Gold answered, with the required grin.

Muriel glowed. Irv chuckled and Victor, Muriel's husband, looked embarrassed. Rose stared from face to face intently. Gold suspected that she had grown hard of hearing, and perhaps did not know. Her husband, Max, a postal worker, was slurring his words of late, and Gold wondered if anyone but himself had noticed.

Esther returned with a plate prepared for him, and a salt-shaker aloft in her other hand. "I brought these all for you," she announced in her trembling voice. "And your own saltshaker."

Gold cringed.

"Don't spoil him," Muriel joked gruffly, spilling ashes onto her bosom from a cigarette hanging from her mouth.

The women in Gold's family believed he liked his food excessively salted.

"Don't salt it until you taste it," Ida yelled from across the room. "I already seasoned it."

Gold ignored her and continued salting the cracker he was holding. Other people's fingers plucked the remaining pieces from his plate. Esther and Rose each brought him more. Sid watched with amusement. So many fucking faces, Gold thought. So many people. And all of them strange. Even Belle, these days. And especially his stepmother.

He would never forget his first encounter with his step-mother. Sid had flown to Florida for the wedding and returned with her and his father for a reception at his home in Great Neck. There was an uncomfortable silence after the introductions when no one seemed sure what to say next. Gold stepped forward with a gallant try at putting everyone at ease.

"And what," he said in his most courtly manner, "would you like us to call you?"

"I would like you to treat me as my own children do," Gussie Gold replied with graciousness equal to his own. "I would like to think of you all as my very own children. Please call me Mother."

"Very well, Mother," Gold agreed. "Welcome to the family."

"I'm not your mother," she snapped.

Gold was the only one who laughed. Perhaps the others had perceived immediately what he had missed. She was insane.

●

SAUL BELLOW

Did I Order a Kosher Meal?

This amusing encounter with the kosher laws constitutes the opening scene of Bellow's only nonfiction book, *To Jerusalem and Back,* published in 1976. The book is a straightforward account of an extended visit to Israel, in which Bellow becomes a student, encountering the land, its people (mostly intellectuals and scholars, in this case), and the intense arguments and discussions which characterize Israeli life.

Security measures are strict on flights to Israel, the bags are searched, the men are frisked, and the women have an electronic hoop passed over them, fore and aft. Then hand luggage is opened. No one is very patient. Visibility in the queue is poor because of the many Hasidim with their broad hats and beards and sidelocks and dangling fringes who have descended on Heathrow and are far too restless to wait in line but rush in and out, gesticulating, exclaiming. The corridors are jumping with them. Some two hundred Hasidim are flying to Israel to attend the circumcision of the firstborn son of their spiritual leader, the Belzer Rabbi. Entering the 747, my wife, Alexandra, and I are enfiladed by eyes that lie dark in hairy ambush. To me there is nothing foreign in these hats, sidelocks, and fringes. It is my childhood revisited. At the age of six, I myself wore a tallith katan, or scapular, under my shirt, only mine was a scrap of green calico print, whereas theirs are white linen. God instructed Moses to speak to the children of Israel and to "bid them that they make them fringes in the borders of their garments." So they are still wearing them some four thousand years later. We find our seats, two in a row of three, toward the rear of the aircraft. The third is occupied by a young Hasid, highly excited, who is staring at me.

"Do you speak Yiddish?" he says.

"Yes, certainly."

"I cannot be next to your wife. Please sit between us. Be so good," he says.

"Of course."

I take the middle seat, which I dislike, but I am not really put out. Curious, rather. Our Hasid is in his late twenties. He is pimply, his neck is thin, his blue eyes goggle, his underlip extrudes. He does not keep a civilized face. Thoughts and impulses other than civilized fill it—by no means inferior impulses and thoughts. And though he is not permitted to sit beside women unrelated to him or to look at them or to communicate with them in any manner (all of which probably saves him a great deal of trouble), he seems a goodhearted young man and he is visibly enjoying himself. All the Hasidim are vividly enjoying themselves, dodging through the aisles, visiting chattering standing impatiently in the long lavatory lines, amiable, busy as geese. They pay no attention to signs. Don't they understand English? The stewardesses are furious with them. I ask one of the hostesses when I may expect to receive a drink and she cries out in irritation, "Back to your seat!" She says this in so ringing a voice that I retreat. Not so the merry-minded Hasidim, exulting everywhere. The orders given by these young Gentile uniformed females are nothing to them. To them they are merely attendants, exotic *bediener,* all but bodyless.

Anticipating a difficulty, I ask the stewardess to serve me a kosher lunch. "I can't do that, we haven't enough for *them,*" she says. "We weren't prepared." Her big British eyes are affronted and her bosom has risen with indignation. "We've got to go out of our way to Rome for more of their special meals."

Amused, my wife asks why I ordered the kosher lunch. "Because when they bring my chicken dinner this kid with the beard will be in a state," I explain.

And so he is. The British Airways chicken with the chill of death upon it lies before me. But after three hours of security exercises at Heathrow I am hungry. The young Hasid recoils when the tray is handed to me. He addresses me again in Yiddish. He says, "I must talk to you. You won't be offended?"

"No, I don't think so."

"You may want to give me a slap in the face."

"Why should I?"

"You *are* a Jew. You must be a Jew, we are speaking Yiddish. How can you eat—*that!*"

"It looks awful, doesn't it?"

"You mustn't touch it. My womenfolk packed kosher-beef sandwiches for me. Is your wife Jewish?"

Here I'm obliged to lie. Alexandra is Rumanian. But I can't give him too many shocks at once, and I say, "She has not had a Jewish upbringing."

"She doesn't speak Yiddish?"

"Not a word. But excuse me, I want my lunch."

"Will you eat some of my kosher food instead, as a favor?"

"With pleasure."

"Then I will give you a sandwich, but only on one condition. You must never—never—eat *trephena* food again."

"I can't promise you that. You're asking too much. And just for one sandwich."

"I have a duty toward you," he tells me. "Will you listen to a proposition?"

"Of course I will."

"So let us make a deal. I am prepared to pay you. If you will eat nothing but kosher food, for the rest of your life I will send you fifteen dollars a week."

"That's very generous," I say.

"Well, you are a Jew," he says. "I must try to save you."

"How do you earn your living?"

"In a Hasidic sweater factory in New Jersey. We are all Hasidim there. The boss is a Hasid. I came from Israel five years ago to be married in New Jersey. My rabbi is in Jerusalem."

"How is it that you don't know English?"

"What do I need English for? So, I am asking, will you take my fifteen dollars?"

"Kosher food is far more expensive than other kinds," I say. "Fifteen dollars isn't nearly enough."

"I can go as far as twenty-five."

"I can't accept such a sacrifice from you."

Shrugging, he gives up and I turn to the twice disagreeable chicken and eat guiltily, my appetite spoiled. The young Hasid opens his prayer book. "He's so fervent," says my wife. "I wonder if he's praying for you." She smiles at my discomfiture.

As soon as the trays are removed, the Hasidim block the aisles with their *Minchah* service, rocking themselves and stretching their necks upward. The bond of common prayer is very strong. This is what has held the Jews together for thousands of years. "I like them," says my wife. "They're so lively, so childlike."

"You might find them a little hard to live with," I tell her. "You'd have to do everything their way, no options given."

"But they're cheerful, and they're warm and natural. I love their costumes. Couldn't you get one of those beautiful hats?"

"I don't know whether they sell them to outsiders."

When the Hasid returns to his seat after prayers, I tell him that my wife, a woman of learning, will be lecturing at the Hebrew University in Jerusalem.

"What is she?"

"A mathematician."

He is puzzled. "What is that?" he asks.

I try to explain.

He says, "This I never heard of. What actually is it they do?"

I am astonished. I knew that he was an innocent but I would never have believed him to be ignorant of such a thing. "So you don't know what mathematicians are. Do you know what a physicist is? Do you recognize the name of Einstein?"

"Never. Who is he?"

This is too much for me. Silent, I give his case some thought. Busy-minded people, with their head-culture that touches all surfaces, have heard of Einstein. But do they know what they have heard? A majority do not. These Hasidim choose not to know. By and by I open a paperback and try to lose myself in mere politics. A dozen Hasidim in the lavatory queue stare down at us.

We land and spill out and go our separate ways. At the baggage carousel I see my youthful Hasid again and we take a final look at each other. In me he sees what deformities the modern age can produce in the seed of Abraham. In him I see a piece of history, an antiquity. It is rather as if Puritans in seventeenth-century dress and observing seventeenth-century customs were to be found still living in Boston or Plymouth. Israel, which receives us impartially, is accustomed to strange arrivals. But then Israel is something else again.

●

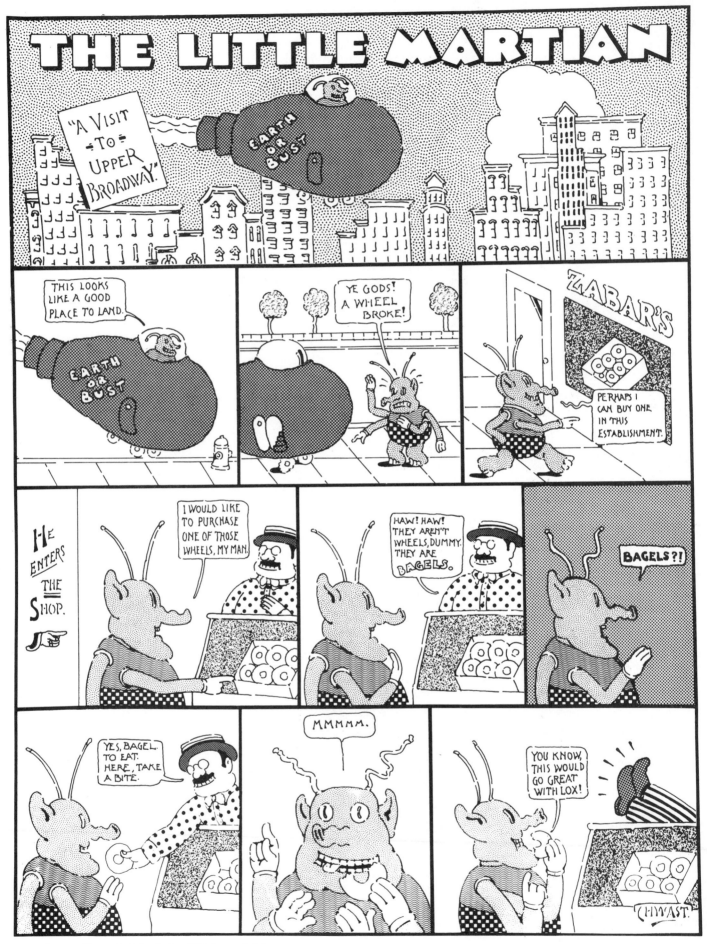

> Rabbi Ishmael ben Yosi and Rabbi Eleazar ben Shimon were both very fat. Their bellies were so round that when they met and stood talking together, a herd of oxen could have gone between them, under their bellies, and not touched either of them. —Talmud (Bava Metsia 84a)

PHILIP ROTH
The Kosher Laws

What else, I ask you, were all those prohibitive dietary rules and regulations all about to begin with, what else but to give us little Jewish children practice in being repressed? Practice, darling, practice, practice, practice. Inhibition doesn't grow on trees, you know—takes patience, takes concentration, takes a dedicated and self-sacrificing parent and a hard-working attentive little child to create in only a few years' time a really constrained and tight-ass human being. Why else the two sets of dishes? Why else the kosher soap and salt? Why else, I ask you, but to remind us three times a day that life is boundaries and restrictions if it's anything, hundreds of thousands of little rules laid down by none other than None Other, rules which either you obey without question, regardless of how idiotic they may appear (and thus remain, by obeying, in His good graces), or you transgress, most likely in the name of outraged common sense—which you transgress because even a child doesn't like to go around feeling like an absolute moron and schmuck—yes, you transgress, only with the strong likelihood (my father assures me) that comes next Yom Kippur and the names are written in the big book where He writes the names of those who are going to get to live until the following September (a scene which manages somehow to engrave itself upon my imagination), and lo, your own precious name ain't among them. Now who's the schmuck, huh? And it doesn't make any difference either (this I understand from the outset, about the way this God, Who runs things, reasons) how big or how small the rule is that you break: it's the breaking alone that gets His goat—it's the simple fact of waywardness, and that alone, that He absolutely cannot stand, and which He does not forget either, when He sits angrily down (fuming probably, and surely with a smashing miserable headache, like my father at the height of his constipation) and begins to leave the names out of that book.

When duty, discipline, and obedience give way—ah, here, *here* is the message I take in each Passover with my mother's *matzoh brei*—what follows, there is no predicting. Renunciation is all, cries the koshered and bloodless piece of steak my

It is as if a Hebrew patriarch, having outlived the wife of his youth, had married the wife of his old age and fathered three sons to say *Kaddish* for him in post-ghetto America:

Bernard, traditional and belated down to the self-protective ghetto humor, a pillar of the synagogue, rather prosaic maybe but steady and reliable, his father's son; then Saul, irresistible talker, promoter, last of the big-time spenders, flashy, willful, hypnotically charming, bottomlessly cynical and sad, home only for the holidays, when he puts on the skullcap and a pious face for services; finally Philip, nervous, vulnerable, the doomed and delicate one, least committed to the past and most troubled by the future, whom all the family fusses over and is apprehensively fond of.

Marvin Mudrick

family and I sit down to eat at dinnertime. Self-control, sobriety, sanctions—this is the key to a human life, saith all those endless dietary laws. Let the *goyim* sink *their* teeth into whatever lowly creature crawls and grunts across the face of the dirty earth, we will not contaminate our humanity thus. Let *them* (if you know who I mean) gorge themselves upon anything and everything that moves, no matter how odious and abject the animal, no matter how grotesque or *shmutzig* or dumb the creature in question happens to be. Let them eat eels and frogs and pigs and crabs and lobsters; let them eat vulture, let them eat ape meat and skunk if they like—a diet of abominable creatures well befits a breed of mankind so hopelessly shallow and empty-headed as to drink, to divorce, and to fight with their fists. All they know, these imbecilic eaters of the execrable, is to swagger, to insult, to sneer, and sooner or later to hit. Oh, also they know how to go out into the woods with a gun, these geniuses, and kill innocent wild deer, deer who themselves *nosh* quietly on berries and grasses and then go on their way, bothering no one. You stupid *goyim!* Reeking of beer and empty of ammunition, home you head, a dead animal (formerly *alive*) strapped to each fender, so that all the motorists along the way can see how strong and manly you are; and then, in your houses, you take these deer—who have done you, who have done nothing in all of nature, not the least bit of harm— you take these deer, cut them up into pieces, and cook them in a pot. There isn't enough to eat in this world, they have to eat up the *deer* as well! They will eat *anything,* anything they can get their big *goy* hands on! And the terrifying corollary, *they will do anything as well.* Deer eat what deer eat, and Jews eat what Jews eat, but not these *goyim.* Crawling animals, wallowing animals, leaping and angelic animals—it makes no difference to them—what they want they take, and to hell with the other thing's feelings (let alone kindness and compassion). Yes, it's all written down in history, what they have done, our illustrious neighbors who own the world and know absolutely nothing of human boundaries and limits.

. . . Thus saith the kosher laws, at least to the child I was, growing up under the tutelage of Sophie and Jack P., and in a school district of Newark where in my entire class there are only two little Christian children, and they live in houses I do not enter, on the far fringes of our neighborhood . . . thus saith the kosher laws, and who am I to argue that they're wrong? For look at Alex himself, the subject of *our* every syllable—age fifteen, he sucks one night on a lobster's claw and within the hour his cock is out and aimed at a *shikse* on a Public Service bus. And his superior Jewish brain might as well be *made* of *matzoh brei!*

Moses asks God to explain the kosher laws:

"THOU SHALT NOT SEETHE A KID IN ITS MOTHER'S MILK."

"Does that mean that we should wait six hours between eating meat and drinking milk?"

"THOU SHALT NOT SEETHE A KID IN ITS MOTHER'S MILK."

"Does that mean we should have two sets of dishes?"

"THOU SHALT NOT SEETHE A KID IN ITS MOTHER'S MILK."

"Does that mean we should check the label of everything we buy, and use only those items made with pure vegetable shortening?"

"THOU SHALT NOT SEETHE A KID IN ITS MOTHER'S MILK."

"Does that mean—"

"OKAY, HAVE IT YOUR WAY!"

THE BARNACLE GOOSE MYTHS

The barnacle goose is a migratory bird, whose winter habitat is the Arctic region, where it is seldom seen outside of the Arctic circle. In summer, however, large flocks are found on the western shores of the British Isles and other parts of the temperate zone.

According to a popular medieval fable, the barnacle goose was produced out of the fruit of a tree, or grew upon the tree attached to its bill (hence called the tree goose), or was produced out of a shell. This fable —the origin of which is obscure—was taken quite literally by both Jews and non-Jews, and in consequence it was a matter of doubt whether it was to be regarded as bird, fish, or a completely different species.

Isaac b. Moses of Vienna *(Or Zaru'a)* quotes R. Tam—who was the first to deal with the subject—as ruling that it may be eaten after ritual slaughtering like poultry. This decision was in opposition to the views of contemporary famous scholars who permitted it to be eaten the same way as fruit.

Samuel he-Hasid and his son Juda he-Hasid of Regensburg agreed with R. Tam. R. Isaac b. Joseph of Corbeil forbade it *(Sefer Mitzvot Katan* no. 210), as he regarded it as a species of shellfish. The Zohar (3:156) states that R. Abba saw a tree from whose branches grew geese. The Shulhan Arukh (YD 84:15) rules that birds that grow on trees are forbidden since they are regarded as creeping things.

The fable was disputed, however, by various scholars but as late as 1862 R. Bernard Issachar Dov Illowy in New Orleans quoted a conflict of authorities whether it might be eaten, and vigorously denounced those who would permit it. He too referred to the belief of many early naturalists that it grows on trees.

(Reprinted in its entirety from the *Encyclopedia Judaica*)

This is an interesting reversal of most Jewish restaurant stories, in which the waiter is testy, proud, and arrogant, and alternates between protecting his customers and afflicting them.

•

Mendel, a popular waiter at Sol's Delicatessen, passes away, and some of his customers decide to visit a spiritualist who will try to communicate with him.

"Just knock on the table as you did when he was with you," says the medium, "and he will appear again."

There is much knocking, but no sign of Mendel. The group bangs louder, and finally they begin to call his name, louder and louder. Finally Mendel appears, with a cloth over his arm.

"What happened, Mendel?" says one of the group. "Why didn't you come when we first knocked?"

"It wasn't my table," says Mendel.

•

A MAN came into the Eppes Essen Delicatessen for dinner, and when he was finished, the owner came over to him. "Was everything all right, sir?" the owner asked.

"Fine, just fine," the man said. "But I would have liked a little more bread."

The manager spoke to the waiter. "How much bread did you give that man?" he asked.

"Two slices," came the reply.

"Well," said the manager, "the next time that man comes in, I want you to give him four slices."

The man returned the next night, and when dinner was over, the owner came over to him. "Was everything all right, sir?"

"Fine, just fine," the man said. "But I would have liked a little more bread."

"How much bread did you give that man?" the owner asked the waiter.

"Four slices," came the reply. "Just like you said."

"Well," said the manager, "the next time he comes in, I want you to give him seven slices."

The next night the man was back again, and after dinner the owner came over and said, "Was everything all right, sir?"

"Fine, just fine," the man said. "But I would have liked a little more bread."

"How much bread did you give that man?" the owner asked the waiter.

"Seven slices, just like you said," said the waiter.

"Well," said the manager, "the next time he comes in, I want you to take a whole loaf of bread, the biggest loaf in the kitchen, and cut it in the middle. Give this man both halves."

After dinner the next night the owner came over to the man and asked, "Was everything all right, sir?"

"Fine, just fine," the man said. "But I see you're back to two slices."

Do not make a stingy sandwich;
Pile the cold cuts high!
Customers should see salami
Comin' thru the rye.

ALLAN SHERMAN

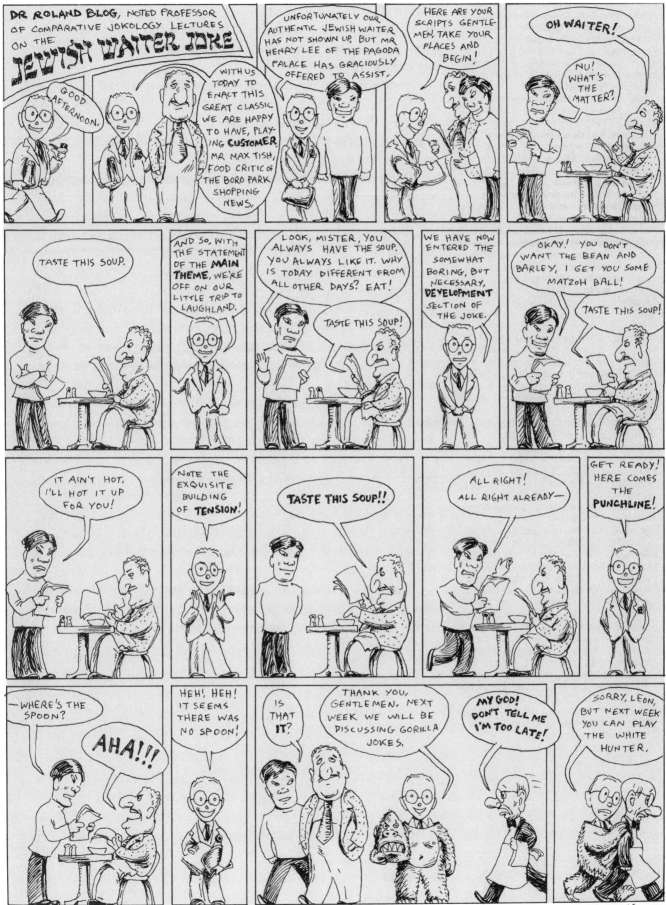

By permission of the artist.

In a variation of this joke, Yossel Kollek is pleased rather than puzzled, and Reb Yonah gives his answer with genuine regret, wishing that Yossel's impression were true, and that, as Reb Sender of Angst used to say, "the reward of being a good Jew in this world is that you can live like a goy in the next." Indeed, there is a minority opinion in the Talmud that the forbidden foods, like pork, will become permissible to Jews in the World to Come, as a reward for their self-denial in the earthly world.

Judaism has traditionally been this-world-oriented, and there are relatively few jokes dealing with an afterlife. One exception is the genre of Catholic-Protestant-Jew jokes, in which, for example, a representative of each group is applying for admission to heaven; in one of these jokes, the Jew is accorded special treatment for being "related to the boss."

•

A pious rabbi passed away and arrived in heaven; he was immediately served a meal of schmaltz herring. Though surprised and a little disappointed at this humble meal, the rabbi said nothing. But later, glimpsing into the Other Place, he noticed that people there were eating bagels and lox, toast, and eggs.

For the next meal the rabbi was again served a plate of schmaltz herring, only this time it was accompanied by a glass of tea. After the meal, the rabbi looked again at the Other Place, and noticed that the people there were feasting on blintzes, soup, sour cream, and berries.

For supper an angel came and brought the rabbi another plate of schmaltz herring and a glass of tea. Later, he looked at the Other Place, where he noticed that the people were eating steak and turkey, and drinking fine wine.

Finally, the rabbi could not control himself, and he turned to the angel and said, "I don't understand it. This is supposed to be heaven, but all I get to eat is schmaltz herring. But in the Other Place, I see that they eat like kings."

The angel gave an uneasy smile and replied, "I know. But to tell you the truth—it doesn't pay to cook for just two people."

•

YOSSEL KOLLEK, a pious and righteous man, was taken from this world at the age of seventy. Upon reaching the celestial gates, he was quickly admitted into Paradise. "Now that you're here," the admitting angel said, "is there anything we can do for you?"

"Indeed there is," replied Yossel. "Most of all, I'd like to see my rebbe from yeshiva, who passed away thirty years ago. He gave me the strength and the inspiration to lead a pious life. He was almost like a father to me, and I would dearly love to see him again."

A moment later Yossel found himself on a spacious avenue with large white mansions. He spotted a mailbox with the name of his teacher, Reb Yonah, on it. Yossel walked up to the front door and rang the bell; a group of servants greeted him, and led him around to the back of the house.

And there, in the lush, green yard, Yossel was thrilled to see his rebbe, looking just as he remembered him: old and wizened, with a handsome white beard. Reb Yonah was sitting in front of an open volume of the Talmud. Behind him was an Olympic-size swimming pool, and at his side was an extravagantly beautiful and voluptuous blonde, clad in the most skimpy of heavenly garments.

Yossel was taken aback to see Reb Yonah in such a setting, but he quickly composed himself and stepped forward to introduce himself to his former teacher.

"Reb Yonah," he began. "I don't know if you remember me, but this is your old student, Yossel Kollek!"

"Yossel!" cried Reb Yonah. "Of course I remember you. It's such a treat to see you."

"Reb Yonah," replied Yossel, "I want to ask you a question. It's not that I don't wish you the very best, but are *these* the fruits of Paradise?"

Reb Yonah looked up at his former student, shook his head slowly, glanced at his companion, and replied: "Yossel my boy, not so fast. It's not my heaven—it's her hell!"

Dick Codor © 1979

I. L. PERETZ

Bontsha the Silent

Here on earth the death of Bontsha the Silent made no impression at all. Ask anyone: Who was Bontsha, how did he live, and how did he die? Did his strength slowly fade, did his heart slowly give out—or did the very marrow of his bones melt under the weight of his burdens? Who knows? Perhaps he just died from not eating—starvation, it's called.

If a horse, dragging a cart through the streets, should fall, people would run from blocks around to stare, newspapers would write about this fascinating event, a monument would be put up to mark the very spot where the horse had fallen. Had the horse belonged to a race as numerous as that of human beings, he wouldn't have been paid this honor. How many horses are there, after all? But human beings—there must be a thousand million of them!

Bontsha was a human being; he lived unknown, in silence, and in silence he died. He passed through our world like a shadow. When Bontsha was born no one took a drink of wine; there was no sound of glasses clinking. When he was confirmed, he made no speech of celebration. He existed like a grain of sand at the rim of a vast ocean, amid millions of other grains of sand exactly similar, and when the wind at last lifted him up and carried him across to the other shore of that ocean, no one noticed, no one at all.

During his lifetime his feet left no mark upon the dust of the streets; after his death the wind blew away the board that marked his grave. The wife of the gravedigger came upon that bit of wood, lying far off from the grave, and she picked it up and used it to make a fire under the potatoes she was cooking; it was just right. Three days after Bontsha's death no one knew where he lay, neither the gravedigger nor anyone else. If Bontsha had had a headstone, someone, even after a hundred years, might have come across it, might still have been able to read the carved words, and his name, Bontsha the Silent, might not have vanished from this earth.

His likeness remained in no one's memory, in no one's heart. A shadow! Nothing! Finished!

In loneliness he lived, and in loneliness he died. Had it not been for the infernal human racket, someone or other might have heard the sound of Bontsha's bones cracking under the weight of his burdens; someone might have glanced around and seen that Bontsha was also a human being, that he had two

I. L. Peretz (1852–1915) was, along with Mendele Mocher Seforim and Sholom Aleichem, one of the founders of modern Yiddish literature. "Bontsha the Silent," his most famous story, has usually been read as a testament to Bontsha's saintliness and submissiveness. But the story can also be seen as expressing the darker, more cynical side of Jewish humor.

As the tale ends, even the angels are ashamed, and the heavenly prosecutor is laughing bitterly. Peretz's black humor invokes an impassioned critique of Jewish passivity in the face of suffering, and, in the general spirit of Jewish humor, it mocks those who submit meekly to injustice.

frightened eyes and a silent trembling mouth; someone might have noticed how, even when he bore no actual load upon his back, he still walked with his head bowed down to earth, as though while living he was already searching for his grave.

When Bontsha was brought to the hospital, ten people were waiting for him to die and leave them his narrow little cot; when he was brought from the hospital to the morgue, twenty were waiting to occupy his pall; when he was taken out of the morgue, forty were waiting to lie where he would lie forever. Who knows how many are now waiting to snatch from him that bit of earth?

In silence he was born, in silence he lived, in silence he died—and in an even vaster silence he was put into the ground.

Ah, but in the other world it was not so! No! In Paradise the death of Bontsha was an overwhelming event. The great trumpet of the Messiah announced through the seven heavens: Bontsha the Silent is dead! The most exalted angels, with the most imposing wings, hurried, flew, to tell one another, "Do you know who has died? Bontsha! Bontsha the Silent!"

And the new, the young little angels with brilliant eyes, with golden wings and silver shoes, ran to greet Bontsha, laughing in their joy. The sound of their wings, the sound of their silver shoes, as they ran to meet him, and the bubbling of their laughter, filled all Paradise with jubilation, and God Himself knew that Bontsha the Silent was at last here.

In the great gateway to heaven, Abraham our Father stretched out his arms in welcome and benediction: "Peace be with you!" And on his old face a deep sweet smile appeared.

What, exactly, was going on up there in Paradise?

There, in Paradise, two angels came bearing a golden throne for Bontsha to sit upon, and for his head a golden crown with glittering jewels.

"But why the throne, the crown, already?" two important saints asked. "He hasn't even been tried before the heavenly court of justice to which each new arrival must submit." Their voices were touched with envy. "What's going on here, anyway?"

And the angels answered the two important saints that, yes, Bontsha's trial hadn't started yet, but it would only be a formality, even the prosecutor wouldn't dare open his mouth. Why, the whole thing wouldn't take five minutes!

"What's the matter with you?" the angels asked. "Don't you know whom you're dealing with? You're dealing with Bontsha, Bontsha the Silent!"

When the young, the singing angels encircled Bontsha in love, when Abraham our Father embraced him again and again, as a very old friend, when Bontsha heard that a throne waited for him, and for his head a crown, and that when he would stand trial in the court of heaven no one would say a word against him—when he heard all this, Bontsha, exactly as in the other world, was silent. He was silent with fear. His heart shook, in his veins ran ice, and he knew this must all be a dream or simply a mistake.

He was used to both, to dreams and mistakes. How often, in that other world, had he not dreamed that he was wildly shoveling up money from the street, that whole fortunes lay there on the street beneath his hands—and then he would wake and find himself a beggar again, more miserable than before the dream.

How often in that other world had someone smiled at him, said a pleasant word—and then, passing and turning back for another look, had seen his mistake and spat at Bontsha.

Wouldn't that be just my luck, he thought now, and he was afraid to lift his eyes, lest the dream end, lest he awake and find himself again on earth, lying somewhere in a pit of snakes and loathsome vipers, and he was afraid to make the smallest sound, to move so much as an eyelash; he trembled and he could not hear the paeans of the angels; he could not see them as they danced in stately celebration about him; he could not answer the loving greeting of Abraham our Father: "Peace be with you!" And when at last he was led into the great court of justice in Paradise, he couldn't even say "Good morning." He was paralyzed with fear.

And when his shrinking eyes beheld the floor of the courtroom of justice, his fear, if possible, increased. The floor was of purest alabaster, embedded with glittering diamonds. On such a floor stand my feet, thought Bontsha. My feet! He was beside himself with fear. Who knows, he thought, for what very rich man, or great learned rabbi, or even saint, this whole thing's meant? The rich man will arrive, and then it will all be over. He lowered his eyes; he closed them.

In his fear he did not hear when his name was called out in the pure angelic voice: "Bontsha the Silent!" Through the ringing in his ears he could make out no words, only the sound of that voice like the sound of music, of a violin.

Yet did he, perhaps, after all, catch the sound of his own name, "Bontsha the Silent"? And then the voice added, "To him that name is as becoming as a frock coat to a rich man."

What's that? What's he saying? Bontsha wondered, and then he heard an impatient voice interrupting the speech of his defending angel. "Rich man! Frock coat! No metaphors, please! And no sarcasm!"

"He never," began the defending angel again, "complained, not against God, not against man; his eye never grew red with hatred, he never raised a protest against heaven."

Bontsha couldn't understand a word, and the harsh voice of the prosecuting angel broke in once more. "Never mind the rhetoric, please!"

"His sufferings were unspeakable. Here, look upon a man who was more tormented than Job!"

Who? Bontsha wondered. Who is this man?

Dick Codor © 1980

"Facts! Facts! Never mind the flowery business and stick to the facts, please!" the judge called out.

"When he was eight days old he was circumcised—"

"Such realistic details are unnecessary—"

"The knife slipped, and he did not even try to staunch the flow of blood—"

"—and distasteful. Simply give us the important facts."

"Even then, an infant, he was silent, he did not cry out his pain," Bontsha's defender continued. "He kept his silence, even when his mother died, and he was handed over, a boy of thirteen, to a snake, a viper—a stepmother!"

Hm, Bontsha thought, could they mean me?

"She begrudged him every bite of food, even the moldy rotten bread and the gristle of meat that she threw at him, while she herself drank coffee with cream."

"Irrelevant and immaterial," said the judge.

"For all that, she didn't begrudge him her pointed nails in his flesh—flesh that showed black and blue through the rags he wore. In winter, in the bitterest cold, she made him chop wood in the yard, barefoot! More than once were his feet frozen, and his hands, that were too young, too tender, to lift the heavy logs and chop them. But he was always silent, he never complained, not even to his father—"

"Complain! To that drunkard!" The voice of the prosecuting angel rose derisively, and Bontsha's body grew cold with the memory of fear.

"He never complained," the defender continued, "and he was always lonely. He never had a friend, never was sent to school, never was given a new suit of clothes, never knew one moment of freedom."

"Objection! Objection!" the prosecutor cried out angrily. "He's only trying to appeal to the emotions with these flights of rhetoric!"

"He was silent even when his father, raving drunk, dragged him out of the house by the hair and flung him into the winter night, into the snowy, frozen night. He picked himself up quietly from the snow and wandered into the distance where his eyes led him.

"During his wanderings he was always silent; during his agony of hunger he begged only with his eyes. And at last, on a damp spring night, he drifted to a great city, drifted there like a leaf before the wind, and on his very first night, scarcely seen, scarcely heard, he was thrown into jail. He remained silent, he never protested, he never asked, Why, what for? The doors of the jail were opened again, and, free, he looked for the most lowly filthy work, and still he remained silent.

"More terrible even than the work itself was the search for

work. Tormented and ground down by pain, by the cramp of pain in an empty stomach, he never protested, he always kept silent.

"Soiled by the filth of a strange city, spat upon by unknown mouths, driven from the streets into the roadway, where, a human beast of burden, he pursued his work, a porter, carrying the heaviest loads upon his back, scurrying between carriages, carts, and horses, staring death in the eyes every moment, he still kept silent.

"He never reckoned up how many pounds he must haul to earn a penny; how many times, with each step, he stumbled and fell for that penny. He never reckoned up how many times he almost vomited out his very soul, begging for his earnings. He never reckoned up his bad luck, the other's good luck. No, never. He remained silent. He never even demanded his own earnings; like a beggar, he waited at the door for what was rightfully his, and only in the depths of his eyes was there an unspoken longing. 'Come back later!' they'd order him; and, like a shadow, he would vanish, and then, like a shadow, would return and stand waiting, his eyes begging, imploring, for what was his. He remained silent even when they cheated him, keeping back, with one excuse or another, most of his earnings, or giving him bad money. Yes, he never protested, he always remained silent.

"Once," the defending angel went on, "Bontsha crossed the roadway to the fountain for a drink, and in that moment his whole life was miraculously changed. What miracle happened to change his whole life? A splendid coach, with tires of rubber, plunged past, dragged by runaway horses; the coachman, fallen, lay in the street, his head split open. From the mouths of the frightened horses spilled foam, and in their wild eyes sparks struck like fire in a dark night, and inside the carriage sat a man, half alive, half dead, and Bontsha caught at the reins and held the horses. The man who sat inside and whose life was saved, a Jew, a philanthropist, never forgot what Bontsha had done for him. He handed him the whip of the dead driver, and Bontsha, then and there, became a coachman—no longer a common porter! And what's more, his great benefactor married him off, and what's still more, this great philanthropist himself provided a child for Bontsha to look after.

"And still Bontsha never said a word, never protested."

They mean me, I really do believe they mean me, Bontsha encouraged himself, but still he didn't have the gall to open his eyes, to look up at his judge.

"He never protested. He remained silent even when that great philanthropist shortly thereafter went into bankruptcy without ever having paid Bontsha one cent of his wages.

"He was silent even when his wife ran off and left him with her helpless infant. He was silent when, fifteen years later, that same helpless infant had grown up and become strong enough to throw Bontsha out of the house."

They mean me, Bontsha rejoiced, they really mean me.

"He even remained silent," continued the defending angel, "when that same benefactor and philanthropist went out of bankruptcy, as suddenly as he'd gone into it, and still didn't pay Bontsha one cent of what he owed him. No, more than that. This person, as befits a fine gentleman who has gone through bankruptcy, again went driving the great coach with the tires of rubber, and now, now he had a new coachman, and Bontsha, again a porter in the roadway, was run over by coachman, carriage, horses. And still, in his agony, Bontsha did not cry out; he remained silent. He did not even tell the police who had done this to him. Even in the hospital, where everyone is allowed to scream, he remained silent. He lay in utter loneliness on his cot, abandoned by the doctor, by the nurse; he had not the few pennies to pay them—and he made no murmur. He was silent in that awful moment just before he was about to die, and he was silent in that very moment when he did die. And never one murmur of protest against man, never one murmur of protest against God!"

Now Bontsha begins to tremble again. He senses that after his defender has finished, his prosecutor will rise to state the case against him. Who knows of what he will be accused? Bontsha, in that other world on earth, forgot each present moment as it slipped behind him to become the past. Now the defending angel has brought everything back to his mind again—but who knows what forgotten sins the prosecutor will bring to mind?

The prosecutor rises. "Gentlemen!" he begins in a harsh and bitter voice, and then he stops. "Gentlemen—" he begins again, and now his voice is less harsh, and again he stops. And finally, in a very soft voice, that same prosecutor says, "Gentlemen, he was always silent—and now I too will be silent."

The great court of justice grows very still, and at last from the judge's chair a new voice rises, loving, tender. "Bontsha my child, Bontsha"—the voice swells like a great harp—"my heart's child . . ."

Within Bontsha his very soul begins to weep. He would like to open his eyes, to raise them, but they are darkened with tears. It is so sweet to cry. Never until now has it been sweet to cry.

"My child, my Bontsha . . ."

Not since his mother died has he heard such words, and spoken in such a voice.

"My child," the judge begins again, "you have always suffered, and you have always kept silent. There isn't one secret place in your body without its bleeding wound; there isn't one secret place in your soul without its wound and blood. And you never protested. You always were silent.

"There, in that other world, no one understood you. You never understood yourself. You never understood that you need not have been silent, that you could have cried out and that your outcries would have brought down the world itself and ended it. You never understood your sleeping strength. There in that other world, that world of lies, your silence was never rewarded, but here in Paradise is the world of truth, here in Paradise you will be rewarded. You, the judge can neither condemn nor pass sentence upon. For you there is not only one little portion of Paradise, one little share. No, for you there is everything! Whatever you want! Everything is yours!"

Now for the first time Bontsha lifts his eyes. He is blinded by light. The splendor of light lies everywhere—upon the walls, upon the vast ceiling, the angels blaze with light, the judge. He drops his weary eyes.

"Really?" he asks, doubtful, and a little embarrassed.

"Really!" the judge answers. "Really! I tell you, everything is yours. Everything in Paradise is yours. Choose! Take! Whatever you want! You will only take what is yours!"

"Really?" Bontsha asks again, and now his voice is stronger, more assured.

And the judge and all the heavenly host answer, "Really! Really! Really!"

"Well, then"—and Bontsha smiles for the first time—"well, then, what I would like, Your Excellency, is to have, every morning for breakfast, a hot roll with fresh butter."

A silence falls upon the great hall, and it is more terrible than Bontsha's has ever been, and slowly the judge and the angels bend their heads in shame at this unending meekness they have created on earth.

Then the silence is shattered. The prosecutor laughs aloud, a bitter laugh.

Translated by Hilde Abel

●

AN elderly Jew is struck by a car and brought to the hospital. A pretty nurse tucks him into bed and says, "Mr. Epstein, are you comfortable?"

Epstein replies, "I make a nice living."

TEUTCH passes away while playing cards with his cronies at a coffee shop. The men don't know what to do; finally, they draw lots and one man is sent to inform the widow.

"How do you do, Mrs. Teutch," he says. "I've come to tell you that your husband has lost a lot of money at cards."

"He should have a stroke," says the angry woman.

"He already had it," replies the messenger.

Jokes about the relaying of the ultimate bad news are common to many cultures. In an American joke, for example, a tough drill sergeant orders: "All men whose mothers are alive, take one step forward," and then: "Not so fast there, Johnson."

DAVE was at death's door, and the family was gathered around him.

"Sarah, my wife, are you here at the bedside?"

"Yes, Dave, of course I'm here."

"And Bernie, my oldest son, are you here?"

"Yes, Dad."

"And Rachel, my daughter, are you here?"

"Yes, Father, at the foot of the bed."

"And Sam, my youngest, are you here too?"

"Right here, Pop."

"Well, then," said the merchant, "if all of you are here, who's minding the store?"

A classic.

Later, when the will is being read:

"And to my wife, Sarah, I leave half of all my assets. To my son Bernie, I leave a third of the remainder. To my daughter, Rachel, the same. To my son Sam, the same. And to my brother-in-law, whom I promised to mention in the will—hello there, Hymie!"

MENDEL was out walking one evening when he saw a man about to jump into the river. "Wait!" he shouted. "What are you doing?"

"Never mind," the man replied. "I'm just fed up with my life, and I don't want to continue living."

"Look, mister," said Mendel. "I don't want to tell you how to run your life, but please do me a favor. If you jump into the river, I would have to jump in after you and try to rescue you. But I can't swim. Can you imagine what would become of my wife and kids if I drowned? Is this the sort of thing you want to have on your conscience? Of course it isn't! So be a good Jew. Go home. And later tonight, in the privacy of your own house, go hang yourself!"

In Woody Allen's movie *Play it Again, Sam,* Allen (called Allen Felix) tries to pick up a girl at the Museum of Modern Art. They are standing in front of a Jackson Pollock painting.

"What does it say to you?" asks Allen.

"It restates the negativeness of the universe," the girl answers. "The hideous lonely emptiness of existence. Nothingness. The predicament of Man forced to live in a barren, Godless eternity like a tiny flame flickering in an immense void with nothing but waste, horror and degradation, forming a useless bleak straightjacket in a bleak absurd cosmos."

Allen: "What are you doing Saturday night?"

Girl: "Committing suicide."

Allen: "What about Friday night?"

Death on Second Avenue

This vivid description of the Yiddish theater brings to mind an old joke in which a real death has occurred:

"Ladies and gentleman," the manager announces, "I am terribly sorry to have to tell you that the great actor Yankel Leib has just had a stroke in his dressing room, a fatal stroke, and we cannot go on with tonight's performance."

At this, a woman in the second balcony stands and cries, "Quick, give him an enema!"

"Lady," says the manager, "the stroke was fatal."

"So give him an enema!" she shouts once more.

"Lady, you don't understand. Yankel Leib is *dead.* An enema can't possibly help."

"It wouldn't *hurt!*"

One of the most marvelous sights to behold in all the world is a death scene in the Yiddish theater. There is Maurice Schwartz, or some other great Yiddish actor, and he has just discovered his wife in bed with another man, and he has a heart attack, and it is the end of him. But he doesn't die just like that. First he screams, *"I am having a heart attack! I am dying!"* Then he falls, and the fall itself takes a full minute onto the sofa, then he moans and groans; then he rises and stumbles across the room, knocking over furniture and all the while yelling, "I am *dying! I am dying! Oh, God, I am dying!"* Then he stumbles offstage, wailing and moaning; then he stumbles back onstage and clutches at the draperies and sinks to the floor. And by now the whole family is standing there watching all this, crying and shrieking, *"My God, he is dying!"* And when he finally lands on the floor, he writhes painfully and he makes a speech, gasping out each word. And this speech includes all the philosophical Talmud learnings of his life, and it is chock full of advice to his sons and farewells to his daughters and his wife, and this speech alone lasts six minutes. And then at long last he gives one great effort to stand up again, and he almost makes it, but just when you think he's going to be all right, he lets out this horrible, croaking groan and stumbles over the entire stage again, knocking over what's left of the furniture and the family, and finally he dies. This death scene always takes about fifteen minutes. If the play is a musical, it is exactly the same, except with singing and dancing and very melancholy music underscoring the whole thing. And the audience, which is composed of Jewish people who have troubles of their own, feel this man's great pain, and *they* moan and groan and weep, and when he is finally dead, they sigh with relief and they feel this wonderful sense of total satisfaction.

•

COHEN approaches the secretary of the burial society. "I'm here because my wife is dead, and I have to arrange for her funeral."

"Your wife is dead?" asks the secretary. "How can that be? We buried your wife two years ago!"

"No, no," says Cohen. "That was my first wife. This was my second."

"Really?" says the secretary. "I didn't know you got married again. Mazel tov!"

MAX GELBERG was seventy-two years old when his wife died. After six months of mourning, Max, who was in good health, decided that life must go on, and so he began a strict program of physical fitness. Within a few months he had become a health nut.

After a few months of regular workouts, Max felt and looked wonderful. Friends would stop him on the street to ask, "Max, is that you? I didn't recognize you! You look sixty!"

With this encouragement, Max continued on the exercise program. He became a vegetarian. Soon he bought himself a hairpiece, and his friends, seeing him on the street, would stop and say, "Max, is that you? I didn't recognize you! You look fifty!"

Max was delighted, and gathering up his savings and his social security checks, he decided to move to Florida, where he could take advantage of the sun. He took up a permanent spot on the local muscle beach. The following winter he met a group of his friends on Collins Avenue. "Max," said one, "I didn't recognize you! You look thirty-five!"

This was all that Max needed to hear; it was time to act on his wish to get married again. And sure enough, within a few months, he met and married a pretty college freshman. At the chapel, the rabbi looked at Max with astonishment and joy. "Max, is that you?" the rabbi said. "I didn't recognize you. You look twenty-five! And I'm so glad that you came to me to marry you again. I'm sure your late wife would be pleased to see you pulling your life together and starting over."

Max was ecstatic. When the ceremony ended, and the bride and groom were about to leave for their honeymoon at Disney World, they stepped into the parking lot, where suddenly—*wham!*—Max was struck down and killed by a black Cadillac.

Reaching the gates of heaven, Max was stunned and angry. He pushed his way past the admitting angels and demanded to speak directly to the Manager. There was no stopping him. He would not stop shouting until he was admitted into the office of the Almighty Himself.

"I don't believe this!" Max shouted. "I finally get my life together, I'm about to start living again, and *poof!* That's it! Tell me, what do you have against Max Gelberg?"

"Max?" the Almighty replied. "Max Gelberg? Is that you? You look terrific—I didn't recognize you!"

•

"Did you hear about Shloime Grossbart?"

"You mean the Shloime Grossbart with the double hernia?"

"That's the one."

"The man with the liver condition and the bad leg?"

"That's him."

"Of course I know him. He has yellow skin, and his head is always bobbing up and down. . . . Anyway, what happened to him?"

"He died."

"Oy! Such a healthy man!"

•

This dark tale seems to be hinting rather strongly at allegory. Kurt Schlesinger, a San Francisco psychiatrist, comments: "Brecht says, 'He who is still laughing has not yet received the bad news.' In the Jewish mode, we have received the bad news and need to laugh, precisely because of that. We are all underwater without proper scuba equipment. It is not 'You schmuck, I'm drowning!' It is rather, 'Fellow schmucks, we are all drowning!' "

•

A new flood is foretold and nothing can be done to prevent it; in three days, the waters will wipe out the world.

The leader of Buddhism appears on television and pleads with everybody to become a Buddhist; that way, they will at least find salvation in heaven.

The Pope goes on television with a similar message: "It is still not too late to accept Jesus," he says.

The Chief Rabbi of Israel takes a slightly different approach: "We have three days to learn how to live under water."

•

GOLDFINE, a garment manufacturer from New York, takes his vacation every winter at the same hotel in Miami Beach, together with a number of his cronies from other cities. He arrives at the hotel and settles into his deck chair on the beach. Recognizing none of his colleagues, he starts to thumb through *Women's Wear Daily,* but he has an uneasy feeling: something is wrong; he is still alone.

Suddenly a strange apparition arises from the sea, dressed in a mask, goggles, and a black rubber suit. Goldfine is mystified as the creature comes toward him, until the goggles come off and the creature says, "Goldfine! What are you doing here?"

Goldfine recognizes Schwartz from Chicago, who has been part of the crowd at this beach for years. "What do you mean, what am I doing here?" asks Goldfine. "I'm getting a tan, relaxing, and waiting for the rest of the fellas. The question is what are *you* doing here, all dressed up like that?"

"Don't you know?" says Schwartz. "Nobody is sunbathing this year. We're all scuba diving. That's what I'm wearing—scuba diving equipment. All your friends are down at the bottom of the ocean."

"How do I get there?" asks Goldfine.

"Here's what you do," says Schwartz. "Go to the equipment store in front of the hotel, and tell them I sent you. They'll take care of everything."

Goldfine goes to the store, and the clerk gets him outfitted in the latest scuba equipment. As Goldfine is writing his check, the clerk throws in an underwater blackboard and special underwater chalk, explaining to the incredulous Goldfine that these tools represent the only means of communication under water.

Back at the beach, Goldfine steps into the ocean and descends into the deep. He sees strange fish and dark shadows—and finally he sees his friends, each dressed just like Goldfine, with tanks of air on their backs, and spears in their hands.

Goldfine stands around waving to everybody, and suddenly he sees Siegel from Seattle. Unlike the others, Siegel is dressed in a pair of slacks, loafers, and a green shirt with a picture of an alligator. Goldfine is shocked. Taking out his special underwater blackboard, he writes: "Hello, Siegel. This is Goldfine. How are you? Why aren't you wearing your special equipment?"

Siegel grabs the chalk from Goldfine's hand and writes: "Schmuck—I'm drowning!"

IN a little town, tucked into the woods and far from the main roads, the Jews were afraid that the Messiah would come and pass them by. They decided to build a tower on the outskirts of town, and appointed one of the town's beggars to serve there as watchman. If the Messiah should come, the watchman would give him directions to the town.

One day a stranger approached the tower, and the watchman came down to greet him. "What are you doing here in the middle of the forest?" the stranger asked.

"I sit on top of the tower and wait for the Messiah," answered the watchman.

"How do you like your job?" the stranger asked. "I'm sure it doesn't pay very much."

"That's true," answered the watchman. "But it's steady work."

ABOUT THE AUTHORS

Moshe Waldoks lectures extensively on Jewish cultural renewal and humor, and performs as a Jewish humorist. He is a media consultant and television producer in the Boston area, where he lives with his wife and three daughters.

William Novak, who lives in the Boston area with his wife and two sons, is probably best-known as the ghostwriter for the memoirs of Lee Iacocca, the Mayflower Madam, Tip O'Neill, and Nancy Reagan. He lectures widely on Jewish humor, singles, and the art of ghostwriting.

William Novak and Moshe Waldoks are also the editors of *The Big Book of New American Humor.*